BIG ISRAEL

How Israel's Lobby Moves America

Grant F. Smith

Library of Congress Cataloging-in-Publication Data

Names: Smith, Grant F., author.
Title: Big Israel : how Israel's lobby moves America / Grant F. Smith.
Description: Washington, D.C. : Institute for Research: Middle Eastern Policy, Inc., [2016] | Includes bibliographical references.
Identifiers: LCCN 2015051291 (print) | LCCN 2016000154 (ebook) | ISBN 9780982775714 ()
Subjects: LCSH: American Israel Public Affairs Committee. | Lobbying--United States.
Classification: LCC E184.36.P64 S637 2016 (print) | LCC E184.36.P64 (ebook) | DDC 324/.40973--dc23
LC record available at http://lccn.loc.gov/2015051291

ISBN 9780982775714

"I know what America is. America is a thing you can move very easily, move it in the right direction."

Benjamin Netanyahu, speaking to Jewish West Bank settlers in 2001.

Table of Contents

Table of Figures

Grant F. Smith

ACKNOWLEDGMENTS

The author wishes to acknowledge and thank the many cited sources quoted throughout this work. Thanks also to Jeffrey Blankfort for developmental editing, Janet McMahon for copy editing, and Henry Norr for proofreading and timely suggestions.

Grant F. Smith

1 THE ISRAEL LOBBY

Asking whether the Israel lobby exercises undue influence has only recently stopped being entirely taboo. If defined as "influence by which a person is induced to act otherwise than by their own free will or without adequate attention to the consequences," then the power wielded by the lobby clearly is undue. In modern-day America there is, however, nothing particularly unique about undue influence since a number of well-funded and highly organized interest groups, representing only a tiny minority, also exercise "undue influence," sometimes in concert with the Israel lobby. These certainly include financial services, the energy industry, and weapons-making elites. However—and unlike most lobbying for Israel—those groups openly exercise undue influence, lobby overtly and are the subject of robust news reporting and public debate. Due to the long and well-remembered history of conflict as Jewish minorities within larger populations, those running the most influential Israel Affinity Organizations—a term that will be defined in detail—that are predominantly Jewish often unfairly characterize attempts to analyze or quantify their influence as driven by anti-Semitism. As a barrier to scrutiny, this charge has effectively prevented a great deal of critical analysis. In particular, it prevents many individuals who are neither Jewish, nor minor insider critics of tactical Israel lobbying issues, nor working to advance more "acceptable" IAO initiatives, from speaking up.

This book proceeds, unapologetically, into this minefield on the principle that IAOs are more than "fair game" and overdue for exhaustive review, particularly to reveal those broader interests negatively affected by their actions. Declaring oneself "pro-Israel" has become as much a litmus test for running for public office as it is a screen to evaluate appointees wishing to work in sensitive positions in agencies such as the U.S. State Department,

Department of Justice or Treasury. The attributes of IAOs—some replicable, others utterly unique—their history, trajectory, battles lost and won, and seeming permanence on the scene, also make them one of the most fascinating players in so-called "special interest" politics in America. A fascinating and timely example is B'nai B'rith.

Established in 1843, B'nai B'rith formed a fraternal lodge system that offered social welfare services and a bridge toward integration to the waves of Jewish immigrants entering the United States. Yet within a decade, B'nai B'rith attempted to use the power of its membership base to change U.S. foreign policy. Its first well-known foray occurred in 1851 when a number of Swiss states refused to permit Jewish residence. B'nai B'rith lobbied against the U.S. secretary of state signing a trade agreement with Switzerland unless the policy was reversed. This effort was celebrated as "the beginning of a B'nai B'rith commitment to fight for and protect Jews and Jewish interests around the world."[1]

In 1903, a Jewish community in the Bessarabian province of the Russian empire (current day Moldova) was attacked by groups spurred on by accusations that Jews were murdering Christians for Passover matzo. In two days of rioting nearly fifty Jews were killed, ten times as many were injured, 700 homes were destroyed, and 600 stores were robbed while police and military stood by without intervening. Response to the 1903 Kishinev pogrom in Tsarist Russia was the second major foreign policy lobbying initiative by an organization that today is only one among hundreds promoting the advancement of Israel by harnessing the influence of the United States government. B'nai B'rith's president, Simon Wolf, met with President Theodore Roosevelt and Secretary of State John Hay—persuading them to use the power of the state—to transmit a petition of signatures gathered by B'nai B'rith lodges through the U.S. Charge de Affairs in Saint Petersburg to the Tsar. The Russian government rejected it

Jewish leaders inside and outside B'nai B'rith then agitated for more U.S. Russia policy "linkage" to what they termed "Jewish interests." They demanded an immediate reduction in American cooperation with the Russian government on a range of vital issues because of Kishinev. Momentum also continued to build for creating a lobby that could credibly be perceived to speak with a unified voice representing all American Jews on domestic and international affairs. This effort by fairly elite and unrepresentative organizations to portray themselves as a unified front continues today, though it faces much greater scrutiny.

In 1910, B'nai B'rith invited President Taft to address its general assembly. B'nai B'rith leaders were, in turn, cordially received in the White House. In

---

[1] Allan J. Jacobs, "A Glorious Future Rooted in a Proud Past" *B'nai B'rith Magazine*, Fall 2013 p. 6

1912, the U.S. abrogated its commercial treaty with Russia, an act for which Taft received B'nai B'rith's annual medal to the "person who had done the most for Jews." B'nai B'rith's success was an important political milestone in Washington. It had elevated the concerns of a new special interest over those of business, cultural and other interests in Russia.

However, the core challenge to those advancing this new special interest was obvious. Initiatives had to be carefully framed as "American interests" so as not to draw too much criticism. These efforts would later become preemptive. Criticism of those writing about organized agitation for the U.S. to fight wars that benefitted the formation and interests of Israel became harsh and immediate—most often characterized as "anti-Semitism" or "hatred of the Jews," or if one was Jewish, "self-hatred." Careers were damaged or destroyed by such charges.

Today, the Israel lobby, defined here as the collective of Israel Affinity Organizations, is more openly considered to be a powerful lobbying force, with some caveats. This has been disturbing to organizations such as the Anti-Defamation League, which branded itself as a Jewish defense organization. Few things have challenged Israel Affinity Organizations and their programs so much as this recent open acknowledgement that such a group of organizations exists and forms an interlocking interest that wields vast—and undue—influence in the United States, primarily to promote Israeli interests. Beyond actual recognition of this fact, proceeding toward any informed criticism of their true and sometimes unflattering history, programs, operational codes, secrecy, interrelations and quantifiable negative impact on other Americans is mostly ignored, suppressed when that fails, or decried as anti-Semitism when it finally breaks into any relevant or high profile public forum.

Yet the public's attention is not waning. The costs of IAO policies in terms of blood and treasure when successfully packaged and sold in the past as U.S. national interests that must be pursued above all others have steadily mounted. Recently, many U.S. states individually passed their own Iran economic sanctions, sent their U.S. law enforcement officials to Israel for training and inserted anti-Boycott Divestment and Sanctions measures into various laws in order to protect Israel's occupation of Palestinian territory in global trade legislation. This is mostly the work of IAO model legislation drives in tight coordination with national organizations with ties to the Israeli government rather than grassroots efforts on behalf of a state's voters. That most Americans reject the many resolutions praising Israel in their name is demonstrable in surveys.

The negative outcome of IAO influence exemplifies what economists have dubbed the "collective action" problem. Small interest groups—and the lobby is small—with a strong interest in a particular issue are better able to coordinate their activities and impact on policymaking than larger groups with diffuse interests.[2] Add to that the ability to coordinate with a foreign government to create incidents abroad and constant external pressure on the United States—without, as the top lobbying IAO the American Israel Public Affairs Committee once boasted "leaving fingerprints"—and an insidious challenge to sensible American public policy emerges.[3] The impact that this "collective action" has on Congress has been significant long before the creation of Israel in 1948. But it is why, the following year—1949, over U.S. State Department opposition and long before any evidence of Israel's value as a "Cold War ally" or country of "shared values" with the United States—Congress delivered a billion dollars in foreign aid (adjusted for inflation). Since then, American taxpayers have—not counting secret intelligence aid—paid a quarter trillion in foreign aid to Israel. Israel receives the largest share of the U.S. foreign aid budget and is historically the largest single recipient. With most of Congress today automatically voting "yes" on any of what members now call an "AIPAC vote"—and IAO revenues reaching dizzying new heights—America's annual foreign aid payment to Israel is poised to return to Cold War levels, if not far, far higher.

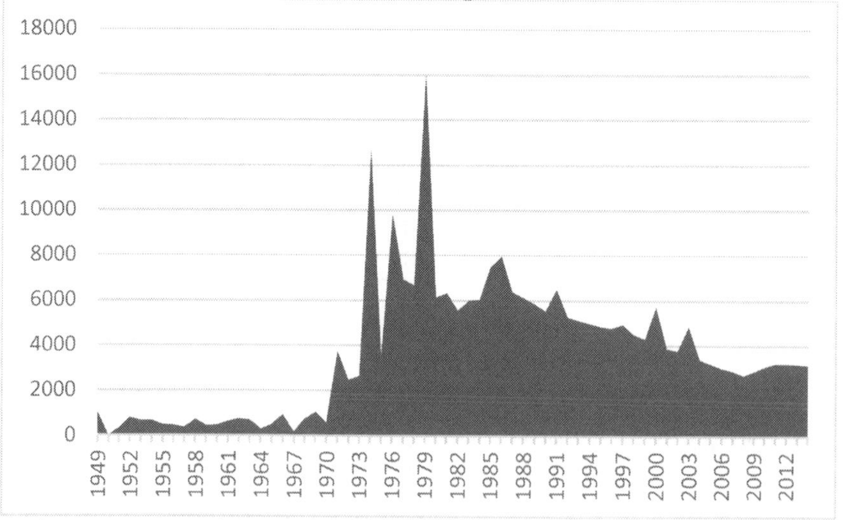

Figure 1 U.S. annual foreign aid to Israel ($ U.S. million, adjusted for inflation)[4]

[2] George Stigler, "The theory of economic regulation" *Bell Journal of Economics and Management Science*, Spring 1971.

[3] An anonymous AIPAC official confided to *The National Journal* that "there is no question that we exert a policy impact, but working behind the scenes and taking care not to leave fingerprints, that impact is not always traceable to us."

[4] These U.S. foreign aid figures are adjusted for inflation using the Bureau of Labor Statistics CPI inflation calculator. The nominal data appears in Jeremy M. Sharp,

This influence is why at the beginning of the last century the United States began punitive trade and other measures against Russia. Additional measures were enacted in the name of facilitating Jewish emigration to Israel from the Soviet Union in the 1980s. It is why in the mid-1980s the United States signed its very first "free trade" agreement with Israel—over the opposition of powerful U.S. corporations like Dow and Monsanto and with a bit of a boost from Israeli espionage—and not a more economically substantial state that had more to offer Americans in return. From a balance of trade perspective, the U.S.-Israel "Free Trade Area" turned out to be a constant headache for U.S. exporters and is essentially yet another assumed, guaranteed, subsidy for Israel. Fear of IAOs is also why the U.S. ignores important laws governing foreign lobbying, fails to prosecute ongoing Israeli espionage campaigns against its nuclear weapons material and technology, national intelligence and other resources of the state. IAOs have been the sole driver of economic boycotts of Iran. IAOs through constant activity monopolize scarce and less tangible resources—saturating the "bandwidth" and "attention span"—of federal government agencies that are supposed to be focused elsewhere. IAOs operating overseas such as the American Jewish Committee often write up a sumptuous program menu and have the table set for a lavish operational banquet, only to pass the bill to Uncle Sam. This occurs when IAOs transfer their own programs over to U.S. agencies to implement and fund with tax resources most would assume were supposed to improve the lives of ordinary Americans living in the United States. Instead scarce resources flow to the Israeli Defense Forces engaging in questionable operations or indirectly supporting Soviet or Brooklyn-born Jewish settlers colonizing the West Bank.

The 2015 battle to subvert the comprehensive agreement on the Iranian nuclear program flushed IAOs such as United Against Nuclear Iran and various highly active Jewish federations out into the open—terrain in which many do not normally wish to be seen exercising their influence. In mid-July of 2015, Iran signed the agreement with the permanent members of the UN Security Council plus Germany (P5 +1) agreeing to additional limitations on its civilian nuclear program in exchange for relief from international economic sanctions. AIPAC, the American Jewish Committee, the Anti-Defamation League and the Conference of Presidents of Major American Jewish Organizations worked in coordination with the Israeli government to try to kill the deal, spurred on by Israeli Prime Minister Benjamin Netanyahu. The Netanyahu administration spied on U.S.-Iran negotiations then leaked details to Israel Affinity Organizations in the United States. Israel even openly

---

"U.S. Foreign Aid to Israel," Congressional Research Service, June 10, 2015, page 30. No estimate for clandestine or intelligence support included.

asked undecided U.S. lawmakers, "What it would take to win their votes."[5]

Though not accurately reflected in mainstream media, the entire Iran nuclear scare was largely a "manufactured crisis" that focused pressure on Israel's regional rivals and away from the longest running—and arguably most damaging to the U.S.—regional conflict—that between Israel and Palestine.[6] That a primary objective of many such IAO initiatives is to divert attention away from the problems created by Israel is a perception increasingly gaining traction among informed Americans.

Quite appropriately, President Barack Obama identified the source of opposition to the Iran nuclear deal as largely the same organizations that advocated for the disastrous 2003 U.S. invasion of Iraq. In an August 2015 speech at American University, Obama even highlighted the naked motivation behind the drive to kill the deal—affinity for Israel. He also began discussing, in a way no doubt alarming to IAOs, Israel's "conventional" military superiority—indirectly implying something IAOs and the Israeli government insist must not be officially recognized by the United States—that Israel also has "unconventional" military capabilities in the form of nuclear weapons.

Although major American news media reported about the parallels between Obama's address and John F. Kennedy's 1963 speech at the same venue, to promote peace and overcome widespread opposition to arms control with the Soviets—they missed the more far more relevant Israel connection. In 1963, the Kennedy administration was secretly fighting Israel's nuclear weapons development program and had even secretly ordered Israel's top—and largely foreign funded—lobbying organization the American Zionist Council to register as a foreign agent and openly report its public relations and secret lobbying expenditures on behalf of Israel.

When Kennedy was assassinated the following November and conspiracy theories about Russian and Cuban complicity began to swirl, nobody of significance speculated about possible Israeli connections. That is because—as has become the norm in such cases—the relevant and highly detailed government records about the administration's initiative to keep Israel's lobby in check were effectively kept bottled up, in this case classified as secret until 2008. The story of JFK's fight against the Israeli nuclear program was similarly withheld from the public until fairly recently. Nevertheless, one outcome is clear. JFK's assassination settled both issues. After Kennedy's death, Israel proceeded at full speed ahead with its nuclear weapons program, smuggling material, technology and know-how out of the U.S. to Israel with

[5] Adam Entous and Danny Yadron, "U.S. Spy Net on Israel Snares Congress," *The Wall Street Journal*, December 29, 2015

[6] See Gareth Porter, *Manufactured Crisis: The Untold Story of the Iran Nuclear Scare* (Just World Books, 2014)

the direct involvement of IAO officials (in this case, the Zionist Organization of America). American presidents, from Nixon onward, agreed to never acknowledge the Israeli program. Presidents subsequently gagged government employees and contractors from discussing it in public. Presidents have refused to enforce a law forbidding U.S. foreign aid to countries with clandestine nuclear weapons programs—because Israel is just such a state. The lobbying division of the American Zionist Council, which was ordered to register as a foreign agent by the Kennedy administration—split off and incorporated six weeks after the AZC order. Today it is known as the American Israel Public Affairs Committee. AIPAC seamlessly took over AZC's activities without ever registering as an Israeli foreign agent.[7] AIPAC's history as a foreign funded agent, and not a representative of the broader American Jewish community, has again became clear as it bucked widespread Jewish support for the Iran nuclear deal and instead sided with the Israeli government in opposition.

Today, unlike JFK's era, the fight between the Obama administration and IAOs/Israel has been public. There are also new factors—alternative media and independent investigative journalism. If unusual circumstances (equivalent to the Niger uranium forgeries used to justify the Iraq invasion) were to arise that seemed to compel immediate U.S. military action against Iran, or the immediate "snap-back" of economic sanctions against Iran, questions would immediately arise about whether IAOs and/or Israel were involved. Such questions would not come from *The New York Times* or *The Washington Post* which history suggests would more likely be channeling disinformation or substantiating a false flag attack than leading a squad of debunkers. Rather, truth squads would emerge on peer-to-peer social media, blogs and the alternative news websites that have expanded to fill the gaping investigatory void left by establishment media. When the Associated Press surfaced a sketchy story in 2015 that secret "side agreements" would allow Iran self-inspection rights under the nuclear agreement, the recitation of obviously suspicious terminology not commonly used in side agreements quickly set off alarm bells. AP's report was quickly debunked in the alternative media by real experts rarely consulted as fact-checkers by establishment media.

The Internet has also finally debunked an IAO canard so integral and longstanding as to be considered the Israel lobby's central pillar of legitimacy—that IAOs are somehow "representatives" that consolidate and channel a "Jewish consensus view" on what actions the United States should

[7] For the only book-length account of the Kennedy administration's battle to register the American Zionist Council as a foreign agent, read Grant F. Smith *America's Defense Line: The Justice Department's Battle to Register the Israel Lobby as Agents of a Foreign Government* (Institute for Research: Middle Eastern Policy, 2008)

take. IAO claims to represent them have been overturned by surveys revealing the tiny percentage of American Jews actually involved in any way with such organizations and chants of "not in my name" from prominent Jewish individuals and non-IAO Jewish organizations. Nevertheless, the Internet also amplified the non-Jewish voices for peace and reason often entirely excluded or drowned out in the debate. Their growing resentment over the subordination of the common good and commonwealth to Israeli prerogatives has grown exponentially even as major demographic shifts suggest that the Israel lobby will have a much harder time maintaining their grip on the levers of power in coming decades. When that happens, it will be a positive beginning. More sensible resource allocation. Peace and justice. Restoring America's image after years of undue and harmful IAO influence on policymaking. This book's little known historical facts and current data place Israel lobby activities and external costs into a proper, unvarnished perspective.

2 ISRAEL AFFINITY ORGANIZATIONS

Not-for-profit Israel Affinity Organizations (IAOs) are entities that support Israel in both common and unique ways. Together, they make up the Israel lobby. Even the smallest organizations engage in multiple tactics, from taking influential Americans on trips to Israel, reactive media pressure campaigns, hosting on-campus Israel advocacy programs, publishing advocacy literature and academic studies, to proactively placing editorials and op-eds in elite and hometown newspapers. They convene non-stop conferences and events aimed at shaping U.S. foreign policy. Some organizations and their leaders have engaged in illegal activities of immense damage to the United States on behalf of Israel. When caught, they argue—mostly from behind the scenes and exercising uncanny influence over enforcement officials—that law breaking in support of Israel should not be punished. IAOs have a major impact not only on U.S. foreign policy, but also on the news media, within political campaigns, and on academia. They also have a significant impact on the U.S. economy and how scarce government resources are allocated at the local, state and federal levels. Much of that impact, as revealed in this book, is negative because it externalizes costs onto millions of American taxpayers who are either not willingly part of the pro-Israel movement, or would oppose such support for Israel if they were allowed to know and do something about it.

Some IAOs are open about their missions, objectives and programs while others are almost completely opaque. The American Israel Public Affairs Committee, or AIPAC, concentrates its efforts on lobbying Congress for massive foreign aid packages and foreign policies that benefit Israel. A much larger network of Jewish federations focuses most of its efforts on raising funds that are transferred to other IAOs, local lobbying organizations, and through subsidy conduits to Israel partner organizations. The internal Jewish federation political operations are called Jewish Community Relations Councils and are usually not separately incorporated. Most are also physically housed within Jewish federations. Although they lobby heavily, they do not declare lobbying as a significant activity and resist attempts to regulate or make them more transparent in their dealings with elected officials.

Debriefing and training U.S. government officials is a particularly unusual IAO activity that borders on intelligence gathering. The Jewish Institute for National Security Affairs, founded in 1976, functioned mostly under the radar for years, quietly influencing the top echelons of the national security state to integrate more closely with the Israeli military. JINSA has achieved on a micro level for Israel what the Central Intelligence Agency labored for decades to accomplish in similar overseas efforts to turn the military leadership in various developing countries and despotic regimes into pro-U.S. assets. The model and tactics are from the same intelligence operations playbook.

This book uses the term "Israel Affinity Organization" when referring to individual organizations in an attempt to be precise. Not all IAOs lobby. A handful of large IAOs—in terms of revenue—are not predominantly Jewish in terms of their leadership, members and donors, though most are. In order to be included in this IAO analysis, an organization must have all of the following attributes. It must be an IRS recognized tax-exempt 501(c)(3) or 501(c)(4) organization. This means a group that incorporated (or in some instances was brought into being by legislative action), then applied to the IRS or its predecessor for tax-exempt status as a social welfare providing organization and now operates with tax-exempt status. Most of the financial data analyzed in this study is only available because the mandatory annual tax returns filed by IAOs must be made publicly available. However, as explored later, many of these organizations are "going dark" and the IRS is either doing nothing about it or facilitating the growing lack of transparency. In addition, although the data should—and easily could—be made available in a digital format that quickly allows cross-referencing transfers between IAOs and foundations—it is not.

To be included an IAO must actively and unconditionally support Israel as a major function. This must either be a formal component of the organization's mission statement or a top priority in programs or observable as its core mission. Some organizations, such as the Foundation for Defense of Democracies, are dedicated to framing Israeli issues as American concerns and hiding their affinity. They make no mention of Israel in their mission statements. We include such organizations if their output on behalf of Israel is so high it can realistically be presumed to be their primary purpose. We also include the main evangelical Christian organizations to the extent possible. One of the highest profile thanks to heavy expenditures on public relations, Christians United for Israel, has hidden behind its status as an "association of churches" to conduct lobbying activities and conceal basic information from the public. Though Christian evangelical influence and entry into the fray are relatively recent and somewhat overestimated, they are an important component of the ecosystem because they tap an entirely different revenue stream and can mobilize large numbers of voters. They also sometimes undertake risky overseas ventures on Israel's behalf that carry a high potential for blowback against the United States.

To be included in our analysis, an IAO must raise the majority of its funding in the United States. Some of the "startup" funding that launched the American Zionist Council and AIPAC was actually foreign money, laundered through various entities, by the Jewish Agency. Today most IAOs appear to raise the majority of their funding in the United States—though there is much consultation with Israeli officials on how it should be spent. This activity creates a quantifiable, largely unexplored, and highly negative impact on U.S. taxpayers tapped to fill the revenue holes created by the tax-deductibility of the billions of dollars moving every year through the system.

Lastly, to pass through the IAO screen an organization must be headquartered in the United States. While many large and small IAOs have offices in Israel and conduct their ongoing private consultations with government officials there, no advantage can be gained by actually headquartering in Israel. The Jewish Agency for Israel ran into innumerable woes and tangles with the Foreign Agents Registration Act office of the Justice Department as a foreign-based entity. While offices in Israel offer prestige and easier private communications with Israeli government officials, there is no longer any worthwhile tax or influence advantage to headquartering in the state of central IAO concern.

Some readers may question such a set of criteria. Under this definition, an organization such as the American Israel Education Foundation, which sends members of Congress (more than 1,000 since the year 2000) and other influential Americans on all-expense-paid trips to Israel is clearly an Israel Affinity Organization. The American Enterprise Institute, a Washington-based think tank with a central pro-Israel doctrine that regularly beats war drums for attacks on Israel's rivals and receives large amounts of funding from Jewish federations, is not counted. Israel advocacy is not its principal function. Frank Gaffney's Center for Security Policy is explored and included in the revenue tallies. Its top priority seems to be portraying Islamic militancy as a threat on par with the former Soviet Union, necessitating an ever-expanding U.S. military budget. It is the recipient of many donors giving to more mainstream IAOs. However, the David Horowitz Freedom Center is not included in our database, since it seems to be mostly about David Horowitz, rather than exerting influence for Israel.

The Jewish Agency for Israel—formerly Israel's government-in-waiting which financed many initiatives toward the establishment of the state in the 1940s and which even has quasi-governmental status bestowed by the Knesset in a 1953 secret covenant—is explored many times in the following pages, but its finances are not counted in this study for other reasons. The Jewish Agency's predecessor, the Jewish Agency for Palestine, was created under a 1922 League of Nations mandate. It has registered as a U.S. foreign agent with the Justice Department at various times and raises substantial funding in the United States, indirectly, through IAOs such as the United Israel Appeal. The Jewish Agency even hauls in huge U.S. government subsidies for "refugee settlement." However, it is not headquartered in the United States. It would also present a significant "double counting" issue to include the Jewish Agency since it a large recipient of IAO funds.

In addition to adding up revenues, employees, volunteers and exploring when IAOs were launched, this book also attempts to reveal what IAOs do—as opposed to examining only what they say they do. This is a major challenge since the most easily available public information about IAOs is public relations spin emitted by the IAOs themselves. Little of that examines their impact on communities beyond ardent supporters of Israel and the benefits bestowed to their country of passionate attachment. Preference is therefore given to their internal communications, mandatory financial disclosures and information divulged in various encounters with regulators.

We have also mostly ignored a large number of minor organizations that—strictly speaking—do fall within our IAO definition. For example, a study conducted by Brandeis University identified 774 organizations raising $1.979 billion in the United States for Israel in 2007.[8] In contrast, this book pegs the total Israel Affinity Organization "industry" size that year at $3.6 billion, counting only 336 IAOs. The differences are a function of study aims and mathematics. The Brandeis study was primarily geared toward identifying whether a plethora of new "American Friends of Israel" organizations giving directly to their Israeli counterparts accounted for a slowing in overall giving to large "umbrella" collection organizations such as the United Jewish Appeal which traditionally collected and transferred funds to Israel. Brandeis also attempted to net out transfers between fundraising and conduit organizations, a task that it found to be impossible in the end.

The aim of *Big Israel* is to provide a bird's eye view of the "industry size" and composition. It forecasts tax-exempt nonprofit resources raised in the United States for Israel and assesses their impact on the majority of Americans. While it includes the largest organizations reviewed by Brandeis in a "subsidy" category, it also analyzes the advocacy and education

---

[8] Eric Fleisch and Theodore Sasson, *The New Philanthropy: American Jewish Giving to Israeli Organizations*, Brandeis University, April, 2012 https://www.brandeis.edu/cmjs/pdfs/TheNewPhilanthropy.pdf

organizations left out by the Brandeis study and the federation fundraising IAOs that power much of the Israel lobby "ecosystem." It does not attempt to "net out" transfers from one organization to another or factor out internal overhead costs such as fundraising. We do however calculate the "revenue externality" IAOs leave for other Americans to pay because of the tax-deductibility of contributions and huge endowments that continually grow with no taxation of interest or capital gains. In short, *Big Israel's* approach yields numbers that are generally not—for good reason—calculated or trumpeted by IAOs to the American public.

There is value in Americans outside the Israel affinity ecosystem knowing how IAOs came into being, what initial social challenges or problems they were designed to confront, and how they have transformed themselves—some gradually, others instantaneously—into the equivalent of mini Israeli embassies and consulates (including sometimes serving as clandestine intelligence service stations) in every major U.S. population center. It is also useful to know why some have been dissolved, regulated out of existence, spun off into new organizations or reconstituted under a different organizational banner.

Just as location, location, location are the three principals of real estate investment and key to merchandising, studying the location of IAOs can also be revealing. Why are so many located in metropolitan New York? Are federations present in every major American population center? Where, exactly, are federations' allegedly separate political and lobbying units—Jewish Community Relations Councils—located? Why are multiple organizations located in a complex at 633 3rd Avenue in New York City that brings together lobbying, banking and the Israeli government into a single seamless agglomeration? What binary IAOs orbit one another at 251 H St NW. in Washington?

IAOs differ significantly from other major American charitable organizations. Many IAOs have common attributes that distinguish them as a group. Most, unabashedly, are nearly entirely led, managed and staffed by Jews. Most of the executives—as is continuously criticized in the Jewish press—are highly overpaid males. Turnover in the top executive positions, whether at the Anti-Defamation League or American Jewish Committee, is glacial. In an America concerned with workplace diversity—or at very least the appearance of it—this is notable, though considered of extremely little importance by IAOs themselves, which are seldom challenged. One exception are photos in brochures and marketing materials for AIPAC conferences and events, which inevitably display ethnic diversity. Many IAO leaders cultivate an environment of secrecy and suspicion, admonishing, "Hostile ears are always listening." That some probably are does not diminish the perception that by acting conspiratorially, they are often perceived by outsiders to, in fact, be conspiratorial. Many IAOs consider their inside information to be as proprietary as an industry-patented manufacturing system, and are as security-conscious as an elite investment bank or embassy—and a great deal of their security infrastructure is provided at no cost by taxpayers. They require employees to sign complex and lengthy nondisclosure agreements. Employees must read and obey intricate employee conduct manuals and never leak or make off-the-cuff remarks to the press. At all costs, they must maintain the secrets of the organization—especially if leaving to join another IAO. Their measures go beyond common practices within the world of charities.

One major inquiry is, "For what purpose was IRS tax-exempt status originally intended, and how do IAOs fulfill their professed mandates as social welfare organizations?" We then ask, "How did the very oldest IAOs qualify?" This second question is becoming less clear with the passage of time. Many pre-1948 IRS and predecessor Bureau of Revenue records on why IAOs were given such status have been destroyed under various government records management guidelines. The IRS seems content not to know why it granted such powerful privileges. Some applications for tax-exempt status from such relatively new organizations as The Israel Project—all are theoretically open to public inspection—cannot be located by the IRS. There are twenty-nine categories of nonprofits and only some of them are charitable.[9] All IAOs examined here—whether as religious, educational, or other categories—claim to be charities and all are tax-exempt. We therefore critically examine what, if any, social welfare benefits IAOs actually bestow in the United States and whether they reduce burdens on the government. Asking whether actual IAO activities vary significantly from those they claimed to the IRS in order to gain tax-exempt status is obviously an important question, despite the ever weaker and under-resourced nature of tax-exempt organization oversight at the IRS. In reality, the brigade of IAOs that subsidize partner organizations in Israel do so questionably, through the tiniest of tax loopholes. Each year, they drive multi-billion-dollar tank trucks bursting with cash through that loophole. There are no weigh stations, speed traps or state patrol cars either, since they are entirely self-regulated.

Funding is the major indicator of the influence and reach of this ecosystem—although, curiously, the tottering Zionist Organization of America recently argued otherwise, in order to provide twice as much compensation to its president than industry benchmarks suggested. We focus on the total amount of revenue raised (and expended) by IAOs every year and forecast the trajectory of each organization in the appendix out to year 2020 using actual data from 2001-2012. Some IAOs are clearly zombie organizations that probably should have shut down years ago. Others are

[9] David Cay Johnston, email message to the author with permission granted to quote. December 10, 2015.

growing at such exponential rates, a few from almost nothing ten years ago, that they will easily pass $100 million in tax-exempt donations by decade's end.

We categorize IAOs by major functions using only four broad groupings. This allows a basic comparative analysis of their growth rates by overall functional category and inference into how varying levels of support affects the success in achieving declared—and sometimes unstated—objectives. In the case of AIPAC, this objective will continue to be delivering the biggest single share of the U.S. foreign aid budget to Israel while periodically agitating for foreign policies such as U.S. economic and kinetic warfare campaigns against Israel's rivals. In the case of the Anti-Defamation League it will be using a global survey to deliver public proclamations on every country's—with the single important exception of Israel—position on what the ADL represents to be the world's definitive anti-Semitism spectrum. Privately, the ADL's number of training sessions for federal and local law enforcement—the contents of which are a closely guarded secret withheld from the broader public and which the FBI has fought against releasing—are internal statistics of vital importance and part of ADL's half-century-long forced collaboration with the FBI and law enforcement nationwide.

Data is presented from news reports, obscure academic journals, websites, over four thousand IRS form 990 tax returns, public statements issued by IAO leaders, legal filings and largely untapped resources such as FBI and military intelligence investigations obtained through the Freedom of Information Act. Where necessary we have filed FOIA lawsuits and appeals against understandably—yet unpardonably—reluctant U.S. federal agencies. We unveil what IAOs have taken from the United States in the past and what they are trying to get in the very near future. A set of statistically significant survey results test whether American popular support for Israel is as high as IAOs claim. Admittedly, by largely focusing only on IAOs, we are only illuminating the lower right-hand piece of a far larger puzzle.

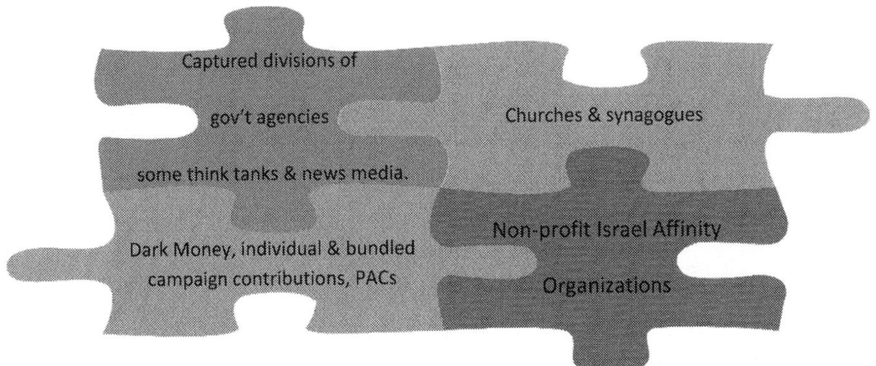

Figure 2 IAOs within the larger pro-Israel ecosystem

Not quantified in this book are three other major institutional "puzzle pieces" of the American "pro-Israel" system. Many synagogues and churches are extremely active in their support of Israel. As mentioned, Christians United for Israel, which raises vast amounts of funding for Israel lobbying, hides behind its church association status to avoid disclosure, and it is far from the only entity concealing activities and financial support. Evangelical and other denominational churches and synagogues are not required to file any tax declaraions. Any activity they may be engaged in is uncountable. This is legal if certain IRS criteria are met, yet in the case of CUFI's actual practices such compliance appears to be highly unlikely.

There are also large individual donors to Israeli causes who forgo tax deductibiity in return for total privacy and do not donate through IAOs. Neither category can be counted or examined in depth because the data is simply unavailable.[10] Extremely influential U.S. think tanks such as the Brookings Institution have let their Middle East policy-analysis divisions, essentially, be taken over or outsourced to pro-Israel forces. At Brookings, this occurred just as the Israel lobby needed "centrist" backing for the 2003 U.S. invasion of Iraq. The friendly takeover was funded by Israeli media mogul Haim Saban who paid Brookings $12.3 million. The Saban Center was created in 2002 and its director—former AIPAC Director of Research Martin Indyk—immediately began issuing calls for war.[11] However the Saban Center has never been segregable from the rest of Brookings for analysis, so it does not meet our strict IAO criteria.[12] We explore a similar "takeover," involving the purging of critical writers reporting on Israel, which occurred at the Center for American Progress (CAP), a Democratic Party linked thinktank, during the runup to the 2016 presidential election. Though now apparently advocating for Israel and firing employees who are not pro-Israel, we also do not include CAP, since such advocacy is not its primary purpose.

Many major and minor news outlets are so compromised in their Middle East reporting and editorializing that their content has largely become indistinguishable from official releases by the Israeli Ministry of Foreign Affairs. We examine the Jewish Telegraphic Agency, which was tasked with turning Israeli government communiques into "news" when appropriate,

---

[10] Churches and synagogues are not required to file revenue or giving reports with the IRS. Individuals making large direct gifts to Israel that do not pass through an IAO can similarly not be counted for lack of data.

[11] Martin Indyk and Kenneth M. Pollack, "Lock and Load: If war with Iraq is inevitable, let it begin sooner rather than later" *The Los Angeles Times*, December 19, 2002

[12] See the author's essay Grant F. Smith "Why AIPAC Took Over Brookings" *Dissident Voice (2007) http://dissidentvoice.org/2007/11/why-aipac-took-over-brookings/* for an analysis on how and why Haim Saban endowed a new center at Brookings on the eve of the U.S. invasion of Iraq.

according to files declassified late in 2015. We review establishment media fear of reporting which can be traced back to "media watch" IAOs such as Facts and Logic about the Middle East (FLAME), the Committee for Accuracy in Middle East Reporting (CAMERA) and Honest Reporting which attack and organize boycotts of media outlets that dare to distribute content critical of Israel—by effectively targeting their sources of revenue. We also present a recent case study of tactics The Israel Project uses to replace pundits it does not like with Israel-approved talking heads inside a U.S. taxpayer-funded global news network.

Some media organizations, like the *Weekly Standard*, were purpose-built to advance a pro-Israel line, pressuring and targeting U.S. government officials to be more deferential to Israeli interests. Still other media outlets are wholly-owned subsidiaries of IAOs. The conservative *Commentary* magazine was founded by the American Jewish Committee in 1945 and has been effecively used to "supervise" the American conservative movement and eject critical voices such as Joe Sobran, Governor William Scranton, and presidential candidate Pat Buchanan because of their positions on Israel.[13]

The liberal *New Republic* has served a similar role in the American Liberal Left, particularly when it was under the ownership of Martin Peretz beginning in the 1970s and extending well into the current century. According to political insider and senior advisor Sidney Blumental, in a confidential memo to then-Secretary of State Hillary Clinton, the *New Republic* (which has apoplogized for its strong advocacy for the 2003 U.S. invasion of Iraq) was little more than an Israeli propaganda organ, used to pump disinformation and overturn peace initiatives, led by pro-Israel activists such as the former American-turned-Israeli-Ambassador and current Knesset member Michael Oren. In an email Blumenthal warned Clinton about Israeli-generated content and pressure campaigns in the *New Republic*:

> *In case you haven't seen it, this is the fully articulated view of the Netanyahu government and Likud about 'the crisis'. The New Republic is a preferred outlet for the highest level likud/ neocon propaganda. Michael Oren, a channel for Israeli intel, was a frequent contributor in the past. On a lower level, so was Michael Ledeen when he was trafficking disinformation. The New Republic was critical in undermining Carter when he pressed Begin. Israel intel used Ledeen and TNY to put out stories on*

[13] Scott McConnell "Did Neoconservatives take over GOP Foreign Policy?" Speech, National Summit to Reassess the U.S.-Israel Special Relationship, March 7, 2014. http://natsummit.org/transcripts/scott_mcconnell.htm

> *Billy Carter. But TNR is only one key being hit in the Wurlitzer.*[14]

Some ostensibly independent or privately-owned media outlets have entire programs actively promoting a single IAO. For example, Conference of Presidents of Major American Jewish Organizations President and CEO Malcolm Hoenlein appears on a weekly radio program to discuss and promote its initiatives called "JM in the AM," which is broadcast from a station airing in New Jersey and New York and via Internet podcast and live audio streams. The Center for Security Policy's Frank Gaffney hosts a daily diatribe against Muslims in America and the alleged threat of Sharia law from his Washington-based American Freedom Radio broadcast and podcast. Non-IAO players in this vast universe of public and privately-owned media outlets—a few purpose-built, but most cajoled or intimidated into becoming more pro-Israel—are also not deeply covered in this analysis.

Although directed by IAO candidate scorecards[15] and secret efforts to channel political action committee funding, we also do not attempt to tally total individual, bundled and aggregated contributions to political campaigns delivered on the "single issue" basis of a candidate's support for Israel. We do review a small number of specialty nonprofits and anecdotal examinations of campaign fundraisers and committees with IAO connections. We mostly steer away from any in-depth analysis of big Israel lobby donors such as Sheldon Adelson, Paul Singer and Haim Saban. A great deal of solid reporting about such donors is becoming available from the mainstream and Jewish press. Despite these many exclusions, studying nonprofit IAOs alone as a system delivers critical insights.

IAOs are the single most visible and quantifiable piece of America's pro-Israel jigsaw puzzle. They are the visible dorsal fin that allows a perceptive marine biologist—even while paddling furiously back toward the safety of his analytical dingy—to accurately estimate the mass, velocity and forces propelling the invisible creature obscured beneath the surface. Without IAOs, captured U.S. government policymakers would receive fewer marching orders conflating Israeli and U.S. interests. News media outlets would not have broadcast so many false stories inflating first the threat of Iraq, then the Iranian nuclear program while constantly distorting Israel-Palestine issues. Israel's nuclear weapons and the doctrine that governs their use would be openly discussed and anaylzed with the resources they warrant. Orwellian acronyms such as "QME"—qualitative military edge, referring to Israel's congressionally mandated entitlement to a military advantage over all

---

[14] Sidney Blumenthal, "Israel, couple of things, Sid" email to Hillary Clinton, March 17, 2010

[15] See an AIPAC candidate scorecard "AIPAC INSIDER Election 2008," http://IsraelLobby.org/AIPAC/AIPACinsider.pdf

presumed rivals—but which never includes a tally of its strategic and tactical nuclear weapons—would not be minted and circulated. Dark money would have fewer obvious candidates furiously contorting themselves to receive funding measured on the basis of their pledged support for Israel through endless repetition of IAO talking points.

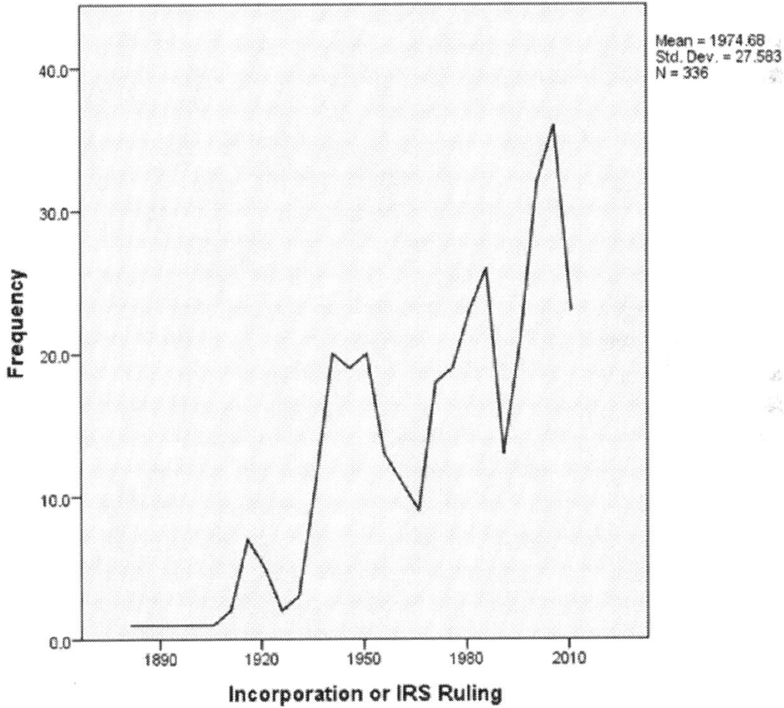

Figure 3 Four waves of IAO formation by year

Crunching the revenue, employee, volunteer, location and incorporation date[16] numbers of the selected IAOs yields some interesting and actionable data. Our very first finding from this *Big Israel* database reveals that Israel Affinity Organizations were created in four distinct waves. It is important to remember that most of the earliest did not begin operations seeking a Jewish state in Palestine. Many at first were even staunchly opposed to the idea. As a group, IAOs resemble the Most Interesting Man Alive formerly portrayed by Jonathan Goldsmith in beer commercials. He "didn't always drink beer, but when he did, preferred Dos Equis." IAOs weren't always Zionist, but when Israel was finally established (or "reestablished" as many IAOs insist)

[16] Or IRS tax-exempt status ruling per determination letter date.

it became a top cause.

The first wave of IAOs were largely formed as social welfare organizations facilitating a smoother flow of Jewish immigrants into the U.S. Only after huge membership and donor growth did such organizations as B'nai B'rith or the Hebrew Immigrant Aid Society attempt to influence policymakers and secure approval of Zionism from elites and institutions.

Wave two was state-building—creating the giant fundraising machines that harvested Jewish charitable largesse and directed some of it to Jewish entities in Palestine, then into newly created Israel. The big transfer and subsidy organizations helped arm and equip a Jewish state in Palestine, sometimes through highly illicit means using disposable front organizations. Yet today, the regulatory basis for what are mostly self-monitored transfers of billions of dollars from the United States to Israel is sketchy, though few activists in the pro-Israel community wish to draw attention to that fact.

The 1980s and 1990s "third wave" organizations were the media pressure groups formed to counteract critical reporting on Israel following its invasion of Lebanon in 1982 and the first Palestinian *intifadah* in 1987. This was the environment spawning a legion of pro-Israel think tanks, including the mitosis of the Washington Institute for Near East Policy (to function as a source for seemingly "disinterested" or even neutral experts prominently hosted across major media) from the American Israel Public Affairs Committee—which lobbied for the policies advanced by WINEP "experts." Holocaust memorialization and awareness programs in this period became a major means for IAOs to combat growing popular discomfort and more informed questions about Israel's policies and actions.

Support for Jewish Immigrant Assimilation & Zionism 1800-1920s	Building State of Israel 1930s-1940s	Israel Justification & Defense 1980s-1990s	Pro-Israel Imposition on Campus Anti-Muslim/Lawfare 2000-Present
Zionist Organization of America	United Jewish Appeal	U.S. Holocaust Memorial Museum	The Israel Project
Jewish Telegraphic Agency	American Society for Technion	Friends of the IDF	Investigative Project on Terrorism
Hebrew Immigrant Aid Society	Jewish Council for Public Affairs	CAMERA/MEMRI	Emergency Committee for Israel
B'nai B'rith	American Zionist Council – which spun off AIPAC	Middle East Forum	Israel on Campus Coalition
American Jewish Committee	American Society for Technion	Birthright Israel	The Lawfare Project
American Jewish Joint Distribution Committee	American Committee for the Weizmann Institute	Washington Institute for Near East Policy	United Against Nuclear Iran

Figure 4 Important IAOs within the four waves

In the final wave, IAOs were formed to tell students how to think about Israel on campus and to label pro-Palestinian grassroots organizations as responsible for creating "unsafe spaces" for Jewish students. They tirelessly work to pass legislation funding Holocaust awareness and Israel Studies programs. The Lawfare Project attempts to cut federal education funding if Middle East studies programs are insufficiently pro-Israel, short-circuiting serious research and intellectual ferment. Any effective challenge to Israel's foreign policies on campus by organized groupings of students can quickly be portrayed as part of a resurgence of "anti-Semitism." The Israel Project and its demonstrably dubious polling—as revealed later—tells Americans that their support for Israel's invasions and security policies are both unflagging and proper. It is this widespread IAO organized imposition of a "pro-Israel" environment as the forced "norm," by silencing opposing views, that earns the fourth wave the "imposition" label.

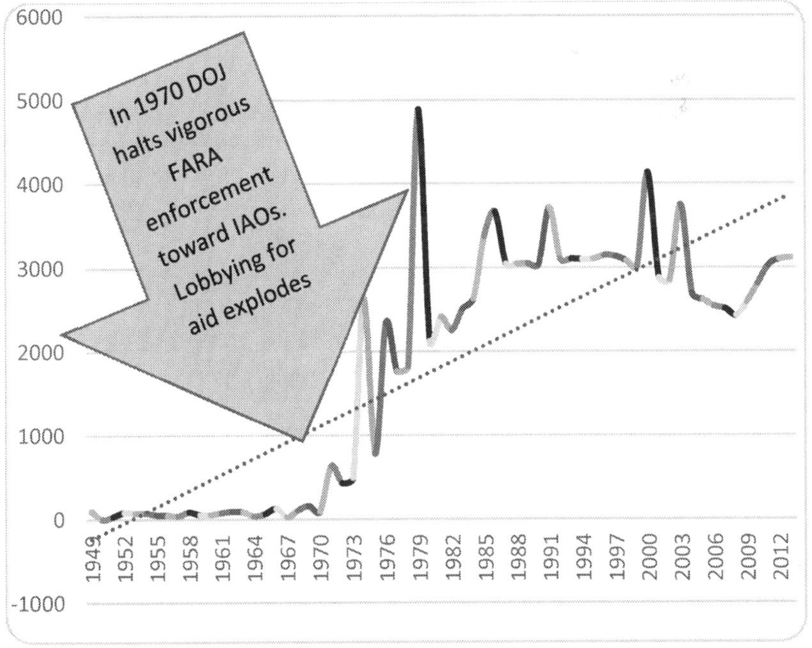

Figure 5 U.S. aid to Israel before & after FARA enforcement[17]

[17] These U.S. foreign aid figures are not adjusted for inflation. They are charted from data as presented in Jeremy M. Sharp, "U.S. Foreign Aid to Israel," Congressional Research Service, June 10, 2015, page 30

Half of the organizations surveyed in this book—again only the 336, including the biggest, most visible and influential but also fairly small and quiet organizations—were created before the year 1975 with the other half launched during and after 1975. Explanations advanced as "conventional wisdom" by IAOs and their proponents say this boom in organizational activity and U.S. aid occurred as a direct result of the 1967 Six-Day War. Israel attacked and scored military victories against Egypt, Jordan and Syria. Military success, goes the story, put Israel into the U.S. camp as an effective Cold War ally, able to defeat Soviet client states in the Middle East and share captured Soviet weapons technology with America. Therefore, a surge in taxpayer-funded U.S. aid to Israel began to flow. But upon closer examination, this "cause and effect" may not be so simple, because an important and little-known transformation in law enforcement was simultaneously underway.

Less well known is that the boom in aid and IAO formation coincides with the *de facto* end of U.S. Justice Department attempts to enforce the 1938 Foreign Agents Registration Act on U.S. entities either funded by, controlled by, or tightly coordinating with the Israeli government. The Department of Justice attempted early on to get the Zionist Organization of America to register as a foreign agent—formally making the demand seven times. Lobbying the attorney general resulted in a Justice Department commitment not to enforce registration. Justice Department functionaries then ordered the American Zionist Council to register as a foreign agent in 1962, only to see the lobbying committee AIPAC split off six weeks later, incorporate as a separate entitity and restart the same activities.[18] After, once again, pursuing the Jewish Agency's foreign agent entity in the United States in 1970, the Justice Department finally threw in the towel and backed away from enforcing FARA—though not in cases involving other foreign countries lacking a network of affinity organizations in the U.S., such as Pakistan.[19] The numbers of IAOs backing unconditional U.S. support and foreign aid for Israel subsequently exploded, as did the actual amount of U.S. foreign aid going to Israel. U.S. leaders grew more aware of Israel's nuclear weapons during this period—which should have ended foreign aid to Israel after 1976, when the Symington and Glenn Amendments were passed prohibiting

[18] Before AIPAC split off from the AZC and incorporated as a separate entity, it was known as the American Zionist Committee for Public Affairs (1954-1959). On August 11, 1959 it changed its name to American Israel Public Affairs Committee. Nevertheless, AIPAC remained an unincorporated committee within the AZC until 1963. "American Zionist Council, American Zionist Council for Public Affairs, American Israel Public Affairs Committee," The Israel Lobby Archive. http://www.israellobby.org/AZCPA/

[19] Grant F. Smith "Selective FARA Enforcement: Pakistan's Alleged Agents Prosecuted, Israel's Ignored" *Washington Report on Middle East Affairs*, September-October 2011, 32-33, 73.

foreign aid to clandestine nuclear weapons states. The degree to which they were coerced by Israel to acquiesce to demands for aid and diplomatic support—despite awareness of the nuclear arsenal—currently cannot be rigorousy studied because of laws banning public briefings by the most informed experts on Israel's nuclear weapons, who are federal government employees or contractors.[20]

IAO demands have evolved and become ever greater over time as they shifted away from providing social welfare for Jewish immigrants, to ideological support for the Zionist cause, toward the immediate recognition and defense of Israel and its claims on Palestinian land and defense against rivals. As mentioned, America's first modern foreign managed [free] trade agreement was with Israel.[21] Today, IAOs have wrangled U.S. terrorism designations for most of Israel's major enemies while constantly agitating—publicly and privately—for U.S. military actions against them. Unbeknownst to most Americans until unearthed by Wikileaks and reported in *The Guardian* newspaper, a secret doctrine is operative across U.S. federal agencies that "the survival of the state of Israel is a paramount goal of U.S. Middle East policy."[22]

One way Israel Affinity Organizations exercise such a great deal of influence in the halls of power is by claiming to represent all Americans who are Jewish. Until very recently they have derived significant political benefits from doing so and have seldom been challenged. Yet open and visible dissent, backed up by major statistical surveys, reveal many IAO policy positions are at fundamental odds with overwheming numbers of Jewish Americans. Pew Research Center's 2013 survey of Jewish Americans found that only 18 percent of American Jews even belong to Jewish organizations. The Steinhardt Social Research Institute at Brandeis University estimated that the 2013 population of Jewish adults in the United States was 4.3 million.[23]

---

[20] Phil Weiss and Grant F. Smith, "Israeli nukes are finally newsworthy—as U.S. gov't both releases and gags info" *Mondoweiss*, August 26, 2015. http://mondoweiss.net/2015/08/israeli-mentioned-releases

[21] See the book by Grant F. Smith *Spy Trade: How Israel's Lobby Undermines America's Economy* (Institute for Research: Middle Eastern Policy, 2009) for a history of how espionage aided the American Israel Public Affairs Committee's fight to pass the unpopular (with industry groups and the public) managed trade measure that favored Israeli exports to the U.S.

[22] Glenn Greenwald, "NSA shares raw intelligence including Americans' data with Israel." *The Guardian*, September 11, 2013 http://www.theguardian.com/world/2013/sep/11/nsa-americans-personal-data-israel-documents

[23] Steinhardt Social Research Institute at the Cohen Center for Modern Jewish Studies. Brandeis University. American Jewish Population Project. http://ajpp.brandeis.edu/

The Pew ratio applies to most IAOs, since most self-identify as Jewish organizations. Many IAOs incorporate the words "Jewish" and "Judaism" in their names, actively reach out to the Jewish community in donation and membership drives, and claim to represent American Jews. The Pew poll percentage applied to the Steinhardt population number reveals that the Jewish (or non-Christian Zionist) member segment of the Israel lobby in the United States probably only numbers around 774,000 adults, or the approximate population of a city like Charlotte, North Carolina or Fort Worth, Texas.

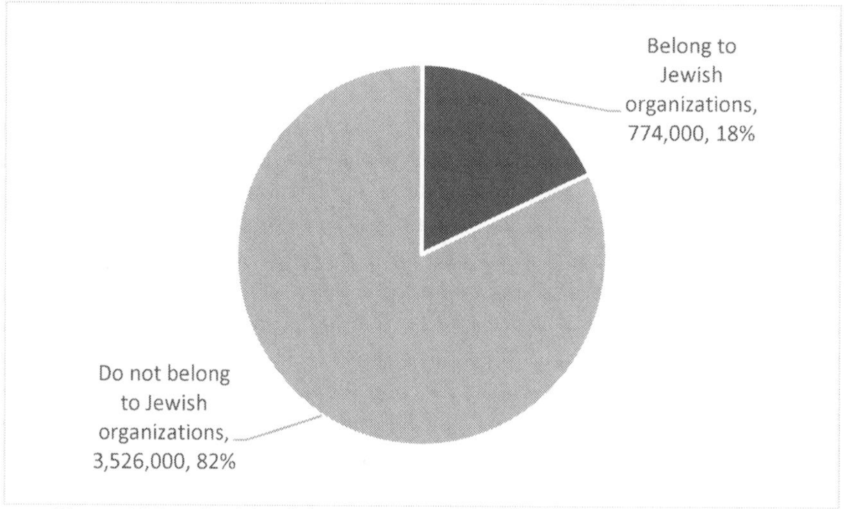

Figure 6 Most Jewish adults are not Israel Affinity Organization members

Those who are IAO members tend to be wealtier than the non-IAO-member Jews—31 percent have incomes of at least $150,000, as opposed to only 24 percent of non-members. IAO members are also more likely to be Republican (18 percent vs. only 12 percent for the non-affiliated). IAO members are less likely to identify as liberal (46 percent versus 53 percent of the general Jewish population). So not only the ideology but political affiliations of most Jewish Americans sharply diverge from the positions held by IAO leadership. In 2013 those who were members of IAOs were more likely to disapprove of President Obama's handling of the Iran nuclear issue, at 42 percent, than the the majority non-member Jewish population, of which only 33 percent disapproved.[24] The multi-billion-dollar lobby nevertheless

[24] Todd Gitlin and Steven M. Cohen, "On the Iran deal, American Jewish 'leaders' don't speak for most Jews." *The Washington Post*, August 14, 2015 https://www.washingtonpost.com/opinions/on-the-iran-deal-american-jewish-

continues claiming to represent people who have never indicated any desire to be affiliated with it.

IAOs self-designating to be the voice of America's Jews, like Israel, disenfranchise multitudes who do not support Israeli policies, the massive aid packages, or the army of hawkish politicians mouthing lobby doctrine in fierce competition for large campaign contributions. As examined in the final chapter, this Jewish majority is victimized twice—first as IAOs "bundle" them into a contrived homogeneous voice for Israel, and then leave them to suffer the potential backlash of being viewed as responsible for corrupt Israel lobby policies emanating from Washington and Israel. IAOs—and Israel for that matter—could reduce this potential backlash by more careful qualification about who they can verifiably claim to represent. But they do not, since such honesty does not serve their cause.

Far more important, as revealed in the final chapters, are the much larger number of Americans who don't happen to be Jewish and who either know nothing about or, when informed, disapprove of major IAO initiatives. Their victimization is similar in some ways to the better known frauds perpetrated by junk mortgate purveyors and large investment banks during the financial crisis. In stage one, small borrowers received mortgages with monthly payments they could not afford. In stage two, these junk mortgages were bundled into triple-A rated securities—graded by heavily compromised major rating agencies—and foisted off on unsuspecting investors, including pension funds. In the final stage, bankers created instruments to bet on mass mortgage default. The bailout, when it came, saved many of the victimizers but not many victims.

Yet like IAOs, many junk mortgage system victimizers claimed the opposite was true. Their clamor for a bailout and government purchase at face value of worthess assets was often portrayed as being entirely on behalf of small mortgage holders. In reality, threats made by the industry, behind closed doors, that soon ATMs would stop working and money market shares would break the buck (go below one dollar) if they were not immediately bailed out, were far closer to their real attitude toward captured politicians than lipservice about saving small mortgage holders.

In stage five, injury was heaped onto insult as American tax dollars were put up to bail out the large banks responsible for the fraud. The backlash against this abuse resulted in protest movements such as "Occupy Wall Street." A fundamental popular perception shift about big finance ensued and is still a major issue in the 2016 presidential race. But a similarly frank discussion has never taken place about Israel's influence.

This is partly due to Americans only rarely being asked relevant policy

---

leaders-dont-speak-for-all-jews/2015/08/14/988e577e-41d5-11e5-846d-02792f854297_story.html questions by pollsters about the amount of U.S. foreign aid to Israel or the impact of unwavering U.S. diplomatic support. Or IAO attempts to direct and interfere with U.S. foreign policy toward armed conflicts and boycotts that externalize costs onto unsuspecting taxpayers. When Americans are informed and asked, most overwhelmingly disapprove, as is explored in chapter 9, "American Public Opinion." This disapproval is likely to accelerate in the near future, as social transformations of tremendous breadth drive large numbers of Americans out of the most easily-influenced groupings—religious institutions—and toward more skeptical views of Israel and unconditional American support.

3 FOUR IAO CATEGORIES

Four major categories of IAOs reveal themselves in the Israel Affinity Organization database compiled for this book and available online at IsraelLobby.org. The year 2012 was chosen as the cut-off for data because that was the latest available year for most IAO tax returns. Tax returns can legally be filed years after the close of a given calendar year. Many IAOs file requests for automatic extensions to delay filing. AIPAC has managed its fiscal year and extensions filing in a way that its returns are delayed as long as possible. The IAO data analyzed and available online and in the Appendix is from the year 2001 to year 2012 returns, unless otherwise noted. The forecast data is projected through the year 2020. Many IAOs do not have fiscal years that begin on January 1 and end on December 31. However, we tally and compile data by the reporting year stamped on the IRS tax form. For example, all IAO filings on an IRS 2005 tax form are tallied and compared as 2005 data.

Subsidy organizations transfer privately raised tax-exempt donations and significant amounts of some congressional appropriations tapping U.S. taxpayers into Israeli institutions, organizations and projects. The largest members in this IAO category are the American Jewish Joint Distribution Committee and United Israel Appeal. A growing segment within our subsidy category are partners to a single recipient organization in Israel. Many of these are incorporated with names that include the words "American Committee for" or "American Friends of," such as "American Friends of the Israel Museum" or the "American Society for Technion, Israel Institute of Technology, Inc." There are nearly 700 "American Friends" organizations. The hundred major subsidy organizations included here raised $2 billion in funding for Israel in 2012.

The "fundraising and local political action" organizations are the second category and include more than 150 federations raising large amounts of cash through their metropolitan fundraising campaigns. The greatest number of large IAO fundraising organizations are, in fact, federations. They give financial support to both local Jewish and non-Jewish organizational recipients and also provide large amounts in direct transfers to Israel. Of greatest concern to Americans worried about stealth lobbying are entities housed inside federations and not generally separately incorporated or filing separate tax returns. These Community Relations Councils are highly politically active, function within a network of media watchdogs to provide "local" media action and reaction on behalf of Israel, and also lobby for cookie-cutter local, city and state legislative initiatives to benefit Israel that are promulgated from national headquarters.

Community Relations Councils are largely invisible as an IAO national lobbying force precisely because most are not functionally, financially or even physically separate from their metropolitan federation host organizations. More troubling is that 91 percent claim on their tax reporting to the IRS that they do not lobby—despite activities on websites and in the press that directly contradict such claims. Federations that house a resident Jewish Community Relations Council reported in total only $1.3 million directed toward lobbying in the year 2012. Unofficially JCRC executives and staff often help favored political candidate campaigns by joining up as "independent" fundraisers and "campaign committee chairs" and then having JCRCs host events for favored candidates to raise funding and their political profile. Hiding inside a large federation means even JCRCs that focus all of their efforts on lobbying can claim to the IRS that the primary activity of the larger organization (the federation) is not lobbying. Remaining unincorporated, as AIPAC did while still a committee within the American Zionist Council, helps hide the footprints of lobbyists.

The third major IAO category—the advocacy organizations—leverage and focus the collective might of the other affiliated IAOs, from federations and JCRCs to the wealthy donors that fund subsidy IAOs, on massive public relations campaigns, targeting Congress and the White House as well as key government agencies. The political clout, focused at the federal level, has made massive annual (and ad hoc add-ons during the year) "aid legislation" providing funding for weapons and programs in Israel such as the "Iron Dome" missile defense system, and non-binding resolutions pledging political and diplomatic support, an entitlement that can never be rationally debated or reassessed. Though often reported in the news media as military "sales" to Israel, the arms deals represent a transfer of tax dollars for Israel to either purchase U.S. arms or invest in its own weapons programs, most of which produce high-margin exports for Israel. IAO advocacy organizations exert pressure on politicians via their indirect and direct influence on campaign contributions and their ability to field opposing primary candidates if an incumbent fails to be sufficiently deferential. A study of lobbying on Capitol Hill that interviewed hundreds of staffers reveals that there is no such thing as being "too deferential" to AIPAC.

Advocacy IAOs publish news and information while continually organizing public events to promote Israel. The American Israel Education Foundation, an arm of AIPAC, takes politicians, journalists and other elites on free trips to promote Israeli policy objectives. Other IAO advocacy organizations attack enemies by censuring, suing and attempting to defund critics of Israel. Linkages have been formed between Israel and advocacy IAOs, and between advocacy IAOs. For example, all executives of an umbrella organization called the Conference of Presidents of Major American Jewish Organizations are automatically members of the American Israel Public Affairs Committee, which does most of the lobbying on Capitol Hill. Media watchdog advocacy IAOs try to buff up Israel's image through story placement and censuring unfavorable press.

The fourth and final IAO category—Education & Training—is directed both inward and outward. The internal component includes spreading "Zionist education" programs from kindergarten through college in the U.S. for Jewish students. It includes the movement for the expansion of Jewish day schools as part of an anti-assimilation campaign and to create closer cultural ties to Israel. It also funds the network of Hillel organizations on campus. Hillel originated as a means for ensuring equal opportunity for Jewish students but today increasingly functions as the primary on-campus advocate for Israel.

The external education campaign is aimed at elites and the general American public. This includes Holocaust memorial museums across the country, law enforcement "tolerance" and counter-terrorism training in Israel (mostly inappropriate for real-world American law enforcement needs) as well as producing and promoting Israel studies departments and Holocaust memorial curricula for public and private schools. These programs create a feeling of affinity with and sympathy for Israel as a refuge, particularly during the formative years of young Americans. It also crowds out far more relevant and useful histories much closer to home.

Ever larger efforts are being made by IAOs, particularly Jewish Community Relations Councils, to secure taxpayer funding at the state level to field "counter-extremism projects" directed entirely toward Muslim communities. Such programs claim to stem the flow of "radicalized" U.S. Muslims leaving the country to join extremist groups in the Middle East. While doing much to heighten tensions about and within Muslim communities, such programs avoid addressing the causes of terrorism and political violence; because to do so would inevitably call into question the U.S. (and Israel's) key role in creating it, according to author and syndicated columnist Rami Khouri:

> *Specifically, the countering violent extremism approach ignores four of the most important drivers of political violence and terrorism in the Middle East: 1) sustained socioeconomic stress, deprivation and marginalization, including rampant official corruption, that leaves several hundred million people destitute and powerless; 2) chronic, Western-supported authoritarianism and dictatorships that leave citizens without any political rights in most of the societies that generate terrorism; 3) the impact of sustained Western militarism in the region over the last few decades, especially the Anglo-American war in Iraq; and 4) the persistent radicalizing impact for the past half-century of the Arab-Israeli conflict, Israeli colonization of Arab lands and U.S.-led Western acquiescence in Israeli policies.*[25]

The fourteen IAOs studied in this education category raised $317 million in 2012 for their indoctrination, public education and training programs. Ironically, within the IAO ecosystem there is a strong—though inconspicuous—recruiting drive that motivates young pro-Israel American Jews to serve in the Israel Defense Forces. This ongoing soft sell recruiting now appears to be diminishing the already-historically low percentage of self-identified Jews in the U.S. armed services, as is explored later. Some IAOs provide direct and indirect financial support for violent West Bank settlers who illegally expropriate Palestinian lands, destroy crops, attack and kill Palestinians from behind a protective phalanx of IDF soldiers. Yet there is no program for countering IAO extremism of this sort. The U.S. Treasury Department has been noticeably absent for a long time whenever questions about cutting off support through denial of tax-exempt status or financial flows are raised. The reasons for that absence are becoming clearer with the passage of time.

---

[25] Rami G. Khouri, "Beware the hoax of countering violent extremism: UN global youth effort is an exercise in delusion." *Aljazeera America*, September 29, 2015 http://america.aljazeera.com/opinions/2015/9/beware-the-hoax-of-countering-violent-extremism.html

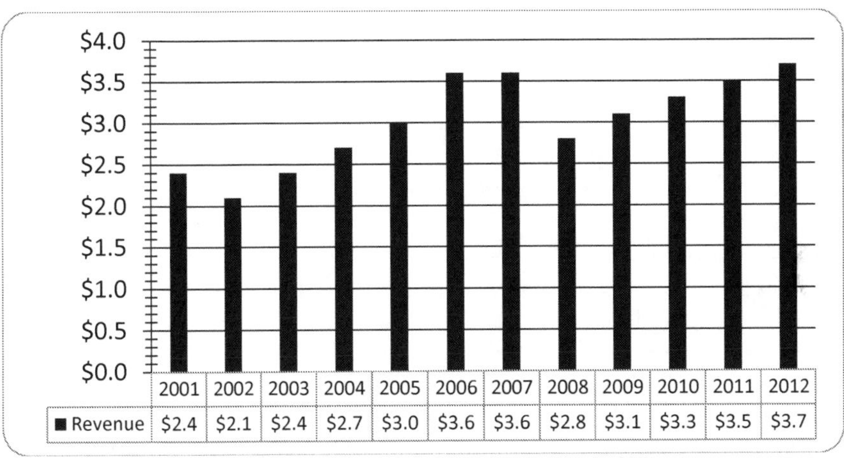

Figure 7 IAO revenue year 2001-2012 ($ U.S. billion)

The total revenue of the 336 "Big Israel" organizations that make up the Israel lobby has been steadily growing since 2008. Revenue suffered a 21 percent decline during the 2008 financial crisis, yet by 2012 total revenue exceeded recent highs at $3.7 billion a year. To put this in perspective, the total charitable sector in the U.S. was $338 billion in 2012 and grew at four percent per year over the past decade. Over the same period, Israel Affinity Organizations have been growing faster—at five percent annually—which is increasing their overall slice of the total American charity pie.

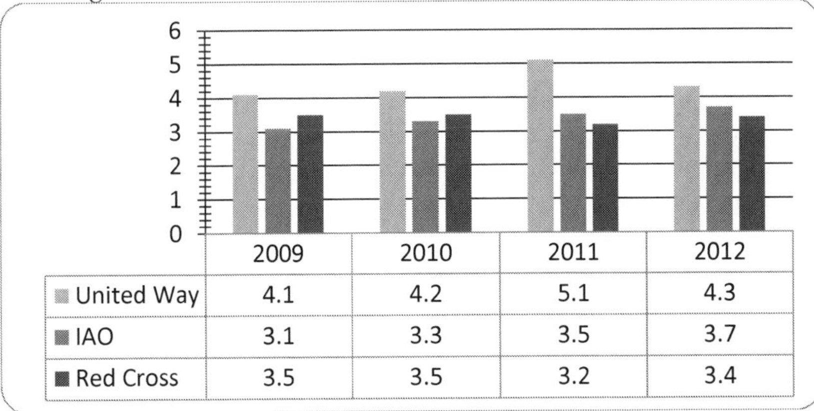

6
5
4
3
2
1
0
2009 2010 2011 2012
United Way 4.1 4.2 5.1 4.3
IAO 3.1 3.3 3.5 3.7
Red Cross 3.5 3.5 3.2 3.4

Figure 8 IAOs & top U.S. charities ranked by revenue ($ U.S. billion)

Collectively IAOs, within the overall ranking of top U.S. charities, in year 2012 were right behind the United Way, America's largest tax-exempt charitable organization, and just ahead of the Red Cross. Given their steady trajectory and faster overall growth rate, it is reasonable to assume that 2015 data will reveal collectively IAOs—the Israel lobby—raised more revenue than any other U.S. charity, but such confirmation will not be possible until 2017, given tax return filing realities.

If categories of IAOs were viewed as a pyramid built of revenue blocks, the large IAO base is made up of subsidy organizations. At the second tier are the fundraising and local political action organizations—the federations and JCRCs. Comprising the next level are the many advocacy organizations like the American Israel Public Affairs Committee, which is often incorrectly discussed in isolation as if it alone constituted the "Israel lobby" in America. The nearly invisible education category organizations, many working assiduously behind the scenes and highly averse to scrutiny, are the capstone.

Some Israel affinity organizations exercise enormous power at the United Nations as officially recognized Non-Governmental Organizations (NGOs). Such official UN status gives IAOs access to UN premises and opportunities to attend or observe many conferences and events at United Nations facilities around the world. Conference of Presidents of Major American Jewish Organizations president Malcolm Hoenlein has described pro-Israel NGOs at the UN as an extremely potent force against the many efforts there to force through peace initiatives and recognize the rights of Palestinians. Hoenlein has discussed how his organization briefs and educates Israeli government officials how to best leverage this IAO-funded lobbying infrastructure at the UN.

Analyzing the growth rate of IAOs reveals important dynamics within the affinity ecosystem. We summarize these organizations briefly in the following pages to reveal the dynamism and breadth of IAO activities. Comparing each IAO's 2012 revenue from tax returns with their revenues a decade earlier reveals the fastest growing IAOs are two large subsidy organizations. Batya-Friends of United Hatzalah is a subsidy IAO that provides funding to Israel's largest non-profit volunteer emergency medical services (EMS) organization. American Friends of Rambam Medical Center funds the fifth largest medical center in Israel, which is also a teaching hospital.

The next two fastest growing IAOs are in the *Aliyah*—Jewish-only migration to Israel—business. Nefesh B'Nefesh Jewish Souls United Inc. was created in 2001 and facilitates *Aliyah* ("going up" in Hebrew) from North America and the United Kingdom. Birthright Israel, launched in 1999, provides free identity-building trips to young Jews in hopes they will marry fellow Jews, personally connect with Israel and possibly make *Aliyah*. The Friends of the Israel Antiquities Authority subsidizes an independent Israeli governmental authority that regulates archeological excavation and conservation. The Foundation for the Charlotte Jewish Community is a federation that has boomed in a North Carolina metropolitan area that is the third fastest growing in the United States and now the second largest city in the Southeast.

World ORT is a subsidy IAO that funds 159 education and training centers in Israel and other countries. The Israel Emergency Alliance is a Los Angeles-headquartered advocacy organization with a large number of programs to promote Israel on campus and to the general public such as B.I.G (Buy Israel Goods) and "Peace Takes Two," which portrays Palestinians as ever unwilling to engage in peace negotiations ardently pursued by Israel. The Israel Venture Network subsidizes small businesses that hire at-risk and disadvantaged populations in Israel. American Friends of Yeshiva Kodshim of Kodshim raises funding for a religious education center in Jerusalem. The American-Israeli Cooperative Enterprise (AICE Inc) was formed in 1993 by Mitchell Bard, the former editor of AIPAC's house organ, the *Near East Report*, to "strengthen the U.S.–Israel relationship." AICE runs the "Jewish Virtual Library," an online encyclopedia as well as a database of joint U.S-Israel projects and academic exchanges. American Friends of the Israel Free Loan Association Inc. (AFIFLA) subsidizes loans to families in need and struggling small businesses in Israel. The Jewish Funders Network attempts to increase collaboration between large donors to make more effective grants and investments into Israeli business ventures. The David Project trains Jewish students to become effective Israel advocates on campus and in other important communities.

Director Jay Marcus runs the Central Fund of Israel out of the Marcus Brothers Textiles store on Sixth Avenue in Manhattan. Itamar Marcus is the former vice president of the fund which, according to *Politico,* funds Israeli pro-settler groups. Friends of Yad Sarah funds services for disabled, elderly and housebound Israelis. The Westchester Jewish Council, Jewish Community Foundation of Greater Long Beach and the United Jewish Community of Virginia Peninsula are additional fast-growing federations that bounced back quickly from the 2008 financial crisis.

Minnesotans Against Terrorism is a small IAO that was launched in 2002 by Ilan Sharon, who was born and raised in Israel and served as a captain in the IDF. Sharon moved to Minnesota after his software company in Israel merged with a Minnesota corporation. Sharon struggled for many years to build the Minnesotans Against Terrorism from a $38,000 operation in 2001 to almost a quarter million a decade later, with major support from local billboard mogul Bob Naegele. According to this new Minnesotan, Ilan Sharon, the radical Islamists were winning over the American media with a:

> *…sweeping victory of the radical Muslim supporters and apologetics in the media. The main stream [sic] media was bending over backward to not portray the Palestinian radical Muslim terrorists as terrorists. This is when I realized how*

dangerous these groups might be and when I decided that I need to do something about it....[26]

A snapshot of the truly "bleeding edge" entities in the IAO ecosystem are the twenty organizations with the highest five-year revenue growth rate. Omitting the federations, which are somewhat homogeneous in focus, as well as IAOs mentioned previously, the five-year growth stars may signal an emerging "fifth wave."

Israel Affinity Organization	10-Year Growth
Batya-Friends of United Hatzalah	742%
American Friends of Rambam Medical Center	350%
Nefesh B'Nefesh Jewish Souls United Inc.	232%
Birthright Israel Foundation	168%
The Friends of the Israel Antiquities Authority	165%
Foundation for the Charlotte Jewish Community	142%
World ORT	133%
Israel Emergency Alliance aka Standwithus	123%
Israel Venture Network	119%
American Friends of Yeshiva Kodshim of Kodshim	102%
American-Israeli Cooperative Enterprise (AICE Inc.)	95%
American Friends of the Israel Free Loan Association Inc. Aka AFIFLA	74%
Jewish Funders Network	58%
The David Project	48%
Central Fund of Israel	46%
Friends of Yad Sarah Inc.	40%
Westchester Jewish Council Inc.	39%
United Jewish Community of the Virginia Peninsula	36%
Jewish Community Foundation of Greater Long Beach & West Orange County	36%
Minnesotans Against Terrorism	35%

Figure 9 Fastest growing IAOs by ten-year revenue change

Leading the pack is the Israel Strategic Alternative Energy Foundation. Many IAOs have a heavy interest in separating the United States from its long alliance with Middle East, North African and particularly Gulf energy-

[26] "Ilan Sharon, Minnesotans Against Terrorism," The Clarion Project, http://www.radicalislam.org/action/ilan-sharon-minnesotans-against-terrorism

producing states. ISAEF, launched in 2008, aims to fund 100 alternative energy research programs in Israeli universities within a decade.

Israel depends on high-tech research, and particularly weapons development, as a major export category. Friends of Israel Sci-Tech Schools is a new (2009) North American non-profit organization supporting an independent network of science and technology schools in Israel. It is determined to maintain Israel at the competitive edge.

J Street debuted to much excitement as a "pro-Israel, pro-peace" organization that advocates for a "two-state" solution, seeks a halt to illegal settlement expansion, opposes cuts to foreign aid to Palestinians and that advocates for a diplomatic resolution to the so-called "Iran nuclear crisis." J Street runs a political action committee (PAC) that funds candidates who adhere to J Street's program. This is unlike its much larger, highly secretive competitor the American Israel Public Affairs Committee, which though not a PAC, instead signals a large network of purposely obscurely-named PACs (e.g. National Action Committee and Northern Californians for Good Government), some of which it helped create, and wealthy individuals to support candidates that adhere to the AIPAC agenda.

The Israeli American Council is an organization launched in 2007 and funded by casino mogul Sheldon Adelson, aimed at mobilizing the estimated half-million Israeli Americans residing in the U.S. to be more active on behalf of Israel. It was the brainchild of Israeli Consul General Ehud Danoch, who wanted more of a public turnout in support of Israel's massive 2006 bombing campaign against Lebanon. Danoch estimated that 200,000 Israeli Americans resided in the Los Angeles area, but had not visibly turned out in support of Israel.[27]

Like the Israeli American Council, the International Israeli Caucus Foundation also sought to build up formal support—in Congress—for Israel amidst huge international pressure for a ceasefire during the 2006 Israeli attack on Lebanon. It plans to form 31 more caucuses, internationally, in the elected bodies of such countries as Brazil, Germany, Australia, Switzerland and Uruguay. IIC's declaration of purpose states members must resolve that:

> *Jerusalem is, and should be, the undivided capital of Israel and the Jewish People, and in recognition of this all the nations of the world should locate their embassies in Jerusalem" and that "the Iranian regime with its developing arsenal of weapons of mass destruction and its stated goal of destroying Israel constitutes a*

[27] "The history of the IAC." Israeli American Council. http://www.israeliamerican.org/national/history-of-iac

clear and present danger to the existence of the State of Israel that must be opposed.[28]

On its website, the organization lists 31 serving members of Congress as caucus members, including Eliot Engel, Louie Gohmert and Alan Grayson.

The Institute for the Study of Global Antisemitism and Policy sees Anti-Semitism everywhere in the top tiers of academia, and is determined to shut down the federal funding that it alleges supports such content. The Institute "studies" and holds public events about the "connections" between "terrorism, BDS and Antisemitism." The institute has never lacked facilities and conference rooms at elite Ivy League law schools and universities to host and webcast events linking anti-Semitism to just about any form of criticism of Israel.

Israel Affinity Organization	**5-Year Growth**
Israel Strategic Alternative Energy Foundation	4194%
Friends of Israel Sci-Tech Schools Inc.	3898%
United Jewish Federation of Utah	334%
J Street Education Fund, Inc.	281%
The Friends of the Israel Antiquities Authority	261%
Israeli American Council	195%
Jewish Federation of Central New York Inc.	154%
North Louisiana Jewish Federation	139%
Jewish Federation of Reading Pennsylvania Inc.	116%
International Israeli Allies Caucus Foundation Inc.	103%
Institute for the Study of Global Antisemitism and Policy	92%
American Friends of the Hebrew University Inc.	85%
Jewish Community Board of Akron	61%
American Friends of the Israel Free Loan Association Inc. Aka AFIFLA	60%
Greater Miami Jewish Federation	57%
Milwaukee Jewish Federation	54%
Scholars for Peace in the Middle East Inc.	54%
Greensboro Jewish Federation	52%
Hadassah, Women's Zionist Organization of America	51%
New Israel Fund	47%

Figure 10 Fastest growing IAOs by five-year revenue change

[28] "Declaration of Purpose and Solidarity with the People and State of Israel" Israel Allies Foundation. http://www.israelallies.org/images/uploads/resources/IIACF_Declaration_of_Purpose.pdf

The Middle East Studies Association, or MESA, is a large, organic association that has in the past never been shy about debating, studying and criticizing Israeli policy. It is definitely not an IAO. That is perhaps why the Foundation for the Defense of Democracies attempted to create a rival organization, The Association for the Study of the Middle East and Africa, which has somewhat fizzled in terms of membership and standing. However, the pro-Israel network of academic scholars, Scholars for Peace in the Middle East, has also stepped up to promote "Israel's right to exist as a sovereign Jewish state within safe and secure borders, and with the rights and legitimate aspirations of her neighbors" and determine whether scholarship critical of Israel is "anti-Semitic."

Hadassah, the Women's Zionist Organization created in 1922, would not seem to be the type of younger, smaller innovative IAO that would post huge jumps in five-year growth scores. Its chaotic revenue could be a sign of its pending demise. After unwise investment allocations to fraudster Bernie Madoff's Ponzi scheme nearly crippled the organization, savvy and fundraising acumen have led to huge gains, from $46 million in 2011 to $101 million in 2012, as the organization regained donor confidence and posted some huge single-year gains that put it on the list. But then things turned sour again.[29] Finally, the New Israel Fund is an organization working for "social justice" in Israel that funds democratic movements toward a "two-state" solution and peace and equality for all—as long as this does not fundamentally change the makeup of Israel as a predominately Jewish state. The organization has suffered barbs from other IAOs, often lambasted for giving to the wrong—meaning, too progressive—groups.

Apart from the federations and Hadassah, the fastest growing, younger IAOs such as Israel Strategic Alternative Energy Foundation, J Street, the International Israel Allies Caucus and Institute for the Study of Global Anti-Semitism and Policy all seem to share overriding common goals—to provide cover for Israel as unconditional support is being challenged in the United States by Americans informed and concerned about Israeli policies.

Weaning America from Middle East energy has long been promoted by IAOs under the innocuous banner of "energy security." Much was premised on not wanting Israel to be blamed for another energy crisis such as was triggered by Arab producer export cuts to the U.S. in response to the 1973 Arab-Israeli conflict. However, some Americans would probably choose Arab energy which is less expensive to produce if they believed domestic alternatives—groundwater polluted by fracking or dirty tar sands refining—

---

[29] A review of the organization's 2013 IRS form 990 reveals investment income collapsed from $63 million in 2012 to $7.2 million in 2013, with total revenue sliding to $13.6 million. Related organizations such as the Hadassah Medical Relief Association and Hadassah Foundation are not included in this study.

were presented as a means to support Israel. From this angle, the Israel Strategic Alternative Energy Foundation and other organizations begin to look quite a bit less charitable.

J Street was initially presented as a progressive and positive organization dedicated to peace in the Middle East. Since 2005, however, it has become increasingly indistinguishable from AIPAC in its support for unconditional and massive foreign aid to Israel, rejection of the right of return for Palestinian refugees expelled from their homes in 1948 and supporting the U.S. obligation to maintain a "quantitative military edge" to Israel, while both misrepresenting and labeling academics John Mearsheimer and Stephen Walt's book *The Israel Lobby and U.S. Foreign Policy* as anti-Semitic. For all of its attempts to brand itself as more palatable to younger, more progressive American Jews displeased with advocacy IAOs, for many former members the organization failed to break away from being just another advocacy IAO. Critics who follow Israel lobby activities closely left J Street. This has led to the exponential growth of Jewish Voice for Peace, an organization that is much more confrontational, emphasizes peace and justice, and insists on ending the Israeli occupation.[30]

The International Israel Allies Caucus, culling away elected representatives from the diverse views of their constituents in order to support a foreign country, is a typical IAO approach to elites and a dangerous development. In crude terms, elected officials who were lavished with pro-Israel donations directed and channeled by the relevant IAOs are "monetized" and used as political currency to push Israeli objectives in Congress in a way that makes a mockery of how the system is supposed to function. This model being exported is based on AIPAC's successful mode of operation on Capitol Hill.

Finally, the Institute for the Study of Global Antisemitism and Policy partially answers the question explored later of, "why do federations lavish so much on Ivy League schools?" One answer may be to "academicize" an ongoing attack aimed at purging scholars who legitimately and authoritatively question the enormous problems that Israel—and IAOs—have created for America. That is what appears to have driven an ISGAS conference titled, "Terrorism, Antisemitism & BDS: Is there a connection?" As a thought experiment, it is difficult to imagine an Ivy League institution allowing a pro-Palestinian (or any other) group to host an academic event titled, "The Israel lobby, Corruption & War: Is there a connection?" The outcry would be immediate, with calls to purge those responsible for allowing it—as donors and alumni heavies were lined up to threaten cutoffs to the university's

[30] JVP does not meet the author's criteria for being considered an IAO and actively exposes and works against many IAO policies. JVP's definition of occupation includes only those territories captured in the 1967 Six-Day War.

endowment. As explored later, there is an observable connection between funding flows from the IAO ecosystem, often channeled to boards of regents rather than general university coffers, and the Israel lobby's ability to muster support from academia, boards of regents and higher education administrators—and even outside watchdogs such as the American Civil Liberties Union (ACLU) and Electronic Frontier Foundation (EFF) as discussed in the final chapter.

4 SUBSIDY

Israel Affinity Organizations subsidizing a sole Israeli partner organization or sending funds to multiple destinations in Israel (and other regions to support Jewish immigration to Israel) in the year 2012 raised over $2 billion in the United States. In comparison, in 1948, the very year that Israel came into existence, the total transfer of charitable support among the fundraising organizations[31] was equivalent to approximately $1 billion in 2012 dollars. Among the top five 2012 fundraisers were American Friends of Bar Ilan University of Israel ($344 million, 31 employees), the American Jewish Joint Distribution Committee–JDC ($316 million, 154 employees), United Israel Appeal ($193 million, 4 employees), the International Fellowship of Christians and Jews ($193 million, 97 employees), and the Feinberg Graduate School of the Weizmann Institute of Science ($114 million, no listed employees).[32]

Americans can take deductions for charitable contributions made to

---

[31] Author inflation-adjusted total of the Jewish National Fund, Keren Hayesod, American Committee for the Weizmann Institute, American Friends of the Hebrew University, American Technion Society, American Fund for Palestine Institutions, Federated Council of Palestine Institutions, Hadassah, Junior Hadassah, National Labor Committee for Palestine, Pioneer Women, Red Mogen David, Ezrath Torah Fund, and the Joint Distribution Committee. Data from appendix IV – American Jewry's Financial Contributions to Palestine, Samuel Halperin, *The Political World of American Zionism* (Wayne State University, 1961)

[32] IRS form 990 filings available from Citizen Audit at http://www.citizenaudit.org

Israel-based tax-exempt entities under the U.S.-Israel tax bilateral treaty.[33] However, most do not because of two treaty restrictions. First, the taxpayer must have substantial income coming from Israel in order for such donations to make good financial sense. Second, the charitable giver can only take a deduction up to 25 percent of their adjusted gross income. Since most donors do not have substantial income from Israel, they prefer to donate through "friends of" organizations based in the United States.

U.S. tax-deductible contributions from American "Friends of" groups amounting to billions of dollars directed to Israel—though going on for decades—are not solidly grounded within the overall rationale for America's tax-exemption policy. The tax-deductibility of charitable donations is a major enabler of overall charitable giving in the United States. Donors giving to qualified U.S. charities can deduct the amount of their donation from the amount they owe in federal income tax up to certain limits. The core rationale for deductibility in U.S. tax law toward charities is that the work of charitable organizations relieves U.S. government burdens.[34] For example, a charity that feeds the homeless relieves government-funded anti-poverty programs.

Congress was initially somewhat inconsistent and reactive about whether tax-deductibility was available for donors of gifts to foreign, as well as domestic charitable organizations. The first Revenue Acts effective from year 1917 to 1935 did not have any geographical limitations. The 1921 Revenue Act began limiting individual deductions to only contributions toward activities within the United States, while the Revenue Act of 1935 further imposed limits on corporate deductions to only those occurring domestically.[35] The "reducing government burden" rationale was formally and comprehensively enacted for individual taxpayers in the Revenue Act of 1938 as stated at the time by the House Ways and Means Committee:

> *The exemption from taxation of money or property devoted to charitable and other purposes is based upon the theory that the*

[33] "Convention between the Government of the United States of America and the Government of the State of Israel with respect to taxes on income." January 1, 1995 https://www.irs.gov/pub/irs-trty/israel.pdf

[34] Other rationales identified by tax experts but that are not encapsulated in IRS regulations include encouraging volunteerism and philanthropy, allowing private citizens to develop and support their individual interests, and the theory that individuals should only be taxed on income that is consumed. See Joannie Chang, Jennifer I. Goldberg and Naomi J. Schrag, "Cross-Border Charitable Giving," New York University, 1996, http://www1.law.nyu.edu/ncpl/pdfs/1995/Conf1995_GoldbergandSchrag_Final.pdf

[35] In the United States, roughly 80 percent of charitable donations are made by individuals, with 20 percent are contributed by corporations.

> *Government is compensated for the loss of revenue by its relief from financial burden which would otherwise have to be met by appropriations from public funds, and by the benefits resulting from the promotion of the general welfare. The United States derives no such benefit from gifts to foreign institutions, and the proposed limitation is consistent with the above theory. If the recipient, however, is a domestic organization the fact that some portion of its funds is used in other countries for charitable and other purposes (such as missionary and educational purposes) will not affect the deductibility of the gift.*

Operating under the rather thin exception in the final sentence of the above-stated rationale, American "Friends of Israel" organizations have proliferated. Despite appearing to prohibit organizations acting as blind "conduits" designed solely to pass funds through to a designated and much larger foreign organization, and also prohibiting donor "earmarks" to a particular foreign destination, the IRS has allowed American "Friends of Israel" organizations to operate in the United States with the understanding that they will provide adequate oversight over their own foreign disbursements. This "self-regulatory" approach now has even been codified. Revenue Ruling 63-252 states:

> *...Friends of donee not be bound to transfer the funds to a foreign entity by virtue of a charter or by-law provision, that gifts made by the U.S. donee to the foreign entity be entirely within the charitable mission and purpose of the U.S. entity, and that the U.S. donor exercise some scrutiny over the foreign donee to ensure that it is an eligible charity within the meaning of Code section 501(c)(3).*

The IRS role to monitor the proper disbursement of funds of such massive fundraising organizations as the U.S. based "Friends of the Weizmann Institute for Science and Technology" has thus been outsourced to the American "Friends of" organizations. Most American "Friends of" organizations with Israeli doppelgangers have no intrinsic purpose in the U.S.—their only function is to raise money. This is clearly revealed in their tax filings. According to its 2012 IRS return, the Friends of the Weizmann Institute for Science and Technology had no employees to perform such self-monitoring. Each employee at the other top "Friends of" and subsidy IAOs is theoretically overseeing anywhere from a few hundred thousand dollars in charitable transfers to up to $14 million. IRS audits of either "Friends of" IAOs or their Israeli counterparts are unheard of within the Jewish news media.[36] In the case of the Weizmann Institute, which had a major role in supporting Israel's clandestine nuclear weapons program, this has led to stunning abuses.

Declassified FBI files[37] on the Weizmann Institute revealed its central role in Israel's nuclear weapons research program and how it has been secretly funded from the United States through its "Friends of" IAO. On April 24, 2012, the FBI released 159 pages detailing a secret 1992 counterespionage investigation into the Weizmann Institute of Science of Rehovot, Israel. The previously unreleased files detailed not only how the U.S. government continually missed opportunities to take timely and warranted law enforcement actions against major IAO counterparts, but how Israel's nuclear fundraising and influence network drags the U.S. out of compliance with the Nuclear Non-Proliferation Treaty and subjects U.S. government non-proliferation efforts to international ridicule.

In October of 1992 military personnel at the Yuma Proving Ground, which tests nearly every significant U.S. ground combat weapons system, detected a University of Buffalo computer system user penetrating their secure computer network via New Mexico State University. A senior at University of Buffalo majoring in Chemical Engineering hacked the university's own system to obtain high-level graduate student access codes. Soon after, according to the FBI, "computers from the Weizmann Institute for Science accessed computers from NMSU to penetrate computers at YPG" using the same access codes stolen at University of Buffalo. FBI investigators suspected the Buffalo University student passed the secret access codes to Weizmann, and Amherst Town police subsequently arrested him on October 8, 1992.

In January of 1993, the FBI interviewed Buffalo University graduate students whose accounts had been misappropriated by the hacker. The FBI began to research the student's connection to other hackers in Texas and Hawaii and his "possible contact/association with the Weizmann Institute of Rehovot, Israel." Investigators also dialed up the Lexis-Nexis online news database for more background on Weizmann. Among their first hits was a 1972 *New York Times* article documenting Soviet charges that Weizmann was nothing more than a front for Israeli nuclear weapons research. Interest piqued, the FBI amassed a lengthy public source file on Weizmann.

They discovered that the Weizmann Institute launched operations at the

---

[36] Josh Nathan-Kazis, "How to be a 'Friend' and get a tax break in return." *The Jewish Daily Forward*, December 19, 2014 http://forward.com/news/israel/210767/how-to-be-a-friend-and-get-a-tax-break-in-return/

[37] "The Weizmann Institute of Science FBI Counterespionage file," The Israel Lobby Archive, Institute for Research: Middle Eastern Policy. http://www.israellobby.org/weizmann/

close of WWII under the direction of Israeli nuclear research pioneer Ernst David Bergmann. It was named after famed chemist Chaim Weizmann, a Russian who immigrated to the UK and revolutionized the production of acetone needed for WWI gunpowder production. The Zionist activist lobbied and charmed Lord Balfour, who issued the famous "Balfour Declaration" calling for the creation of a Jewish homeland in Palestine. Weizmann became Israel's first president in 1949. The FBI noted the Weizmann Institute had:

> *...an 'American Committee for the Weizmann Institute' which operates in the United States from New York City, Chicago, and possibly other metropolitan cities. The Committee engages in fund-raising, hosts lectures on topics of interest and engages in public relations on behalf of the Weizmann Institute. CI-3B [counter-intelligence] believes that the Weizmann Institute is an academic organization which conducts research in high-technology issue areas, including theoretical aspects of nuclear and conventional weapons development.*[38]

Like many such FBI investigations, the efforts were quickly suppressed and shut down because the trail led to Israel. On March 8, 1993 the Assistant District Attorney of Erie County reduced the unnamed Buffalo University hacker's "misuse of a computer" charge to "disorderly conduct," fined him $145 and sentenced him to 40 hours of community service. Buffalo University officials were not "overly anxious" to have their student charged with a serious crime, including possible espionage on Weizmann's behalf, rather than a mere campus computer access violation. This tendency to cover for students caught attempting thefts, or actually stealing, for Israel has been repeated over the years, with the most recent publicized incident involving a Technion University student at UCLA, discussed later. The FBI continued its Weizmann Institute spy network investigation, obtaining a Grand Jury subpoena on March 19, 1993, served on an unnamed suspect at his place of business. The Counter Intelligence Division obtained logs of Yuma Proving Ground data that may have been passed to Weizmann. Late in 1994, the investigation was closed due to the "rudimentary" level of the "computer cracker" intrusion. The "Weizmann Espionage" case was thus officially closed.

In hindsight, what the FBI uncovered in the 1990s about the Weizmann Institute reveals that it was involved both in nuclear weapons development and fundraising through a U.S. non-profit charity. That pile of evidence has

---

[38] "The Weizmann Institute of Science FBI Counterespionage file," The Israel Lobby Archive, Institute for Research: Middle Eastern Policy. http://www.israellobby.org/weizmann/

only deepened in intervening years. If the FBI had kept digging, and the Justice Department upheld its mandate, the threat posed to American Nuclear Non-Proliferation Treaty compliance could have been mitigated by shutting down the Weizmann Institute's U.S. fundraising arm over documented IRS charitable purpose violations.

However, Weizmann's vast support network in the United States means that it has never been an easy target. Since its very beginning, the Weizmann Institute invested significant resources courting and cultivating elite allies and collaborators spread across U.S. government and scientific communities. Isidor Rabi worked on the Manhattan Project, providing key leadership developing America's first atomic bombs alongside the legendary Robert Oppenheimer at Los Alamos. When dispatched by a nervous JFK to visit Dimona in 1961, Rabi stated unequivocally he had found "no evidence of weapons related activity." Thomas C. Reed and Danny B. Stillman, co-authors of the 2009 book *Nuclear Express,* skeptically noted, "Rabi was already a member of the board of governors (and presumably on the payroll) of Israel's Weizmann Institute of Science, the incubator of most nuclear weapons work in Israel." Rabi's misleading testimony took some JFK administration heat off of Israel as it raced to finalize the Dimona reactor to produce plutonium and build a nuclear arsenal.

At the very center of the U.S. IAO support network in the 1940s was Abraham Feinberg, a major Democratic Party operative and David Ben-Gurion's designated North American nuclear weapons fund-raising coordinator. Feinberg began courting Nobel laureate Glenn T. Seaborg on behalf of the Weizmann Institute in the early 1950s. After becoming head of the Atomic Energy Commission (AEC) during the Kennedy administration, Seaborg played a key role in derailing AEC and FBI criminal investigations into the Israeli theft of AEC-owned weapons-grade U-235 from a contractor facility in Apollo, Pennsylvania. Upon leaving the AEC in 1971, Seaborg accepted Weizmann Institute Chairman Feinberg's invitation (and an honorarium equivalent to nearly 10 percent of his annual salary) to keynote the organization's annual Waldorf Astoria fundraising event. Seaborg returned the favor by foreshadowing a soon-to-be adopted U.S. policy of dissembling and covering-up for Israel's arsenal. According to the Weizmann Institute's official transcript of the event, Seaborg said:

> *During my tenure as Chairman of the AEC I was asked on numerous occasions whether I thought Israel was a nuclear power — or less euphemistically — did she have the bomb?...Now in retrospect, I often wished I had said, 'Yes, she is a nuclear power, the kind that knows of, and makes use of, the atom's power for peace.'*

Seaborg was a major obstacle to Justice Department investigations into how weapons-grade uranium was stolen from an AEC contractor called the Nuclear Materials and Equipment Corporation (NUMEC). When the NUMEC uranium theft diversion investigation was rejuvenated by Attorney General Edward Levi in 1976, Seaborg refused to talk to FBI agents, even after being informed by DOE officials that traces of U-235 of a particularly rare signature supplied by the AEC to NUMEC had been recovered in Israel.

Major efforts have been formalized within the federal government to institutionalize a "no comment" policy toward Israel's nuclear weapons—thereby avoiding a discussion of the illicit support and funding that built them. During the Nixon administration, Henry Kissinger played a key role in crafting the U.S. policy of "nuclear ambiguity" designed to keep Israel's nuclear arsenal from ever becoming an "established international fact." In 1969, Kissinger penned a classified strategy document that even noted the NUMEC uranium diversion, "There is circumstantial evidence that some fissionable material available for Israel's weapons development was illegally obtained from the United States by about 1965," he wrote. However, while Kissinger and Nixon had many good policy options that could have reversed the Israeli nuclear program and preserved the American drive for non-proliferation—especially by withholding U.S. military equipment shipments to Israel—they chose to pursue none of them. Instead, they mandated that the U.S. government simply should never officially acknowledge Israel's nuclear weapons, if Israel never tested them or formally made their existence public. Shortly after stepping down as U.S. Secretary of State in 1977. Kissinger graciously received a Weizmann Institute of Science honorary degree as a "messenger of peace" and "principal architect of international conciliation." Recently declassified Nixon administration files reveal that fears of a "Zionist campaign to try to undermine" his administration—not U.S. national security—was behind the so-called "ambiguity" policy.[39]

In 1987, the Department of Defense contracted a study titled "Critical Technology Issues in Israel" led by Dr. Edwin S. Townsley, Deputy Director of the Science and Technology Division of the Institute for Defense Analyses. According to leaks to the press, Weizmann scientists developed a cutting-edge high-energy physics and hydrodynamics program "needed for nuclear bomb design." Weizmann also worked on advanced methods for enriching uranium to weapons-grade through the use of lasers. As U.S. foreign aid for Israeli conventional weapons purchases and development surged, so too did Weizmann's U.S. charitable funding for secret weapons development.

The Israel affinity ecosystem's core lobbying organization, the American

---

[39] Israel's Nuclear Weapons Program, ISCAP declassification, Nixon Administration papers, March 18, 2014 http://www.archives.gov/declassification/iscap/pdf/2009-076-doc1.pdf

Israel Public Affairs Committee, features Weizmann programs at its annual policy events and has been organizationally intertwined through chairman emeritus Robert Asher's ties to both organizations. AIPAC would no doubt muster the full might of its 50-plus executive committee organizations to derail any attempt to regulate charitable funding to Weizmann as a non-proliferation initiative. Yet by knowingly turning a blind eye toward Weizmann's role within Israel's clandestine nuclear program, the U.S. specifically appears to have violated Article 1 of the Nuclear Non-Proliferation Treaty, which states:

> *Each nuclear-weapons state undertakes not to transfer, to any recipient, nuclear weapons, or other nuclear explosive devices, and not to assist any non-nuclear-weapon state to manufacture or acquire such weapons or devices.*

It is clear that the Justice Department did not follow the Weizmann investigation through to its logical conclusion, even after discovering the U.S. weapons-funding front. The IRS is similarly studiously uninterested in formally ruling on whether clandestine funding for laser enrichment and ballistic missile development even qualifies as a tax-deductible social welfare purpose.

In 2012, the author filed a "Request for Miscellaneous Determination" and paid a $1,000 fee to obtain a formal IRS determination about whether he could mirror the role of the American-Friends-of-Israel nuclear funding pipeline by setting aside a $50,000 tax-exempt donation for the Weizmann Institute of Science in Rehovot from a 501(c)(3) organization. The authors request for and IRS approval or denial was explicit:

> *Our set-aside is designated to experimentally laser-enrich 12 kilos of uranium to 90% pure, weapons-grade U-235, sufficient for one nuclear warhead that will then be experimentally mounted on a ballistic missile. This charitable project will enable the successful culmination of two publicly-reported Weizmann nuclear weapons development programs by bringing them both together in an applied configuration.*[40]

A nervous IRS agent called and informed the author by telephone that the IRS would not be able to make a formal written determination, though "he doubted" such a transaction would comply with IRS guidelines.[41]

---

[40] Form 8940 "Request for Miscellaneous Determination" filed with the IRS by the author on May 23, 2012

[41] The author, on the IRS agent's advice, withdrew his request. On December 30, 2014 the IRS confirmed it had not refunded the $1,000 for a "determination

However, not all "Friends of" funding flows are so exciting.

Given the size of the operation—$344 million in revenue in 2012—American Friends of Bar-Ilan University's fundraising operations in the United States receive staggeringly little publicity. Fundraising events are spread across various regions of the United States. Since this IAO claims only thirty-one employees on its 2012 tax return, it is unclear why the IRS believes this IAO is capable of exercising much oversight over its foreign partner, or why the employees could possibly be pursuing any intrinsic social welfare purpose in the United States. In other words, it does not appear to have the infrastructure to satisfy the "conduit" standard, given that its sole observable purpose is raising tax-exempt donations for Bar-Ilan University in Israel. The university was established in 1955 and is the second largest academic institution in Israel, with over 26,000 students and more than 1,300 faculty members.

Tools in its fundraising kit include conferring honorary doctorate degrees at annual dinners to major donors such as Mortimer Zuckerman of *The New York Daily News* and *U.S. News and World Report* and Harvey Kruger of Lehman Brothers.[42] The American "Friends of" group ran into corporate image trouble with Bar Ilan University in 1996, when it published a pamphlet featuring twelve pictures capturing the university's most infamous student. The fundraising dinner was thrown to honor the late Prime Minister Yitzak Rabin, but the brochure featured pictures of his confessed assassin, Yigal Amir, who shot him in 1995. On campus at the time, professors such as Hillel Weiss were agitating that Rabin's peace policies may have been an indicator that he was a traitor.[43] Nevertheless, the photo dustup had no long-term effect on fundraising.

Another major subsidy IAO is nicknamed "the Joint," though none of its officials has done time for their role in documented ongoing illegal seizures of Palestinian land. Founded in 1914, the American Jewish Joint Distribution Committee was originally a non-Zionist agency that focused on post-WWI Jewish relief in Europe. Though principally focused on assisting needy Jewish populations, it also supported non-Jewish refugees in need, often contributing to Catholic, Protestant, Quaker and non-religious organizations.

The "Joint's" original philosophy mirrored the worldview at that time of major German-American philanthropists backing the organization such as Felix M. Warburg, Paul Baerwald and James Rosenberg. They instilled the

---

whether your organization can set aside tax-exempt donations to fund a weapons program." The IRS checked its records and apologized that "you should receive your refund shortly."

[42] "News in Brief" *The Jerusalem Post*, March 3, 2006

[43] Joshua Brillian, "University official: Amir photos 'mistake'" *UPI*, February 4, 1996

mission as "helping Jews to help themselves" and that most Jews would stay "in country" while working to overcome whatever persecution or discrimination they faced. It was their right, in the view of donors, to both supervise the administration of received aid and live in their country of birth. The rise of Hitler abruptly overturned this largely non-Zionist mission.

Initially significant funding allocations to Jewish projects in Palestine grew to $63 million (inflation adjusted) in 1921-1932 before falling to $30 million during the Great Depression. After multitudes of displaced Jewish refugees accumulated in shelters in Switzerland, France and Spain the American Jewish Joint Distribution Committee broke with its non-Zionist stance and begin building a "rescue" pipeline of WWII Jewish displaced persons and refugees. In 1939 alone, it spent $8.5 million creating an underground railroad to Palestine.[44] In 1949, the Joint Distribution Committee allocation to Israel peaked again at almost a quarter-billion in today's dollars.[45]

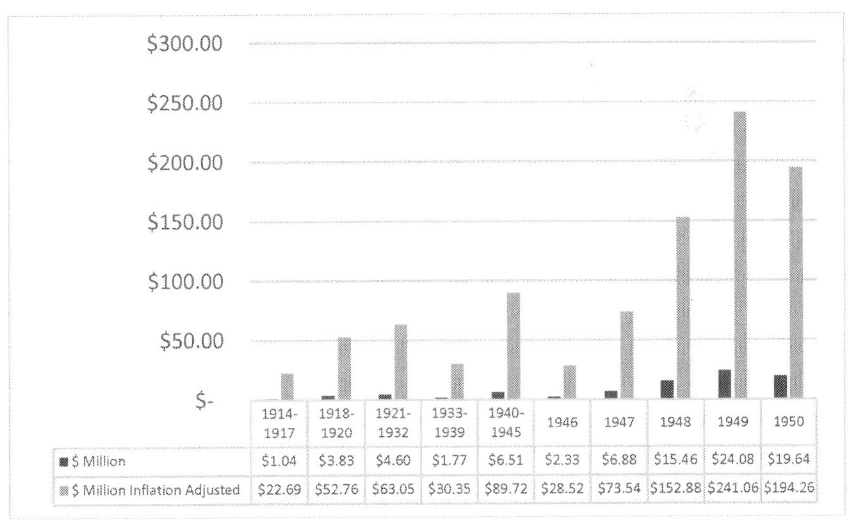

	1914-1917	1918-1920	1921-1932	1933-1939	1940-1945	1946	1947	1948	1949	1950
$ Million	$1.04	$3.83	$4.60	$1.77	$6.51	$2.33	$6.88	$15.46	$24.08	$19.64
$ Million Inflation Adjusted	$22.69	$52.76	$63.05	$30.35	$89.72	$28.52	$73.54	$152.88	$241.06	$194.26

Figure 11 JDC contributions to Israel/Palestine ($ U.S. million)

As the Soviet Union crumbled, the Joint again sprang into action to influence the future of Soviet Jews to Israel's advantage. More than a million Soviet Jews were relocated to Israel in the decade between 1990 and 2000, though many of these immigrants had every right to seek their future in the United States or Germany. While the huge population influx "saved" Israel,

---

44 Yehuda Bauer, *My Brother's Keeper: A History of the American Jewish Joint Distribution Committee, 1929-1939* (Philadelphia: The Jewish Publication Society of America, 1974)

45 Reports of executives submitted to the 23rd Zionist Congress at Jerusalem, 1951, p. 29

it was partially achieved by limiting the choices and taking advantage of the psychological state of the Soviet asylum seekers, according to Yaakov Kedmi, one of the Israeli officials in charge of the operation:

> *It was the right moment to take the people and turn them in our direction, Yaakov Kedmi said. If we'd have missed the moment very few would have come to Israel…In Romania we reached an agreement with dear [Romanian dictator Nicolae] Ceausescu, may he rest in peace, that Jews who reached him would go in only one route, to Israel, and in most instances they didn't even leave the airport, he said. The herd-mentality obedience of the immigrants, the psychological pressure and Soviet education all played into our hands.*[46]

In hindsight, the IAO campaign in the United States toward the public, and particularly directed at Congress, to characterize the plight of Soviet Jews as more deserving of U.S. assistance than the average Soviet dissidents and would-be emigres is not persuasive. As "Cold Warfare," the U.S. government interest in casting its superpower opponent in the worst possible light was, as a propaganda interest, harnessed by IAOs elevating the plight of Soviet Jews. IAO leaders such as Elie Wiesel, according to historian Mark Chmiel, constantly:

> *…exaggerated the condition of Soviet Jews, who suffered from some discriminatory policies in post-Stalin Soviet Union that affected their cultural and religious practices as well as jobs and education.*[47]

The USSR anti-religious campaign, which began in 1928, targeted above all others the Russian Orthodox Church, which had the largest number of followers. Russia's communist government sought to eliminate all religion and replace it with atheism by shutting down places of worship and persecuting religious leaders.[48] Limitations on expressions of religious belief by Jews in the Soviet Union were certainly as harsh as those imposed on Christians and Muslim worshippers. However, the exit visas that IAOs campaigned for were clearly discriminatory in that they did not broadly

---

[46] Gil Shefler, "Ex-Aliya representative says Russian Jews were free to emigrate wherever they wished. Retired Israeli official: Country misled Soviet Jews into making Aliya. Agency insists: There was no scam," *The Jerusalem Post*, April 15, 2011

[47] Mark Chmiel, *Elie Wiesel and the Politics of Moral Leadership* (Philadelphia, Temple University Press, 2001)

[48] Dimitry V. Pospielovsky, *A History of Soviet Atheism in Theory and Practice and the Believer* (St. Martin's Press, New York, vol. 1, 1987)

extend rights to emigrate to non-Jews. Perhaps in gratitude for the U.S. government's role in prioritizing Jews, luminary Wiesel kept quiet about the plight of groups under repression or outright extermination by U.S. allies such as the Ache of Paraguay who were liquidated by Paraguayan dictator General Alfredo Stroessner and the multitudes of Vietnamese and Indochinese displaced victims of the Vietnam War. Wiesel firmly emphasized that some victims were inherently more worthy than others, a view shared by some IAO leaders today toward Syrian refugees:

> *...there is no comparison...Those who talk about 'Auschwitz in Asia' and the 'Cambodian Holocaust' do not know what they are talking about.*[49]

Israel's Mossad, which, in small part, influenced the formation of AIPAC,[50] also ran a special operation parallel to the IAOs publicizing the "plight of Soviet Jews" issue in order to boost Israel's population, according to a leaked 1979 CIA report, which reported:

> *Mossad [has] a small unit whose sole objective is to remind the Soviets through propaganda and contacts about the Jewish question at any point throughout the world. All sorts of people, even Cyrus Eaton [a Canadian-American investment banker, businessman and philanthropist], have been stimulated to raise the subject. Israeli efforts must at times be effective because the Soviets often attack the Israeli service in their propaganda with detailed revelations of Israeli plots against allegedly innocent Soviet citizens.*[51]

Also during the 1980s, Operation "Moses" began an airlift transferring Ethiopian Jews, known as Beta Israel, from the Sudan to Israel during a famine. By 1993, under pressure from IAOs, which also put the plight of the Beta at the top of their agenda, most of the community—45,000—had been relocated in Israel. Eventually U.S. government resources followed, such as a CIA airlift named Operation Sheba and Operation Joshua, which further aided efforts to save stranded migrants in Sudan trying to make it to Israel.

---

[49] Mark Chmiel, *Elie Wiesel and the Politics of Moral Leadership* (Philadelphia, Temple University Press, 2001) 63.

[50] Grant F. Smith, "The Mossad Has Long Given Marching Orders to AIPAC" *Antiwar.com*, February 28, 2012 http://original.antiwar.com/smith-grant/2012/02/27/the-mossad-has-long-given-marching-orders-to-aipac/

[51] "Israel: Foreign Intelligence and Security Services," Central Intelligence Agency, March, 1979. Document can be browsed at: http://www.serendipity.li/cia/counterspy/secret_cia_documents_on_mossad.htm#1

In 1990, as 20,000 Ethiopian Jews concentrated themselves in the capital, Addis Ababa, the Jewish Agency, Israeli government and American Jewish Joint Distribution Committee provided aid.[52] In the midst of civil war and rebel forces closing in, operation "Solomon" airlifted 14,000 Ethiopians to Israel.[53] There have been many other initiatives, domestic and foreign, that began as IAO programs that were later transferred to and funded by U.S. government agencies, without much legitimate congressional debate about whether any American interest would be served.

The American Jewish Joint Distribution Committee runs the "Hesed Welfare Centers," which it claims have served 165,000 people across "the former Soviet Union." Cuban Jewish communities regularly received religious articles, medicine, educational materials and other supplies. In 2010, following the 7.0 magnitude earthquake in Haiti, the American Jewish Joint Distribution Committee claims it became the biggest single Jewish fundraising conduit to that nation, distributing $7.7 million into a multitude of projects, including hospitals, middle schools and medical supplies.

The Joint never left Eastern Europe. In 2015, it became heavily involved in both resettling "internally displaced" Jewish refugees fleeing Russian anti-coup federalists in Ukraine and facilitating their immigration to Israel. According to the Jerusalem Post, the Joint had a partnership with the Israeli "Diaspora Affairs Ministry," which provided a half-million dollars:

> *'The State of Israel and the ministry see a responsibility for every Jew who lives in the Diaspora,' the official said.*
>
> *'We see it as our responsibility to guard them as much as possible. I very much hope that beyond the budget that we have for this emergency project we will expand [our aid] and help more because it is never enough.'*[54]

The American Jewish Joint Distribution Committee's actions as a *de facto* agent of the Israeli government are rarely acknowledged in the United States, but are openly discussed in Israel, again according to the *Jerusalem Post:*

> *The Post understands that the JDC will act as Israel's intermediary, passing funds on to local organizations working*

---

[52] Another organization, the North American Conference on Ethiopian Jewry, first identified the Ethiopian Jewish groups, publicized their attempted conversion by various Christian missionary groups active in Africa, and mobilized for their transfer to Israel. The organization ceased operations after 25 years.

[53] Steven Kaplan and Chaim Rosen, "Ethiopian Jews in Israel" in *The American Jewish Year Book* (Vol. 94, 1994), 59-109

[54] "Diaspora Ministry official calls for expanded aid to Ukraine Jews," *The Jerusalem Post*, January 19, 2015

> *with refugees. Instead of directly providing aid on the ground, the money the government provides will be used to reimburse organizations for their outlays. Community leaders in Kiev, Odessa and Dnepropetrovsk have all confirmed being contacted by the JDC. 'There is a new programme by the Israeli government... which will fund 75 per cent of the costs to care for a refugee,' said Rabbi Refael Kruskal, CEO of Odessa's Tikva organization. 'The other 25 per cent will be paid for by the JDC or the organization that is helping the refugee.'*[55]

The Israeli government acts through the best-positioned American IAOs to accomplish its foreign policy aims. This is a charge that is always met with a wall of silence, especially when the activities in question are conducted within the United States. Yet, as examined later, such actions have and continue to be commonplace and are completely ignored by the Justice Department's Foreign Agent Registration Act office.

Whenever armed conflict flares up between Palestinians and Israel—the American Jewish Joint Distribution Committee—in chorus with other IAOs—is quick to issue news bulletins in conjunction with the Jewish Federations of North America about their efforts to deliver trauma counseling, medical services and removal of Israeli civilians from conflict zones. Attacks on Gaza or Lebanon are often characterized coarsely as "mowing the grass" within Israeli circles. Nevertheless, IAO information campaigns in the U.S. quickly elevate the profile of victims of Palestinian violence and portray Israel as the victim rather than aggressor, no matter how the conflict started or lopsided the casualty figures. That Palestinians are primarily to blame for such crises is the targeted message of such public relations campaigns.

Through the quite appropriately designated "Entwine" and "Next Generation" programs, the Joint recruits young adults to participate in immersive "Jewish service experiences." This involves shipping 400 Jewish volunteers overseas to destinations such as Rwanda and Peru. These training programs may come in response to a looming paradox. A comprehensive survey of young Jewish Americans found that while many volunteered for social welfare projects, few connected this realization of the value of volunteering with their own Jewish identity. Most also did not choose to volunteer, when they did, with Jewish-identified organizations.[56]

The United Israel Appeal is another massive subsidy IAO, and the central fundraising body for Israel around the world, though it no longer reigns supreme in the United States. The United Israel Appeal outside the United

---

55 "Israel to provide aid to displaced Jews in Ukraine," *BBC Monitoring Middle East - Political*, Supplied by BBC Worldwide Monitoring, October 31, 2014

56 "For Young Jews, It's About Serving, Not Judaism," *The Forward*, July 8, 2011

States is referred to as "Keren Hayesod" ("The Foundation Fund") and manages fundraising campaigns in 45 countries.

This largely fictitious U.S. vs foreign fundraising separation in the past has allowed Israel to claim (of course, with no independent verification) that funds channeled into Israel and used in ways that contradicted U.S. foreign policy were not actually raised in the United States. For example, when the U.S. State Department discovered Soviet Jews, who under U.S.-supported policy were transferred to Israel, were in fact being settled in the occupied Golan Heights, Israel calmed U.S. officials by highlighting an alleged "glass wall," according to an unclassified cable released by WikiLeaks:

> *Spokesman emphasized settlements not rpt [repeat] not sponsored by Jewish Agency but by World Zionist Organization which does not receive funds from Jewish Agency nor from us or Canadian sources. WZO raises funds through Keren Hayesod, which is fund-raising arm operating in countries outside United States. WZO was split off from Jewish Agency (with which it had been united) in major reorganization in 1971: (a) to provide additional measure of security of fund-raising apparatus in united states vis-a-vis us tax laws; and (b) to obviate complications in connection with [Foreign Agent Registration Act] registration…*[57]

In its latest IRS form 990 filing, the American Israel Public Affairs Committee disclosed a relationship with Keren Hayesod, but did not clarify whether it receives funding (indirectly, as it once did from the Jewish Agency) or other details.

The little-known fact that the Jewish Agency's American Section claimed to be a subsidiary of the World Zionist Organization, when placed under scrutiny in the United States by the Justice Department, should have raised U.S. State Department charges that such hocus-pocus financial claims—never subject to outside audit—were irrelevant. Nevertheless, U.S. policy against illegal settlements has mostly been a matter of lip service, and rarely been of major concern to most IAOs. This was verified by the leadership of the United Israel Appeal's Director Irving Kessler who:

> *…confirmed that the ban on spending Jewish Agency funds donated by American Jews in the [occupied] territories had no*

[57] "Settlement of Soviet Immigrants in Occupied Territories," Unclassified U.S. Department of State cable, marking Confidential, Tel Aviv, June 19, 1973 https://search.wikileaks.org/plusd/cables/1973TELAV04829_b.html

> *basis in American law or in restrictions imposed by the U.S. Internal Revenue Service.*[58]

Whatever "paper" reorganizations may have accomplished have been undone, in reality, by IAO leaders' simultaneous multiple board memberships in different key organizations. When Richard N. Bernstein, of the Miami law firm Greenberg Traurig, became chairman of the United Israel Appeal in 2012, he was also a member of the Board of Governors of the Jewish Agency. Such arrangements are commonplace across the IAO ecosystem. As a bonus, one of Greenberg Traurig's legal specialties is establishing offshore international entities that conceal or minimize taxable income from various jurisdictions, though usually for corporations engaged in for-profit activity.

The birth of the United Israel Appeal is as murky and convoluted as any of the more ancient major IAOs. In 1963 hearings before the Senate Foreign Relations Committee, its representatives claimed the organization was the result of a 1927 merger between two competing U.S. organizations raising and sending money to Jews in Palestine prior to 1927: The Palestine Foundation Fund and the Jewish National Fund. The Jewish National Fund nevertheless still exists as a separate entity. In 2005, the organization designated nearly half a million dollars toward improving facilities at Ramon Airforce Base in Israel.[59]

The United Israel Appeal raised funds until overseas funding needs triggered a reorganization in 1938 in which the United Jewish Appeal emerged to raise funds for the United Israel Appeal and the American-Jewish Joint Distribution Committee. In the 1960s, it functioned as a conduit or "standby fund" for transmitting funds raised by other organizations to Israel.[60] During congressional hearings, and no doubt here as well, these complicated and continuous changes in the Israel lobby Rubik's cube cause eyes to glaze over and induce slumber. They are nearly impossible to keep straight.

The United Israel Appeal's current mission, according to Richard Bernstein, a well-situated leader occupying board seats on the Jewish Federations National Association, the United Israel Appeal and others, is simple: boosting immigration to Israel:

> *Aliya is a central part of our fundraising mission in support of Israel and the Jewish Agency. It is a cornerstone of the Diaspora-*

---

[58] "From our Archives," *The Jerusalem Post*, December 20, 2012

[59] Jewish National Fund year 2004 IRS form 990.

[60] Activities of Nondiplomatic Representatives of Foreign Principals in the United States, Hearings before the Committee on Foreign Relations, United States Senate, Eighty-Eight Congress, First Session. pp 1232-1233 http://www.israellobby.org/Senate/05231963pt1.pdf

> *Israel relationship and the efforts of building global Jewish identity with Israel at its center.*[61]

That *Aliyah* mission is ever ready to take advantage of a crisis, no matter how gruesome. In the wake of the 2015 attacks on the French satirical magazine *Charlie Hebdo*, the Israeli Ministry of Absorption allocated $4-5 million toward Jewish Agency, World Zionist Organization and United Israel Appeal programs promoting the emigration of French Jews to Israel.

The United Israel Appeal is also a conduit for U.S. tax dollars, quietly appropriated by Congress and placed into the U.S. State Department's Migration and Refugee Assistance account, which is earmarked for Israel. The State Department transfers the appropriated funds to the United Israel Appeal, which in turn claims to transfer the entirety to the Jewish Agency for Israel. Between 1973 and 1991, U.S. taxpayers ponied up $460 million for resettling Jewish refugees from the Soviet Union and other locations to Israel. If this were truly a national priority of the United States, it is interesting to speculate why a U.S. agency or special division was not launched to oversee and execute such a large program. The Congressional Research Service also reveals that between 2000 and 2013 the Jewish Agency received $534 million ($41 million per year) in funding from Congress–none of it easily auditable by U.S. taxpayers.[62] Even a cursory review of tax filings reveals many suspicious transactions, such one as in 2007, where the United Israel Appeal paid $144 thousand to an untraceable business with no identifiable employees run out of a residential dwelling in Washington, DC. As of 2012, the names of all overseas recipient organizations of United Israel Appeal grants are censored in publicly released form 990s under a new IRS guideline, discussed later, that guarantees zero accountability. Despite all the U.S. donations and taxpayer-financed revenues, the Jewish Agency is a black box to outside watchdogs.

As a member organization of the JFNA, the United Israel Appeal also sponsors speaking tours for authors or personalities the Israel government would like to place before international audiences, including the authors of the book *Start-Up Nation* that portrays Israel's heavily subsidized high-tech sector as a modern day example for the world. Avi Melamed was sent around to groups to discuss the threats of the "Arab Awakening" and reframe the exuberance surrounding the "Arab Spring." However, not all such IAO tours, speaking invitations or sponsorships work out well. Former President George W. Bush canceled a planned keynote speech on "freedom" at a gala United Israel Appeal fundraiser in Geneva, Switzerland under protests and

---

61 "U.S. Jewish leaders criticize Israel's plan for private corporation to oversee European Aliya" *The Jerusalem Post*, June 11, 2014

62 "U.S. Foreign Aid to Israel," Congressional Research Services, April 13, 2013 http://fpc.state.gov/documents/organization/209258.pdf

legal complaints filed in Swiss courts by the Center for Constitutional Rights and Amnesty International over the Bush administration's widespread use of torture.

Christian Zionist organizations were not IAO pioneers within the first or even second wave, and generally do not maintain a constant mass presence in Washington like Jewish IAOs. They also do not raise anywhere near the money. Their primary influence is through a large and activist voting base. Nevertheless, they are becoming financially important. While subsidy revenue from Christian Zionist organizations in the United States is not a major component of total charitable inflow for Israel, they have come to the rescue of faltering IAO programs. More importantly, they in a small way diversify the revenue base of the IAO ecosystem. Past attempts by evangelical Christians to display the Ten Commandments on government properties such as the local courthouse or rewrite laws to allow school prayer squared off against powerful consortiums of IAOs working for separation of church and state. Today IAOs contribute seed money to grow and harness the political and financial support of evangelical Christians and to prioritize Israel within Christian IAOs that have become active players. Christian evangelical IAOs are unique within the Israel lobby for their targeted, often tasteless, fundraising campaigns graphically portraying Jewish suffering and infused with dispensationalist allegories.

The International Fellowship of Christians and Jews is an IAO founded in 1983 by Rabbi Yechiel Eckstein which now claims more than a quarter million adherents. When the Soviet Union fell apart, Christian evangelical organizations stepped up their fundraising to transport and resettle Soviet Jews in Israel. These "lord's travel agent" programs continue, with Eckstein trumpeting his organization's Christian funding stream as largely "untapped" and less affected by the travails of those Jewish IAO donors who are heavily exposed to financial sector volatility such as the 2008 financial crisis. It has even taken on funding commitments originally financed by the Jewish Agency for Israel and the Israeli government such as Jewish studies programs in Eastern Europe, a medical center in Ashkelon, welfare centers for abused children in Israel, and anti-violence programs in public schools.

A 2004 poll conducted by the International Fellowship of Christians and Jews estimated the population of "born again" and evangelical Christians in the U.S. at 105-135 million. This number is inflated when compared to more credible Pew Research findings, interpreted later, which peg the number closer to 80 million. According to the International Fellowship of Christians and Jews, 31 percent of its base identified U.S. support for Israel as a "primary consideration" for selecting a presidential candidate, with 64 percent saying it was an "important factor."[63] The organization maintains offices in Chicago and Jerusalem. Like the American Jewish Joint Distribution Committee, the International Fellowship of Christians and Jews has moved decisively into Ukraine, pouring millions into programs that fly planeloads of Ukrainian Jews to Israel.

Many Israeli organizations and IAOs have been wary of Christian evangelicals over fears that they were proselytizing Jews to convert to Christianity. Dispensationalist theology, embraced by many evangelicals, prophesizes the mass destruction of Jews who do not convert during the "end of days." IAO leaders and supporters have raised eyebrows over Christian evangelical theme park building in Israel, large real estate purchases in Jerusalem, and the ideological framework of exhibits offered in various museums. Rabbi Eckstein frequently attempts to impose limits on the expression of evangelical support for Judaism and Israel through adoption of rituals, according to an interview with the *St. Petersburg Times*:

> *There are limits, said Rabbi Yechiel Eckstein, founder and president of the International Fellowship of Christians and Jews, which is based in Chicago. I am vehemently opposed to Christians usurping the Jewish traditions by taking the seder and giving it new Christological meaning.* [64]

A 2008 program donating $11 million to 28,000 Holocaust survivors for Rosh Hoshanah amounted to $392 per person, which the organization presumably judged to be an affordable "per donor" telethon solicitation amount. International Fellowship of Christians and Jews "On Wings of Eagles" fundraising telethons also tie a specific dollar donation level that will allegedly determine the number of Jews "rescued." Few other efforts—except perhaps Atlantic City boardwalk pitches—are so specific as the Fellowship about what magic can be accomplished through a specific dollar amount:

> *For only $350 you can help air lift one desperate Jew to safety and freedom in the holy land of Israel. Seven hundred dollars will pay for a needy married couple and $1,400 for a family of four. When you call with a gift of $350 or more, when the person or people you sponsor arrive, you will receive a postcard from Israel with their names and where they are from in the former Soviet Union so that you can continue to bless them with your prayers.*

---

[63] Robert Weitzel, "Hillary's 'Dr. Strangelove' Shtick" *The Capital Times*, May 16, 2008

[64] Sheryl Kay, "Church Blends Beliefs at Seder," *St. Petersburg Times*, April 10, 2009

The unnerving catch from the perspective of Jewish partner organizations—the conclusion of the appeal refers to "the End Gathering of the Jewish exiles"—is that creating the conditions necessary for Armageddon is the main perceived benefit for Christian evangelical donors.

Similar to some of its elder IAO allies, the International Fellowship of Christians and Jews has participated in overseas covert actions, financing a "rescue operation" for forty Jews, it claimed were in danger if they continued living in Iran, "a country whose president questioned whether the Holocaust ever happened and asserted that Israel must be wiped off the map."[65] The forty disappeared from Iran only to reappear in Israel. Though conducted by the Jewish Agency, the International Fellowship of Christians and Jews "raised millions of dollars" for the operation.[66] Each Iranian was also given a stake of $10,000 to make a new life in Israel.

The foreign policy ramifications for such actions are enormous. Although U.S. relations with Iran at the time were not warm, they were presumably not improved by an American charity financing the quiet disappearance of Iranian citizens, only to trumpet their almost magical reappearance in Israel as a major public relations victory. Iranian Jewish community leaders called the operation a "misinformation campaign," claiming the 25,000-member minority population was not endangered in Iran and was free to operate "20 synagogues, eight [kosher] butchers, five schools, four youth organizations and two restaurants."[67]

The Jewish Agency has not always treated the International Fellowship of Christians and Jews as the major partner its financial contributions suggest it should be, leading to controversy. In 2008, a dispute arose after the two organizations signed an agreement that the Jewish Agency list the Fellowship on its letterhead and in strategic marketing programs as a major partner. Bilateral Jewish Agency-International Fellowship of Christians and Jews programs rankled Jewish federations, which are the Jewish Agency's major funders, as well as Anti-Defamation League head Abe Foxman, who stated:

> *To make giving charity conditional to how much praise you are going to receive, I find inappropriate and offensive.*[68]

---

65 "McCain Emphasizes Military Service in New Ad; Bill Clinton Campaigns for Hillary," CNN, December 26, 2007

66 Andy Soltis, "Jews in a Great Escape; Iranians Flee to Israel in Secret Exodus," *The New York Post*, December 26, 2007

67 "Iranian Jewish leader calls immigration of 40 Jews to Israel a 'misinformation campaign'" Associated Press International, December 26, 2007

68 Gal Tziperman Lotan, "Eckstein's IFCJ halts donations to Jewish Agency. Dispute swirls around delayed joint marketing plan and fellowship's place in agency publicity," *The Jerusalem Post*, May 30, 2008

A 2012 survey of American Jews also found Christian evangelicals, with their propensity to proselytize and their end-times agenda, to be somewhat suspect. They ranked lowest on the spectrum of religions viewed favorably (20.9 percent), far behind Mormons (47 percent) and even Muslims (41.1 percent).[69]

A far murkier Christian Zionist organization is led by the televangelist and pastor of the 19,000-member Cornerstone Church in San Antonio, Texas, John Hagee's Christians United for Israel (CUFI). Following the 2005 publication of his book, *The Jerusalem Countdown: A Warning to the World*, Hagee formed CUFI. The book calls for a pre-emptive nuclear strike on Iran, a policy popular with many CUFI followers. Such a drastic step would fulfill God's plan for both Israel, argues Hagee, and "the West." Hagee's journey toward forming an influential IAO began when he traveled to Israel in 1976, later confessing, as reported by *The New York Times*:

> *I was literally moved to tears as I began to walk the streets of Jerusalem and I remembered the historical nightmare that the Jewish people were forced to live because of organized Christianity's brutality.*[70]

Hagee's personal narrative about this "spiritual homecoming," with photos at the Wailing Wall and appearing with sundry Israeli politicians, is spread across CUFI promotional materials. In 1981 Hagee was still just a non-denominational preacher at the 3,000-member Church of Castle Hills. Claiming shock over widespread condemnation of Israel's attack on Iraq's Osirak nuclear reactor, Hagee sprang to action. He organized what would be the first of many "Night to Honor Israel" events, an evangelical revivalist road show complete with an 80-member choir and orchestra that traveled the Southwest. On stage, Hagee hosted Christian and Jewish leaders for interdenominational prayers, and in the early days took a collection for Hadassah.

Hagee still raises funds through "John Hagee Ministries," a nonprofit religious organization. Christians United for Israel is a separate organization incorporated in Texas as the "CUFI Church Association." CUFI is housed in the same facilities as John Hagee Ministries, to which it pays rent amounting to $11,880 per year. Though given tax-exempt status in 2007 as a philanthropic grant-making organization, no annual IRS form 990 tax filings are required from CUFI, because it applied for and received special IRS tax-exempt status as a religious church association exempt from disclosure.

---

[69] "American Jews Still View the Christian Right with Concern," *The Forward*, April 20, 2012

[70] Richard Bernstein "Evangelicals Strengthening Bonds With Jews," *The New York Times*, February 6, 1983

In 2006, CUFI's "association of churches" was present in fifteen states, with eight members in Texas and two members each in California, Colorado, Georgia, Minnesota, Oregon and New Mexico.[71] The bylaws of CUFI forbid the organization having corporate members and vests all authority in the individuals sitting on the board of directors. In terms of important decision-making, churches are mere "associate members" that apply to enter the association, but then have no real decision authority, take on obligations to send parishioners to annual gatherings in Washington, and continue to be subject to summary expulsion by the CUFI board.

CUFI's 2007 application for tax-exempt status[72] reveals it expected to raise $5.3 million between 2006 and 2008. CUFI reported $1,884,250 in actual 2006 revenue. That year the Goldhirsch Foundation—a major reliable source of IAO support[73]—provided $100,000 in startup capital to build up CUFI's fundraising infrastructure targeting Christian evangelicals. CUFI signed a $302,646 contract (plus 3 percent of all transacted funds) with leading constituent relationship management solution provider Convio, for online and offline fundraising and donor development campaigns. Concerned about its image, CUFI's other major expenditure was a $25,000 per month retainer with Burson-Marsteller public relations services. BM develops all CUFI messaging, provides training for spokespersons, fields media requests, manages publicity for Hagee's books, contracts facilities (such as the Walter E. Washington Convention Center in Washington, DC) for annual CUFI events, and writes "wrap reports and transcripts" for the news media. Burson-Marsteller also monitors events in Israel for immediate "opportunities" to "leverage CUFI's position," according to the contract executed with CUFI on August 3, 2006. Burson-Marsteller's flat fee for Night to Honor Israel events is an additional $30,000 per event.

This means, under the terms of the contract, in 2007 CUFI's payments to BM were approximately $360,000, or 18 percent of total estimated revenue ($2,040,000). Adding in the Convio contract, CUFI was committed to spending 32 percent of revenue just on PR and its fundraising infrastructure.

CUFI's professed long-term goal is to increase Christian support for Israel based on its selective interpretation of passages in the bible and emphasize to Christians its Jewish roots. CUFI has license to engage in public

---

[71] Other states with a single CUFI church member organization were Alabama, Colorado, Florida, Georgia, Idaho, Missouri, Virginia, Wisconsin and New Hampshire.

[72] Obtained from the IRS and available from The Israel Lobby Archive at: http://IsraelLobby.org/CUFI/cufi.pdf

[73] In 2006, the foundation provided $76,000 to Friends of the IDF, and $20,000 to American Friends of Hebrew University, and also donated to the U.S. Holocaust Museum, Friends of Israel Disabled Veterans, the Jewish National Fund and Simon Wiesenthal Center.

relations, lobby, raise and distribute funds without publicly disclosing any activity, according to the mission CUFI presented to the IRS:

> *CUFI is an association of Christian churches created to proclaim the Bible-based Christian view of the relationship between the Christians and Jews, the United States and Israel; to provide a place for public worship, religious training, and education; and to render Christian services, both material and spiritual, as the Lord directs. Specifically, CUFI is organized to advance the understanding of all Christians working with and through associated church congregations to address the need to understand and support the Old Testament and those who follow its beliefs in order to understand and complete the calling of the New Testament. In carrying out such purposes, CUFI will serve its 'Member Church' (described below) congregations, institutions, agencies, and associates (collectively referred to herein as 'Affiliated Members') by contributing to or otherwise assisting in the work of each Member Church congregation in ways that are consistent with CUFI's purposes.*
>
> *CUFI is dedicated to the promotion of education of fellow Christian churches regarding the Nation of Israel and the Jewish people. CUFI recognizes the growing need to unite the Christian community behind the promise of Genesis 12:3 which is believed to be an eternal covenant, which Christians have an obligation to uphold, between God and the seed of Abraham to which God is faithful.*

Tearing a page out of the annual conferences of AIPAC and Federation General Assemblies, CUFI also hosts gatherings to train members as "Watchmen for Israel" in order to ask politicians to support Israel during mass lobbying across Capitol Hill while "Watchmen" communicate with the news media. CUFI averred to the IRS that such lobbying should "not be characterized as a substantial part of CUFI's activities." Yet in 2006, 3,500 delegates attended the summit.

The IRS wanted CUFI to clarify precisely how much lobbying it would engage in and asked CUFI to commit to a special test by setting expenditure ceilings, twice asking the organization, "Are you willing to sign 5768, enclosed…?"[74] CUFI's lawyer from the firm Loeffler Tuggey Pauerstein Rosenthal LLP in San Antonio, Blakely Fernandez, responded negatively to the IRS:

---

[74] IRS form 5768 "Election/Revocation of election by an Eligible Section 501(c)(3) Organization to Make Expenditures to Influence Legislation"

> *...as an association of Churches, CUFI is not required to submit form 5768....Based on the information described above, it is my understanding that the CUFI application for tax-exempt status, as filed with your office, is complete.*
>
> *In our conversation, you asked to me to further explain the notion that CUFI anticipated that it might engage in legislative advocacy which was insubstantial to its overall program of work. CUFI is dedicated to promoting the Biblical imperative of supporting the Nation of Israel and the Jewish people. It furthers this mission primarily through holding events, in conjunction with its member churches, all over the country honoring Israel. One such event is an annual summit in Washington, DC.*
>
> *CUFI recognizes that at such events policy discussions sometimes occur incidental to the CUFI mission and that, in some instances, reference to certain legislative items or remedies of direct interest to the Association and its members may be made in furtherance of the broader purpose. In light of the scope of the events and the overall CUFI program of work, such instances would not be characterized as a substantial part of CUFI's activities. The narrative attached to the 1023 Application provides greater discussion of CUFI's program of work.*

The IRS folded and gave CUFI special IRS tax-exempt status that not only allowed it to raise fully tax-deductible donations from donors, but did not require CUFI to file any annual form 990 forms for IRS or public review. This is a level of legal opacity no other IAO has ever achieved. It is the reason no outsiders can answer the kinds of basic questions they can easily ask about most nonprofit tax-exempt organizations. How much do CUFI's leaders pay themselves, and is that in line with industry compensation levels? How much are they still paying outside contractors, and who are those contractors? What is the ratio of large to small donations? How much overhead does the organization have? Did the organization annually certify it was not lobbying, or provide a dollar amount of contributions spent on lobbying? Does the organization have foreign bank accounts or send money overseas? Does CUFI give money to other organizations, and if so, which?

Moreover, although unlike AIPAC, CUFI does not apparently pay a stable of full-time lobbyists to push legislation it drafts for recipients of heavy pro-Israel donations to introduce, CUFI's Washington Summit is now a mini Christian evangelical version of the annual AIPAC policy conference. It in no way resembles a gathering of church association members. Politicians and elected officials are called upon to make formal presentations about their positions on Israel, while attendees are trained how to effectively lobby, and are then given a set of lobbying issues and sent off to meet their representatives in Congress.[75] This is the AIPAC and JCRC model.[76]

American Friends of Technion is consistently a top ten subsidy IAO sending funds to Israel. Similar to the Weizmann Institute flaps, the uncomfortable question of whether the "friends" subsidy organization was financing espionage against the U.S. surfaced in 2014. A scholar from Technion, Israel's oldest university, came under an intensifying legal spotlight over allegations of espionage. According to information made public in a civil harassment suit filed on November 13, 2014 in the Superior Court of the State of California for the County of Los Angeles, an Israeli scientist transferred information from the government-funded Jet Propulsion Lab at the University of California Los Angeles to Technion–Israel Institute of Technology in violation of the Arms Export Control Act. He used the same tactics—computer hacking and uploads to Israel—that Weizmann's student friend at the University of Buffalo employed decades earlier.

According to court filings,[77] Dr. Amir Gat—an Israeli national—executed a Technology Control Plan (TCP) under the International Traffic in Arms Regulations (ITAR) registration in order to participate in the U.S. taxpayer-funded JPL "electrospray" space propulsion project at the University of California Los Angeles. The TCP obligates signers not to disclose ITAR-restricted technical data to foreign persons or countries without prior approval from the U.S. State Department. Failure to comply is supposed to trigger criminal fines and penalties. In this case, it did not.

Gat allegedly "stored project-related files and technical information on his personal laptop, rather than on his safeguarded office computer, in violation of the TCP and ITAR." On May 25, 2010, a virus attacked project leader Dr. Sandra Troian's computer network at Caltech, causing hundreds of project files to be uploaded in rapid succession to an unknown internet protocol (IP) address outside of Caltech. Dr. Troian traced the virus that caused the network problems to Dr. Gat's computer, and notified Caltech officials of this fact. On May 28, 2010, Dr. Gat admitted to Dr. Troian that he had been sharing details of the electrospray project with Dr. Daniel Weihs, his Ph.D. advisor at Technion, without the required U.S. State Department approval.

On June 3, 2010, Dr. Troian found Dr. Gat wandering alone,

---

[75] "10th Annual Summit" CUFI website http://www.cufi.org/site/PageServer?pagename=2015Summit_Itinerary

[76] Because CUFI is categorized as a grant-making organization, it is included in this chapter. If information about the organization revealed a significant portion of revenue was used for grassroots lobbying, it would be in the advocacy chapter alongside such groups as AIPAC.

[77] Sandra Troian, PhD v. California Institute of Technology, Superior Court of the State of California for the County of Los Angeles, November, 2014

unauthorized, in one of her access-restricted experimental laboratories. Dr. Gat explained that Dr. Weihs from Technion had recommended that he "look around" to see what other aerospace projects were ongoing at Caltech in collaboration with JPL.

The FBI investigated but made no arrest. On June 28, 2012, Special Agents Kelly M. Sullivan and David Tsang of the FBI Counterintelligence Division told Dr. Troian there had been "several security breaches at JPL" and that "Dr. Gat was a focus of a larger investigation involving ITA violations and possibly espionage." Troian provided the FBI with information about Gat's activities at Caltech. Nevertheless, Gat was never indicted and left the United States to work at Technion. If Troian's civil complaint ultimately proves Caltech was negligent in its handling of Gat, it will probably follow the trajectory of other Israel espionage-related incidents and not result in any accountability for Technion, the instigator of the misbehavior. The U.S. Department of State apparently has not taken any action.

According to researchers, U.S. intelligence officials and congressional sources, Israel has been caught carrying out aggressive espionage operations against American targets for decades—and shows no sign of slowing down. *Newsweek* reported on May 7, 2014 that:

> *American counter-intelligence officials told members of the House Judiciary and Foreign Affairs committees at the end of January [2014] that Israel's current espionage activities in America are 'unrivaled and unseemly,' going far beyond the activities of other close allies, such as Germany, France, the U.K. and Japan.*[78]

Congress never holds Israel accountable, for espionage or any other behavior, by withholding foreign aid. It is currently unknown, but similarly unlikely, that unprecedented levels of secret U.S. intelligence support budgeted for Israel are in any way affected by such activity.

Israeli espionage—if one includes monetary benefits gained through espionage during negations of the U.S.-Israel Free Trade Agreement—costs the U.S. economy billions of dollars annually, not only by undermining U.S. national security as Israel sells or otherwise transfers stolen proprietary U.S technology to American rivals. It also adds unnecessary burdens to U.S. taxpayers, who are funding aid flows that should have been cut off long ago over Israel's violations of various U.S. laws and IRS regulations. However, due to a stunning lack of bona fide espionage prosecutions, there is a detectible sense within the FBI that such investigations—if they are even

[78] Jeff Stein, "Israel's Aggressive Spying in the U.S. mostly Hushed Up," *Newsweek*, May 8, 2014 http://www.newsweek.com/israels-aggressive-spying-us-mostly-hushed-250278

authorized by the Justice Department—will never win convictions. Since IRS oversight is outsourced to IAOs and becoming more lax with each passing year, seemingly nothing can be done.

California appears to be the epicenter of a new outbreak of espionage targeting American nuclear-weapons-related technology. In 2010, the small multi-national corporation Telogy illegally exported Tektronix oscilloscopes that are vital for nuclear weapons design through a front-company network to Israel. California-based Mattson, during the years 2006-2008, skirted export controls to divert dual-use pressure transducers to Israel. Pressure transducers can be used to convert natural uranium into highly enriched uranium in gas centrifuges.[79] No criminal indictments were ever handed down. Moreover, not only American secrets and technology, but also American citizens are flowing into Israel's military complex.

Friends of the Israel Defense Forces (FIDF)is a subsidy IAO founded in 1981 that would be unique if it were providing similar military support services to any country other than Israel. With revenues of $68 million in 2012, its high growth rate suggests FIDF will surpass $300 million in revenues by 2020.

FIDF claims that it does not supply any form of lethal aid to the IDF. However, it does subsidize and provide services that reduce the burden of government—the Israeli government, that is—by providing educational and recreational facilities for soldiers and their families. Like many other IAOs, it idolizes the IDF as the "most moral army in the world," subtly encouraging young American Zionist Jews thinking of military service that their time would be far better spent protecting their "homeland," Israel, than where they were born and live, the United States.

Blockbuster fundraisers held at the Waldorf-Astoria hotel in New York and similar events in Los Angeles raise large amounts but do not attract much media coverage. In year 2013 FIDF raised $27 million in a few hours, while in 2012, $26 million in funds were raised at the hotel, and $23 million the year before. On November 4, 2015 in Beverly Hills, FIDF raised $31 million, with $8.4 million supplied by the International Fellowship of Christians and Jews. According to journalist Jeffrey Blankfort, the group's lofty mission, "Their [IDF's] job is to look after Israel. Ours is to look after them" appears to help support the very occupation-related activities for which Israel is most widely criticized. According to Blankfort:

---

[79] "Case Study – U.S. Company Charged with Pressure Transducer Sales: Who Were the End Users?" Institute for Science and International Security, May 14, 2012. http://isis-online.org/uploads/isis-reports/documents/Mattson_14May2012_1.pdf

> *True to that motto, the money this 'charity' raises benefits exclusively the soldiers of a foreign country that has not fought a war longer than 33 days in 40 years and whose primary duties have been to protect Israel's illegal settlements, demolish Palestinian homes, make the lives of ordinary Palestinians miserable, and suppress Palestinian resistance to its ongoing ethnic cleansing by whatever means necessary.*[80]

FIDF also brings Israeli soldiers to the U.S. to visit synagogues and lecture at schools and universities. According to the IAO's website, "These events offer a great opportunity to meet IDF soldiers and hear the stories of these brave young men and women." Although it is far from the only IAO to sponsor such tours, the glamorization of the IDF within educational programs across the United States for both Jewish and non-Jewish audiences serves as a powerful recruitment tool for the IDF, even though it is illegal to directly recruit in the United States. Major donors prioritize IDF service over service in the American military. A top IAO and Republican candidate funder, casino mogul Sheldon Adelson, expressed regret, during a 2010 speech, that he had ever worn an American military uniform rather than that of Israel, saying:

> *I am not Israeli, the uniform that I wore in the military unfortunately was not an Israeli uniform, it was an American uniform, although my wife was in the IDF, and one of my daughters was in the IDF, and my two little boys — our two little boys one of whom will be bar mitzvahed tomorrow… hopefully he'll come back [to Israel], his hobby is shooting and he'll come back and be a sniper for the IDF.*[81]

More graphic than Adelson's words were those of former President Bill Clinton, who simultaneously managed to hype the near-impossible threat of an Iraqi ground invasion of Israel from the east while transcending his own failure to join any branch of the U.S. military despite ample opportunities to do so. At a 2002 fundraiser for Hadassah-Women's International Zionist Organization in Toronto, the former U.S. president stated:

---

[80] Jeffrey Blankfort, "Friends of Israel Defense Forces Raises $27 million under NY Media's Radar," *Counterpunch*, April 23, 2013

[81] Paul Woodward, "Israel-Firster Sheldon Adelson regrets serving in U.S. instead of Israeli military," *War In Context*, February 6, 2012, http://warincontext.org/2012/02/06/israel-firster-sheldon-adelson-regrets-serving-in-u-s-instead-of-israeli-military/

> *If Iraq came across the Jordan River…I would grab a rifle and get in the trench and fight and die.*

This has presented a problem for elite media pundits and reporters. Ethan Bronner, who for years served as the *New York Times* Jerusalem bureau chief, failed to publicly disclose that his son was serving in the IDF or respond to charges of biased reporting until called out by the alternative news organization *Electronic Intifada*. The newspaper's ombudsman recommended that the newspaper find Bronner another assignment, but the advice was long ignored. David Brooks, even while using his many media perches to justify Israel's violent 2014 invasion of Gaza, failed to disclose as context for his own reporting that his own son was also serving in the IDF.

In 2014, the IDF confirmed that out of 4,000 non-Israeli born troops then serving, "roughly" 1,000 were dual-citizen Americans.[82] Such arrangements are rare, and presumably made with much calculation. Only three other countries let U.S. citizens serve in their armies. Israelis are required to perform military service, and young Americans living there under dual Israeli-American citizenship are not exempt. Garin Tzabar is a program that gives Israelis and Jews living outside Israel the opportunity to serve in the IDF. It was founded in 1991 by the Friends of Israel Scouts, an American IAO, and is largely funded by Israel's Ministry of Immigrant Absorption. Garin Tzabar also receives money from the U.S. government funded Jewish Agency for Israel and from private donors.

Whether such IAO programs are subtly, but effectively, encouraging American Jews to serve in the IDF rather than the U.S. armed forces is thus a fair question, given that the number of American Jewish troops in Israel is on the increase, while in the U.S. it is falling. At the same time as American Jews are vastly overrepresented at Ivy League universities, they are becoming vastly under-represented as a percentage of the U.S. armed services. According to Defense Manpower Data Center statistics for 2014, 300 more Jewish Americans were serving in the Israeli armed forces than in the U.S. Marine Corps. The "roughly" 1,000 Jewish Americans serving in Israel, if transferred into the U.S. armed services, would account for fully 20.8 percent of all Jews currently serving in the U.S. military. Or, put another way, more American Jews are serving in Israel than are present in either the U.S. Air Force, Marines Corps, or Navy (though more are present in the U.S. Army).

---

[82] Chris Allbritton, "1,000 Americans Are Serving in the Israeli Army and They Aren't Alone" *The Daily Beast*, July 22, 2014.

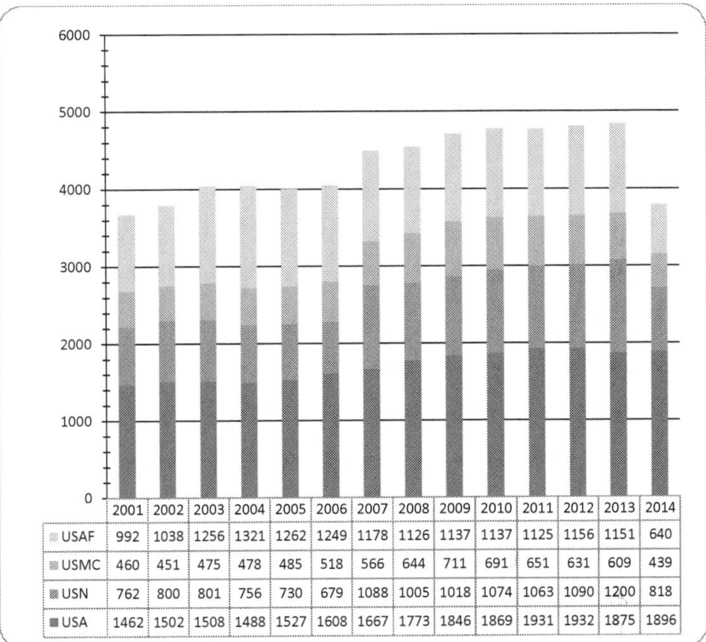

	2001	2002	2003	2004	2005	2006	2007	2008	2009	2010	2011	2012	2013	2014
USAF	992	1038	1256	1321	1262	1249	1178	1126	1137	1137	1125	1156	1151	640
USMC	460	451	475	478	485	518	566	644	711	691	651	631	609	439
USN	762	800	801	756	730	679	1088	1005	1018	1074	1063	1090	1200	818
USA	1462	1502	1508	1488	1527	1608	1667	1773	1846	1869	1931	1932	1875	1896

Figure 12 Jewish active duty U.S. military personnel by service[83]

Given IAOs' established record in calling for U.S. military interventions either directly or indirectly on Israel's behalf (Iraq and Iran, in particular) through highly coordinated and lavishly funded campaigns framed as American interests, it is not surprising just how touchy the subject of Jewish non-participation in the U.S. military can be. Some American Jewish pundits, such as Arnold I. Goldman writing in *The Jewish Ledger*, are concerned about such numbers and urge greater participation:

> *I contend that American Jews have a special responsibility to defend this country, perhaps beyond that of other ethnic groups. It is in our self-interest as Americans, of course, but it is also the right thing to do. We expect, demand and insist on sharing in all that this country has to offer, however, when it is time for our children to serve in defense of it, indeed perhaps in harm's way, we often discourage participation, or at least we do not encourage it. We let others do it for us. This makes us appear to be 'takers,' not the 'givers' we pride ourselves on being. When it comes to the defense of America and of American-ensured freedom around the world, we Jews owe this country something.*

[83] Defense Manpower Data Center, Office of the Secretary of Defense, Freedom of Information Act 14-F-0928 response received on August 26, 2014.

> *The United States liberated Europe for our ancestors and then accepted many of its refugees, including a sizable number of Jewish refugees. It would do so again, and indeed may yet have to, should existing threats become realities. We should be just as willing as others to defend that which we benefit from, our country.*
>
> *There is another reason why we ought to encourage military service among Jewish youth: it is in the best interest of all the world's Jews to do so. We expect, demand and insist that America stand ready to defend Israel against all threats, even when doing so may be at cross purposes with United States national interest or result in divisive American public opinion. Yet those who must stand ready to be in the forefront of this defense are overwhelmingly not Jewish. It should not be so.*[84]

Predictably, an Israel affinity trumpet called *The Algemeiner*[85] sees any exercise researching who is counted and how as a throwback to Nazi Germany and a census conducted by the German Military High Command known as the *Judenzahlung* (Jew count), designed to assess the actual numbers of Jews in the German military, thundering:

> *Throughout history, a common anti-Semitic method of incitement has been to accuse Jews of being unpatriotic. This was often largely expressed in the accusation that Jews were unwilling to join their military.*[86]

Using anecdotal evidence that some Jews entering the military refuse to indicate a religious preference (as more than 25 percent of all active duty service members did in the year 2012), the *Algemeiner* recommends assuming that up to 40 percent of Jews in the military do not indicate a preference. This, however, does not mean as the *Algemeiner* claims, that "the Jewish representation in the military equals at least the Jewish representation of the American population." Assuming 40 percent are not claiming an affiliation brings the 2014 American Jewish active duty number up to only roughly

[84] Arnold I Goldman, "Should More Jews Join the U.S. Military?" *The Jewish Ledger*, November 25, 2009

[85] A New York publication, successor to a Yiddish newspaper, funded by the Gershon Jacobson Jewish Continuity Foundation

[86] "Jews in the Military" *The Algemeiner*, July 18, 2011, http://www.algemeiner.com/2011/07/18/jews-in-the-military/

8,000, not the 28,000 a U.S. population percentage of 2.1 percent[87] suggests would be truly representative.

Even so, Goldman's final idea that boosting the proportion of Jews in the military to a representative number would increase American acceptance of the need to military defend Israel, even when it would go against the American interest or public opinion, is fundamentally flawed. Most Americans would not accept military crusades overtly on behalf of the Roman Catholic Church, despite the fact that the denomination comprises twenty-two percent of the U.S. population and the same percentage of the U.S. military in 2014. In America, that is just not how it works.

However, Americans have already unknowingly been pledged to prioritize Israel by their own federal government. This truth is controversial enough that it was a tightly held secret, indirectly released to Americans by NSA whistleblower Edward Snowden. That IAOs have been the vanguard of promoting the "defend Israel at any cost" concept is certainly no secret, though upon close scrutiny the value of Israel to the United States as an non-treaty ally has never been convincingly substantiated and few IAOs even try to make a public case for it today.[88] As explored in the final chapter, former Israeli Ambassador to the United States Michael Oren struggled mightily to make the case in his 2015 book, *Ally: My Journey Across the American-Israeli Divide*—only to finally concede that the so-called alliance "is not, of course, symmetrical."[89] Again, according to documents released by Edward Snowden, the transfer of raw NSA intercepts on American citizens to Israel was authorized under the prevailing secret doctrine that "the survival of the state of Israel is a paramount goal of U.S. Middle East policy." This policy was probably kept secret because it is a blank check obligating American blood and treasure to a controversial commitment American citizens never approved via advice and consent or any type of representative government exercise.[90] Public opinion polls suggest many, if not most, would oppose it.

---

[87] "Vital Statistics: Jewish Population in the United States by State," The Jewish Virtual Library https://www.jewishvirtuallibrary.org/jsource/U.S.-Israel/usjewpop.html

[88] The American Israel Public Affairs Committee did at one time attempt to justify aid to Israel in a series of "Strategic Value of Israel" papers that appeared in the 1980s. These may be viewed online at http://www.israellobby.org/reagan/

[89] See Grant F. Smith "Ask not what Israel can do for America," *Washington Report on Middle East Affairs*, September November 2015 http://www.wrmea.org/2015-september/two-views-israeli-knesset-member-michael-oren-from-native-born-american-to-u.s.-ally.html

[90] Glenn Greenwald, "NSA shares raw intelligence including Americans' data with Israel," *The Guardian*, September 11, 2013 http://www.theguardian.com/world/2013/sep/11/nsa-americans-personal-data-israel-documents

Not every subsidy IAO is a multi-million-dollar enterprise, and the smaller IAOs are worth examining. The Land of Promise Foundation raised $228,000 in 2012 for U.S. funding of tree planting and providing water to various Jewish groups in Israel. American Friends of Koret Israel Economic Development Funds raised half a million dollars in 2012 to move Israel "toward a free market economy and enhance economic expansion in Israel's private sector."[91]

Yet a darker underbelly of the subsidy IAO sector has periodically been exposed—even by establishment media. In 2010, *The New York Times* reported on forty American tax-exempt nonprofit corporations that had sent more than $200 million to support Jewish settlements in the West Bank and East Jerusalem over a ten-year period. In 2015 an Israeli newspaper found U.S. donors gave $220 million to illegal settlements during 2009-2013.[92] Although the U.S. government prohibits expenditures of foreign aid on Israeli settlement building, Internal Revenue Service and State Department officials duck questions about the legality of such transfers when made by tax-exempt nonprofits. They—in private—apparently give assurances to such IAOs as the United Israel Appeal not to worry. In 2007, the One Israel Fund and Christian Friends of Israeli Communities openly and defiantly sent tens of thousands of dollars to keep illegal settlements active even after permanent home building was temporarily suspended by the Israeli government.[93]

Unofficial enforcement agencies "looking the other way" follows a pattern set toward the original subsidy IAOs that set up fronts to illegally smuggle weapons, recruits and war supplies to Jewish fighters in Palestine, bearing such names as the Sonneborn Institute, Martech, Materials and Manpower for Palestine, and Foundry Associates. These IAOs are long gone and not included in the *Big Israel* dataset. Yet their spirit of defiant lawbreaking activities is periodically resurrected. Recently an IAO was set up to scour the greater Washington, DC region for military industrial secrets of value to Israel. Unsurprisingly the IAO's foreign partner was Israel Aerospace Industries, established by a convicted felon, Adolph "Al" Schwimmer, who smuggled military planes and engines to Israel in the 1940s using a for-profit front called "Service Airways." The first truly "subsidy-oriented" IAOs both willfully and clandestinely violated arms export control and neutrality acts, confident that they would never be prosecuted or suffer

---

[91] Official website http://www.afkiedf.org/

[92] Uri Blau, "U.S. Donors Gave Settlements More Than $220 Million in Tax-Exempt Funds Over Five Years" *Haaretz*, December 7, 2015

[93] "Tax-Exempt Funds Aid Settlements in West Bank" *The New York Times*, July 5, 2010
http://www.nytimes.com/2010/07/06/world/middleeast/06settle.html?_r=0

any consequences.[94] One of their modern-day reincarnations, which we explore later, was called the Alliance for Competitive Technology. After being tipped off, the FBI struggled mightily—probably under guidance of the Justice Department—to compartmentalize its counterespionage investigation so that Israel escaped accountability when the IAO's true purpose was finally exposed.

[94] See Leonard Slater's book *The Pledge* (Pennsylvania, Simon and Schuster, 1970)

5 FUNDRAISING & LOCAL POLITICAL ACTION

Jewish federations are the financial backbone of many Israel Affinity Organizations in America. Federations also house their own politically active mini-AIPACs called "Jewish Community Relations Councils."[95] Present in every major city, the primary role of federations—as declared to the IRS—is raising money, which they do with an intense focus. In 2015, the national federation headquarters organization—the Jewish Federations of North America—claimed there were 152 federations in its network. According to scholar Norman Finkelstein, federations have not always been named in a uniform way, but have traditionally been more than fundraising machines:

> *The Federation movement's role grew and evolved as it assumed the responsibility of being the "address" for local communities, carrying on a long-standing tradition of lay leadership that embodied the American principle of separation of church and state. Whether known as The Associated in Baltimore, United Jewish Federation in Pittsburgh, or Combined Jewish Philanthropies in Boston, the local federation evolved into more than just a fund-raising organization. It became the major policy-setting umbrella under which other community groups gathered. No longer limited to the largest Jewish population centers, federations sprang up wherever Jews were, whether in Sarasota (1959), Orange County (1964), or Las Vegas (1973). Local*

[95] Not to be confused with Jewish Community Centers.

> *federations, in turn, were loosely connected through the national organization, United Jewish Communities.*[96]

Through the year 2013, federations (along with the United Jewish Appeal) automatically provided financial support to both the Jewish Agency for Israel and the American Jewish Joint Distribution Committee. Federations have moved to terminate a longstanding policy of splitting funds allocated for overseas initiatives, 75 percent to the Jewish Agency and 25 percent to the American Jewish Joint Distribution Committee. This meant that the $182 million in allocations from year 2011 federation fundraising was split: $136.5 million to the Jewish Agency and $45.5 million to the American Jewish Joint Distribution Committee. Although the American Jewish Joint Distribution Committee has been able to tap its own donor network, the funding allocation decision left the Jewish Agency, a foreign organization with the troubled but largely secret history in the United States, suffering a major crisis and even partnering with evangelical Christian organizations to fill in budgetary gaps.

Rather than automatic percentage allocations, a new mechanism, branded the "Global Planning Table," tried to satisfy IAO needs and performance-based appeals for funding through a complex committee structure with more individual federation input. Some insiders quoted by *The Jerusalem Post* framed this new funding allocation mechanism as a kind of disintermediation:

> *If in the past federations entrusted the Jewish Agency, JDC and other philanthropic "managing agencies" with the decisions, in recent years, federations have opted for more self-empowerment by giving directly to their favorite causes, without go-betweens. In part, this is because the agency and JDC are no longer the indispensable intermediaries between the grantors in America and the grantees in Israel...*
>
> *But perhaps the demand by Jewish federations for a funding shake-up is also the result of changing relations between Israel and U.S. Jewry. Once upon a time, Israel was dependent on U.S. Jewry's largesse. But this is no longer the case. If anything, the two countries now share mutual economic interests. The Jewish state has become a strong, prosperous nation with a high standard of living, a good quality of life and an innovative*

[96] Norman H. Finkelstein, *American Jewish History: a JPS Guide* (Indiana, The Jewish Publication Society, 2007), 150.

> *business sector. Israel's economy actually managed to weather the financial crisis better than the U.S.'s.*[97]

The shift in funding allocations has meant that aggressive start-up IAOs, such as The Israel Project and United Against Nuclear Iran, can come onto the scene suddenly, and then apply to federations for large amounts of venture capital after pitching their projects or showing some promising initial results. A mountain of cash pre-positioned on the sidelines, ready to enter the federation system from special purpose financial vehicles, is currently estimated to be approximately $4.3 billion. This is largely due to the efforts of a federation activist with the curiously appropriate name of Norman Sugarman, who helped influence a change in IRS rules in 1969 to make such a tax-free accumulation of "sugar" entirely "normalized."

Sugarman worked on the staff of the Bureau of Internal Revenue (the IRS predecessor) in the 1940s and 1950s, helping to draft a major change in tax code. Later working as a lawyer, among his clients were the Jewish Community Federation of Cleveland and other Jewish foundations. Sugarman wanted donors to be able to place their assets into philanthropic funds (now known as "donor advised funds") and obtain an immediate tax deduction. The principal would generate interest and capital gains, tax-free, even though it had not actually been transferred from the account into an IRS-recognized tax-exempt charity. The donor retained authority over when, and to what charity, they would release the funds. Sugarman requested a formal IRS ruling on his broad (and somewhat self-serving) interpretation of the 1969 Tax Reform Act, and won approval. He told delegates at the 1970 national General Assembly of Jewish Federations that the act could be put at their service "with some imagination and use of initiative," presumably via the services of former inside tax specialists such as himself.[98]

This special-purpose vehicle, the Donor Advised Fund (DAF), is why many Jewish federations are not hand-to mouth operations like so many other nonprofits where the money raised during any given year almost immediately flows right back out. By becoming "sponsoring organizations" and setting up one or more DAFs, Jewish federations can lock down resources while still delivering tax benefits coveted by the wealthy donor. The aggregation of resources in federation DAFs mean resources are there for emergencies and to fund strategic long-term initiatives. However, during the almost half-century DAFs have been multiplying and harvesting cash with little oversight, they have become subject to widespread abuse and self-dealing, according to an alarming report produced by the IRS:

---

97 "Changing Charity," *The Jerusalem Post*, November 7, 2011

98 Lila Corwin Berman, "How Norman Sugarman Became $50B Godfather of Charitable Funds," *The Jewish Daily Forward*, November 14, 2015

> *The IRS is aware of a number of organizations that appeared to have abused the basic concepts underlying donor-advised funds. These organizations, promoted as donor-advised funds, appear to be established for the purpose of generating questionable charitable deductions, and providing impermissible economic benefits to donors and their families (including tax-sheltered investment income for the donors) and management fees for promoters.*[99]

In plain English, the already enormous tax bill passed on to other taxpayers by the Israel lobby and explored in the final chapter may be even larger as ultra-wealthy donors take inappropriate deductions. According to a mandatory Treasury Department report to Congress, until 2006 DAFs in general had been largely a black hole in terms of how many assets they accumulate and whether those assets are even properly transferred to qualified recipients.[100]

Fundraising is, again, not the only thing federations do. Jewish federations have been quick to conduct immediate public relations and predictably one-sided reporting on armed flare-ups between Israel and Palestinians. They follow up with branded parallel fundraising campaigns, such as the "Israel Terror Relief Fund." Such public relations campaigns often overwhelm and saturate American establishment news outlets, generating massive empathy for Israel even as the Palestinian narrative is misrepresented or completely blacked out. This "forced empathy" through saturation has been augmented in recent conflicts as Israelis holding dual American citizenship and serving in the IDF are rotated to the front lines of armed conflicts. When these armed combatants become casualties, their citizenship status is quickly trumpeted over the American airwaves, along with Israeli civilian casualties who also held American citizenship. Such was the case of 21-year-old Nissim Sean Carmeli of Texas and 24-year-old Max Steinberg of California in 2014. Federations also liaise directly with Israeli government propaganda units to ensure the Israeli government view is well propagated over American broadcast media, as was reported in 2012 (but ignored by the Foreign Agents Registration Act office). One typical newscast reported:

> *Lt. Col. Avital Leibovich, head of the International Media and Communications Branch of the IDF Spokespersons Unit,*

---

[99] "Donor-Advised Funds," The Internal Revenue Service, https://www.irs.gov/Charities-&-Non-Profits/Charitable-Organizations/Donor-Advised-Funds

[100] "Report to Congress on Supporting Organizations and Donor Advised Funds," Department of Treasury, December, 2011 http://www.treasury.gov/resource-center/tax-policy/Documents/Supporting-Organizations-and-Donor-Advised-Funds-12-5-11.pdf

encouraged the global Jewish community to "go to a media war," during a call yesterday hosted by JFNA and the Jewish Council of Public Affairs. It's critical to promote Israel in both mainstream outlets and social media, she said, to counteract the "false rumors and false pictures" being disseminated from the Palestinian side.

"The Israeli point of view must be represented," Leibovich said. "With our joint efforts, we can influence the narrative."

Up to 20 Federation lay leaders and executives will leave for Israel this weekend to assess the needs on the ground and see firsthand the work of our partner agencies. The mission will tour Israel's southern region, and include meetings with Israeli leadership and visits to those affected by the rocket attacks.[101]

A constant flow of large and small missions to Israel is another federation mainstay. In 2012, the "Miami Mega Mission Israel" sent more than 700 people to religious and historic landmarks, to meet with Israeli leaders and view federation-funded projects in Israel. Such trips are billed as boosting Israel's economy as much as bringing people together.

JFNA "General Assemblies" have long been important political gatherings in the United States. They are an opportunity for IAOs to pitch advocacy and subsidy programs to federation leaders in hopes of gaining financial support. The conferences also can feature the American president, vice president and Israeli prime minister. General Assemblies have served as the launching pad for major initiatives such as winning U.S. government backing for the mass migration of Soviet Jews to Israel and the United States, fighting school-prayer initiatives and spreading Holocaust awareness education and infrastructure-building projects.

In 2001, Israeli Prime Minister Ariel Sharon used the General Assembly as a soapbox to declare to Americans that after the September 11 attacks, "we are all Israelis now." By 2014, the general assembly was softening its harsh and longstanding anti-assimilation narrative (but not policies) and to "search more inclusive entry portals" for more religiously mixed families that were low-cost or even free, in hopes of preserving unchallenged political power. As Michael Siegal, Chair of the Board of Trustees of Jewish Federations North America General Assembly, worried in 2014:

Being Jewish is a numbers game. And some of the numbers should be keeping all of us up at night. Here are some numbers

---

[101] "Update on the Situation in Israel," *Late Edition States News Service,* November 16, 2012

> *for you to think about. Six million Jews in North America, eight million Jews in the rest of the world. Fourteen million people total. One-fifth of one percent of the world's population. And now less than two percent of the North American population. Just on those numbers alone, we will be challenged as a community.* [102]

Stripped bare, federation initiatives could be uncharitably challenged as at best insular or at worst a modern day "anti-miscegenation" drive that runs entirely against the concept of an American "melting pot." When Barack Obama addressed JFNA on August 28, 2015, in a last ditch bid to gain support for the Iran nuclear deal, he was addressing a body that has long openly promoted policies discouraging Jews from marrying non-Jews—people such as himself or his daughters. In the face of the "assimilation" threat, the IAO nevertheless seeks to ensure that unrestricted funding flows and elite access will continue to enact the prerogatives that raw voting power cannot.

Intelligently, IAOs have not been very loud or overt about such discrimination. They do not call attention to this central issue on their program agenda by publicly issuing warnings against "fraternization." There is no equivalent to the word "miscegenation" bandied about in the anti-assimilation campaign, because if there were, Jewish federations and other IAOs in the anti-assimilation business, like Birthright, would probably no longer be given a pass. Nevertheless, in modern-day America, it is hard to find any similar internal discussion and campaign underway in major tax-exempt organizations to promote "hard" or "soft" discrimination as a means of preserving political influence.

General Assembly calls to action are often hostile to the disenfranchised. During the Clinton administration, the GA warmly backed the president's appeal for tougher Iraq sanctions in the face of growing humanitarian calls to ease the suffering of the victims—mostly Iraqi women and children. The same stance is already emerging in some corners of the Israel lobby towards Syrian refugees.

---

[102] Michael Siegal, Chair of the Board of Trustees, Jewish Federations North America, speech to the General Assembly 2014

Federation Policy Initiatives	Rationale
Fight restrictions on the 100 percent deductibility of charitable donations during tax-reform initiatives.	A large percentage of federation revenue comes from a relatively small percentage of donors.[103]
Fight the intermarriage of Jews and non-Jews. Fund anti-assimilation programs.	According to federation and other studies, the Jewish population (and therefore its influence) will decline if the intermarriage rate continues to grow. Publicly, the JFNA now takes a softer line of "inclusiveness," but funding continues.
Urge unconditional U.S. support for Israel	Actions and resolutions demanding constant public statements, politician forums and meetings for voicing unconditional support.
Holocaust awareness, memorialization and education	A means to generate general U.S. popular backing of Israel, particularly from younger generations.
Jewish refugee resettlement	Seek U.S. Jewish donor support, then government backing as the core means to transfer Jewish refugees to Israel, other countries and sometimes the U.S.
Fight laws seeking to limit lobbying by federal aid recipients	Federation member agencies receive federal aid but do not want their lobbying activities limited.

Figure 13 Jewish federation initiatives

The great majority of available information about Jewish federations is emitted by federation press offices or through the JNFA, which annually trumpets the combined amount of funds raised, especially during "super Sundays," to each federation. However, annual funds raised are not often trumpeted in mainstream media, but rather only to audiences that matter and that will not question how it is spent. One such forum is Congress. In testimony to the House Ways and Means Committee on February 14, 2013, Jewish Federations of North America's William Daroff claimed the federations, alone, were the second largest philanthropic network in the nation. He did not—of course—calculate or divulge the nearly $162 million hole that other taxpayers who were not benefitting from federation initiatives had to pay in order to make up the loss in tax revenue. That is the amount the IRS had to find elsewhere, assuming an average household tax rate of 17.3 percent and excluding capital gains and interest on assets held by federations. The total tax bill passed on by the Israel lobby to other taxpayers is discussed in the final chapter.

---

[103] House Ways and Means Committee Hearing; "Itemized deduction for charitable contributions as part of comprehensive tax reform," Testimony by William Daroff, Vice President for Public Policy, Jewish Federations of North America, Washington, D.C., February 4, 2013

Metric	Amount
Claimed number of donors	400,000
Annual fundraising	$950,000,000
Annual planned giving and endowments	$1,200,000,000
Federation endowment assets	$14,000,000,000
Tax impact[104]	$161,500,000

Figure 14 Jewish Federations of North America

A great deal of Jewish federation and IAO political power derives from the quite logical assumption that federations are gateways that politicians can pass through to reach a big Jewish donor community and politically active lobbyists. Because these IAOs are also authoritarian and fundamentally unrepresentative in nature, any political support available to politicians comes from a relatively small number of donors who make their demands along with each campaign contribution. Despite all the very impressive bylaws that ostensibly govern federations, the recent reorganizations and ambitious strategic operations plans, federations are simply not the member-representative agencies they claim to be, according to J.J.Goldberg:

> *The new system does not change one of the basic flaws in the federation system—lack of democracy at the local level. Federations often claim to speak for the entire Jewish community, but most are run by boards representing big givers.*
>
> *Most communities hold elections for the board, but challenges to the board's own slate of nominees are almost unheard of—largely because of public apathy. And in some cities, including New York, the board chooses its own members with no pretense of an election.*[105]

The IRS demanded that the Zionist Organization of America have an effective board during the organization's quest to reinstate its tax-exempt status. Nevertheless, it is silent on this much larger problem of federation governance. A more public discussion—particularly in U.S. metropolitan

---

[104] Calculated by the author using a .173 mean household tax rate only on annual funds raised, excluding forgone taxes on interest and dividends on sheltered assets.

[105] J.J. Goldberg "Changing the Rules" *The Jerusalem Report*, July 1, 1993

areas with large federations—is required about federation influence peddling via "grants" and the negative financial impact federations have on "other" taxpayers. The details of this externality become stark through analysis of the largest federation with an equally unwieldy name, the Jewish Community Foundation of the Jewish Federation Council of Greater Los Angeles (JCFGLA). Such analysis reveals both questionable giving patterns and huge negative externality transferred to other taxpayers because of federation activities.

JCFGLA made 100 grants, averaging $65 thousand each, directly to unknown recipients (presumably in Israel) categorized as being located in the "Middle East North Africa," according to its 2013 tax return.[106] It made 159 grants to California-based Jewish religious, educational and social welfare organizations averaging $155 thousand each, and even more grants (194) to local non-Jewish nonprofit organizations each averaging $34 thousand. JCFGLA also made 113 grants to non-California based Jewish and IAO groups ($3.9 million total) and sixty-seven to non-California non-Jewish non-IAOs, most notably to elite Ivy League universities totaling $1.2 million.

2013 Grants by Region/Group	Total	Mean grant amount	Number of Grants
Israel/region direct	$ 6,604,004	$65,386	100
Non-Israel/region direct	$435,930	$54,491	7
Local Jewish/Israel Affinity	$24,851,753	$155,323	159
Local Non-Jewish/Israel Affinity	$6,667,701	$34,193	194
Non-Local Jewish/Israel Affinity	$3,879,864	$34,033	113
Non-Local Non-Jewish/Israel Affinity	$ 1,245,520	$18,589	67
Total	**$43,684,772**		**640**

Figure 15 2013 JCFGLA grants by category

Given its direct holdings of over a half-billion dollars in endowments that produce steady investment returns and preserve the principal as a healthy financial cushion, JCFGLA can pay out more in grants and overhead than annual donations support, as it did in 2013. An important but rarely asked public policy question is, "what influence do federations like JCFGLA seek through grants?" Another is, "what is the overall impact of a federation's operations on taxpayers outside the Israel affinity ecosystem?"

---

[106] IRS revisions of reporting requirements in 2008 now makes it harder for the IRS and outsiders to understand what federations (and all other nonprofits giving overseas) are actually doing with the money. This is discussed in the final chapter.

JFGLA	2013
Revenues	$91,333,422
Grants paid	$49,512,127
Salaries	$4,041,204
Other expenses	$1,848,841
Total expenses	$97,233,467
Net Assets	$578,465,393
Total tax impact[107]	$16,257,349

Figure 16 JCFGLA tax impact

Like most federations, JCFGLA provides many five-figure grants to elite universities such as Harvard ($43k), Brown ($25k), Princeton ($20k) and Yale ($10k). Jewish students make up a disproportionately large percentage of the undergraduate and graduate school populations at many of these same schools, such as Harvard (25 percent, 61 percent), Yale (28 percent, 22 percent), and Brown (15 percent, 8 percent).[108] The admissions policies which have contributed to the transformation of the student body from heavily Protestant in the past to those favoring admissions benefitting the offspring of alumni "promising higher rates of return" may be signs that "human nature hasn't changed," according to pundit and columnist David Brooks who once tried to explain away Jewish overrepresentation.[109]

Presumably, the funding influences the level of hostility[110] with which universities respond to pro-Palestinian or Middle East activism on campus by groups without such donor affiliations. Donations to local universities, public school foundations, and private schools can also be assumed to grease

---

[107] Calculated by the author using a .173 mean household tax rate only on annual funds raised, excluding forgone taxes on interest and dividends on sheltered assets.

[108] "2013 Top Schools Jews Choose," *Hillel News*, August 21, 2013 http://www.hillel.org/about/news-views/news-views---blog/news-and-views/2013/08/21/2013-top-schools-jews-choose The 61 percent graduate figure for 2013 seems to be an outlier for Harvard. Hillel's frequently updated database in 2016 indicates 12 percent Jewish undergrads, and 20% graduates.

[109] David Brooks, "The Chosen: Getting In," *The New York Times*, November 6, 2005

[110] Amani Al-Khatahtbeh, "Daring to Speak Out on Campus" speech at the conference, The Israel Lobby, National Press Club, April 10, 2015 http://israellobbyus.org/transcripts/3.1Amani_Al-khatahtbehT.htm

the skids for new Holocaust awareness curriculum, pro-Israel speakers and Israel-centric studies centers.

It is less clear what JCFGLA gets out of making a grant to the mostly federal government-funded RAND Corporation. Can $52,000 per year buy more favorable treatment of Israel at a $289 million per year Air Force-founded think tank? Perhaps it is aimed at countering studies chartered by David K. Richards, who funded a 2005 RAND study on how to achieve a viable Palestinian state. The RAND Corporation released another Richards-funded study that estimated Israel could lose $47 billion over a ten-year period to the "Boycott, Divestment and Sanctions" movement.[111] It is not clear whether JCFGLA's grant was tied to, or combined with donations from other IAOs, toward any specific research project. The IRS does not provide this kind of relational data in useful form.

Non Local Jewish/Israel Affinity grant recipients include J Street Education Fund ($19,850), CAMERA ($13,100), Birthright Israel ($12,532), the World Jewish Congress ($11,550), United Jewish Appeal ($11,000) and The Israel Project ($6,800). This review of JCFGLA's giving reveals it does not send significant amounts for the umbrella national organization, the Jewish Federations of North America, to redistribute.

For taxpayers who are engaged neither with organized Jewish communal life, nor IAOs, nor are beneficiaries of largesse to non-Jewish/Israel Affinity Organizations—the Federation's impact is entirely negative. Again, assuming a mean household tax rate of 17.8 percent,[112] the amount of unpaid taxes on $91 million in deductible annual contributions is $16,257,349. Or, put another way, average U.S. taxpayers must pony up an extra $16.3 million to make up for the shortfall created by a non-profit heavily involved in steering funds to a country and organizations supporting Israel that it deems worthy. The donations are also aimed at generating actions that will create new taxpayer subsidies through Israel advocacy and lobbying.

This tax impact does not include revenue forgone over the tax-favored treatment of JCFGLA's investments in terms of zero taxation on a tax-exempt nonprofit's investment capital gains, interest and dividends. That impact is also significant. In 2013, JCFGLA earned $8.2 million on its investments, $33 million of which were maintained offshore in Caribbean and Central American tax havens. Because there is no taxation on such holdings, privacy and opacity may be the reason they are maintained offshore.

---

[111] "The Costs of the Israeli-Palestinian Conflict," RAND, 2015 http://www.rand.org/content/dam/rand/pubs/research_reports/RR700/RR740/RAND_RR740.pdf

[112] "Historical Average Federal Tax Rates for All Households," The Tax Policy Center, A Joint Project of the Urban Institute & Brookings Institution. http://www.taxpolicycenter.org/taxfacts/displayafact.cfm?Docid=456

It also does not calculate benefits to Israel from taxpayer-funded economic development initiatives, state government holdings of Israel bonds, passage of resolutions, and other initiatives promoted by federations but approved by state legislatures and paid for by all of a state's taxpayers.

Federations are alike in terms of tax externalities. Yet they can differ in subtle ways. The Jewish Federation of Greater Philadelphia, unlike JCFGLA, does not report any direct grant making to Israel, and instead funnels all Israel subsidy grants through American "friends" subsidy organizations such as American Friends of the Weizmann Institute for Science ($10,249 total) and Technion ($4,589). JFGP gives a great deal more to Birthright Israel ($333,854) and the ADL ($66,139) than does even the much larger JCFGLA.

Grant breakdown - 2012	Total	Mean grant amount	Number of Grants
Local Jewish/Israel Affinity	$ 9,055,906	$ 113,199	79
Local Non Jewish/Israel Affinity	$ 986,798	$ 21,929	44
Non-Local Jewish/Israel Affinity	$ 1,142,422	$ 19,363	58
Non-Local Non Jewish/Israel Affinity	$ 431,310	$ 15,974	26
Total	**$11,616,436**		**207**

Figure 17 2012 JFGP grants by category

JFGP gave $207,500 to the Trustees of the Germantown Public School, $75,800 to the trustees of the University of Pennsylvania, and $50,950 to Temple University. It also granted $8,100 to "Friends of the IDF," $6,000 to Hadassah and $33,062 to the Hebrew Immigrant Aid Society. On the policy side, the Philadelphia-based Middle East Forum, led by Daniel Pipes, received $5,960, while the more broadly focused Greater Philadelphia Urban Affairs Council took in $5,052. The Aspen Institute in Washington received $10,000. JFGP's grants also included $15,000 for Hawaii Public Radio.

Metric	Year 2012	
Revenues	$	36,742,007
Grants paid	$	17,639,526
Salaries	$	8,422,664
Other expenses	$	9,582,271
Total expenses	$	35,644,461
Net Assets	$	185,228,394
Total tax impact[113]	$	6,540,077

Figure 18 JFGP financial overview and tax impact

For unaffiliated taxpayers the Federation's negative impact is $6.5 million, not including lost capital gains, dividend and interest taxation and the sum of government allocations for initiatives quietly lobbied for by the JCRC.

According to its 2012 return, the Greater Miami Jewish Federation was at the very top of the federation mountain, raising $65.7 million. It funds the College of Judea and Samaria in the Israeli-occupied West Bank ($12,500), American Israel Education Foundation congressional junkets to Israel ($132,500), the Anti-Defamation League ($118,750), and Birthright Israel Foundation youth trips to Israel ($235,000), in addition to Friends of the Israel Defense Forces ($85,300) and the Holocaust Memorial Committee ($245,900).

Like many other federations, Greater Miami makes largely token, smaller contributions to non-Jewish regional charities such as the Diabetes Research Institute ($10,000), Florida Grand Opera ($16,000), and Florida International University ($13,100), though there are some exceptions, such as a substantial gift to the Miami Museum of Science ($300,000).

According to a former employee of the AIPAC lobbying division who contacted the author after leaving the organization in 2014, "Federations are incredible astroturfing resources for AIPAC."[114] With this in mind, it does not take long to uncover evidence of the extensive AIPAC activities within and across many of the largest Federation activity rosters. The Jewish Federation of Los Angeles felt it necessary to issue a disclaimer on a website event announcement for the American Israel Public Affairs Committee. This

---

113 Calculated by the author using a .173 mean household tax rate only on annual funds raised, excluding forgone taxes on interest and dividends on sheltered assets.

114 "Astroturfing" refers to the political tactic of concealing the sponsors or creators of a message or piece of legislation in order to make it appear as though it originates solely from and is supported by local grassroots organizers.

is likely designed to protect the organization's own 501(c)(3) deductibility on donor contributions—even while promoting the non-deductible AIPAC's event. (Contributions to AIPAC, as a lobbying organization, are not tax-deductible although corporate contributions to AIPAC, as discussed later, can be expensed—serving the same purpose for donors running corporations and partnerships.)

The ability of AIPAC and new IAOs such as United Against a Nuclear Iran to promote model legislation from their policy operatives right into state houses through JCRCs and federations is revealed in the large number of similar to identical anti-Iran and anti-Palestinian measures passed by state legislatures. Though in theory limited as 501(c)(3) organizations in their ability to lobby, in addition to reporting almost no lobbying expenditures, JCRCs and federations conduct advocacy training to prepare legions of politically active donors to push legislation in favor of Israel through state legislatures.

The Jewish Federation of Greater Washington is of obvious strategic importance due to its location. It often takes the most aggressive stance to pilot costly new initiatives for Israel's benefit through government appropriations processes. The fourth largest federation by revenue, it gives slightly more than token payments to top Washington-area universities. These include American University ($35,840, 23 percent Jewish undergrads, 22 percent graduate students) and George Washington University ($44,000, 29 percent Jewish undergrads, 10 percent grads). This presumably creates good will and the opportunity to continue to wield heavy influence in schools that produce huge numbers of diplomats, policy wonks and government functionaries. Yet these academic gifts pale in comparison to allotments to such top recipients as The Israel Project ($322,100) and American Friends of Hebrew University ($203,467). Like so many others, the JCRC of Greater Washington is co-located in the same building as the federation and receives the majority of its funding from the federation. Among its program accomplishments it lists "secured millions in government dollars for Jewish agencies...galvanized the community in support of Israel during times of calm and crisis...outreach in public schools, and Holocaust remembrance and education."[115]

This JCRC "monitored more than 200 bills in regional state legislatures," and in partnership with the Baltimore Jewish Council obtained more than $1

[115] Jewish Community Relations Council of Greater Washington, Annual report 2012-2013 http://www.jcouncil.org/site/DocServer/JCRC12Annual_Report.lowres.singlepages.TP3.pdf?docID=8810

million allocated from Maryland's budget[116] to expand the Hillel building at the University of Maryland in College park (see figure below). An additional $275,000 in taxpayer funds were directed into the "Maryland/Israel Development Center."

(K) Hillel Center for Social Justice. Provide a grant to the Board of Directors of Hillel: The Foundation for Jewish Campus Life, Inc. for the demolition of the existing center and the design, construction, and equipping of the Hillel Center for Social Justice, subject to the requirement that the grantee provide an equal and matching fund for this purpose (Prince George's County) 1,000,000

Figure 19 MD House Appropriation Committee - House Bill 101

The JCRC of Greater Washington also boasts of tightening the sanctions noose around Iran through the "Procurement Investment Activities in Iran—Board of Public Works Authority to Adopt Regulations." It also worked to obtain $516,420 in Department of Homeland Security grants to protect Jewish organizations. It arranged for police presence at "Jewish community institutions in the event of a military conflict between Israel and Iran." Given Hillel's role promoting Israel on campus, and admission that security is being sought to protect assets if IAO pressure to launch unwarranted attacks on Iran succeed, these expenditures are representative of the "double tap" undue influence IAOs can have on taxpayers. First, they promote unjustified attacks on Iran, then insist police isolate them from any resultant protests—all at taxpayer expense. The Maryland Hillel is clearly not interested in "social justice' for all, since it plays a major role as an on-campus "monitor" of Students for Justice in Palestine programs. Hillels do so in coordination with the Zionist Organization of America and "other pro-Israel activists" labeling pro-Palestine activities as "bias and hate speech" while unabashedly hosting their own "Israel Week."[117]

However, Hillel's allocations are not the only tax dollars JCRC extracted. JCRC also lobbied for and received funding for Jewish elder care, education and other benefits not obviously related to Israel. The JCRC vetted candidates for an open Virginia senate seat based on their support for Israel. As part of a larger network, this JCRC also pressures the media, when so tasked by yet another IAO network layer, the Israel Action Center, which claims:

[116] MD House Appropriations Committee – House Bill 101, 2013 http://mgaleg.maryland.gov/pubs/budgetfiscal/2013rs-budget-docs-capital-house-reprint-budget-bill.pdf

[117] "Initial Statement to the Jewish Community about Palestinian Solidarity Week," April 11, 2011, Maryland Hillel news release. http://www.marylandhillel.org/2011/04/3003/

> *The Israel Action Center's media communications group monitors local and national news coverage of Israel and responds when bias is detected. JCRC activists sent letters to The Washington Post to protest anti-Israel bias when the paper displayed prominently on the front page a horrific photograph of a Palestinian father holding his deceased child taken out of context and without a balanced perspective. This letter-writing campaign was such a success that it prompted a response from the paper's ombudsman on the editorial page of The Washington Post.* [118]

According to its annual report, the Jewish Federation of Greater Washington also scored a major victory at the Newseum, which bills itself as a private interactive museum of journalism and the news that is located near Capitol Hill in downtown Washington:

> *The media communications group also acted when the Newseum, planning its annual Journalists Memorial Rededication Ceremony, announced its plan to honor two photographers, Hussam Salama and Mahmoud al-Kumi, who were killed in an Israeli air strike in Gaza. When killed, they were working for Al-Aqsa Television, the media arm of Hamas, a group recognized by the U.S. government as a terrorist organization. Moments before the ceremony was to begin, Newseum officials announced that they had reconsidered their decision to honor the two members of Hamas' propaganda wing. After fielding criticism from the JCRC and other activists, the museum decided to uphold the integrity of its memorial by excluding the slain terrorists and honoring those who truly lost their lives in pursuit of a free press.*

It is perhaps revealing that the Newseum has a balcony running above Pennsylvania Avenue named after and in honor of media mogul Hank Greenspun. According to his FBI file, Greenspun made a fortune smuggling illegally purchased and stolen U.S. WWII surplus arms to Jewish fighters in Palestine in the 1940s.[119] A convicted felon who never went to prison, Greenspun used the illicit proceeds to purchase the *Las Vegas Sun* and become a Nevada political power broker who campaigned tirelessly for Israel.

---

[118] Jewish Community Relations Council of Greater Washington, Annual Report 2012-2013 http://www.jcouncil.org/site/DocServer/JCRC12Annual_Report.lowres.singlepages.TP3.pdf?docID=8810

[119] "Herman Milton Greenspun AKA Hank, Green, Greeny FBI file," The Israel Lobby Archive, http://israellobby.org/greenspun/

Despite the extensive 2012 legislative agenda, the JCRC of Greater Washington claimed it spent only $80,535 lobbying on its 2012 IRS form 990, out of a total budget of $1,135,738. Put another way, for every dollar of revenue going into the JCRC of Greater Washington, $1.58 was extracted from unsuspecting U.S. state or federal taxpayers and privately moved toward Israel's benefit. Alternatively, if one believes this JCRC really only spent $80,535 lobbying, every lobbying dollar spent shook loose $22.24 in taxpayer funds.

Taxpayer-Funded Program	Amount
Expand Hillel building at University of Maryland at College Park	$1,000,000
Maryland/Israel Development Center	$275,000
DHS grants to pay for security at Jewish nonprofits	$516,420
Total Israel-related Tax Dollars Obtained by JCRC	$1,791,420
JCRC Budget	$1,135,738
Israel Tax Dollars divided by JCRC Budget	$1.58
Tax Gap (17.8 percent mean household tax rate)	$202.161
Total Impact on U.S. Taxpayers (Tax gap plus total tax dollars obtained by JCRC)	$1,993,581

Figure 20 Greater Washington JCRC tax impact

Because of such lobbying, Israel has been a significant beneficiary of Maryland taxpayer dollars. For Israel's benefit, the University of Maryland's Biotechnology Institute (UMBI) and Israeli research institutions received a $750,000 grant for aquaculture research paid out in the years 2004 and 2005.[120] The Maryland-Israel Development Corporation received $100,000[121] per year to develop projects with Israeli companies and the Israeli Ministry of Economy and Trade.[122] MIDC grants in 2014 went primarily to Israeli military telecom developers, software cybersecurity and online companies, and medical device manufacturers.[123] Maryland's 2013-2015 budget forecasts MIDC grants increasing to $275,000 per year. Because it does not provide

---

[120] Maryland Higher Education Commission, Operating Budget Data, 2005 http://mgaleg.maryland.gov/pubs/budgetfiscal/2005fy-budget-docs-operating-r62i0001-maryland-higher-education-commission.pdf

[121] Maryland Higher Education Commission, Operating Budget Data, 2005 http://mgaleg.maryland.gov/pubs/budgetfiscal/2005fy-budget-docs-operating-r62i0001-maryland-higher-education-commission.pdf

[122] Maryland/Israel Development Center https://www.marylandisrael.org/about-midc

[123] MIDC 2014 Year in Review, https://www.marylandisrael.org/news/midc-2014-year-review

financial information and is not tax-exempt or required to file IRS form 990, MIDC's total revenue and whether it receives anything other than taxpayer funding cannot be determined. None of this funding is counted in tallies of Israel's billions in foreign aid or totaled across state legislatures in order to provide Americans with a clear picture of how many dollars are actually flowing to Israel. Presently, it is both time-consuming and difficult to determine precisely how much each state appropriates for Israel. This benefits JCRCs, which do not appear at all interested in trumpeting in aggregate these achievements to the American public.

Because most JCRCs are embedded inside federations, they are difficult to research. However, that Israel is their top concern is not difficult to discern. A glance at their websites or piles of local letters to editors will suffice. In response to a local upstart conservative competitor, the Jewish Community Relations Council of Indianapolis was compelled to highlight its pro-Israel anti-Palestinian bona fides on its website:

> *'…to maintain strong support for Israel and its right to exist in peace and security' is clearly stated in the governing bylaws of the JCRC. Further, the home page of our website (www.indyjcrc.org) clearly states, 'We advocate for Israel.' The first of two goals in our mission statement, also accessed on the website, notes our responsibility to 'safeguard the rights of Jews here, in Israel, and around the world.' 'Our documents are clear about the centrality of Israel to our mission…Our Israel programming does not contain Palestinian voices.'*

IAOs have both sought and received the majority of Department of Homeland Security funding ostensibly issued to protect nonprofits. This includes new lighting, video surveillance systems, blast and bulletproof doors and windows as well as other security enhancements. For example, the Zionist Organization of America obtained a DHS grant to install an advanced video security system at its New York City national headquarters even as it was losing its non-profit status over failure to file tax returns.[124] Begun in 2005, the Nonprofit Security Grant Program administered by DHS provides funds for nonprofits to be better prepared for terrorist attacks. Over time, the majority of funding from the program has gone to Jewish nonprofits, prompting *The Jewish Daily Forward* to label it an "earmark."

> *This disproportionate distribution is no accident. Examining the grants program provides a window into Jewish organizational and*

[124] Zionist Organization of America application for reinstatement of tax-exempt status. The Israel Lobby Archive. http://IsraelLobby.org/ZOA/ZOA_taxexempt.pdf

> *political power. It is this power that allowed a small community to create and maintain a government program tailored specifically for its needs and catering almost exclusively to its members.* [125]

The political appointees charged with disbursement have no qualms with the proportion going to IAOs. In a 2012 conference call, DHS director Janet Napolitano even justified the imbalance citing, "intensified rhetoric" between Israel and Iran, and a bomb plot against Saudi and Israeli embassies as heightening normal levels of "hate crime type of activity" directed at Jewish nonprofits. A total of $151 million has been distributed to quite wealthy IAOs through 2014.[126] In 2015, a Senate subcommittee doubled the annual amount to $25 million.[127]

Do crime statistics support such skewed grant distribution? Data on extremist attacks compiled since 9/11 by the New America Foundation revealed that while clearly a target, Jewish or Israel-identified facilities have not suffered anywhere near the levels of deadly casualties inflicted on church, police, Sikh and other targets.[128]

Target	Total Killings	Rightwing	Jihadist
Other	61	17	44
Church	11	11	0
Police	10	10	0
Sikh	6	6	0
Jewish/Synagogue	5	4	1
Total	93	48	45

Figure 21 Post-9/11 homegrown extremist attacks by target

However, that the funds enrich board members of Israel Affinity Organizations who provide security services to their own and other IAOs is not in doubt. In 2006, the Simon Wiesenthal Center felt compelled to report

---

[125] Eileen Reynolds, Maia Efrem and Nathan Guttman, "How an anti-terror program became a Jewish earmark," *The Jewish Daily Forward*, September 29, 2011 http://forward.com/news/142542/how-an-anti-terror-program-became-a-jewish-earmark/

[126] "Jewish Institutions Awarded $12 Million In Vital Nonprofit Security Grants," *States News Service*, July 25, 2014

[127] "Senate Panel Doubles 'Jewish Earmark' to $25 million," *The Jewish Daily Forward*, June 17, 2015

[128] Homegrown Extremists, Deadly Attacks database, New America Foundation consulted by the author on December 6, 2015 http://securitydata.newamerica.net/extremists/deadly-attacks.html

on this expensive taxpayer-funded cronyism in a statement buried deep in its IRS form 990, it is revealed that:

> *The organization utilized the services of Guardsmark, Inc., a security services company that is owned by a member of the Board of Directors. Guardsmark was paid fees in the amount of $1,061,945…*

In light of the comparative data, the "earmark" raises important questions. Could the delivery of security grant funding to government law enforcement agencies charged with protecting the entire community—rather than only one politically-empowered segment—prevent such attacks more effectively? Alternatively, should proportionate, similar "earmarks" be granted to the Sikh, police, church and organizations that are much greater victims of deadly extremist attacks?

The security earmark is only the tip of the IAO cronyism iceberg. In reviewing the flow of dollars to other IAO service providers and contractors, including research firms, accountants, lawyers, auditors, caterers, and information technology service providers, it is impossible not to notice that many are Jewish-owned, operated and staffed. It is similarly rare to see non-Jewish surnames appearing on board, staff or managerial rolls of IAOs. If the sector were any other, warranted public inquiries into workplace diversity and compliance with the Title VII of the Civil Rights Act of 1964 would be made. Instead, a comfortable and "closed loop" Mobius strip of hiring and contract cronyism recirculates administrative overhead to a favored few. The typical equal hiring declaration carried on most nonprofit job postings is mostly an empty formality at IAOs. That declaration states:

> *As an EQUAL OPPORTUNITY EMPLOYER, it is our policy to abide by all Federal and State laws prohibiting employment discrimination. We do not discriminate on the basis of a person's race, color, creed, national origin, religion, age, sex, marital status, or veteran status, the presence of non-job related medical condition or disability, or any other legally protected status and no question on employment applications is used for the purpose of excluding any applicant for the consideration for employment.*

From the Israel lobby's perspective, key U.S. states, such as California, are large and important enough to warrant extra infrastructure. IAOs constantly lobby the California state legislature to resolve—in Israel's favor—highly controversial issues that most of the world believes are still open for serious negotiation between the directly involved parties. The IAO resolutions are unabashed in their claims that they represent the entirety of the state's Jewish population—presumably since the time of riveted jeans maker Levi Strauss—and therefore should receive due deference on issues affecting the direct parties to the Israel-Palestine conflict, the region and rest of the world:

> *WHEREAS, California's Jewish community has been active socially, economically, and politically in the state's formation since the gold rush, and that involvement has had a positive impact on the state's multicultural and economic development; and*
>
> *WHEREAS, California is home to an estimated 2,000,000 Jews, making it the second largest concentration of Jews in the United States; and*
>
> *WHEREAS, For years, California and Israel have established business partnerships and trade relations with each other, and those partnerships have helped enhance the agricultural, educational, energy, entertainment, health, medical, scientific, and water policies in California, Israel, and the United States…*
>
> *RESOLVED, That the Legislature believes that Israel's borders should be determined by the Government of Israel.*[129]

Lending money to Israel and guaranteeing its debt, in addition to giving outright foreign aid, is now an important IAO California initiative, as well as in the other states. By 2012, over eighty state, municipal and public pension employee funds and treasuries had invested more than $2 billion in State of Israel bonds.[130] Many states passed laws lifting investor protective restrictions on foreign bond holdings specifically to buy Israel bonds.[131] In 1998, New York held $93.5 million in State of Israel bonds and another $592 million in the U.S. Agency for International Development (USAID) fund securities earmarked for Israel.[132] The State of Minnesota in 2014 held $10 million in State of Israel bonds and another $15 million in USAID securities. Ohio

---

[129] Official California State Legislative Information, Bill ACR 65, introduced June 2, 2011 but never voted on http://www.leginfo.ca.gov/pub/11-12/bill/asm/ab_0051-0100/acr_65_bill_20110602_introduced.html

[130] Advantages of Investing in Israel Bonds, Israelbonds.com http://www.israelbonds.com/getattachment/Invest/Institutional-Investors/States_eBrochure_Oct12_final-%281%29.pdf.aspx

[131] Max Boot, "States Buy Israeli Bonds, Stirring Up Controversy," *The Christian Science Monitor,* July 14, 1993 http://www.csmonitor.com/1993/0714/14072.html

[132] Stewart Ain, "State Buys $5 million in Israel Bonds," *The Jewish Week*, September 25, 1998 http://www.thejewishweek.com/news/new_york/state_buys_5_million_israel_bonds

Treasurer Josh Mandel purchased $42 million in Israel bonds for the state in 2013, a record at the time. In 2014, the 36-year-old purchased another $47.8 million, again breaking the record, as he thanked "credit leaders on both sides of the aisle for enabling our office to make this investment." Restrictions that had to be done away with for the purchase to be made include the Ohio Revised Code, which forbade investment in foreign bonds, and a law in effect until it was overturned 2010, restricting debt earnings in foreign nations to one-half of one percent.[133]

Guaranteeing Israel's debt against default is yet another important lobbying initiative that has leveraged both state and federal IAO muscle. In April 2003, the U.S. Congress approved guarantees with a $9 billion face value for three years to enable easier Israeli access to international debt markets. Bonds issued by the Israeli government and backed by such U.S. government guarantees enjoy a credit rating similar to that of the U.S. government. In fact, such bonds are sold at a yield that is only slightly higher than the yield of U.S. government bonds. Such guarantees are renewed when needed.

In 2005, the guarantee program was extended until 2008, and in 2006, despite the lack of any looming deadline, it was further extended until 2011, with a carryover option to 2012. On July 17, 2012, the U.S. House of Representatives approved an extension to the program. Ten days later, President Barack Obama signed into law a program extension to 2016, allowing the United States to provide access to up to $3.8 billion in future loan guarantees on top of the previously referenced $9 billion commitment made in 2003. On October 24, 2012, the United States entered into a memorandum of understanding for establishing a new framework to administer the extended program. The U.S. guarantee program serves the Israeli government as an extremely important financial "safety cushion."[134] It provides nothing to the United States except jeopardizing its own credit rating and creating an obvious obligation to ensure the Israeli government never has a severe financial crisis.

The amount of Israel bonds backed by the U.S. government constituted 41 percent of foreign currency debt guarantees in December 2011. The USAID bonds and notes guaranteed under the Israel Guarantee Program are regulated by law (22 U.S.C. 2186), and agency information about them should be readily available under the Freedom of Information Act.[135] However,

---

[133] Ed Wittenberg, "Ohio buys $47.8 million in Israel bonds," *Cleveland Jewish News*, June 12, 2014

[134] Israeli Ministry of Finance, The Government Debt Management Division, External Debt. http://ozar.mof.gov.il/debt/ext/funding.asp

[135] Obligations issued and fully insured or guaranteed by the United States Government or a United States Government Agency, U.S. Treasury

USAID did not respond to a Freedom of Information Act request filed by the author to provide the total 2015 value of these commitments in time for publication. Like a great amount of similar data, the cost, time and effort needed to extract what could easily be reported quarterly on an agency website but is not, is a barrier to transparency and accountability.

Jewish Community Relations Councils are two-way transmission belts. They can quickly and effectively put into action, at the state and local levels, the nation-wide initiatives of their titular national policy organization, the Jewish Council for Public Affairs (JCPA). They can serve as lily pads for receiving Israeli government officials who wish to give speeches in a particular region of America, enlist JCRCs in information management campaigns, or host major AIPAC functions. JCRCs also transmit timely information back to JCPA's national member organizations whenever there is a productive opportunity to highlight some perceived slight to Israel or to punish the source. Like AIPAC's connection to each member organization of the Conference of Presidents of Major American Jewish Organizations, the Jewish Council for Public Affairs is also composed of member organizations in addition to representing the network of JCRCs.

American Jewish Committee	Jewish Women International
American Jewish Congress	National Council of Jewish Women
Anti-Defamation League	ORT America Inc.
B'nai B'rith International	The Rabbinical Assembly
Hadassah	Union of Orthodox Jewish Congregations of America
Jewish Labor Committee	Union for Reform Judaism
Jewish Reconstructionist Federation	United Synagogue of Conservative Judaism
Jewish War Veterans of the U.S.A.	Women's League for Conservative Judaism

Figure 22 Jewish Council for Public Affairs member organizations

However, the JCRC national headquarters—the JCPA—is not a heavyweight in terms of revenue. The office is staffed by only 35 employees and saw its budget decline from $4.5 million in 2004 to $3.1 million in 2012. Jewish federations—which, as previously mentioned, provide most JCRC

http://www.treasurydirect.gov/instit/statreg/collateral/collateral_acc31cfr202.pdf

funding and facilities—have periodically threatened to entirely cut off JCRC funding, spin them off into independently incorporated organizations or at least require them to compete for resources based on results rather than automatic allocations.[136]

As an umbrella group, JCPA's pronouncements attempt to carry the combined power of the 16 national member agencies and more than 100 JCRCs. When JCRCs speak locally on matters of importance, they may also claim to speak on behalf of other in-state organizations. For example, the St Louis JCRC claims it is the umbrella for yet another eighteen local organizations.

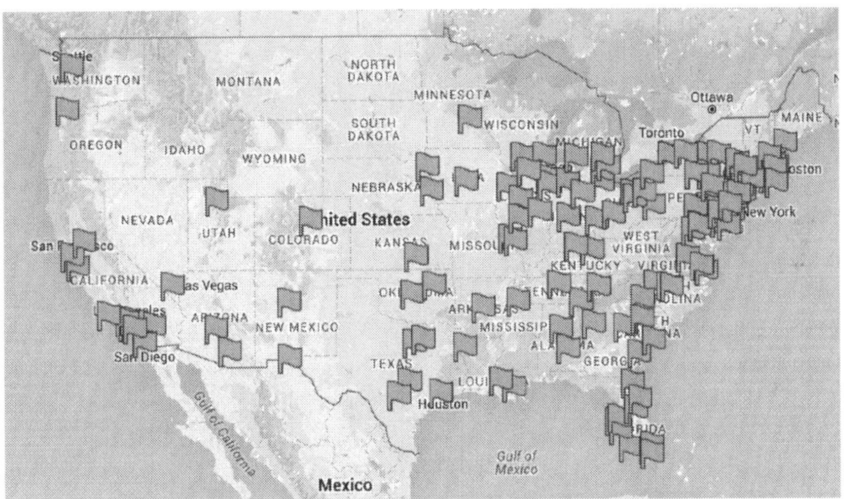

Figure 23 Year 2015 JCRC distribution across the U.S.

That JCPA and JCRCs advocate for Israel is not in doubt. The JCPA's second mission statement goal is, "To dedicate ourselves to the safety and security of the state of Israel." JCRC mission statements echo this mission, "to maintain strong support for Israel and its right to exist in peace and security." Many JCRC websites state openly and unabashedly, "we advocate for Israel."[137]

AIPAC's influence on politicians is buoyed in that it is seen as a gateway to tap major campaign contributors. Its stature as "representative" of Jewish communities is boosted by its member organizations— which again are the

136 "Jewish Federation planning an ambitious restructuring; Member agencies, including the Jewish Community Relations Council, are fearful about their futures," *The Philadelphia Inquirer*, June 8, 2003.

137 Todd Maurer, Marcia Goldstone, David Straus, Adam Kessler, Sharon Levy, Yitzchak Ben-Shmuel, Anthony Luder, "JCRC's behind Israel," *The Jerusalem Post*, May 20, 2011

member organizations of the Conference of Presidents. This power is deployed to pass AIPAC-drafted resolutions and laws in Congress. JCRCs do the same at the state and local levels. Nevertheless, reviewing JCRC activities is not as easy as pulling an AIPAC lobbying declaration from the Clerk of Congress website. That is, again, because most are co-located within Jewish federation offices and are not separately incorporated. JCRCs function more as ongoing "projects" or "departments" of the federations, somewhat like AIPAC did under the umbrella of the Jewish Agency-funded American Zionist Council.[138] This makes studying individual JCRC finances and initiatives difficult if not impossible, particularly for state and local news outlets that might be interested in tracking such a powerful influence on state legislatures.

JCRCs describe their "advocacy days" to promote their legislative agenda, urging state and local lawmakers to pass pro-Israel legislation in this way:[139]

> *There's nothing more important than (for) voting constituents to show up in the offices of legislators and let them know what they think, said Nancy K. Kaufman, executive director of the Jewish Community Relations Council of Greater Boston.*

Only a minority of JCRCs or federations report spending funds on lobbying in their annual IRS filings, even though face-to-face contacts between JCRC staff, executives and members pushing the legislative agendas aimed to benefit Israel are ongoing. Portraying Iran as a major nuclear threat to the United States and Israel has been as important to JCRCs as to AIPAC. In December of 2005 the executive director of one of the most visible JCRCs, again of Greater Washington, informing members about a future anti-Iran rally, claimed that:

> *Iran is potentially months away from developing nuclear weapons technology, and currently has missiles that can reach U.S. troops in the region as well as the State of Israel.*[140]

That it was not true did not appear to staunch the enthusiasm of attendees. Supporting economic boycotts that target Israel's enemies has been a longtime activity of JCRCs that did not start with Iran. When human rights organizations sought to lift Iraq sanctions in the late 1990s because of their devastating impact on Iraqi civilians, JCRCs fought back, again claiming

---

138 "New York Day by Day," *The New York Times*, June 28, 1983

139 "Jewish activists press case in Boston," United Press International, March 24, 2004

140 "Freedom Over Tyranny: JCRC of Greater Washington to Hold Chanukah Candle lighting in Front of Iran Interests Office Dec. 27," *U.S. Newswire*, January 23, 2005

to represent the local Jewish community as report in the San Jose Mercury News.[141]

> *Jewish Community Relations Council, which represents 80 synagogues and Jewish organizations in the Bay Area, argued that lifting the sanctions against Saddam Hussein's regime would threaten security in the Mideast and fail to improve the plight of the Iraqis.*

Operating under the radar, JCRCs were the active lobbying organizations pushing passage of model legislation targeting Iran's economy in key state legislatures across the United States. The "Iran Divestment Act of 2012," modeled after a California law, was passed by the New York State Assembly in late 2011. The law prohibited companies providing goods, services or credit worth $20 million or more to Iran's energy industry from signing or renewing state and local government contracts.[142] The law required the state to maintain a list of those with more than $20 million invested in Iran's energy sector, and those bidding for contracts had to certify they were not on the list. The negative impact of such a patchwork of state legislation on the American economy is severe. American exporters have been seriously hurt by sanctions on Iran and the complicated punitive secondary boycotts. In 2010, a coalition representing the U.S. Chamber of Commerce, the Business Roundtable, Coalition for American Trade, the National Foreign Trade Council and others, urged Congress not to enact sanctions provisions they estimated would cost $25 billion and 210,000 American jobs.[143] The pleas were largely ignored by legislators and the mainstream news media.

JCRCs are the implementation engine behind the massive number of pro-Israel resolutions and laws passed by state legislatures and city councils beyond Iran sanctions. Presenting such measures as if they enjoy broad popular support, rather than being a patch for intense "Astroturf" lobbying as part of a national network, is important to JCRCs. Nevertheless, as presented later, polling reveals absolutely no broad public support for such resolutions.

The success of JCRC lobbying is in part a function of how underreported it all is, especially compared to AIPAC—which, although it should be registering as a foreign agent of the Israeli government—at least is registered

---

141 "Supervisors urge an end to sanctions on Iraq," *San Jose Mercury News*, September 1, 1999 Wednesday Morning Final Edition

142 "Speaker Silver Introduces Sweeping Iran Divestment Legislation," State News Service, October 27, 2011 Note: Silver was convicted of corruption in 2015.

143 Business Roundtable Coalition for Employment through Exports, March 30, 2010 Letter to Nancy Pelosi http://www.nam.org/Issues/Trade/Export-Controls/NAM-s-Analysis-on-the-Impact-of-the-Iran-Sanctions-Legislations/

and reporting as a domestic lobbyist. JCRCs are concerned that someday the veil of secrecy will be lifted. Douglas Bloomfield—a former AIPAC lobbyist once investigated by the FBI for his role in the 1985 theft of American corporate trade secrets in league with an Israeli diplomat[144]—sounded an alarm over the potentially negative impact of public disclosure of the actual—as opposed to reported—levels of JCRC lobbying, writing that:

> *The president's proposal to 'require lobbyists to disclose each contact' may result in treating 'citizen lobbying' by groups such as local Jewish community relations councils the same as corporate and labor interests.*
>
> *The proposals in Obama's State of the Union address to 'require lobbyists to disclose each contact' with Congress or the administration on behalf of a client will create an avalanche of paperwork for the small groups that can least afford it.*
>
> *On the surface the president did not call for restricting the activities of unpaid volunteers who engage in grassroots lobbying for nonprofit groups, which is critical for most Jewish charitable organizations. But that could be the result if he succeeds in removing the current exemption from registration for groups where less than one- fifth of the lobbyist's time is spent lobbying.*
>
> *Disclosure: I am biased. I've spent many years lobbying, mostly for Jewish organizations and causes. They depend on a grassroots network of deeply committed, well-informed citizen lobbyists; many are also campaign contributors, which already requires detailed reporting to the Federal Election Commission.*
>
> *In this era of gotcha politics and 24/7 cable media, it's easy to imagine a report of lobbyist contacts being used by an incumbent's opponents to attack him or her as a tool of the special interests.*
>
> *Some lawmakers may be hounded into also producing lists of unpaid / unregistered lobbyists, including constituents, they meet, even though there are no plans to require such disclosure, according to a source close to the White House. That could easily inhibit the willingness of lawmakers to meet more rarely even with constituents and discourage participation by citizen lobbyists who fear becoming public targets.*

---

[144] "FBI investigates AIPAC for espionage and theft of government property in 1984," Israel Lobby Archive, http://www.IsraelLobby.org/economy

Another former high-level AIPAC executive, Steven J. Rosen—who, unlike Bloomfield, was actually indicted for espionage in 2005—long ago warned that secrecy and darkness are key to IAO success. "A lobby is like a night flower, it thrives in the dark and dies in the sun."[145]

It is highly likely that if Americans were provided with ongoing, comprehensive, accurate information about the amount of time legislators spend meeting with IAO activists and the special benefits those meetings produced at taxpayer expense, they would become alarmed and take action. This is something IAOs and longtime lobbyists like Bloomfield want to prevent. So far, they have been successful.

Like AIPAC, JCRCs are also heavily involved in political campaigns. One of the JCRCs' most powerful functions is one that all deny engaging in, in order to preserve their tax-exempt status: vetting and supporting favored candidates for office. JCRCs host political debates, town hall forums, and in other ways screen candidates for political office. The tremendous fundraising might of the foundations and—most important—individual donors behind the foundations and JCRCs make them "must attend" gatherings for those aspiring to office.[146] JCRC—sponsored events pit candidates in a race for campaign contributions that can move them toward extreme positions to "out-Israel" their opponents.[147] Bill Clinton was once a prime example in 1992:

> *On Tuesday, Clinton made an appeal for votes by strongly criticizing U.S. policies toward Israel. 'This administration [George H.W. Bush] ever so subtly has broken down the taboo against overt anti-Semitism,' Clinton said, speaking to New York's Jewish Community Relations Council. Clinton also said that the United States should not interfere with peace talks in the Middle East on the question of Israeli settlements on the West Bank.*

Often, candidates will be pitted against one another in what several congressional staffers have described as an "ambush debate:"

> *Candidate X is invited to speak before a predominately Jewish audience, let's say at a temple or synagogue. The candidate arrives and discovers, without prior notification, that his or her opponent has also been invited. The candidates are then entreated to speak*

---

[145] Jeffrey Goldberg, "Real Insiders," *The New Yorker*, July 4, 2005

[146] Azi Paybarah, "Ray Kelly Makes the Rounds Some More," *The New York Observer*, June 23, 2008

[147] Bill Labrecht, "New York Primary," *St. Louis Post-Dispatch* (Missouri), April 1, 1992

on the issues, including the matters relating to the conflict…there was no point of contention here vis-à-vis Israel…it was set up there to make sure they hear what the congressman says. It was a very large, influential group of people; there was no way our opponent could oppose us on this issue.[148]

JCRC presidential candidate forums present an opportunity for candidates to echo policy positions and historical narratives pushed by IAO advocacy organizations. Candidate Rudy Giuliani in a 2007 presentation to a JCRC claimed that the history of terrorism started with attacks on Israel, only then to spread to the rest of "the West":

You would think after these two somewhat different but similar situations in not seeing the real intent of people at an early enough stage in dealing with it, you'd think by the time we came to Islamic terrorism, we would have gotten the point. But we didn't.

People think it all started on September 11, 2001. It did not start on September 11, 2001. It started somewhere back in the 1960s, with first the attacks on Israelis, then the attacks on Americans. The first big, big dramatic international incident was the killing of the Israeli athletes at the Munich Olympics. You remember that. Do you know how long ago that was? That was 1972.

Most historians would point to the Jewish Sicarii of the first century, who assassinated their targets with daggers, as the world's first terrorists. In more recent history, two terrorists went on to become prime ministers of Israel—Menachem Begin and Yitzhak Shamir. However, such a history would certainly not produce any upside for candidates addressing JCRCs. JCRCs can be pivotal in indirectly financing and providing resources to candidates who have sufficiently proven their pro-Israel bona fides. For example, Democrat John Delaney of Maryland's sixth district did and said all of the right things to win such support in 2012, including trips to meet top Israeli officials and the required public pledges to work on behalf of Israel and strengthen its U.S. agencies, saying a number of things everyone in the room wanted to hear as quoted in the press:[149]

…the Jewish agencies provide critical services to all-comers, regardless of religious affiliation. The agencies are a great example

---

[148] Kirk J. Beattie, *Congress and the Shaping of the Middle East* [New York, Oakland: Seven Stories Press, 2015], 42

[149] "Delaney Campaign Launches Jewish Community Advisory Board," *Targeted News Service*, September 24, 2012

> *of the importance of public-private partnerships and how the government and private sector can come together to work for the common good... Millions of Americans feel a close spiritual and emotional bond with Israel. After visiting the country, I now have a fuller understanding of the relationship between our two countries. Israel is our strongest ally in the region, and in Congress I will work to make sure we have a strong partnership for years to come.*

The common denominator of nearly the entirety of Delaney's fundraising and promotion committee members was their current and former positions as JCRC, Federation, JCPA or other IAO corporate employees and directors.[150] According to FEC records, Delaney raised nearly $2 million in pre-primary funds for his campaign. Even so, he only barely beat his Republican competitor, Dan Bongino, who also found it to be in his interest to voice passionate support for Israel, since taking a realist or noninterventionist stance carries no financial upside.

Trumpeting "passionate support" for Israel has observably become the norm. It has long been an IAO priority that support for Israel not become a partisan political issue, and JCRCs play a major role in ensuring that all competition will center on who can promise Israel the most support. JCRCs are the Israel lobby's invisible army that has fought to advance the following set of core activities over the past decade. Most JCRC initiatives are similar in tone to the programs of other IAOs, with one important difference: federations and JCRCs have 7,701 employees and 58,000 volunteers trained to vet candidates and pressure state and local governments to pass legislation. It is impossible to know how many of them actively lobby because it is simply

[150] Marchy Cohen, Vice President for Financial Resource Development, Jewish Federation of Greater Washington; past president, JCC of Greater Washington; Yvonne Distenfeld, Board member, Jewish Federation of Greater Washington; David Farber, President, Washington Chapter, American Jewish Committee; Michael Friedman, Vice President, Jewish Community Relations Council of Greater Washington; Board Member, Jewish Federation of Greater Washington; past President; Michael Gelman, past President, Jewish Federation of Greater Washington; Chair, Executive Committee of the Board, Jewish Federations of North America; past Chair, The Israel Project; Board Member, Washington Institute for Near East Policy; Board of Governors, Hillel; Ralph Grunewald, Maryland Hillel; Board Member, Jewish Community Relations Council of Greater Washington; co-founder, AIPAC Washington Regional Council; Abbe David Lowell, Jewish Community Center of Greater Washington; Ryan Spiegel, former Board Member, Maryland Hillel; Stuart Tauber, Board Member, Jewish Federation of Greater Washington; Susan Turnbull, Chair, Jewish Women International; Vice Chair, Jewish Council for Public Affairs; Rabbi Stuart Weinblatt, Board Member, Jewish Federation of Greater Washington

not disclosed. JCRCs have worked on:

1. **Massive public pressure campaigns to release Jewish prisoners**. JCRCs held vigils, rallies, circulated petitions and waged other campaigns to release Alan Gross, a USAID worker jailed in Cuba for alleged espionage activities. It has done the same for captured Israeli soldier, Gilad Shalit, and teenage Jewish settlers kidnapped and presumed alive before the onset of Israel's "Cast Lead" invasion of Gaza. Domestically, JCRCs long campaigned for the pardon of American spy for Israel Jonathan Pollard and his "return" to Israel.
2. **Instant resolutions supporting Israeli military campaigns**. Before many Americans have even digested the most recent news of an Israeli military operation, they will likely find their local city council or state legislature has already passed a resolution defending it as within "Israel's right to protect itself."
3. **Countering BDS**. JCRCs are supporters of boycotts when they target Israel's perceived enemies, but strongly oppose the Boycott, Divestment and Sanctions movement launched by Palestinian civil society groups. This ranges from opposition to local co-ops banning Israeli goods to New York assembly legislation to ban outright any education funding to institutions that divest from Israel. In 2010, a JCPA/JCRC anti-BDS resolution was passed creating a permanent body—the Israel Action Network—ready to immediately respond to BDS activities in order to keep them from undermining "goodwill."[151]
4. **Holocaust memorialization and remembrance** JCRCs promote public funding for Holocaust and Jewish studies centers at state universities. They work jointly with the ADL to protect the word Holocaust as exclusively referencing events surrounding WWII and not allowing the Holocaust to be used in analogies. JCRCs also release statements of annual "anti-Semitic incidents" in U.S. states, and suggested remedies.
5. **Anti-Palestinian efforts** Palestinian bids to join UN bodies, achieve statehood, or take matters to the General Assembly and Security Council are strongly condemned in JCRC petitions, media placements and public rallies. Flotillas designed to raise awareness of and challenge Israel's naval blockade of Gaza are characterized by JCRCs as "violence instigated by the misnamed 'Free Gaza' flotilla."

---

[151] "JCPA Taking Direct Aim at Anti-Israel Boycotters," *The Forward*, March 5, 2010

6. **Pro-Israel media pressure** Many JCRC leaders automatically view all critical news coverage of Israel as "distorted" and work hard to suppress criticism and insert pro-Israel spin. Because they are vigilant and local, JCRC op-eds calling for support of Israel are commonplace while their constant pressure likely increases the perceived "cost" for any news outlet considering publishing serious journalism concerning Israel.
7. **Support for State-to-Israel economic development councils** JCRCs are the primary lobbies for establishing and securing annual appropriations at the state level for joint economic development centers.

One of the most important challenges confronting all IAOs is whether they will be able to maintain credibility when claiming they are the voice a unified Jewish community in the future. The trajectory of Jewish federations, the financial core of the IAO ecosystem, suggests they will not. From 1895 to 1945, Jewish federations were primarily devoted to funding health, social and welfare services, with the aim of integrating the Jewish community into mainstream America. Their purpose was assimilating, through language instruction, values inculcation and cultural programs, Jewish participation in the "American dream." No more.

The gradual adoption of Zionism by major Jewish institutions and the establishment of Israel in 1948 fundamentally altered the mission and programs of federations. Federations subordinated a large amount of their own funding disbursement discretion to the United Jewish Appeal/United Israel Appeal joint campaigns. This increased the flow of resources formerly going toward local Jewish organizations and community needs by sending resources to Jews in Israel and other overseas locations, such as former Soviet states, and using resources to lobby the U.S. government.

Federations in the period 1967-1990, bursting with pride over Israel's 1967 Six-Day War victories, began promoting Holocaust awareness as the second pillar (alongside Israel) of communal identity. They began funding major increases to Jewish education programs and day schools where before many institutional insiders considered them to be "un-American" or ethnic initiatives unworthy of support. However, by the 1990s, such allocations by federations reached 25 percent of revenue.

Federations observably began a 180-degree turn away from their founding purpose of integration and assimilation. As the financial enabler of IAOs in America, and following Israel's own example of discriminating against non-Jews, federations quietly combat intermarriage. Jewish day schools, summer camps, and Jewish studies programs at universities are considered by federations to be "the most important insurers of Jewish continuity and intra-marriage." Federations and IAOs intensely track the demographics of that

"Jewish continuity," and even the precise date when Israel's Jews will outnumber America's, as a kind of "doomsday clock."[152] The impact of this fundamental, extreme mission change at the IAO's financial core opens up the entire ecosystem to justifiable outside criticism.

Again, however they may wish to spin it, an open modern-day fight against intermarriage by the elite leadership of organizations operating under the mantle of social welfare has bad optics. As IAOs reach out to different constituencies for support on their major initiatives, internally they anticipate they will increasingly be challenged over obviously anti-assimilation programs such as Birthright, more subtle socialization programs in Jewish day schools, and programs encouraging intramarriage at Hillel. This kind of ethnocentrism appears hypocritical on principle given the ADL's covert efforts to shut down Arab student organizing in the late 1960s by challenging ethnic exclusivity within their organizations as illegal and prohibited in education settings.

IAO defenders have attempted to shield Israel from criticism and backlash over Israeli actions by labeling any suggestion of it as "blaming the victim" and "anti-Semitism." This, too, has become more difficult, because what were formerly benign Jewish social welfare organizations focused on human betterment have mostly completed their transformation into Israel Advocacy Organizations. Israel is not seen as weak and vulnerable, but rather a powerful global actor. Clinging to discredited notions, prominent pundit Jeffrey Goldberg chastised the executive director of Human Rights Watch for commenting that, "Germans rally against anti-Semitism that flared in Europe in response to Israel's conduct in Gaza war. Merkel joins." Goldberg was livid, writing that:

> *[Human Rights Watch executive director] Roth's framing of this issue is very odd and obtuse. Anti-Semitism in Europe did not flare "in response to Israel's conduct in Gaza," or anywhere else. Anti-Semitic violence and invective are not responses to events in the Middle East, just as anti-Semitism does not erupt "in response" to the policies of banks owned by Jews, or in response to editorial positions taken by The New York Times. This is for the simple reason that Jews do not cause anti-Semitism.*
>
> *It is a universal and immutable rule that the targets of prejudice are not the cause of prejudice. Just as Jews (or Jewish organizations, or the Jewish state) do not cause anti-Semitism to flare, or intensify, or even to exist, neither do black people cause racism, nor gay people homophobia, nor Muslims Islamophobia. Like all prejudices, anti-Semitism is not a rational response to*

[152]Norman Linzer, David J. Schnall, Jerome A. Chanes, *A Portrait of the American Jewish Community* (Westport, CT: Praeger, 1998) 70-73

> *observable events; it is a manifestation of irrational hatred. Its proponents justify their anti-Semitism by pointing to the (putatively offensive or repulsive) behavior of their targets, but this does not mean that major figures in the world of human-rights advocacy should accept these pathetic excuses as legitimate…A question: If a mosque in Europe or in the U.S. were to be attacked (God forbid) by Islamophobic arsonists, would Ken Roth describe such an attack as a manifestation of 'anti-Muslim hatred that flared in response to the conduct of Muslim groups in the Middle East?'*[153]

Goldberg is widely considered a top advocate for Israel and was a ubiquitous proponent of the U.S. invasion of Iraq, yet he enjoyed both unprecedented and uninterrupted access to the Obama White House and top elected officials, who often respond unquestioningly to his demands to answer questions of "communal importance." In the early 1990s, Goldberg served as a prison guard at Israel's largest detention camp for Palestinian political prisoners, where he admitted to covering up for guards who beat prisoners, and famously said, "I never hit a Palestinian who wasn't already hitting me." Goldberg conflates, as is common practice among IAO pundits, Jews, Jewish organizations, and the Jewish state. He also ignores drastically different levels of empowerment between minority groups, in his claim that Israeli actions can never trigger a wider backlash toward those who may or may not want anything to do with it. For this Raphael Magarick took him to task, writing:

> *It is deeply implausible that black people cause American racism, because black people do not hold power in American society. How women dress or behave is unlikely to cause rape, because women don't hold power in their interactions with potential rapists. And for the same reason, German Jews' actions likely have nothing to do with German anti-Semitism. It's delusional to think powerless people are the cause of what powerful people do. But the Jewish state is (thank God!) a powerful force, whose actions have worldwide reverberations. Lumping "Jews" with gay or black people is argumentative Three-card Monte: European Jews are often victimized, and Israel is a powerful, majority Jewish country. A better parallel is Islamophobia in America,*

[153] Raphael Magarick, "Do Jewish Actions Ever Cause Anti-Semitism?" *The Atlantic*, September 24, 2015 http://www.theatlantic.com/international/archive/2014/09/does-human-rights-watchs-kenneth-roth-understand-the-nature-of-prejudice/380556/

> *which targets an oppressed minority, but is sometimes caused (not justified!) by the actions of Muslims who wield power elsewhere.*[154]

Israel's spokespeople often do overtly or indirectly claim to speak for all Jews, a message that mainstream media has echoed, as is explored in the final chapter. The idea that Israel's claiming to speak for all Jews, while continually engaging in outrageous actions and violence, might endanger those it inaccurately claims to speak for does not seem quite as outrageous as the Jeffrey Goldbergs of the world claim it to be.

As this book reveals, IAOs are well on their way to resurfacing as the largest tax-exempt nonprofit collective in the United States and wield immense, disproportionate power. They do not provide the social welfare services many formerly provided and for which they received special tax privileges. They have become, instead, the primary catalyst of U.S. support for Israel and of its virtually unconditional support by the news media. IAOs are active in shaping U.S. policies that primarily benefit Israel an American expense at every level. The characterization of IAOs as disenfranchised victims representative of all American Jews, or somehow unconnected to Israel's actions, is no longer tenable. Having turned sharply away from the social welfare programs that once actually did reduce dependence on government resources—in favor of the advancement of Israel through advocacy that *increases* U.S. government expenditures—IAOs have exposed themselves to growing, well-founded opposition that is not going to be intimidated by false charges of "anti-Semitism" or diverted by trite and overused conflations of "Israel" and "the Jews."

---

[154]Raphael Magarick, "Do Jewish Actions Ever Cause Anti-Semitism?" *The Atlantic*, September 24, 2015 http://www.theatlantic.com/international/archive/2014/09/does-human-rights-watchs-kenneth-roth-understand-the-nature-of-prejudice/380556/

6 ADVOCACY

In the 1970s, major acknowledged wins for Israel advocacy organizations included ousting staunch opponent Senator William J. Fulbright, the 1973 Yom Kippur war arms and aid airlift from the U.S., and getting the Jackson-Vanik amendment to the Trade Act of 1974 passed, which cut "most favored" nation status to the Soviet Union until Jewish émigrés were allowed to leave the USSR and East Bloc countries.[155] In the 1980s, IAOs publicly claimed the major role in ousting from elected office two critics of U.S. policy toward Israel—representatives Paul Findley and Pete McCloskey.

Some past victories went unacknowledged because to celebrate would have publicly raised questions about undue IAO power and influence. These included unpunished diversions of nuclear weapons material and technology from the U.S. to Israel, finally achieving the suspension of Foreign Agents Registration Act enforcement attempts against IAOs, and passage of an extremely one-sided "free trade" agreement favoring Israel that had a boost from Israeli espionage. This came at America's expense, and over the opposition of major U.S. corporations such as Monsanto and Dow Chemical. The ability to effectively coordinate and control messaging reflects the advanced developmental state of IAOs. The oldest, introduced in the first chapter, has operated continuously since the mid-19th century and passed "best practices" and strategies for success down to new generations of leaders.

That first and oldest Israel Affinity Organization, B'nai B'rith, was formed

---

[155] J.J. Goldberg, *Jewish Power: Inside the American Jewish Establishment* (Addison-Wesley Publishing Co., 1996)

in 1843, almost a generation before Theodore Herzl was born.[156] Although the organization has been in decline in recent decades, it is useful to understand its original mission as a genuine social welfare organization, its creation of the Anti-Defamation League, and its gradual transformation into yet another Israel advocacy organization.

A wave of 140,000 Jewish immigrants entered the U.S. from German-speaking countries between 1840 and 1870. The "lodge" system that enabled mutual aid, social networking, economic opportunities and identity building was ascendant at the time, with Freemasonry and the Independent Order of Odd Fellows at the top. In the fall of 1843, middle class German Jewish immigrants in New York, after considering forming a Jewish chapter of the Odd Fellows lodge, instead designed rituals and codes for an entirely new Jewish lodge dedicated to community and identity-building. This lodge movement spread to other major metropolitan areas with large German-Jewish immigrant populations in Baltimore, Cincinnati and Philadelphia.[157]

As mentioned, its first known foray into foreign policy occurred in 1851 when a number of Swiss states refused to permit Jews to reside there. B'nai B'rith lobbied the U.S. secretary of state not to sign a trade agreement with Switzerland unless the policy were reversed. This was "the beginning of a B'nai B'rith commitment to fight for and protect Jews and Jewish interests around the world."[158]

The order opened the Maimonides Library for civic betterment in New York in 1852 and other orders quickly followed suit, expanding their own member services. Non-members could use materials in the reading room, though only members could check them out. By 1858, Maimonides Library held over a thousand volumes, presented lecture series and even hosted musical events.

Fulfilling its mission as a mutual support group, B'nai B'rith founded a hospital in Philadelphia in 1864. Movement leaders wanted a network of hospitals that would not violate Jewish burial rites by performing autopsies, providing non-kosher food to patients, or burying Jews with non-Jews. A competitive drive also existed to show that the rising Jewish community could provide hospitals on par with Christian facilities. The greater mobility of B'nai B'rith members and the inability to place orphans with family members, as was common practice in the "old country," also led B'nai B'rith to provide modern orphanage services.

B'nai B'rith membership peaked in 1880 at 24,000 members. Thereafter,

---

[156] In the year 1860.

[157] Cornelia Wilhelm, *The Independent Orders of B'nai B'rith and True Sisters: Pioneers*, (Wayne State University Press, 2011) 28-29

[158] Allan J Jacobs, "A Glorious Future Rooted in a Proud Past," *B'nai B'rith Magazine*, Fall 2013, 6

a membership decline became a major concern, as flows of new immigrants slowed and second and third generations failed to become active dues-paying members in high numbers. This, in turn, caused some actuarial difficulties in maintaining one of its core membership benefits: life insurance. Nevertheless, as a vehicle for opening spaces closed to American Jews, and a pathway toward a successful, middle class life, B'nai B'rith claimed success, proudly proclaiming itself, "The most influential Jewish association in the United States and, indeed, in the world."[159]

Another million and a half Jews arrived in the United States between 1900 and 1914 from Russia, Galicia and Romania, escaping poverty and anti-Semitism. B'nai B'rith provided assistance, but instilled an American Jewish identity among recipients whom, it insisted, had to place this new identity at the "front and center." It also engaged in "immigrant distribution," placing new arrivals in Ohio, Missouri, Illinois, Pennsylvania, Indiana, Colorado and Texas.[160] B'nai B'rith Washington, DC lobbyist Simon Wolf crafted the regional distribution policy entirely in response to 1891 immigration laws aimed at excluding people who could become an economic burden on the U.S. He felt that spreading them around to places with greater opportunities than the Eastern seaboard would keep America's doors open. However, many within the lodges also wanted to lobby for changes to U.S. foreign policies that would improve the situation of Jews still living in Russia and Romania.[161]

B'nai B'rith did not originally embrace Israel as a central concern in its mission statement, though it did designate members "Israelites," stating:

> *B'nai B'rith has taken upon itself the mission of uniting Israelites in the work of promoting their highest interests and those of humanity; of developing and elevating the mental and moral character of the people of our faith; of inculcating the purest principles of philanthropy, honor, and patriotism; of supporting the science and art; alleviating the wants of victims of persecution; providing for, protecting, and assisting the widow and orphan on the broadest principles of humanity.*[162]

The paid membership-based system provided financial resources for programs, and organic chapter growth was highly encouraged. Any lodge that grew too large to house new members could spin off new lodges. A hierarchy

---

159 "The Order of B'nai B'rith," *Jewish Times*, February 15, 1879

160 Cornelia Wilhelm, *The Independent Orders of B'nai B'rith and True Sisters: Pioneers,* (Wayne State University Press, 2011) 224-225

161 Jack Gazier, *Dispersing the Ghetto: The Relocation of Jewish Immigrants across America* (Cornell University Press, 1998) 20ff, 42ff

162 Edward E. Grusd, *B'nai B'rith: The story of a covenant* (Appleton-Century, 1966) 20

of district and grand lodges emerged. By the 1870s, the organization had coast-to-coast coverage and nearly 17,000 members. It provided inexpensive death benefits, as well as widow and orphan support, on a profitable basis, given that revenues submitted by a predominately younger membership outpaced payments to the elderly. However, epidemics of yellow fever did occasionally devastate some lodges and strain finances.

One of the most pressing early issues faced by B'nai B'rith was not international or foreign policy, but how to shore up Jewish day schools and establish a proper rabbinical college. Such schools were in decline, with immigrant Jewish parents often sending their children to public schools, where the books that were provided came at no direct cost, rather than in addition to Jewish day school tuition. However, high-level debates about limiting the role of religion—meaning Judaism—were also common in the order. The organization's own identity as a predominantly religious or predominantly charitable organization was often openly debated within the leadership. These were formally subordinated to B'nai B'rith's principal role, elevating the social and moral character of members, as set down in a resolution passed in 1859.[163] However, regional battles over whether to admit Jews married to non-Jews, and the use of religious regalia and identity rituals, continued.

Beginning in 1865 the idea of internationalizing the American organization started floating around the lodges. Cross-border mutual aid and solidarity and protection initiatives began with the 1883 formation of a Grand Lodge in Berlin. German lodges had to promise the government they would not engage in political activities. Lodges spread throughout Europe and even reached Cairo in 1886.

As noted, responding to the 1903 Kishinev pogrom in Tsarist Russia was B'nai B'rith's first major foreign policy lobbying initiative. The Jewish community in the Bessarabian province of the Russian Empire (current day Moldova) was attacked, spurred by accusations that Christians had been murdered for Passover matzo. In two days of rioting nearly 50 Jews were killed and ten times as many injured, with 700 homes destroyed and 600 stores robbed, as police and military stood by.

B'nai B'rith president Simon Wolf met with President Theodore Roosevelt and Secretary of State John Hay. The U.S. government officially transmitted a petition of signatures gathered by B'nai B'rith lodges through the St. Petersburg Chargé d'Affaires. The Russian government rejected it. Jewish leaders outside of B'nai B'rith wanted more "linkage" of such issues to overall U.S. policy and less deference to the Russian government. Pressures continued to build for a lobby that could credibly be perceived as

---

[163] Cornelia Wilhelm, *The Independent Orders of B'nai B'rith and True Sisters: Pioneers,* (Wayne State University Press, 2011) 90-91.

speaking for American Jews on domestic and international affairs. In 1910, B'nai B'rith invited President William Taft to address its general assembly and B'nai B'rith leaders were, in turn, received at the White House. In 1912, the U.S. abrogated its commercial treaty with Russia. This was an act for which Taft received B'nai B'rith's annual medal for the person who had done the most for Jews in a given year.

B'nai B'rith's successful role in the abrogation of the treaty was an important political milestone. However, the organization would subsequently yield the lead lobbying responsibility to other organizations in order to focus in the initial decades of the 20th century on integrating the first American-born generation of European Jews through social services, later building assisted living facilities. It did, however, establish a permanent lobbying presence at the United Nations.[164]

B'nai B'rith was present at the founding of the United Nations in San Francisco in 1945. Its president, Henry Monsky, was an official public advisor to the UN conference's U.S. delegation, while also lobbying for the creation of Israel. Beginning in 1947, B'nai B'rith became an accredited non-governmental organization to multiple UN bodies, including the Economic and Social Council, the Department of Public Information, and UN Educational, Scientific and Cultural Organization. Today it is still the "Coordinating Board of Jewish Organizations" at the UN, maintaining a full-time "Office of United Nations Affairs."

B'nai B'rith helped orchestrate a meeting between future president of Israel and head of the Zionist Organization Chaim Weizmann and President Harry Truman, by leveraging Truman's relationship to failed haberdasher and the president's former business partner, Eddie Jacobson. The meeting and other lobbying initiatives resulted in Truman's recognition of the new state, over the opposition of his top diplomatic and military advisors.

From its UN perch in 1960, B'nai B'rith began a campaign to secure freedom of movement for Jews living in the Soviet Union. However, the organization had a blind spot for other refugees. B'nai B'rith countered allegations of mistreatment of Palestinians by Israel and lobbied to rescind a 1975 UN General Assembly resolution equating Zionism with racism. According to B'nai B'rith, its staff meets continually with important UN officials and diplomats, and in 2005 launched an annual Holocaust Remembrance Day observance.[165]

---

164 Cornelia Wilhelm, *The Independent Orders of B'nai B'rith and True Sisters: Pioneers,* (Wayne State University Press, 2011) p 250-251.

165 "B'nai B'rith International – Office of United Nations Affairs," B'nai B'rith International http://www.bnaibrith.org/uploads/7/8/5/9/7859990/q145_2014_bbi_un_affairspublication.pdf

Today, the organization's venerable system of lodges has fallen into disrepair as dues-paying-member revenue plummeted, replaced by entirely voluntary charitable contributions and infusions of federal funds for its assisted living facilities. Faced with plunging membership dues, in the 1960s the organization began to solicit and receive federal funds to build affordable senior housing. The Internal Revenue Service finally revoked the tax-exempt status of 500 B'nai B'rith lodges in 2011 as part of an initiative to clear the rolls of organizations no longer filing required annual tax returns, or that the IRS believed to be defunct. B'nai B'rith's pension scheme was bailed out by the Pension Benefit Guaranty Corporation in 2012, when the IAO's pension assets were determined to have only $30 million to cover $56 million in liabilities. Though it continues to be popular in Latin America, B'nai B'rith International has only 50 remaining lodges in communities around the world as a political base upon which to promote its agenda. Between 2002 and 2011, B'nai B'rith's net assets fell from $6.2 million to negative $13.5 million.[166]

The organization's fight for Jewish integration and against discrimination is largely over, since it recognizes that "few jobs or places in universities or corporations are denied to Jews." However, B'nai B'rith is not prepared for newer, more daunting challenges. In 2013, the organization readily admitted it cannot do much about what it identifies as the most pressing single challenge—low Jewish birth rates. B'nai B'rith's executive vice president notes that Jews are an older demographic and that Jewish families have less than two children per family, lamenting, "the world population continues to grow exponentially…The not-so-good news is that except for our co-religionists in Israel, we're not replacing ourselves."[167] As a result, B'nai B'rith has finally prioritized an entirely Israel-centric set of programs, as stated by its current president: "Now our focus is on political activism, primarily protecting Israel and Jews around the world, and fighting for human rights for all; protecting and advocating for seniors; and providing critical assistance to the victims of disasters globally."[168]

Another major challenge identified by B'nai B'rith is BDS, the Boycott Divestment and Sanctions movement. This problem, as with so many that came before it, in the view of B'nai B'rith, can be overcome by the old, trusted tactic of lobbying powerful non-Jewish elites. As Daniel S. Mariaschin puts it, "efforts to counter such threats have produced several international gatherings of Jewish leaders. But, we'll need to enlist more important friends—and we have a number of them—in the non-Jewish world, if we're

---

[166] "B'nai B'rith's Disaster Aid Mostly Donated Drug Handouts," *The Forward*, January 10, 2014

[167] Daniel S. Mariaschin, "Tasks that Lie Ahead," *B'nai B'rith Magazine*, Fall 2013, 10

[168] Allan J Jacobs, "A Glorious Future Rooted in a Proud Past," *B'nai B'rith Magazine*, Fall 2013, 7

ultimately to succeed."[169] One key partner in this battle, the Anti-Defamation League, is a B'nai B'rith spinoff.

The Anti-Defamation League has positioned itself to exert influence on behalf of Israel across America and to monitor global trends. It maintains 30 regional offices coast-to-coast that consume over half of its budget. While the group has long claimed its core mission is to fight anti-Semitism and bigotry, the ADL's secrecy, use of undercover investigators, and covert action on behalf of Israel are now a matter of public record. The League's long and ultimately successful attempt to establish a formal relationship with the Federal Bureau of Investigation has left a trail of records shedding light on the organization's determination to undermine Arab organizations and diplomats, civil society organizations working for Palestinian rights and even those that worked against apartheid South Africa when that country was a major Israeli ally. It all began with a lynching following a crime that is still shrouded in mystery.

Leo Frank was a Jewish factory superintendent for the National Pencil Company in Atlanta who served as the Atlanta chapter president of B'nai B'rith. Frank was charged with the murder of 13-year-old employee Mary Phagan, who was found strangled in the basement of the pencil factory on April 26, 1913. He was convicted on August 25, 1913, and his defense team lost their final appeal to the U.S. Supreme Court in April of 1915. After Governor John M. Slaton commuted Frank's sentence to life imprisonment, a group of armed men kidnapped Frank from prison and lynched him in Marietta, Georgia. The Georgia State Board of Pardons and Paroles posthumously pardoned Frank in 1986, although the body did so "without attempting to address the question of guilt or innocence."

Frank's innocence was never in doubt within B'nai B'rith, which formed the Anti-Defamation League of B'nai B'rith on October 20, 1913, in response to Frank's first conviction. In its initial announcement the League identified the "defamation of Jews on the stage, in moving pictures" as having created "an untrue and injurious impression of an entire people and to expose the Jew to undeserved contempt and ridicule" as leading sources of prejudice in immediate need of redress. The League proposed pressuring producers and managers of theaters prior to the staging of such defamatory productions, thus correcting "evils before any harm is done." Defamatory newspaper and magazine articles would also be met with "protest to the editor" and "subsequent articles upon the same subject matter, thereby reaching the same reading public and correcting errors." An economic boycott would be made "by appealing to the patrons and advertisers for co-operation" to confront the most egregious cases of willful abuse. The League would also "eliminate" any "defamation in textbooks which pervert the minds of children and tend

[169] Daniel S. Mariaschin, "Tasks that Lie Ahead," *B'nai B'rith Magazine*, Fall 2013, 11

to prejudice."[170]

The Chicago ADL headquarters was housed within the law office of lodge member Sigmund Livingston and started out with "a $200 budget and two desks."[171] In order to ramp up a membership large enough to deliver on such tactics—particularly pressure campaigns—the newly formed Anti-Defamation League offered free membership to "any reputable person, regardless of sex or creed" that simply signed a membership card.[172] In 1930, the ADL successfully persuaded *Roget's Thesaurus* to remove an entry equating the word "Jew" as synonymous with "cunning rich, usurer, extortioner, heretic." In 1944, Livingstone published a book titled *Must Men Hate?* refuting claims of Jewish responsibility for the punitive Versailles Treaty, financing the Russian Revolution, and controlling the American press and radio industries, among other accusations.[173]

Even as Livingstone labored to refute such beliefs in his book, ADL representatives and investigators worked diligently to ingratiate themselves with an initially unreceptive Federal Bureau of Investigation. Over the coming decades, the ADL would offer its membership rolls to the FBI as informants, submit its files and publications to the Bureau—and, in turn, attempt to gain access to the FBI's own files to avoid "duplication of effort." FBI regional offices would be ordered by director J. Edgar Hoover to liaise with ADL regional offices. Not all FBI special agents trusted the ADL or wished to bring it fully into their confidence. This is revealed in a large trove of FBI files released under the Freedom of Information Act in 2013 and 2015 and referenced in the following pages.[174]

In order to alert the FBI to "un-American activities," Rice A. Pierce, formerly an Anheuser-Busch employee, became an investigator for ADL's St. Louis chairman, Samuel Sievers. Pierce "submitted several hundred written reports" to the regional FBI office "regarding persons suspected by him of un-American activities." The special agent in charge advised FBI director Hoover that Sievers "is regarded as mentally unbalanced by agents of this office who have contacted him." Arnold Forster subsequently undertook the training and professionalization of ADL investigators.

Forster, born Arnold Fastenberg on June 25, 1912, became ADL's chief investigator in the early 1940s. This was after he twice applied to become a FBI special agent, once in 1937 and again in 1939. Forster received

---

[170] "Anti-Defamation League," *B'nai B'rith News*, October 1913, Vol VI, No. 2

[171] "ADL's Centennial Year: Imagine a World Without Hate" ADL http://www.adl.org/centennial/?referrer=https://www.google.com/#.Va57g_1VhHw

[172] "Anti-Defamation League," *B'nai B'rith News*, October 1913, Vol VI, No. 2

[173] Sigmund Livingstone, *Must Men Hate?* (Crane Press, 1944)

[174] "The FBI and the Anti-Defamation League," The Israel Lobby Archive http://www.israellobby.org/ADL/

unfavorable recommendations because he "dressed poorly, did not appear resourceful, would probably not develop, and was not mentally alert." The FBI formally rejected him on October 18, 1939. Nevertheless, the ADL was determined to get inside the FBI.

On August 8, 1940, the ADL delivered a confidential list of hundreds of ADL members, compiled by Miles Goldberg, to the FBI director for use as informants and information resources. The cover letter advised that "the persons named in the lists will cooperate and will make available any files in their possession; also if requested would endeavor to secure information on individuals in whom a particular field office is interested." Some ADL members on the list, such as Abraham Feinberg, later appear in FBI files as possible agents of a foreign government, and in Feinberg's case for using cash payouts to quash arms-smuggling investigations underway inside the Justice Department. Forster also had his own brushes with the law while conducting ADL activity.

According to New York Police Department files, in 1941 Forster used a press pass stolen by *New York Post* reporter Hyman Goldberg to infiltrate and disrupt an anti-war rally in Madison Square Garden. After he was arrested, Forster's friend, the famous newspaper pundit Walter Winchell, ran a November 3, 1941 article, that the FBI thought was "planted" by the ADL to bring "pressure to bear on Commissioner Seery and the Mayor's Committee on Press Cards to drop the Forster incident of the preceding night." Forster was never prosecuted for unauthorized use of a press card. Winchell continued to be a reliable ADL media ally, publishing gushing reviews of Forster's investigative books on anti-Semitism in the United States, such as his 1950 *Measure of Freedom.* The ADL would go on to position itself as doing major work to combat Nazi skinheads, rightwing extremists, and most recently (and ironically) "anti-bullying." Yet many times the ADL's own bullying and other non-publicized activities came under official scrutiny.

The ADL played up its relationship with the FBI. A memo from the special agent in charge of the Chicago office, A.H. Johnson reported this the FBI director on January 16, 1942, writing:

> *One Jerry Friedman advised forty women from the different lodges [presumably Hadassah] that the League was recognized by the FBI as the most effective civilian intelligence gathering organization. He read in confidence a few lines from a letter of the Military Intelligence to 'a certain government agency." Friedman also told these women that the Anti-Defamation League had turned over from their files 30,000 names to the*

> *FBI; that they were active in working with the FBI on Naval and Military recruit information."*[175]

The FBI received yet another report of ADL undercover investigators claiming the ADL acted as "unofficial auxiliaries of the Department of Justice." FBI internal analysis that the ADL and related groups were "interested only in their own material benefit and their work is directed more in the line of persecution and of framing their enemies than the exposing of Nazism and Fascism…" The FBI issued a complaint to the ADL in 1942 that it was circulating false reports that ADL had conducted 373 investigations on behalf of the FBI during a one-year period. The FBI director privately expressed his view "that private investigative agencies had no excuse for existence, that they only created hysteria and contributed to vigilantism and a mob spirit…the FBI had never asked the ADL to conduct an investigation…"[176]

But the ADL was unfazed. Two operatives from the ADL Chicago office, over lunch with local Special Agent in Command S. J. Drayton, requested permission to periodically check FBI files in order to avoid "duplication" of investigatory efforts. The FBI internally reported that:

> *As the Bureau can see, under the procedure suggested by Gross, the Anti-Defamation League would have an opportunity to learn of the informants being utilized by the Bureau and would also be in a position to learn of those under investigation. I cannot understand the reason that Mr. Gross would make such requests of us at this time inasmuch as his organization undoubtedly already knows the policy of the Bureau with reference to such matters.*[177]

Undaunted, in 1947 the ADL again asked for confidential FBI information. The ADL's Paul Richman, who was headquartered on K Street in Washington, sent a list of names on its speaker's bureau asking for a check of FBI files so that the bureau could "tell him very confidentially and off-the-record if they should knock any names off." The FBI rebuffed him, which angered Richman. "He did not like this at all and seemed to be of the opinion that we should tell him whether the names are good or bad, which obviously we cannot and should not do." But the FBI had reasons for not trusting the

---

[175] The FBI and the Anti-Defamation League, The Israel Lobby Archive. http://IsraelLobby.org/ADL/ See file 100-HQ-530

[176] The FBI and the Anti-Defamation League, The Israel Lobby Archive. http://IsraelLobby.org/ADL/ See file 100-HQ-530 Section 4

[177] The FBI and the Anti-Defamation League, The Israel Lobby Archive. http://IsraelLobby.org/ADL/ See file 100-HQ-530 Section 5

ADL.

Within its files about the ADL, the FBI retained a copy of a congressional hearing that explored damage to reputations caused by secret "investigatory" files circulating within the Civil Service Administration about "individuals who were neither federal employees nor applicants for positions coming under the jurisdiction of the Civil Service Commission." Within the Commission's eight truckloads of files were some, "made up in cooperation with the American Jewish Committee and the Anti-Defamation League." The ADL/AJC files were causing controversy and had no justification for being comingled with official government personnel and applicant-related files. According to Committee Chairman Clare E. Hoffman, a Republican congressman from Michigan, "It is all hearsay...I will tell you they are smear artists."[178]

During WWII the ADL continued to proclaim victories against antisemitism and trumpet its protection of small ethnic and religious community rights in its news releases and bulletins. In reality this protective umbrella did not extend, however, over Japanese Americans. Imperial Japan, of course, was allied with Nazi Germany. Japanese Americans, for the most part, were neither affiliated with Imperial Japan nor Nazi Germany. However, the concentrated nature of the League's funding gave the ADL a reason to agitate for the continued internment of Japanese Americans—in order to divert growing congressional investigators' attention away from large Hollywood film studios.

Almost immediately after the Japanese attack on Pearl Harbor, the FBI established its Special Service Contact (SSC) program. SSCs were highly placed individuals who volunteered proprietary inside information to the FBI during periods of national emergency. Once such contact, Jack Holmes, was the personnel director at Warner Brothers Studio, provided inside information about the ADL's major funding source, and how—even though ADL was opposed to it in principle—the ADL financed actions in support of the internment of Japanese Americans in order to protect its most important financial asset.

John R. Lechner, born in Innsbruck, Austria in 1900, immigrated to the United States and moved to California in 1924. In 1927 Lechner founded the Americanism Educational League to promote various conservative causes and public demonstrations of loyalty to the United States on the part of other immigrants. Lechner was initially aligned with various California-based Japanese American groups such as the Nisei and Japanese Chamber of

[178] "Congressional Hearings of the Subcommittee of the Committee on Expenditures in the Executive Departments of the House of Representatives" Eightieth Congress, October 3, 6 and 7 of 1947. The Israel Lobby Archive http://israellobby.org/ADL-CA/1947_Congress_Hearings.pdf

Commerce. The West Coast was where the majority of Japanese Americans lived. Three weeks after Pearl Harbor, Lechner became a proponent of the mass removal of Japanese Americans. Lechner gave a series of speeches, and authored pamphlets such as *The Inside Story of Our Domestic Japanese Problem.* On February 19, 1942, President Franklin D. Roosevelt signed Executive order 9066 authorizing the internment of Japanese Americans in designated camps. Lechner later became the star witness on the topic of Japanese Americans in testimony before the congressional Joint Fact-Finding Committee on Un-American Activities in 1943.[179]

According to Holmes, Lechner was "employed by the Anti-Defamation League and paid out of their secret fund." Lechner was sent to Washington to interest Congress in the Japanese American problem in order to divert the very same committee's upcoming "series of hearings at Los Angeles to determine the extent of Communist infiltration into the motion picture industry." Lechner conducted his campaign "to interest those committees in the Japanese problem and to set up a smoke screen so as to cause the suspension of the proposed inquiry into the motion picture industry." The ADL furnished information about Japanese American activities "at Manzanar and the Tule Lake" internment camps for Lechner to present.[180]

Why did the ADL aid the campaign to incarcerate and maintain Japanese Americans in internment camps as a diversion? Protecting ADL's Hollywood funding. At the time, most of the ADL's $3 million per year budget (equivalent to $41 million today) "was contributed by major motion picture studios and by prominent Jewish motion picture actors, directors, and others prominent in the industry." According to Holmes, "Warner Brothers Studio alone contributed $60,000 to the fund." This is $700,000 in today's dollars. Did the ADL/Lechner "smoke screen" work? Yes, although the results were mixed. [181]

In 1947, the House Committee on Un-American Activities subpoenaed witnesses named by *The Hollywood Reporter* as communist sympathizers. Actors, screenwriters and directors were blacklisted. But the major studios mostly escaped scrutiny. Acting under the umbrella of the Motion Picture Association of America, a group of studio executives fined artists accused of being communist sympathizers, issued statements condemning them and thereby avoided the brunt of the financial and reputational fallout of the "Hollywood blacklist" until it fizzled out in the 1960s. Today the ADL offers

---

[179] "John R. Lechner" Dencho Encyclopedia, http://encyclopedia.densho.org/John%20R.%20Lechner/#cite_note-ftnt_ref2-3

[180] The FBI and the Anti-Defamation League, The Israel Lobby Archive. http://IsraelLobby.org/ADL/ See file 100-HQ-530 Section 5

[181] The FBI and the Anti-Defamation League, The Israel Lobby Archive. http://IsraelLobby.org/ADL/ See file 100-HQ-530 Section 5

up the Japanese-American internees as case study to help students understand discrimination and the Civil Liberties Act of 1988—without disclosing its own sordid role in targeting Japanese-Americans.[182]

Japanese internees were not the only casualties of the ADL. The list of ADL operatives given to the FBI director in 1940 to use as resources and informants proved irresistible. An early casualty of the FBI's conversion from suspicious observer to full partnership with the ADL was Senator Rufus Holman. Holman served as a Republican United States Senator for Oregon during WWII, after previously serving as the state's treasurer and on a board of commissioners. However, Holman was an isolationist. Although he supported WWII, he was critical of the expansive foreign policies of President Franklin D. Roosevelt. Holman clearly would have been an obstacle to U.S. support for the formation of a Jewish State in Palestine. From the ADL's perspective, Holman had to go.

On April 10, 1944, Holman asked for an FBI and Justice Department investigation into the ADL's orchestration of a boycott against his business and reelection campaign via a primary challenge. According to an internal FBI memo:

> *Senator Holman stated he understood that the purpose of the organization was to uncover anti-Jewish statements and that the Jews would then boycott people who were reported to make such remarks without a hearing or chance to be heard...He further remarked that there was no check upon the activities of the Anti-Defamation League...*

Before running any check into whether statutes had been violated, the Portland FBI office confirmed it had a problem. It was carrying attorney David Robinson, head of the ADL Oregon office, as Confidential Informant #7 "on the Bureau's records..." The FBI's confidential informant "Robinson is endeavoring to line up the Jewish vote behind Wayne Morse [Homan's primary challenger]." FBI Special Agent David A. Silver of Portland reported that the pressure was on from the ADL, "Jack Barde of the Barde Steel Company and Abe Gilbert of the Gilbert Hardware Company, both of Portland, and both Jews, gave a dinner for Senator Holman. Silver said he was heard that Robinson chided them for doing so."

Holman wanted an investigation into the core purpose of the ADL, listing four key questions. "Is the Anti-Defamation League recognized officially by the Government and the United States? How do they determine who is Anti-Semitic? What is their weapon? Who finances it? Who contributes to it and

---

182 "Voices of Japanese-American Internees" ADL Curriculum Connections. Anti-Bias Lesson Plans and Resources of K-12 Educators. http://archive.adl.org/education/curriculum_connections/summer_2008/

in what amounts?"[183]

The Department of Justice refused to investigate, and the FBI retained the services of its confidential informant. Senator Wayne Morse defeated Holman in the primary and won the general election in November of 1944. He was unwavering in his drive to deliver ever larger U.S. aid packages to Israel, claiming it was the moral obligation of every American. Addressing a Zionist group in 1954, Morse claimed,

> *Israel is a nation surrounded by the economic system of feudalism of the Middle East. a nation that is practicing the personal dignity of man. a nation that recognizes that it is the individual who counts...Yet there are forces in American that seem to think that this freedom can be traded for Arab oil at a bargain price. Americans have a stake in the freedom of Israel because it is a stake also in the freedom of every American...Yet whenever a proposed grant-in-aid to Israel comes up. the movement in the Senate cloakrooms is to cut it down. You must not give them cause to cut it down or they will eliminate it entirely. And you will give them cause if you fail to keep faith with the principle of supporting Israel to the best of your ability.*[184]

In the run-up to the creation of the state of Israel, the ADL was also worried about American organizations presenting informed, non-fiery and principled opposition to organized Jewish activities in Palestine. Destroying organizations opposed to the formation of Israel by going after their donors required obtaining tightly held confidential information. According to its own monthly newsletter, the ADL obtained just such information directly from personnel at banks providing service to opponent organizations. The ADL did this during its undercover investigation of the Institute for Arab-American Affairs. The organization's crime, according to the ADL, was successful public education "refuting the Jewish point of view on Palestine." The ADL compiled a comprehensive dossier on the IAAA's internal operations including confidential banking information, recording that:

> *The bank sources revealed that this organization solicits only membership dues of $10.00 from their mailing list of about*

[183] The FBI and the Anti-Defamation League, The Israel Lobby Archive. http://IsraelLobby.org/ADL/ See file 100-HQ-530 Section 5

[184] "Sen. Morse Urges More Aid to Israel; Hits Anti-Israel forces in U.S." The Jewish Telegraphic Agency, March 10, 1954 http://www.jta.org/1954/03/11/archive/sen-morse-urges-more-aid-to-israel-hits-anti-israel-forces-in-u-s

> *3,500, of which they receive only a small fraction of paying dues. As of last week, their bank balance was $9,000…*[185]

However, the FBI remained under intense pressure to work with the ADL. In 1951, the FBI was tasked by the U.S. State Department to investigate allegations against Saudi Arabia and Egypt raised in an ADL report titled "Workers for the Arab League in the U.S." The FBI interviewed the ADL's paid undercover operative who was working to surveil Arab activities at the UN while posing as a foreign correspondent, the preferred cover for many ADL undercover operations. Then the ADL discovered its undercover operative was compromised and unreliable. The FBI, which was not involved in any way with the ADL's investigation, upon receiving this information rejected the State Department recommendation and never opened its own investigation. FBI Director John Edgar Hoover wrote, on November 23, 1951, that "material which the Anti-Defamation League has been channeling to this Bureau in the past is now believed by the officials of the League to be absolutely unreliable...the B'nai B'rith organization had been fraudulently duped by the informant."

In 1957, Forster provided the FBI with materials from the Committee to Secure Justice for Morton Sobell. Sobell, a former American engineer and military contractor, was found guilty of spying for the Soviet Union. Material provided by Forster to the FBI included legal analysis, opinion columns urging Sobell's release, news releases, and petitions to President Eisenhower. Sobell was jailed until 1969 and finally admitted his guilt to *The New York Times* in 2008.[186]

In 1957 Forster personally delivered to the FBI an information package on ADL's own initiatives, including its press releases, pamphlets, press clippings, plans for legal actions, book review clippings and calendar of social events. Presumably, the ADL's chief investigator hoped to impress the Bureau and its long-serving director that the ADL was an organization with elite access and investigatory capabilities aligned with the FBI's own anti-Communist mandate.[187] Nevertheless, it took the FBI director another decade to order formal liaison with the organization. On January 17, 1968, Hoover at last ordered FBI field offices to establish liaisons with ADL's regional offices:

---

185 The Facts: Reported monthly by the National Fact-Finding Department, Anti-Defamation League of B'nai B'rith. June, 1946 edition, http://IsraelLobby.org/ADL/ See file 100-HQ-530 Section 5

186 The FBI and the Anti-Defamation League, The Israel Lobby Archive. http://IsraelLobby.org/ADL/ See file 100-HQ-367944

187 The FBI and the Anti-Defamation League, The Israel Lobby Archive. http://IsraelLobby.org/ADL/ See file 100-HQ-367944

> *The ADL...maintains regional offices throughout the United States. As you know, this organization, like the Bureau, is opposed to groups and individuals espousing bigotry, prejudice and extremism. It seeks to bring the true facts concerning such groups and individuals to light...*
>
> *In furtherance of these worthy objectives, the ADL receives considerable information of interest to this Bureau and has been very cooperative in the past in referring such data to us. You are to immediately make certain that you have established liaison with the head of the ADL regional office in your territory and explain the jurisdiction and interests of this Bureau. For your information, there is attached a list of ADL regional offices…*
>
> *You should, of course, review your office indices prior to making contact. Advise Bureau if contact is not deemed advisable...*[188]

In 1968, acting under this ADL liaison program, the FBI Dallas field office received ADL reports on the American Nazi Party, United American Klans, and the Minutemen. That same year, the FBI Minneapolis field office received an ADL liaison report on University of Minnesota professor Mathew Stark's involvement with the "Negro integration movement in the Twin Cities area." ADL advised, conspiratorially, that "Stark may have certain political aspirations in view of his recently avowed discontent with the policies and action of Mayor Naftalin and Calvin Hawkinson, Chief of Police, Minneapolis." By 1973, Stark, who is Jewish, left the university to head the American Civil Liberties Union of Minnesota and work on church-state separation, free speech and gay rights.[189] In addition to keeping an eye on African-American political movements, the ADL worked to keep FBI crosshairs trained on Palestinian and Arab political movements in the U.S. By 1979, the ADL began contacting the FBI urging it to work on certain terrorism threats, sending its "Special Report" on the "P.L.O. and Arab Terrorism; a Decade of Violence." Secretly, the ADL continued its own covert actions against similar targets.

In 1969, the Anti-Defamation League infiltrated and spied on a national gathering of Arab students in the United States. Internal FBI documents reveal how ADL surveillance against the Organization of Arab Students (OAS) in 1969 coalesced into plans for infiltrating the OAS national

---

188 The FBI and the Anti-Defamation League, The Israel Lobby Archive Http://IsraelLobby.org/ADL/
See file 1199215-000 --- 100-IP-16164 --- Section 1

189 The FBI and the Anti-Defamation League, The Israel Lobby Archive. http://IsraelLobby.org/ADL/ See file 62-4098 and 157-362

headquarters in New York in order to bring down the organization.

In the late 1960s, OAS was working to unite visiting Arab international students studying in the U.S. with their Arab-American counterparts interested in connecting to developments in the region, primarily in Palestine. Formed in 1952 as the nonprofit Organization of Arab Students of the United States and Canada, by the late 1960s. OAS was hosting its eighteenth annual national conference, with a reported 200 participants. Like modern-day groups such as Students for Justice in Palestine, the OAS was not at all shy about criticizing U.S. media coverage of the region or issuing direct challenges to Israel Affinity Organization public relations efforts.

The OAS's growing capacity to organize major events eventually sounded alarm bells at the ADL, which dispatched undercover investigators to penetrate the OAS national convention held in 1969 at Ohio State University. The ADL agents assigned to the convention filed reports under the codenames Buckeye, Adam and Eve. "Buckeye" tirelessly worked the entire seven days of the event, presenting himself as a reporter, often for the *Spectator* newspaper. He claimed to be sympathetic to OAS objectives in order to gain access to events and high officials and have a pretext for inquiring about "back office" issues such as the state of OAS finances.

The ADL agents covering the conference inquired about alleged OAS links to the armed Palestinian group Fatah, and were skeptical toward one OAS spokesperson's claim that "there was no real relationship between them, that the OAS was merely letting them sell their literature there." The name of the spokesperson was redacted from the ADL file by the FBI, along with most other names.

Buckeye's reports sounded an ADL red alert: "The political activity of Arab students in the U.S. will increase significantly in the coming school year (1969-1970) with increasing effectiveness. They are beginning to display a much greater understanding of how to present their arguments to the various levels of the American public (church groups, New Left, lower middle class, etc.); and any successes are certain to increase their confidence and, hence, their activity." Buckeye recommended this "threat" be confronted "directly" as growing numbers of OAS chapters achieved and shared successes with other student groups, especially those on the Left.

In those pre-Internet days, Buckeye had to manually gather and compile information on the location, officers, phone numbers and membership strength of each OAS chapter. To ingratiate and provide cover for himself to a group of Buffalo University students, Buckeye claimed all his questions were for a future *Columbus Citizen Journal* story.

Students were candid in telling Buckeye they viewed such major media outlets with growing skepticism. They claimed *The Christian Science Monitor* and *The New York Times* were biased in their coverage of the Middle East, and urged Buckeye to read *The Guardian* and *Le Monde* to get a more balanced view of regional issues. Buckeye carefully recorded the most effective Arab public relations strategies, the main points of Arab media critic presentations, strategies to deploy to counter negative media, and each session speech from Palestine Liberation Organization and Arab Information Office representatives.

On his own, Buckeye had a hard time penetrating closed OAS sessions. Security at the 1969 OAS conference was tighter than in previous years. Only ethnically Arab students who had been members of a local OAS chapter for one year could attend closed sessions. Non-Arab members needed the recommendation of five Arab chapter members to enter closed sessions. Buckeye's wife attempted to enter closed OAS convention meetings posing "as a Canadian divorcee and assumed an alias for which she had proper identification." The spies also saw such exclusionary security mechanisms as an opportunity to wage an attack on OAS chapters:

> *On many campuses there are rules against discriminating on the basis of race, etc. Therefore it is illegal for the OAS to require its membership to be of Arab descent. In these places pro-Israeli forces could join and take over the machinery of the organization, its funds, etc. and at the same time dismantle it as a base for dissemination of propaganda….concentrate on getting an Arabic-speaking Jew into the national machinery of the OAS. At the recent convention, for example, we had difficulty finding anyone who could attend and understand the arabic [sic] sessions where finances, policy, etc. were discussed. This is a crucial factor in combating the students.*[190]

Buckeye reported that there was some competition "combatting the students" on the clandestine front, and enviously noted "the attached article from the *Near East Report* indicates that the American Israel Public Affairs Committee had somebody on the inside of the OAS who covered the convention." Given its activities, covert action to destroy the OAS was entirely warranted, in Buckeye's view. He recommended that the ADL recruit an Arabic-speaking agent from the nonprofit Hebrew Immigrant Aid Society to work inside the OAS national headquarters in New York, in order to be "privy to important national OAS information."

After obtaining the ADL's OAS report in 1969, the FBI—which had also surveilled the conference—came, to its credit, to its own more objective conclusions. The FBI felt not only that the ADL report was "biased," but also that such ADL-sanctioned activity "possibly represents a violation of the Foreign Agents Registration Act."

---

[190] The FBI and the Anti-Defamation League, The Israel Lobby Archive http://IsraelLobby.org/ADL/ See file 62-4098 and 157-362

Based on its own long-term observations of the ADL, the FBI felt it would be incredible "to assume it [the ADL's report on the OAS] is not furnished to an official of the government of Israel due to the extremely close ties between ADL and Israel." Buckeye suggested in his report that "this information may be of interest to our official friends." Within ADL investigator files, the term "Official Friends" refers to law enforcement personnel and federal government agency employees friendly to the ADL. Some of these officials cultivated by the ADL provide sensitive, personal and even classified information about alleged adversaries. Confirmation of this came out of an investigation into how the ADL ran its undercover operations in California.[191]

The FBI also seemed to resent the ADL's self-appointed authority as a competing counter-intelligence agency using tradecraft. "This report shows investigation conducted by the ADL, using codename sources, pretexts such as local news reporters ... recruiting of [Arabic-speaking] Jewish refugees ... to infiltrate the OAS in New York." In the end, the FBI did not obtain permission from the Justice Department to conduct a foreign agents investigation of the ADL. The OAS eventually went into decline as a serious challenge to IAO programs in the U.S.

By the late 1980s, coordinated OAS media pronouncements, conferences and national organizing waned, as chapters increasingly dedicated themselves more to local social and education functions than to politics. As desired by the ADL, they finally did open up to all students claiming an interest in Arab culture. Many OAS chapters even passed individual charters renaming their organizations, adopting new logos and severing national affiliations. Few conducted any major events beyond the boundaries of their individual campuses.

However, the ADL also soon hit a rough patch when hard evidence surfaced that it was illegally obtaining confidential information about pro-Palestinian and anti-apartheid activists in order to counter their effective organizing. The police even raided the ADL's major California offices. The ADL's covert agent, Roy Bullock, was caught in the middle of an operation, and it soon became clear he had also worked closely with apartheid South Africa's intelligence services.[192] Civil suits against Bullock and the ADL filed

---

[191] From San Francisco Police Department Inspector Ron Roth's 1993 investigation of the ADL in the Files Affair: "Based on the evidence, exhibits and facts in this affidavit I believe that Roy Bullock (an undercover ADL investigator) and the ADL had numerous peace officers supplying them with confidential criminal and DMV information." Criminal investigation and successful civil lawsuits against the ADL over privacy right violations – 1992-1993. Israel Lobby Archive: http://www.israellobby.org/ADL-CA/1993_dec_insp_ron_roth.pdf

[192] Robert I. Friedman, "The Enemy Within: How the Anti-Defamation League turned the notion of human rights on its head," *The Village Voice*, May 11, 1993

in the 1990s were eventually settled out of court in 2002 for tens of thousands of dollars. Nevertheless, the ADL never admitted to doing anything wrong, and never had to face any serious penalty, even though it was known to be in possession of illegally obtained, classified FBI files.

In the aftermath of 9/11, all past problems between the FBI and the ADL were finally smoothed over. During his April 28, 2014 remarks to the ADL National Leadership Summit, incoming FBI director James B. Comey was unequivocal about his affinity for the ADL, dubbing it a "love letter." The FBI has also wholly committed to the ADL training of special agents, according to Comey:

> *The FBI works with the ADL to host civil rights and hate crime training for our state and local counterparts through a number of programs. We have made [ADL] Law Enforcement and Society training mandatory for all National Academy participants, just as it is for all new agents. Together, we created the Hate Crimes Training Manual—a fantastic resource for our law enforcement partners across the country.*
>
> *And the ADL, of course, has even greater reach; you trained more than 12,000 law enforcement personnel last year alone, and I want to thank you for that. This past January, your North Texas/Oklahoma office worked with the FBI's Dallas Division to sponsor a one-day seminar for more than 160 federal, state, and local law enforcement officers from 40 different agencies.*
>
> *And of course, we are educating ourselves, too. Since 2010, FBI employees have participated in more than 105 training sessions sponsored by the ADL on extremism, terrorism, and hate crimes, in 17 states and here in the District. Your own Michael Lieberman, director of the Civil Rights Planning Center, will speak at an FBI civil rights conference in Boston on May 13, and in San Francisco in June.*[193]

By late 2015, ADL claimed to have trained more than 1,000 government officials from 250 agencies across the country in an "Advanced Training School" focusing on "Extremist and Terrorist Threats."[194] Given the ADL's

---

[193] James B. Comey, FBI Director, speech to the ADL National Leadership Summit, April 28, 2014 https://www.fbi.gov/news/speeches/the-fbi-and-the-adl-working-toward-a-world-without-hate

[194] "FBI, San Bernardino Police Chief among law enforcement trained by ADL," ADL website, http://la.adl.org/2015/06/09/fbi-san-bernardino-police-chief-among-law-enforcement-trained-by-adl/

history, Americans should be concerned about its ever-closer liaison with the FBI. Though branded as civil rights and hate crime training, the actual ADL curriculum has never been disclosed by the FBI, despite repeated Freedom of Information Act requests. The FBI's own case log of suspicious prosecutions using undercover informants to entrap Muslims on terrorism charges is on the upswing, a trend the ADL, quite likely, privately welcomes. Similarly, although Israeli espionage against the United States has shown no signs of abating, the FBI has either refused to properly pursue prosecution (as discussed later in the case of Ben Ami Kadish) or altered its investigations so as to shield Israeli principals and organizations, such as Israeli Aerospace Industries, from liability (as reviewed in the case of Stewart Nozette.)

IAOs may also influence the FBI in other ways. Guardsmark Security, mentioned earlier, has become one of the largest outside contractors to the Simon Wiesenthal Center ($687,000 in year 2001 expenditures, according to the IAO's IRS form 990). The privately held company is run by Ira A. Lipman. Guardsmark is also a large employer of former FBI special agents. Barbara Greenspun serves on the center's board. Her late husband, Hank, was relentlessly pursued by the FBI for smuggling stolen weapons in the 1940's,[195] but she apparently feels no irony in this arrangement.

As a thought experiment, can one imagine the FBI welcoming an organization offering training in "effective counter-intelligence" that focuses entirely on Israel, since it is a highly capable and ongoing espionage threat? Such a training arrangement would be politically impossible. Or on "false front smuggling" that trained special agents in the art of detecting and rolling up front organizations engaged in smuggling on behalf of Israel, using case studies from the 1940s to the present day? This is also impossible to imagine, despite the fact that such training would be well warranted by any fair criminal history review. The fact that the ADL is so well ensconced inside the FBI and that its training is completely secret it is not subject to outside review and that no similar opportunity is imaginable for counterbalance, is evidence of the League's undue influence. That the ADL itself so easily escaped well-warranted espionage prosecution after obtaining and possessing classified information on behalf of Israel, discussed later, is further evidence. Another organization, active for only half the lifespan of the ADL, has been entangled in three separate espionage investigations, and similarly has never paid any criminal penalty.

The American Israel Public Affairs Committee is today the most important advocacy IAO, because its mandate is to focus the collective power of most of the IAO ecosystem on Congress. Its rise is poorly understood and receives little due attention from establishment media

---

[195] "Herman Milton 'Hank' Greenspun" The Israel Lobby Archive http://www.irmep.org/ila/greenspun/

outlets. Only after burrowing into recently declassified government files does it become clear that AIPAC was an entirely foreign creation, set up and seed-funded to advance Israel's interests at the expense of the United States.

In the beginning, much of AIPAC's financial support was laundered from a pool of donations from international Jewish communities through Switzerland as it struggled to build up a support base in the U.S. Like a JCRC, AIPAC at first functioned as an unincorporated lobbying division within a larger organization, the American Zionist Council (indeed, it was once known as the American Zionist Council for Public Affairs.) Most of AIPAC's funding, like many IAOs, is still largely provided by a small group of ultra-wealthy donors. AIPAC would not exist in its present form had its parent organization not been ordered by the Kennedy administration to begin registering as an Israeli foreign agent under the 1938 Foreign Agents Registration Act. AIPAC successfully thwarted the order.[196]

AIPAC's dorsal fin periodically breaks the surface in espionage scandals, election manipulation flaps and insider accounts of wrongdoing. These hint at the scope and direction of the Israeli government policies that have always driven its U.S. lobbying. The most recent evidence that AIPAC is a foreign agent is how it sided with the Netanyahu government in opposition to the U.S. Iran nuclear deal. It clearly did not represent majority Jewish public opinion in the United States, which supported the deal. Representing Israel over all other possible interests is AIPAC's norm rather than a departure.

Theodore Herzl's original grand Zionist vision, as promulgated in his book *The Jewish State,* contemplated a corporation that would lay the necessary groundwork for the state by raising money, organizing orderly Jewish emigration and managing programs. The Jewish Agency was chartered in Switzerland in 1925 as just such an organization for achieving statehood, and was often characterized as a "government in waiting" that lobbied in the United Nations for the division of Palestine and later the creation of Israel. The Jewish Agency established its first U.S. representative office, "The American Section," in New York in 1944. By September of 1948, the Bureau of Internal Revenue granted the Jewish Agency tax-exempt status, though the IRS no longer possesses any records documenting its basis for doing so.

Isaiah L. "Si" Kenen, a naturalized Canadian, who began life as a journalist, was the Jewish Agency's public relations official as it battled for the creation of Israel in the United Nations. As a lobbyist and public relations man working on behalf of foreign entities, Kenen initially took the Foreign Agents Registration Act quite seriously. FARA was passed in 1938 to protect Americans from the undue influence of foreign governments. It netted up

---

[196] For the full account, see Grant F. Smith, *America's Defense Line: The Justice Departments Battle to Register the Israel Lobby as Agents of a Foreign Government* [Washington, DC Institute for Research: Middle Eastern Policy, 2008]

assorted Communists with Soviet connections and Nazi agents corresponding with the Third Reich in the 1940s. They were prosecuted, not for their activities, but rather for their failure to properly notify Americans of true foreign government sponsors, and for failing to file the required disclosures at a public FARA office visited often by reporters. On April 21, 1947, Kenen registered as an agent of the American Section of the Jewish Agency for Israel. After Israel was founded, he became a foreign agent of the Israeli Ministry of Foreign Affairs, working at the "Israel Information Services" office from October 12, 1948 through May 13, 1951.[197]

Kenen's mission—to send arms, diplomatic support and foreign aid from the United States to Israel—never changed. However, he and many other Israel supporters immediately concluded that it was a mistake to follow the rules and go through diplomatic channels as representatives of a foreign—even a new and unique—government. As stated in his biography, *Israel's Defense Line,* "Embassies talked to the State Department, and American voters talked to their congressmen." Kenen wanted to pressure Congress, the best source for what Israel desperately needed, not as a foreign government lobbyist, but as a concerned American. The advantages were, and continue to be, obvious. A foreign government soliciting American help would have to deliver something the United States wanted in return. Israel had—and continues to have—very little to offer commensurate with the billions of dollars and political support it has received. However, it did have an organized, vocal, politically active, higher-than-average wealth, Jewish Zionist American support base that could be focused on agitating through myriad means for what Israel wanted. To accomplish this, Israel's government and agencies needed to set up and fund an organization that could frame the fulfillment of Israel's needs as an American interest. This was the purpose of the American Zionist Council. Today, it continues to be the purpose of AIPAC.

Because there were already several American Zionist organizations in existence, the Jewish Agency began funding a consortium comprising the Zionist Organization of America, Hadassah (the Women's Zionist Organization) and other now, mostly defunct, organizations[198] to coordinate and conduct the public relations and lobbying necessary to provide Israel what normal diplomatic relations could not. The AZC did not take direction or receive funding from its member organizations. Rather, AZC was principally a vehicle for—largely secret—Jewish Agency funded programs.

---

[197] Isaiah L. Kenen, "Foreign Agent to Founder of AIPAC." The Israel Lobby Archive. http://www.irmep.org/ila/kenen/

[198] American Jewish League for Israel, B'nai Zion, Religious Zionists of America, Labor Zionist Movement, Progressive Zionist League, United Labor Zionist Party, United Zionist-Revisionists of America

The big-name organizations and figures on the AZC letterhead would ostensibly impress the rest of the political elite and keep investigators at bay.

The American Zionist Council filed to begin lobbying Congress to pass the Israel Aid Act of 1951 to help pay for Jewish immigration to Israel. The AZC issued pamphlets arguing that America would benefit by giving aid to Israel, and that it was Israel, not Arab states, that was earnestly pursuing peace.[199] The Eisenhower administration communicated its displeasure that the AZC initially lobbied for foreign aid using tax-exempt donations. According to UCLA scholar Steven Spiegel, opposition from the president was intense:

> *The tension between the Eisenhower administration and Israeli supporters was so acute that there were rumors (unfounded as it turned out) that the administration would investigate the American Zionist Council. Therefore, an independent lobbying group was formed within the auspices of the American Zionist Committee.*[200]

A special lobbying division was formed within the AZC, led by Kenen and internally referred to as "the Kenen Committee." It was officially dubbed the American Zionist Council for Public Affairs. Although AZCPA claimed in tax filings to the IRS that it used non-tax-deductible donations for lobbying, such money was scarce and hard to come by, though unsavory sources such as mobster John Factor (aka Jake the Barber) and Meyer Lansky associate Aaron Weisberg of the Sands Casino stepped up with contributions. Still, the indefatigable Kenen worked members of Congress and obtained approval of a $15 million foreign aid allocation to Israel in the face of robust State Department opposition.

In celebration of the 1951 passage of a $65 million aid bill, Kenen inaugurated what would become a Washington tradition—congressional junkets to Israel. In November 1951 Kenen was paid $2,518 by the Israeli government to escort "visiting Congressmen: Ribicoff, Fugate, Keating, O'Toole, Barrett and Fein..." around Israel. Given the fungible nature of such aid, it is hard to imagine that none of it was ultimately paid by American taxpayers.[201]

---

[199] "The Mutual Security Program in the Middle East" American Zionist Council, 1953, "Who is for Peace in the Middle East?" June, 1953, Herbert Levy Printing Company

[200] Spiegel Steven, *The Other Arab-Israeli Conflict: Making America's Middle East Policy, From Truman to Reagan* [Chicago: The University of Chicago Press, 1985] 87-89

[201] Grant F. Smith, "The First Congressional Junket to Israel," originally published by *Online Journal*, available at *Intifada-Palestine*, August 22, 2009

The American Zionist Council, like AIPAC today, recommended planks to be inserted into both party platforms during presidential election campaigns and conventions. A July 1, 1952, AZC memorandum to the Republican Party urged adopting a plank pledging continued support to Israel. On July 17, a similar resolution was submitted to the Democratic National Convention. Both were adopted.[202]

In addition to funding a wide variety of public relations activities through the American Zionist Council, the Jewish Agency began paying Isaiah Kenen under the table in order to keep his lobbying operation afloat. Kenen launched his privately owned lobbying newsletter called *The Near East Report*.[203] Sent to every member of Congress and influencer he could identify, the publication nakedly promoted why U.S. aid to Israel was such a sensible endeavor, while belittling and chastising Arab leaders. It took no prisoners, excoriating senators and congressional representatives who did not approve of Israel aid packages, which later led to trouble with Senator J. W. Fulbright. Most importantly for Kenen, the Jewish Agency in Jerusalem funded the publication with $5,000 quarterly earmarks, made to the American Zionist Council, which the Jewish Agency directed to be sent on to its former employee, Kenen, the newsletter's owner.[204]

Fred Scribner, a U.S. Undersecretary of Treasury, confidentially warned during a 1959 meeting with key Zionist organizations operating in the U.S. that they needed to restructure themselves in order to avoid problems with the Eisenhower administration, the IRS, and the U.S. Department of Justice. Subsequently, that same year, Kenen again changed the name of his lobbying organization, this time from the American Zionist Committee for Public Affairs to the American Israel Public Affairs Committee, to better reflect that, according to him anyway, it "raised its funds from both Zionists and non-Zionists." Yet it still remained just a committee, unincorporated and run inside the AZC.

In addition to subsidizing public relations expert Kenen, the Jewish Agency was secretly providing much bigger funding flows to the AZC for a comprehensive campaign aimed at generating enough grassroots support for Israel that Congress would continue funding aid packages. The incredible 1962-1963 plan of the AZC "Committee on Information and Public

---

http://www.intifada-palestine.com/2009/08/the-first-congressional-junket-to-israel/

202 Louis Shub, "Zionist and Pro-Israel Activities," *The America Jewish Yearbook*, Vol. 54, 1953, 157

203 *Near East Report* was acquired by the nonprofit IAO Near East Research, which dissolved, according to its last IRS filing, by "resolution on September 22, 2008 and merged into the operations of the American Israel Education Foundation."

204 American Zionist Council and American Zionist Committee for Public Affairs tax filings, Israel Lobby Archive http://israellobby.org/AZCPA/

Relations" pressed every lever to influence public opinion in the United States, including magazines, TV, radio, films, Christian groups, academic circles, news dailies, books, public speakers, visitors to Israel, and measures counteracting opposition groups. It must be read to be believed.[205] The lobbying campaign for favorable public relations and media coverage included strategically directed gifts and grants to U.S. colleges and universities for new Israel-centric "Middle East Studies" departments. Many groups, including evangelical Christian religious organizations, now highly active in AIPAC-like affairs, were initially indifferent to or even suspicious of these initiatives. They were only gradually won over by the intensity, longevity, and financial resources dedicated to the campaign.

One senator, who intensely felt the barbs of *The Near East Report* and building pressures to do ever more for Israel, was the chairman of the Senate Foreign Relations Committee, J.W. Fulbright. Fulbright's understanding of U.S. law and foreign agent registration requirements were anchored in his legal studies. He earned a degree from George Washington University Law School in 1934. That year he was admitted to the Washington, DC bar and became an attorney in the U.S. Department of Justice anti-trust division. This legal expertise would serve Fulbright well as he sought to unravel one of the most complex and opaque chains of interlinked nonprofit corporations ever assembled in the United States. Fulbright chartered an investigation into the forces and money behind Israel lobbying in America. His March 17, 1961 three-page memorandum (only declassified late in the year 2010!) outlines why the Senate Foreign Relations Committee focused much of its investigation on the Jewish Agency, the American Zionist Council and the American Israel Public Affairs Committee (still functioning as the unincorporated lobbying division of the AZC). It reads:

> *In recent years there has been an increasing number of incidents involving attempts by foreign governments, or their agents, to influence the conduct of American foreign policy by techniques outside normal diplomatic channels…there have been occasions when representatives of other governments have been privately accused of engaging in covert activities within the United States and elsewhere, for the purpose of influencing United States Policy (the Lavon Affair).*

The "Lavon Affair" referred to a botched 1954 false flag Israeli terrorist bombing plot against U.S. and other targets in Egypt code-named "Operation Susannah." It was intended to reverse the Eisenhower administration policy of pressing for a British withdrawal and returning

---

[205] American Zionist Council 1962-1963 U.S. Public Relations Plan, The Israel Lobby Archive http://www.israellobby.org/azc2/

control of the Suez Canal zone to Egypt. A group of Egyptian Jews who had been recruited by Israeli military intelligence targeted American and British cultural centers. The agents, dressed as Arabs, were discovered, arrested and criminally prosecuted in Egypt after the explosives malfunctioned. This led to a crisis in the Israeli government and minor disruption in relations with the U.S. The Senate Foreign Relations Committee charter of the 1960s foreign agents investigation, which mentioned the Lavon incident twice in three pages, expressed caution about investigating such sensitive matters and proposed three avenues for Senate investigation:

> *There would undoubtedly (even with care) be instances which would lead to foreign governmental protests, to violent attacks by special groups in the United States...*
>
> *I. Public receipt of testimony from Department of Justice and Department of State....II. Public receipt of testimony from selected law and public relations firms....III. Executive (perhaps public) receipt of testimony on the Lavon Affair, and similar 'grey area' activities...*[206]

Ultimately, no testimony on the Lavon Affair was ever given during the Israel lobby investigation. However, after initiating its investigation in 1961, the Senate used subpoena power to seize sensitive Jewish Agency files. The files revealed the full extent of the Jewish Agency's subsidies to the American Zionist Council and its secret earmarks to Kenen. Apparently fearing arrest, Kenen fled the U.S. for a lengthy international tour. He wrote:

> *In 1961, it was rumored that Fulbright intended to investigate foreign agents. I was subjected to a barrage of inquiries from friends and foes wherever I went, and while I was confident that I would survive the attack I decided to vanish from the scene. Coincidentally, I was invited that year to visit Iran as a guest of the Iranian government. I accepted the invitation and from there I flew on to Africa to learn more about the people of that continent. I was happy to find most African countries friendly to Israel and*

[206] The Eisenhower library has released National Security Council files detailing high-level meetings in 1954. It has never released any files about the cabinet's reaction to "Operation Susannah." Archivist Herb Pankratz claimed to the author in 2011 that much information from the administration has still not been properly indexed for research.

> *was more relaxed in Africa than in Mr. Fulbright's Washington.*[207]

Under pressure from the Senate investigation, on March 31, 1962 the Jewish Agency's American Section finally admitted in its mandatory filings to the Justice Department a fact it had kept hidden for over a decade: that it was channeling large amounts of funding to the American Zionist Council for public relations and lobbying activities. On November 21, 1962, the Department of Justice ordered the American Zionist Council to begin registering as a foreign agent, touching off an intense battle in which the AZC summoned every resource to fight being regulated for what it was—a foreign-funded stealth political operation.[208]

The Senate record of the May 23 and August 1, 1963, hearings on Israel lobbying outlined the many Jewish Agency-funded public relations and lobbying programs. During testimony, the Jewish Agency American Section director made it clear that the start-up funding provided to the American Zionist Council, $700-800,000 per year, were foreign funds, raised by interested foreign Jewish communities, and not diverted from United Jewish Appeal charitable relief funds raised in the United States. The American Zionist Council director and legal team, throughout the May hearing, refused to acknowledge what Senator Fulbright certainly knew, since he was keeping in close touch with the administration—that the AZC had already been ordered to register as a foreign agent. Legal counsel obliquely characterized it as "a request for some more detailed information with respect to specific items, I think it was in September or October, I do not recall, 1962." [209] Throughout the hearings, Jewish Agency representatives stressed their intention to make the American Zionist Council and its programs financially self-sustaining, as if fully domestic funding would brush away the trail of foreign seed money that started the operation.

The airing of dirty laundry in the hearings did not stop foreign-directed public relations and lobbying efforts for Israel, as the 1970 Dow Jones weekly newspaper, the *National Observer*, neatly summarized:

> *In 1963 the Senate Foreign Relations Committee investigated the Jewish Agency and uncovered a conduit operation run by an*

---

[207] Isaiah L Kenen,.*All My Causes in an 80-Year Life Span* [Washington, DC: Near East Research, 1985] 103

[208] "DOJ orders the AZC to Register as a Foreign Agent," Israel Lobby Archive, http://israellobby.org/AZCDOJ/

[209] Senate Foreign Relations Committee Investigation into the Activities of Agents of Foreign Principals in the United States, 88th Congress, 1st session, Washington, U.S. Government Printing Office, May 23, 1963, 1242-1245 http://israellobby.org/Senate/05231963pt1.pdf

> *organization called the American Zionist Council. Over an eight-year period, this council received more than $5,000,000 from the Jewish Agency to create a favorable public opinion in this country for Israeli government policies. The Senate investigation closed down the conduit, but the extensive propaganda activities still go on.*[210]

The "extensive propaganda activities" continued because AZC's unincorporated lobbying division, the American Israel Public Affairs Committee, quickly split off and then took over the entire operation. Just six weeks after the 1962 FARA order, AIPAC incorporated in Washington, DC. It applied for tax-exempt status in 1967 and achieved a surprising concession from the IRS (one the ZOA itself later attempted, but failed to obtain). Without admitting association with any predecessor tax-exempt organization on its application to the IRS (thereby avoiding questions about whether it, too, should register as a foreign agent, like the AZC), it was granted tax-exempt status retroactive to 1953 in acknowledgement of the year it debuted as the unincorporated American Zionist Committee for Public Affairs inside the AZC.[211]

By 1973, Kenen was able to claim that AIPAC had boosted U.S. aid to Israel to $1 billion per year. When he retired in 1974, Kenen retained his "editor emeritus" title at the *Near East Report.* The spirit of AIPAC's hardball and often legally questionable tactics would continue long after Kenen left the scene, and the results are staggering. At the time of Kenen's death in 1988, U.S. aid to Israel exceeded $3 billion a year, and remains the highest amount of U.S. aid allocated to any country.

Fulbright was right to be concerned about these Jewish Agency seed-funding operations, for which he did not see "precedent of anything like it in any other instance."[212] IAOs worked hard to defeat Fulbright and ultimately ousted him by backing Arkansas governor Dale Bumpers. Nevertheless, Fulbright continued to speak out against the clandestine activities of Israel lobbying organizations in America. He brandished a confidential internal May 6, 1974 B'nai B'rith memo written to its national board of directors from Secretary-General Herman Edlesberg. It stated, "…all of the indications suggest our actions in support of Governor Bumpers will result in the ousting of Mr. Fulbright from his key position in the Senate."[213]

---

210 Mosher Lawrence, *National Observer* (Dow Jones), May 19, 1970

211 The American Israel Public Affairs Committee (AIPAC), Israel Lobby Archive http://www.israellobby.org/AIPAC/

212 Senate Foreign Relations Committee investigation into the Activities of Agents of Foreign Principals in the United States May 23, 1963, 1,307-1,312

213 Paul Findley, *They Dare to Speak Out: People and Institutions Confront Israel's Lobby* [Chicago, Lawrence Hill Books, 1986] 91

IAOs derive a great deal of influence claiming to represent the majority of American Jews, which they clearly do not, as revealed by evidence cited throughout this book. Just as Jewish federations have been charged by insiders as being captive to a small number of wealthy donors with no real pretense of constituent governance. The American Israel Public Affairs Committee is also extremely narrowly funded, a fact it has tried hard to hide.

For fiscal year 2006, AIPAC's top contributor gave $650,000. The rest of AIPAC's donors gave on average $16,772 each. Donors giving more than $5,000 numbered just over 1,700 individuals. This group of wealthy donors provided the majority (56 percent) of AIPAC's total claimed direct public support. If—as AIPAC claimed—it had approximately 50,000 paying members that year, the rest gave on average only $464 to make up the total of $50,920,792 in public support.[214] An imperfect IRS redaction of AIPAC's schedule of contributors revealed that one donation was actually paid from a law partnership. This likely meant the donor deducted the payment as a business expense, thereby creating a "tax-deductible" donation to an organization that—because it lobbies Congress and is a 501 (c)(4) organization—is not tax deductible for individual donors. Given that AIPAC is segmenting its donor base into professional groups, such as "real estate" and "high-tech," it is reasonable to assume it is also urging members to make "expensed" donations from their business revenue, rather than contributing personal after-tax dollars to fund the organization.

AIPAC has filed misleading tax returns in the past, including its original application for tax-exempt status, which as previously mentioned failed to state it was a subsidiary of the American Zionist Council. AIPAC plays games with responses to questions on IRS 990 forms, claiming no expenditures for lobbying and trying to consolidate donors into broad categories to hide how many $5,000-plus donors it has. Though required, like any nonprofit, to individually list every donor giving more than $5,000, in the year 2009 it listed only two: one contributor of $48,542.187, and the other (which was obviously the American Israel Education Foundation) that reimbursed AIPAC $13,503,472 for its supposed "education-related" endeavors.[215] AIPAC was probably trying to consolidate and hide the actual number of $5,000-plus contributors—perhaps because they likely had shrunk in number following the 2005 indictment of two AIPAC executives for espionage, and a subsequent defamation lawsuit filed by one of those two employees.[216]

---

[214] Grant F. Smith, "Does AIPAC Have Only Two Major Donors?" *Antiwar.com* August 10, 2011

[215] AIPAC's 2009 IRS Form 990 Schedule of Contributors, view online at: http://www.irmep.org/990/2009_AIPAC_Sched_B.pdf

[216] Although the author has solicited AIPAC's 2009 schedule of contributors a number of times, no corrected schedules have been forthcoming, indicating that the IRS has not pursued the issue.

AIPAC "funny numbers" games continue. For the year 2012, AIPAC filed two returns, one in August and the other in October, with $23 million in accounting differences.

Like many of the Jewish federations, AIPAC does not claim to spend any funds for lobbying on its tax reports to the IRS. However, as a domestically registered lobby, it must file quarterly lobbying reports with the Clerk of Congress. These disclosures indicate that approximately $3 million in expenditures per year are generated by the activities of a staff of about ten lobbyists. Obtaining and compiling the lobbying reports into useful annual data requires knowing where to look and is more arduous to researchers than looking up a single yearly IRS 990 report. However, like examining ZOA lobbying disclosures or peering into Christians United for Israel startup operations, the effort is somewhat fruitless because it does not capture the principal way AIPAC pressures Congress, or the actual funds this consumes.

AIPAC puts many of its lobbying eggs into a single basket, spending almost $40 million per year on a three-day spring policy conference that attracts as many as two-thirds of the sitting members of congress and key administration officials. The 14,000 attendees at the 2015 conferences are then scheduled into "lobbying appointments" with their members of Congress to "speak to them about issues of concern to the pro-Israel community." This "paper trail-less" model of "grassroots" lobbying that is practiced by Jewish Community Relations Councils, and now CUFI, maximizes the power of activists, donors and members of AIPAC while minimizing public disclosure. It has a huge impact to those on the receiving end, according to congressional staffers interviewed by author Kirk Beattie:

> *In contrast to Arab groups, AIPAC comes in and they all say the same thing. When they have their annual convention, 7,000 people are at the dinner—everybody in Congress is there. There was a big pro-Israel rally recently and 10,000 people showed up. They're so good at choreography, with everyone doing their role. The Arabs all want to do their own thing. AIPAC has a good understanding of when to play hardball and when not to do so.*[217]

Analysis of giving patterns between AIPAC board members, known donors, and a legion of "stealth" PACs with names that give no indication that they exclusively promote pro-Israel candidates also reveals a high degree of coordination. However, the Federal Election Commission and courts, even when made aware of the written orders of an AIPAC official coordinating such funding flows in the 1980s, have never taken concrete steps to patrol the boundaries between charity status and generally prohibited

---

[217] Kirk J. Beattie, *Congress and the Shaping of the Middle East* [New York, Oakland: Seven Stories Press, 2015], 152

support for particular candidates.[218] AIPAC scorecards clearly reveal which candidates are favored for donations. That AIPAC's power derives both from its role representing major IAOs and ability to mobilize donors in a senator's state or a congressional district is readily admitted by a former AIPAC staffer:

> *AIPAC is really shorthand for the whole network. They have their rote answer regarding noninvolvement in politics, but they do help candidates get money. I know, I used to work for them. But AIPAC also plays or makes a 'pain in the butt calculus.' The national level lobbyists will come in, five or six of my big Jewish donors back home will call in and threaten to cancel events, or the rabbi calls, or 40 to 50 constituents will call—so is it worth it to buck this group? It's a pain in the butt. That's their strength on the bill, versus, 'if I vote with them, I can make points and get money.'*[219]

Like the B'nai B'rith's spinoff, the Anti-Defamation League, AIPAC has also incubated other organizations. The American Israel Education Foundation is an organization that sends members of Congress (more than 1,000 since the year 2000) and other influential Americans on all-expense-paid trips to Israel. AIEF was incorporated in 1988 to promote a more "balanced and realistic" understanding of American interests in the Middle East among policy-makers, academics and journalists. Although it promised the IRS in its application for tax-exempt status that "All research produced and published will be made available to the general public," AIEF has never complied. Its still-relatively new, single-page website contains no information on education programs.

AIEF's activities ramped up after legislative reforms banned much lobby-sponsored travel following the Jack Abramoff affair, while still allowing "educational" trips by educational nonprofits.[220] AIEF is housed in the same facilities as AIPAC, has no staff, and in 2009 sixty-six percent of its board of directors were also directors of AIPAC.[221] Existing only on paper, AIEF uses

---

218 Janet McMahon, "Fiddlesticks! Federal Judge dismisses case against FEC," *Washington Report on Middle East Affairs*; December 2010, Vol. 29 Issue 9, 26

219 Kirk J. Beattie, *Congress and the Shaping of the Middle East* [New York, Oakland: Seven Stories Press, 2015], 157

220 The 2007 Honest Leadership and Open Government Act of 2007. The allowance for AIPAC-sponsored travel through AIEF is commonly referred to on Capitol Hill as "the AIPAC exception."

221 IRmep - Center for Policy and Law Enforcement complaint to Nanette M. Downing, Director, Exempt Organization Examinations. Friday, September 9, 2011 http://irmep.org/09092011AIEF.pdf

AIPAC-developed education materials and sends AIPAC staff (such as its "Israel Seminars Assistant" and "Grassroots and Missions Director) to accompany members of Congress on trips to Israel.

AIEF, like AIPAC, echoes the rhetoric of the Israeli government. Members of Congress on junkets are told by AIEF—and in its official briefing book—that "Jerusalem is Israel's largest city—not a 'settlement.'" There are no longer any final status issues to be negotiated—despite UN insistence to the contrary because, according to AIEF, "Israel later incorporated the eastern half of the city and declared the unified Jerusalem to be the capital of Israel." AEIF's "case closed" approach to what the rest of the world considers to be open issues impresses congressional visitors, many of whom have little international experience, views on the region, or alternative sources of information.[222]

The AIEF briefing book is full of flattery to Congress, and declares "Congress has regularly recognized Jerusalem as Israel's capital in various resolutions and law." Interviewed anonymously, one congressional staffer who had lived in Israel stated, "the termination of such trips would be ruinous to pro-Israel interests"[223]

Another spinoff by AIPAC employees and donors is the Washington Institute for Near East Policy. WINEP (or TWI, as it now calls itself) is also somewhat narrowly funded. In the year 2001, it reported that just six donors provided 30 percent of its $4.2 million in donations. Those seeking background information about WINEP on its official website are informed that WINEP was founded "in 1985" by a small group of visionary Americans committed to advancing U. S. interests in the Middle East. Like much of the website's content, the information is not accurate. WINEP was incorporated during an espionage investigation crisis that suddenly enveloped AIPAC in 1984. The process of AIPAC spinning off WINEP is reminiscent of AIPAC's own crisis-driven incorporation just two decades earlier.

Between 1982 and 1985, English-born Australian immigrant to America Martin Indyk busily served as deputy research director at AIPAC. Under Indyk's reign, AIPAC pumped out a steady flow of lobbying booklets arguing for ever greater U.S. military support to Israel, such as *The Strategic Value of Israel* (1982), *Israel and the U.S. Air Force* (1983), *Israel and the U.S. Navy* (1983), *Israeli Medical Support for U.S. Armed Forces* (1983) and *U.S. Procurement of Israeli Defense Goods and Services* (1984).

Securing non-reciprocal duty-free Israeli access to U.S. consumers was the AIPAC research division's most important project in 1984. However,

---

[222] Grant F. Smith, "Israel Junkets Pump Disinformation into Congress," *Antiwar.com*, April 23, 2015

[223] Kirk J. Beattie, *Congress and the Shaping of the Middle East* [New York, Oakland: Seven Stories Press, 2015], 39

trade negotiations were going badly at the beginning of that year. Undercutting the arguments of many in the lobby who insist that U.S. industry is always an eager driver of entangling economic and military deals, the majority of U.S. companies providing formal input did not want any special U.S. trade preferences granted to Israel, an economy then dominated by state-run industries. Monsanto even suggested that if the U.S was going to bother with negotiations to boost trade volumes through comparative advantage, it should do so with a worthwhile economic partner such as Taiwan, Hong Kong or Japan.[224]

Help for Israel soon arrived in the form of Israeli Minister of Economics Dan Halpern. Halpern provided AIPAC with a stolen copy of a secret U.S. International Trade Commission report outlining the precise objections supported by internal domestic industry, and secret market data provided in absolute confidence to the U.S. government by American companies opposed to concessions to Israel. It was an indispensable resource for AIPAC's counter-lobbying and public relations. Unfortunately for AIPAC, on August 3, 1984, *The Washington Post* broke the news that the FBI was investigating how AIPAC "obtained a copy of a classified document that spells out the American negotiating strategy in trade talks with Israel…" An August 13, 1984, FBI report stated, "Files contain an unsubstantiated allegation that a member of the Israeli Intelligence Service was a staff member of AIPAC…" November 1, 1984, the U.S. Bromine Alliance was in urgent talks with the International Trade Commission chairwoman, publicly demanding to know how much of their industry's secret trade and market data had been leaked to AIPAC and Israel's own state-run producer.

Later that month on November 14, 1984 WINEP suddenly incorporated in Washington, DC, formed not by "prominent individuals" but rather by Martin Indyk's wife, Jill, along with Marilyn Edeson and Elizabeth Chotin, according to the original articles of incorporation filed at the DC Department of Consumer and Regulatory Affairs. This suggests that the incorporation process was hurried along even as the FBI's espionage and theft-of-government-policy dragnet tightened around AIPAC during the so-called "Year of the Spy."[225] The year earned that designation, spurred by revelations of Jonathan Pollard's espionage bonanza against the Defense Intelligence Agency. Martin Indyk jumped the AIPAC ship and quietly relocated his research production within WINEP. By 1986, WINEP was doing public relations work for yet another disastrous program—the Lavi jet fighter—

---

224 "AIPAC, espionage and the U.S.-Israel Free Trade Agreement," The Israel Lobby Archive, http://www.israellobby.org/FTA/

225 Law enforcement agencies arrested so many spies for foreign governments operating inside the United States that the news media referred to 1985 as the "Year of the Spy."

while providing a Washington perch for a visiting Shimon Peres to chastise Soviet immigration policy. Thwarted by Israeli diplomatic immunity claims, the FBI quietly shut down its investigation in 1987 after learning much about AIPAC and Israeli officials' various roles in obtaining, reproducing and handling classified economic documents—to the detriment of democratic process in the U.S.[226]

Although WINEP's founding myth is that its "scholars" simply wanted to do serious research independent of AIPAC (not mentioning they would still be funded by AIPAC's own major donors), history indicates that survivability was also a compelling reason for its quiet launch in November of 1984. In a worst-case scenario, espionage or theft of government property indictments would have likely disbanded either AIPAC or WINEP but probably not both. One would surely survive and make sure the massive trade concessions were implemented. Splitting off was the same survival strategy that led to the spinoff of AIPAC just six weeks after its parent organization, the American Zionist Council, was ordered to register as an Israeli foreign agent in 1962.

WINEP's history and role as an Israel lobby think tank is never mentioned when the organization's ubiquitous pundits fan out across the American news media. Such disclosures would undermine WINEP's and the media host's credibility. Like AIPAC, WINEP often beats war drums for Israel. A 2012 video clip features WINEP's Research Director Patrick Clawson listing "crisis initiation" triggers, such as the Gulf of Tonkin torpedo attacks (later proven to be a false alarm), or pinning blame on the Spanish for the sinking of the U.S.S Maine in 1898 (which likely was an accidental boiler explosion). Clawson advised that an effective false flag attack, such as taking out an Iranian submarine, could drag a then-reluctant United States into war with Iran. Israel lobby stalwart Dennis Ross struggled mightily to answer reporter Barbara Slavin's question about how WINEP could move the U.S. beyond diplomatic "red lines" against Iran, when polls revealed the majority of Americans had already grown tired of costly elective wars in the Middle East. He could not answer.

Just as WINEP effectively ingratiates itself with the media through proactive marketing of its "experts" as news sources and pundits, media pressure groups are even more aggressive. CAMERA is one such media pressure group that emerged during Israel's ill-fated 1982 invasion of Lebanon, a conflict that produced ghastly images of massacres and death. In the 1980s, a CAMERA advisor in an opinion column issued a blunt

---

[226] For the full story, see Grant F. Smith *Spy Trade: How Israel's Lobby Undermines America's Economy* [Institute for Research: Middle Eastern Policy, Washington, DC, 2009]

assessment that set the tone for CAMERA's stylebook.[227] Those who would defend Palestinian human and civil rights should be dismissed as "Palestinian propagandists" and "PLO propagandists."[228] This labeling, according to one observer, was necessary because the Palestinian narrative was becoming too effective according to a report in *The Jerusalem Post*:

> *They court and/or threaten foreign journalists [and] send back naive Western visitors with pitiful usually uncheckable tales of Israeli oppression ready-made for op-ed pages, and encourage cabinet ministers to publish their own lies in those spaces. Though the answer to Israel's public relations problem might be a separate new government ministry, "creation of a nationwide monitoring organization is already in place. It's called CAMERA: Committee for Accuracy in Middle East Reporting in America. Its many members, professional staff and dedicated volunteers are fighting the public-relations war every day.*[229]

In the aftermath of 9/11, former Israeli President Moshe Katsav, who in 2011 was sentenced to seven years in prison for rape, advised CAMERA that simplification was in order:

> *The world must be divided into two sections…those who fight against terrorism, and those who don't. Furthermore this is not a time to be silent…whoever remains silent and does not join the struggle, legitimizes terrorism. Tuesday's terrorist attacks in the United States were not just an attack against America but a war against the free world.*[230]

CAMERA, eager to enforce the advice, had little patience with any news outlet insufficiently branding various resistance or insurgency groups as "terrorists." According to the CAMERA view reported in *The Washington Post*, history itself gave Israel a license to take extraordinary measures that should not be questioned in the Western press:

> *After 2,000 years of persecution and being at the mercy of others, the state of Israel determined to take extraordinary measures to rescue Jews. That Israel acts in this manner should be praised*

---

[227]In print media, this is a book containing rules of usage in typography, punctuation, etc., employed by printers, writers, and editors

[228] George Jawad, "Who is the 'Propagandist?'" *The Washington Post*, April 16, 1989

[229] Richard D. Wilkins, "Smile for the CAMERA," *The Jerusalem Post*, August 24, 2001

[230] Greer Fay Cashman, "Sbarro reopens after bombing" *The Jerusalem Post*, November 13, 2001

> *and lauded as the highest form of human rights and concern for others.*[231]

That does not leave much room for criticism of Israel's actions or for affinity with Palestinians. CAMERA has taken many a journalist's scalp for reporting on the wrong subject, or even marrying the wrong person. Part-time NPR reporter Maureen Meehan, who was married to Palestinian official Jiries Atrash, was summarily fired after being exposed by CAMERA. "We didn't have adequate information about her husband's relationship with the Palestinian government, which she was covering," apologized NPR's Editorial Director John Dinges. In 2001, CAMERA organized a boycott of major underwriters and smaller donors of Boston NPR radio affiliate WBUR during a critical membership fundraising campaign, costing the station over a million dollars. CAMERA demanded the removal of certain NPR programming, charging that WBUR's international rebroadcasts of the BBC were not balanced or objective. CAMERA also demanded the ouster of NPR foreign editor Loren Jenkins over his "long record of partisanship in favor of Palestinian views." Jenkins, NPR and WBUR all rejected the demands.

NPR Ombudsman Jeffrey Dvorkin called CAMERA "absurd" for demanding Jenkins' firing and accused the group of engaging in "McCarthyism" over its public claims when CAMERA refused to share its quoted studies with NPR. NPR's own internal assessment, presented to the board of directors, showed NPR's coverage was actually skewed toward Israel, reporting, "CAMERA's views are subjective as any lobbying group's arguments are likely to be. They choose facts to suit their arguments."[232] The network also declined to remove CNN founder Ted Turner from its board of directors after CAMERA complained that he suggested in 2002 that the Palestinians were fighting Israelis with the only weapons available, and that both sides engaged in terrorism. Turner said:

> *The Palestinians are fighting with human suicide bombers, that's all they have. The Israelis...they've got one of the most powerful military machines in the world. The Palestinians have nothing. So who are the terrorists? I would make a case that both sides are involved in terrorism.*[233]

The U.S. media routinely fails "to mention the long pattern of Palestinian

---

231 Stuart Weinblatt, "The Shadow of the Holocaust," *The Washington Post*, February 3, 1990

232 "NPR rejects demand for removal of foreign editor Loren Jenkins" *Public Broadcasting Report*, June 14, 2002

233 "CNN Chief accuses Israel of Terror," *The Guardian*, June 18, 2002 http://www.theguardian.com/media/2002/jun/18/terrorismandthemedia.israel

incitement that puts the conflict in context," according to CAMERA contesting accepted narrative that an official visit to the Al Aksa Mosque in Jerusalem touched off the second Palestinian intifada in 2000, claiming:

> *Instead of dating the start of the conflict from the time of the visit of Likud leader Ariel Sharon, which was coordinated in advance with Palestinian security chief Jibril Rajoub...intense violence between Israelis and Palestinians didn't start until the next day, when Moslems were falsely told that the Jews wanted to tear down al-Aksa mosque."*[234]

ABC news anchor Peter Jennings and his reporter Gillian Findlay acted "as advocates for the Palestinians" by asserting such a cause-and-effect relationship, according to CAMERA.[235] Jennings was also guilty of inserting qualifiers and pesky statistics about actual casualties, while failing to provide adequate details on the "bloodlust" of Arabs, according to CAMERA. "This was the entire coverage Jennings gave to the murders of Koby Mandel and Yossi Ishran" (May 9, 2001, Jennings report in quotes, then CAMERA):

> *"At a Jewish settlement in the West Bank funerals for two Israeli teenagers. They had skipped school and gone for a hike. Their badly beaten bodies had been found in a cave near Bethlehem. The Israeli government says Palestinian terrorists were responsible. Since last September...six Israelis under the age of 18 have been killed and 143 young Palestinians have died."*
>
> *ABC flashed a video clip of a rocky valley where distant figures were seen while Jennings's own commentary offered immediate damage control for the Palestinians. Omitting the shocking details widely reported by other media—the bloodlust of the murderers who bludgeoned their victims to pulp then smeared the boys' blood on cave walls—he immediately injected the protective language practiced over more than a decade. Israel 'says' Palestinians were responsible he notes, as though the identity of the killers were in dispute. And lest even his own minimal comments point too clearly at the savagery—and diminish sympathy for the Palestinians—Jennings hastened to remind viewers that many more Palestinian young people 'have been killed.'*

CAMERA Executive Director Andrea Levin was not averse even to

---

234 Gil Hoffman, "Fighting for the Best Angle," *The Jerusalem Post*, October 20, 2000

235 Andrea Levin, "The Peter Jennings bias show," *The Jerusalem Post*, October 27, 2000

turning CAMERA's fusillade against other, much larger members of the Israel lobby, even taking to task the long-term director of the ADL, Abraham Foxman, writing in *The Jerusalem Post*:

> *Have the media distorted recent Israeli-Palestinian clashes? Supporters of Israel believe the answer is an emphatic yes, but the ADL's Abe Foxman has repeatedly declared news coverage of the crisis to be essentially sound and entirely free of bias. His assertions are not only at odds with widespread opinion, but with the data as well. While much of the reporting has been accurate and professional, all too often influential outlets have made serious factual errors, tilted stories with an unbalanced array of interviewees, omitted Israel's voice entirely and excluded vital information.*[236]

However, the long-time head of the ADL saw something problematic with CAMERA's categorical denunciations, telling yet another Israel lobby media outlet, the Jewish Telegraphic Agency:

> *...when we accuse...anyone... of bias, we are saying that they are coming together to decide or conspire to slant a story...That's a very, very serious charge. It's the opposite charge of Jews controlling the media or Hollywood. And that's irresponsible.* [237]

Responsible or not, CAMERA's reactive approach has recently been upstaged by a more proactive public relations IAO, also with objectives indistinguishable from the Israeli Ministry of Foreign Affairs or an Israeli-run public relations effort.

Is an Israeli intelligence or military official suddenly getting blanket U.S. media coverage? Is the Israeli prime minister or ambassador to the U.S. again saturating the airwaves at a critical juncture? The Israel Project (TIP) may have been working behind the scenes to arrange it. The organization started operations in the heart of Washington's lobbying sector, at 2020 K Street. TIP has placed Major General Israel Ziv in front of news conferences to explain how Jordan's foreign policy affects Israel's security, Major General Amos Yadlin to express doubt over Western negotiations on the Iranian nuclear program, and Intelligence Agencies Minister Dan Meridor to explain why Israeli military forces should never withdraw from the West Bank. The Israel Project has been a *de facto* public relations firm for a long list of Israeli

---

236 Andrea Levin, "Honest, Abe, there's media bias" *The Jerusalem Post*, December 2, 2000

237 Andrea Levin, "Honest, Abe, there's media bias" *The Jerusalem Post*, December 2, 2000

government officials.

Why was TIP created? In the words of former *Jerusalem Post* reporter, Jeremy Ruden, it emerged because of Israel's extremely poor media relations. Although the country consistently wins battlefield military victories, lamented Ruden in 2012, "a lot of time, effort and resources are being put into spreading anti-Israel hatred. It worked and it's still working."

> *Israel has been losing the 'media/public opinion/hearts-and-minds battle and are now in a position from which it is very unlikely we can change the tide.' Mass media is a new phenomenon in Israel, and its leaders and advocates still don't understand it. 'The Israel Project came out of necessity...[they are] a testament to just how bad the situation is...it's so bad it's absurd...Can anyone even imagine citizens from a Western country putting together a non-profit organization designed solely to explain their government's policies and actions to members of the press?'*

It is the position of TIP—along with many nodes of the Israel affinity network—that U.S. media is inherently anti-Israel. Its own carefully worded (but never independently verifiable) polling claims that Americans blame Palestinians two-to-one for the long-lasting conflict. Presumably, so should the news media. So TIP ramps up news releases and media analysis whenever questionable Israeli actions direct unwanted attention toward Israel in the United States. TIP often portrays the executive branch as "out of touch" with members of the Congress and the American public, demanding ever closer U.S. relations with Israel and, of course, demanding that more taxpayer-funded weapons stockpiles be located in the country in conjunction through increased aid flows.

The Israel Project organizes many conference calls between Israeli government officials and journalists, elite briefings and one-day conferences in the U.S. and Israel on topics in vogue with the larger Israel affinity ecosystem. Such events have little academic balance. The many that focused on the Iranian nuclear program invariably portrayed it as a weapons program, all the while studiously avoiding the very real regional impact of Israel's own clandestine nuclear arsenal. Most of TIP's Iran nuclear events helped underscore the Israeli government's position of skepticism over U.S. and Western negotiations with Iran and concluded with a position that Israel will "not see itself bound by an agreement" it did not feel would "keep Iran from getting nuclear arms." TIP promoted the Israeli position of maintaining a constant military option against Iran, that only the total abandonment of Iran's nuclear program was acceptable, and that U.S. economic warfare measures be maintained, if not increased, to confront Iranian terrorism.

Like the American Jewish Committee, TIP is concerned about and runs programs focusing on other countries, such as a "China Affairs" program established in 2011, aimed at transmitting core talking points and getting Chinese support for economic warfare against Iran. TIP's "India Programs" aimed to diminish traditionally deep Iran-India trade ties. TIP research found that the "Chinese believe Jews are good with money, strong in science and exert a tremendous amount of influence on the world—all Jewish stereotypes, but meant in a positive way." These somewhat backhanded compliments nonetheless warrant further monitoring, according to TIP, since "the world changes very fast."

TIP's chief executive Josh Block was a former AIPAC spokesperson and has been quoted often in the Jewish press arguing against the legitimacy of grassroots movements such as Boycott, Divestment and Sanctions. Block left AIPAC after AIPAC was embroiled in an expensive lawsuit filed by former executive Steve Rosen, who claimed AIPAC defamed him in the news media. This costly public relations disaster, however, did not teach Block to refrain from labeling as "anti-Semites" prominent critics of Israeli policies such as Max Blumenthal and non-Jews such as Rula Jebreal and Roger Waters. Block characterized Secretary of Defense nominee Chuck Hagel as "well outside the mainstream of both Democratic and Republican positions" during his confirmation battle, while questioning Hagel's willingness to negotiate with Hamas and his Senate votes against designating the Iranian Republican Guard a terrorist group, which were all AIPAC positions.

Before AIPAC, Block was a spokesperson in the Clinton administration. After he took over from TIP's well-connected founder, Jennifer Lazlo Mizrahi, the organization's year-to-year fundraising became chaotic, even as TIP continued to pay Lazlo nearly $100,000 a year to keep the funding stream flowing. That TIP was led by a woman is remarkable in the IAO universe, which insider critics often skewer for almost never allowing females to lead the most visible organizations. This fact has not kept IAOs from heaping criticism upon the Arab and Muslim world over its treatment of women.

TIP attempts to discredit the Palestinian right of return to their homes and land seized by Israel in 1948. Africans should not enter or live in Israel as refugees, according to TIP, but the "birthright" of any Jew living outside of Israel to immigrate, or "make *Aliyah*" to Israel as a citizen is sacrosanct. TIP generally strives for "positive" as opposed to "negative" messaging. "Shared Values" is one such TIP campaign that emphasizes the ostensibly shared values of Israel and major western countries, "openness, pluralism, family and democracy."

However, whether Israelis actually do share common values with the West or any other country is an open question. The gold standard for measuring and comparing values is a survey administered by the World Values Survey Association. It has almost never been conducted in Israel because of alleged lack of funding—although this is not a barrier in much poorer countries. Organizers of the survey also claim there has been no local partner willing to carry it out.[238] However, if Israeli values truly matched up with the West, TIP would certainly get behind a push to have the Global Values Survey consistently fielded in Israel so that "shared values" could be quantifiably validated. The fact that TIP, with so much polling and survey inertia, does not actively work to enable the survey speaks volumes about the likely true state of Israeli values and the damage their reporting could do to TIP and overall Israel lobby messaging.

Whatever the disadvantages of negative messaging and inconsistency with efforts to legitimize even the most harmful Israeli government policies, TIP conferences consistently emphasize the need to delegitimize and have Hezbollah and Hamas listed as a terrorist organization by groups and individual countries that do not already categorize them as such. TIP painted European tolerance of such groups as a lack of "moral clarity." It encourages not responding to Hamas proposals despite the fact that the group's creation was originally encouraged by Israel. That Hamas tactics closely resemble those of early Israeli leaders accurately labeled as terrorists by the British government and historians is not a history that ever makes it into TIP regional analysis.

Aside from publicizing the Iran nuclear program as the "challenge of our generation," TIP was also vital in amplifying a message that Jews are physically endangered in the West. In February 2014, TIP chartered a poll of French Jews, reporting "26 percent said they have considered emigrating due to worsening French anti-Semitism and 13 percent were seriously considering leaving."

When Israel rattles sabers for an aggressive policy that could plunge it into

---

[238] The author emailed several people in charge of fielding the survey. Two of them responded with essentially the same answers:

Response #1

"Many thanks for making us aware of this discussion. As concerns your question, the only reason why the survey has been only conducted once in Israel and why responses to many of the questions we usually ask are missing is deficient funding. If we were able to raise sufficient funds, we had [would have] surveyed Israel more frequently and with a more complete questionnaire. I hope this explanation answers your questions."

Response #2

"We would love to have more complete data from Israel. The problem has simply been one of obtaining funding. The World Values Surveys are generally funded from within each country and up to now, it has been difficult to obtain funding there. Nevertheless, we hope to include Israel in the present wave…the University of Haifa is currently seeking funding to carry out the [complete] current wave of the World Values Survey in Israel."

war, TIP almost inevitably releases "polling results" showing that Americans firmly back Israel. "Americans increasingly back the U.S. aiding Israel militarily should it come under attack from Iran after a [Israeli] strike on Tehran's nuclear facilities," stated a November 2012 TIP poll finding 71 percent American approval for blindly following Israel into war.[239] Perhaps so as not to waste any ink, the survey's press release also claimed American voters opposed "unilateral UN recognition of a Palestinian state and continuing aid to the Egyptian government if it does not honor its peace treaty with Israel."

Is The Israel Project polling its own supporter email list with leading questions, or allowing multiple responses to get such results? No audit data is ever made available. However, other pollsters frequently contradict TIP findings. A CNN/ORC poll,[240] conducted only a few months later, showed the majority of Americans in fact supported "not getting involved" or were "unsure," rather than being ready to plunge into war following an Israeli sneak attack on Iran. TIP was also surveying the wrong population about support for Palestinian entry into the United Nations. The stakeholders who mattered, Israelis (70 percent) and Palestinians (83 percent), overwhelmingly supported UN membership for Palestine, according to credible polling conducted in Israel.[241] TIP appears to consider campus poll numbers pitting Palestinians vs. Israelis as a competition in which TIP's role is to drive down one side, while improving the other team's score. In March 2012, TIP announced:

> *College students also show less interest in the Palestinian narrative than we might expect. According to a recent poll conducted by The Israel Project and American Israel Cooperative Enterprise, only 1% of college students believe that Palestinians share American values, compared to 32% who believe Israel does. There's plenty of room for Israel's numbers to go up; there's very little room for Palestinian numbers to go down.*[242]

In 2012, a TIP poll found 82 percent American support for increased

---

239 Hilary Krieger, "Americans increasingly support coming to defense of Israel should it be attacked by Iran. Poll commissioned by The Israel Project says 71% of respondents feel this way," *Jerusalem Post*, November 29, 2012

240 "Iran Polling Report," CNN/ORC Poll, 3/15-17/2013 http://www.pollingreport.com/iran.htm

241 "Poll: 70% of Israelis say Israel should accept UN decision," *The Jerusalem Post*, September 21, 2001 http://www.jpost.com/Diplomacy-and-Politics/Poll-70-percent-of-Israelis-say-Israel-should-accept-UN-decision

242 David Bernstein, "The Problem with Going Negative," *The Jerusalem Post*, March 22, 2012

"sanctions" on Iran, with only 16 percent opposition. A Pew survey presuming Iran had a nuclear weapons program found 75 percent U.S. support for "tougher international sanctions on Iran to try to stop it from developing nuclear weapons."[243] Another function of TIP polling may be to set a standard for the type of presumptive questions being asked. TIP questions assumed Iran had a nuclear weapons, as opposed to a civilian research and power, program. That no major western intelligence community, including the United States, as stated in the annual National Intelligence Estimates, confirmed that Iran had an active nuclear weapons program in the previous decade makes the questions asked by TIP and Pew more hypothetical than useful, unless one is pushing Israel lobbying objectives. However, as bad as the mainstream pollsters are, TIP's more extreme polls tend to prevail only when no similar survey is fielded by more established, credible—and most importantly, more disinterested—organizations.

TIP always attempts to position itself as a counselor, claiming "top leaders of both the government and the opposition regularly receive briefings on global attitudes toward Israel from TIP,"[244] TIP often serves as a *de facto* spokesperson for the Israeli government. In fall of 2012, The Israel Project issued a statement about properties seized for Israel's controversial "separation wall," claiming:

> *The barrier in the Beit Jala area was constructed on [Catholic] Church lands, based on an explicit agreement reached between Israel and the Vatican...The route of the barrier in this segment was constructed at the request of the Vatican, and with consent (at that time) with local priests, in a way that leaves the Cremisan Monastery, along with most of its lands, on the Israeli side of the fence.*[245]

The Assembly of Catholic Ordinaries of the Holy Land disputed TIP's characterization and facts. "The Catholic Ordinaries deny the existence of any explicit or implicit agreement between the Vatican, the local church and Israeli authorities regarding the construction of this illegal wall," said the press statement condemning the wall's construction and horrific impact on local farmers.

---

[243] "Polls show support for tougher sanctions against Iran, but not for Military Force," *World Public Opinion.org*, July 17, 2012 http://www.worldpublicopinion.org/pipa/articles/international_security_bt/718.php

[244] "Image and Reality," *The Jerusalem Post*, May 23, 2011

[245] Tovah Lazaroff, "Vatican denies deal with Israel on security barrier," *The Jerusalem Post*, October 24, 2012

TIP writers can be counted on to categorize most Israeli military incursions as a "response to terror," dispute reported civilian vs. combatant figures, and question international news portrayals of inevitably lopsided and massive civilian Palestinian casualties. One case study was media reporting on the 2002 IDF military operation in Jenin, which TIP characterized as "malreporting." According to TIP's Israel office executive director,

> *My own organization was founded during this period to ensure that the facts reached the press. One can only hope that 10 years on from the battle of Jenin, the media, too, is different; that journalists have learned the lessons of Jenin.*[246]

Essays from TIP writers appear most frequently in the *Jerusalem Post.* Most closing taglines characterize TIP as "an educational organization that provides factual information about Israel and the Middle East to the press, public officials and public." Nevertheless, TIP is also portrayed as "an advocacy group that promotes the positions of the Israeli government" even in establishment news sources such as *The New York Times.*[247] The group's observable services—arranging press and promoting Israeli government policies—raise questions as to why, unlike Washington-based Qorvis Communications, which handles public relations for the Saudi Government in the U.S., TIP is not registering with the Justice Department under the 1938 Foreign Agents Registration Act. TIP, like AIPAC and other IAOs, might respond that they are raising all of their financial support from American donors. Nevertheless, FARA does not require foreign funding to compel registration, only that organizations are in fact operating in concert with a foreign government. In public relations terms, TIP is demonstrably acting as an Israeli government foreign agent.

One Israeli critic writing in the Jerusalem Post chastised TIP for not knowing when to stop growing, duplication of the efforts of other affinity organizations, and stepping on larger toes in the perpetual race for donations:

> *A case in point is The Israel Project that started off with a very specific niche, very discreetly and very effectively. It gauged public opinion on key Israel-relevant issues, and worked out appropriate answers. It also provided helicopter tours over Israel for visiting journalists, which I can attest is one of the most sophisticated and smart ways of explaining Israel's strategic problems to fresh eyes.*

---

246 Marcus Sheff, "A decade since the battle of Jenin, 'the myth of Jeningrad,'" *The Jerusalem Post*, April 19, 2012

247 "Former Israeli Premier Assails Netanyahu on Iran," *New York Times,* April 30, 2012

> *Now, because it has been so successful, and its leadership so energetic in raising funds, from its website one can assume it is the forefront of the fight against global anti-Semitism, a major player in the UN, a key articulator of Israel's foreign policy, a replacement for the Israel Government Press Office and, apparently, for Israel's diplomats abroad. It claims credit for CNN doing this, and for the New York Times doing that, and claims to have the last word on what Israel's message on Iran should be.*
>
> *But instead of fighting anti-Semitism now, it seems, from its own promotional materials, that this once fast, smart, different and niche Israel-action group is fighting the Anti-Defamation League, AIPAC and indeed the Israel government itself over turf and resources, thus creating needless animosity along the way.*
>
> *By the very nature of things, how can it not get dirty when all of these organizations, with basically the same cause in mind, are fighting for the same philanthropic dollars? And this can only become aggravated when justifying new money, more often than not, means duplicating to some degree what is already being done.*[248]

The Israel-Egypt peace treaty cannot be reevaluated or renegotiated as a consequence of evolving Egyptian governance, at least according to the Israeli government, and therefore according to TIP. Speaking at a press conference organized by The Israel Project, Intelligence Agencies Minister Dan Meridor said on February 20, 2012, that "objectively" there is no reason for either Israel or Egypt to change the peace agreement that has served both sides for more than 30 years. "If people are rational and act for the good of their country, both Israel and Egypt should keep the agreement." Meridor made this claim while simultaneously denying the need to establish any contact with Egypt's then Muslim Brotherhood-led government, which was soon ousted in a military coup, the leaders of which were immediately recognized by the U.S. and Israel.

TIP conducts extensive polling about American political party support for Israel, and helps inject Israel issues into U.S. presidential elections. In November 2011, Israel Project founder and President Jennifer Laszlo-Mizrahi said, "This [TIP 2009] poll shows that Israel is significantly more popular among American voters than either the president or Congress." What purpose does such polling and analysis serve if not to pit the two major parties in a "concessions race"? It may suppress voting Americans wishing

[248] "When big becomes too big," *The Jerusalem Post*, March 16, 2012

for a Middle East paradigm-shift, by confirming that they will have no candidates for whom to vote. TIP's polling also sometimes seems to be used to issue stark warnings to U.S. presidents. One TIP poll claimed:

> *"Days before Obama, in a conversation with French President Nicolas Sarkozy, was caught expressing frustration with Netanyahu's efforts on the peace process, a majority of American voters (60%) said that Netanyahu and Israel are committed to peace, while 52% say that President Mahmoud Abbas and the Palestinian Authority are not committed to that end."*[249]

A pattern guided by doctrine can be distilled by reviewing TIP's messaging. Israel can never be allowed to become a "partisan" issue in the U.S. political system: "support for Israel should not divide Americans; rather it should unite them—whether they be liberal or conservative, Democrat or Republican." Like AIPAC, TIP works hard to make it appear that the majority of Americans do not favor increased annual aid to Israel, or do not choose sides in the conflict, will never get to actually cast a vote based on their convictions.

TIP trumpets alleged "common values" between Americans and Israelis, although, as noted above, polls that could validate such common values are simply not conducted, and such values remain an assertion rather than fact. TIP insists that Israel and the U.S. are facing "common enemies." Israel is always portrayed as a cutting-edge development center for agricultural productivity and medical innovations. TIP harps on the danger of U.S. isolationism, the overall desirability of a hawkish foreign policy and the taboo of U.S. talks with enemies of Israel such as Hamas, Hezbollah or Iran. TIP is supportive of walkouts during Iranian speeches at the UN These are portrayed as an adult, rather than a childish, reaction.

Other TIP doctrine includes forcing U.S. political candidates to clearly, publicly and frequently state their views about the U.S.-Israel "special relationship." It helps if they echo TIP stating that Palestinians are perpetually "not ready for peace," and their leadership promotes "unacceptable" solutions. Palestinian bids for UN recognition and status are an extreme "UDI, unilateral declaration of independence" that should be deterred by the U.S. Popular support and sympathy for Israel is therefore "rational," while popular support and sympathy for Palestinians is "clouded by anti-Semitism."

Beyond the helicopter rides in Israel for journalists, TIP also organizes and funds tours to Israel for foreign ambassadors accredited to the United States and serving in Washington. In 2011, TIP arranged for William Bull,

---

[249] Rebecca Anna Stoil, "Americans' support for Israel rising" *The Jerusalem Post*, November 11, 2011

Liberia's Ambassador to the U.S., and nineteen other Washington-based foreign ambassadors to travel to Israel on a five-day trip to meet with Israeli Prime Minister Netanyahu and other officials. The visit included presentations on Israeli security concerns, tours of religious sites and economic talks.[250] What was TIP hoping to accomplish?

Africa is the major source of uncut diamonds that Israel cuts and exports. Israel hoped to dissuade developing-country support for Palestinian statehood bids by pressing the idea of Israel's "willingness to negotiate," while subtly communicating that the U.S. was fully behind Israel's major export industry—whether or not it actually was—and that voting with Palestinians would be a mistake. As one Israeli official remarked, "This is a group not known for voting for Israel, so the goal is to engage them, and any change in their voting pattern would be a plus." Other country ambassadors airlifted from Washington to Israel by TIP were representatives of Albania, Barbados, Belize, Burkina Faso, the Dominican Republic, Haiti, Macedonia, St. Lucia and Uganda. That TIP was acting on behalf of the Israeli government to sway U.N votes with this program is almost certain.

Unlike TIP's news and updates appearing in the *Jerusalem Post*, TIP's effect on Western news media is less visible. Even as the Israeli government increasingly restricts press access to conflict zones, TIP's public relations operatives coordinate specific messages, applying pre-approved terminology and talking points. One analyst writing in *The Guardian* bluntly stated that news about Israel was becoming essentially one-sided:

> *In 2004 the Glasgow University Media Group published a major study on TV coverage of the Second Intifada and its impact on public understanding. We analyzed about 200 programs and questioned more than 800 people. Our conclusion: reporting was dominated by Israeli accounts. Since then we have been contacted by many journalists and told of the intense pressures they are under that limit criticism of Israel. They asked us to raise the issue in public because they can't. They speak of 'waiting in fear for the phone call from the Israelis,' of the BBC's Jerusalem bureau having been "leant on by the Americans," of being 'guilty of self-censorship' and of 'urgently needing an external arbiter.'*
>
> *In a new project, we have analyzed more than 4,000 lines of text from the main UK news bulletins of the attack, but there was no coverage in these of the killing by the Israelis of more than 1,000 Palestinians, including hundreds of children, in the three years*

[250] "Liberia: Amb. Bull Visits Israel—Meets Prime Minister Netanyahu," All Africa News, August 9, 2011

> *before it. In TV coverage, Israeli statements on the causes of action overwhelmed those of the Palestinians by more than three to one. Palestinian statements tended to be only that they would seek revenge on Israel. The underlying reasons for the conflict were absent, such as being driven from their land when Israel was created.*[251]

Professor Greg Philo of the Glasgow University Media Group joined others in assessing how a secret TIP media strategy guide distributed to IAO allies has helped transform facts into disinformation distribution. "Images of suffering do not now in themselves affect how audiences see the validity of actions in war. People see the images as tragic, but judgments as to who is right and wrong are now firmly in the hands of the spin doctors."[252]

The spin-doctor contracted by TIP in 2003 and paid $60,000 to produce its first strategy guide was pollster and political operative Frank Luntz. The Israel Project's *2009 Global Language Dictionary* was a Luntz update that leaked to the press and was immediately dissected by the alternative media. Founder Laszlo Mizrahi's bellicose opening comment in the 2009 *Dictionary* further disrobes TIP of its tax-exempt social welfare cloak and reveals it as a sharp information warfare and propaganda weapon. She wrote:

> *On behalf of our board and team, we offer this guide to visionary leaders who are on the front lines of fighting the media war for Israel. We want you to succeed in winning the hearts and minds of the public. We know that when you achieve your mission that you are helping both Israel and our global Jewish family. Thus, we offer these words with our sincerest wishes for your every success. May your words help bring peace and security to Israel and the Jewish people!*

The guide is a masterpiece of how to change the subject while broadcasting talking points tested by Luntz, who recommends:

> *No matter what you are asked, bridge to a productive pro-Israel message. When asked a direct question, you don't have to answer it directly. You are in control of what you say and how you say it. Remember, your goal in doing interviews is not only to answer questions—it is to bring persuadable members of the audience to Israel's side in the conflict.*

---

251 "Truth is still the casualty: Our latest analysis of news bulletins reveals how Israel continues to spin images of war," *The Guardian*, May 31, 2011

252 "Truth is still the casualty: Our latest analysis of news bulletins reveals how Israel continues to spin images of war," *The Guardian*, May 31, 2011

TIPs guidance to spin-doctors urges the de-contextualization of the conflict by ignoring, or diversion away from, uncomfortable historical facts, such as the displacement of Palestinians from their own land during the creation of Israel. Luntz recommends activists:

> *Talk about the future, not the past. Spending time giving the public a history lesson on the maps of Israel will put your audience to sleep—at best. At worst, if you spend your communications capital (time and money) on history lessons of who got what land when and who promised what to whom, it will be viewed by Americans and Europeans as a game of gotcha and not a vision for a better future. Remember—communications is not a test for who can remember the most facts. Listeners want simple messages that will answer their simple, silent question: 'What is in it for my country and for me to support Israel?'*

Luntz's suggestions follow the Israeli government's line. No discussion of borders until there is "peace," Iran as racing toward a nuclear weapon that it can proliferate to terrorists; no recognition of the lopsided casualties suffered by Palestinians at the hands of Israel, and empty repetition of empty words such as "hope" in the same sentence as "children;" rejections of timelines revealing Israel as often an instigator of "tit-for-tat" violence; Israel as perpetually seeking peace; avoiding the most caustic quotes of Israeli leaders, such as their long historical denial that Palestinians were even a people; contrasting what Washington would do if under attack by rockets, without citing how or why it would happen.

On how to refute American agreement that Israel should give back land captured in 1967, for example, Luntz suggests:

> *Israel should not give any more land for peace, because every time it does, it just gets more war.*

Luntz justifies the ongoing expansion of Israeli settlements on occupied Palestinian land "Settlements are necessary for the security of Israel" but recommends changing the subject to jobs, prosperity and "a better future for children." Luntz and TIP, as is common across the Israel lobby, support and justify Israeli control of the entirety of Jerusalem.

Upon close examination, The Israel Project's *2009 Global Language Dictionary* is not educational material or a means for promoting greater understanding of the issues. It is, as stated by TIP's own director, a guide for supporters to locate, overwhelm and "win over" people to the Israeli side of the argument. It clearly uses deceptive rhetoric and logical fallacies. It is obviously not the nonprofit educational material for which TIP received IRS tax-exempt status as an organization dedicated to "promoting international understanding."

TIP's challenge is not rebranding Israel; it is about undercutting entirely valid and warranted global popular perceptions about Israeli actions. TIP has a difficult task, given that its message conflicts with public opinion revealed in surveys such as that conducted for the BBC:

> *The 2011 Country Rating Poll, a large, annual, 28-country study for the BBC World Service, asked about a number of countries, and whether that country has a negative or a positive influence in the world. The results show that among more than 28,000 respondents, Israel's influence is viewed favorably by only 21% and negatively by 49%. Although this is a meager two-point rise from the previous 2010 Country Rating Poll, overall the poll shows very little change from when the survey began asking about Israel in 2007. As we have often heard in ominous news reports over the last few years, only countries of great ignominy were rated lower than Israel: Pakistan, North Korea and Iran....The heavily endowed Israel propaganda campaigns largely focus on Israel's positive impact in a range of fields beyond the diplomatic sphere—science, technology, arts, emergency aid-and perhaps these have contributed to the two-point rise from 2010. But the overall picture is not encouraging.*[253]

Rather than change Israel and its lobby's provocative and unproductive actions, through trickery and slick PR frames TIP is trying to change minds. The most important are those of elites it believes "will offset the heated and conflicting emotions surrounding Israel with a large dose of pragmatism." However, over the long term, even the most sophisticated campaign will probably fail, since no "pragmatic" (or captured) leader or institution can indefinitely remain immune from growing popular awareness and calls for change demanded by an increasingly informed citizenry.

TIP, as a new upstart IAO with sharp elbows, has not been able to enter the most establishment club of all umbrella IAOs—the Conference of Presidents of Major American Jewish Organizations. The Israel Project applied to become a member organization immediately after completing the five-year mandatory waiting period required of all new organizations and after showing an ability to financially sustain itself. Told that its application was still "pending" in 2012, TIP began agitating for a vote on its application. Perhaps as a backhand to newbies such as TIP that compete with the older established order, and even his own stature with Israeli and American officials, Conference President and CEO Malcolm Hoenlein told his radio listeners that:

---

[253] "Image and Reality," *The Jerusalem Report*, May 23, 2011

> *I had an opportunity to speak last Sunday with the JDC [American Jewish Joint Distribution Committee's] meeting. And the truth is they do remarkable work. We partner with them all over the world. We do the political stuff, they're the ones on the ground. Working behind the scenes, often quietly, doing such remarkable things, providing food. They're not some people, some organization, some efforts [that] spend all their money on publicizing very little. They do very little publicity but have great activities in the community.*[254]

Despite lacking its own large membership base, TIP has managed to corral a contingent of 25 current and 11 former members of Congress onto its advisory board. They include Representative Elliot Engel (D NY); Senator Ben Cardin (D MD); Senator Mark Kirk (R IL), Representative Joe Wilson (R SC), Senator Joe Lieberman (I CT), Senator Ron Wyden (D OR) and Representative Howard Berman (D CA).[255] The Israel Project's formal organizational connections to so many former and current members of congress differentiate it from the majority of other IAOs. Why does it go to such lengths to maintain a large congressional advisory board? It may be that it provides an extra layer of necessary insulation against what would be entirely justified investigations by the currently dormant Justice Department as to whether it is really just another not-so-stealthy public relations firm for the Israeli government. One vital component of such an investigation would be to compare the organization's actual activities against those declared to the Internal Revenue Service on its application for tax-exempt status.

Of all the required filings an IAO makes (or any other tax-exempt organization that received such status from the IRS), its application for tax-exempt status can be the most revelatory. It must include the articles of incorporation that formed the organization, bylaws that reveal how the corporation is governed, responses on an IRS application that asks whether an organization is a subsidiary or has ties to other organizations, and if it will be engaged in lobbying. There is also usually back-and-forth written communication with IRS examiners. Although the IRS must provide full copies of such applications for tax-exempt status documents to any requester (taking up to a year to do so), the IRS claims it cannot locate The Israel Project's filing:

> *We are unable to locate a copy of the application or determination letter for this organization. While we were unable to provide*

[254] "Weekly Update" with Nachum Segal and Malcolm Hoenlein, May 22, 2015, http://wfmu.org/playlists/HE

[255] TIP's Board of Advisors, TIP website http://www.theisraelproject.org/tips-board-of-advisors/

> *copies of these documents, our records indicate a determination letter was issued in March, 2004.*[256]

The media pressure contingent of the Israel lobby adds members whenever conditions warrant. The Los Angeles-based Israel Emergency Alliance, also known as Standwithus, was formed to combat "misinformation about the Middle East conflict and inappropriate, often anti-Semitic language used about Israel and the Jewish people." Standwithus devotes a major amount of time to college campuses, where it claims it has:

> *...been working on campuses since it officially became a non profit organization. A significant portion of our work is dedicated to making sure that college students are not confused by the misinformation about Israel and Jews that is being promoted on college campuses throughout the United States. For example, many speakers who come to American campuses talk about Israel's security fence. They don't explain why Israel built the fence. Terrorism, rockets into Israel and violence against Israel are not mentioned. Much of the information distributed on campuses has been one-sided anti-Israel material. Students have felt intimidated and confused. The misinformation often morphed into anti-Semitism on campuses and sometime resulted in violence. IEA provides students with written materials that they can use to educate their campus communities. IEA provides them with speakers who travel to their campuses in an effort to diffuse anti-Semitic anti-Israel misinformation.*[257]

Times are good at StandWithUs. The organization's revenue grew from $347,000 in 2002 to over $8.7 million in 2012: adding a $22,000 vehicle to its listed assets in 2008: and opened an office in Israel and relocated its U.S. headquarters to trendy Wilshire Boulevard.

Yet another media pressure group, Facts and Logic About the Middle East (FLAME, 2012 revenue $465,000) runs full-page ads in liberal and Jewish publications, presenting pro-Israel talking points. It demonstrated its no-holds-barred approach in its 2009 campaign against *The Berkeley Daily Planet.*

FLAME launched a campaign to get the newspaper to stop publishing op-eds and articles critical of Israel. The newspaper was founded in 1999 as a progressive daily that often endorsed liberal candidates and policies. After the newspaper published a letter to the editor by an Iranian student criticizing

---

[256] Letter to the author, U.S. Department of Treasury, Internal Revenue Service, March 18, 2015

[257] Standwithus 2008 IRS form 990

Israel's invasion of Lebanon, FLAME set out to shut the paper down. FLAME Vice President Jim Sinkinson sent letters to all of the newspaper's advertisers, along with a form he developed to cancel their ads.

As a long-time professional publicist and owner of the *Bulldog Reporter*, Sinkinson's personal business was producing media directories, webinars, conferences and award programs. A Sinkinson colleague, Dan Spitzer, called and visited the *Daily Planet's* advertisers, demanding that they drop their contracts. Another fellow traveler, John Gertz, set up the website "DPwatchdog.com" to capture and warn web readers searching for *The Berkeley Daily Planet* of its "anti-Semitism and Journalistic malfeasance" and question whether individuals working for the newspaper were "anti-Semites." An April 21, 2009, email to the executive editor from Gertz said, "Reform, or close, or bleed money until you are forced out of business or die broke." Sinkinson contacted the newspaper's advertisers as a representative of "East Bay Citizens for Journalistic Responsibility" without referencing his association with FLAME or the *Bulldog Reporter*, and urged advertisers to visit the website. According to *The Daily Planet*, the campaign had mixed results:

> *Some Daily Planet advertisers, incensed at the threats, have renewed their contracts. Others have fled, at least one prompted by the loss of paying clients.*[258]

In 2010, the perpetually financially challenged *Daily Planet* ceased print publication, but managed to continue its online reporting. During the lengthy FLAME attack, the *Daily Planet* fought back by publishing articles about who was orchestrating the campaign and why. It issued successful front-page appeals for funding and challenged the legitimacy of ideologically driven censorship.

In the end, it may be FLAME that flames out. A revenue forecast trending the group's declining revenues reveals it probably will go out of business by 2017 (see appendix). According to *The Wall Street Journal*, in 2014 Sinkinson's PR firm went bankrupt, with $178,000 in assets and $784,000 in liabilities. The newspaper did not mention his role in FLAME.[259] Yet while such aggressive fights for Israel in the news media have been going on for a long time, there is a new emphasis on taking the fight into courtrooms.

The Lawfare Project, Inc. (TLP) was created by the Conference of Presidents of Major American Jewish Organizations. It gained its own

---

[258] Richard Brenneman, "The Campaign Against The Daily Planet," *The Berkeley Daily Planet*, June 4, 2009

[259] Sara Randazzo, "Bulldog reporter bankruptcy leaves trail of unpaid journalists," *The Wall Street Journal*, November 26, 2014 http://blogs.wsj.com/bankruptcy/2014/11/26/bulldog-reporter-bankruptcy-leaves-trail-of-unpaid-journalists/

independent tax-exempt status in 2011. It claims not to conduct lawfare, but rather combat it. In an official announcement, the Conference of Presidents stated:

> *The Lawfare Project is the only organization of its kind dedicated solely to identifying, analyzing, and facilitating a response to lawfare in all of its manifestations.*
>
> *The primary goals of The Lawfare Project are: (i) to raise awareness about the phenomenon and specific instances of lawfare, assuring the subject matter receives the credibility and immediacy that it warrants; (ii) to facilitate (legal and non-legal) responses to the perversion and misapplication of international and national human rights law; (iii) to identify potential lawfare threats and mobilize human and institutional resources to combat them; and (iv) to bring diverse and interested parties together in a common forum to discuss the phenomenon.*[260]

TLP claims that Israel is the major target for activists abusing the Western legal system for political ends. Lawfare project head Brooke Goldstein continually attacks groups such as the Council on American-Islamic-Relations (CAIR) as "terror-connected" entities working to stifle critical debate through labeling critics as "Islamophobic."[261] The Lawfare Project (TLP) raises awareness of the "campaign to silence critics of militant Islam" through educational videos and other programs. It issues open letters to hotel chains such as Hyatt, urging them to cancel gatherings of groups such as American Muslims for Palestine because, it alleges, they are defenders of terrorism and are "involved with terrorism financing."[262] According to TLP, the United States federal government has been penetrated by Muslim operatives, as evidenced by its refusal to brand CAIR as a "front for Hamas."

> *This is a State Department that itself staffs Muslim Brotherhood sympathizers, for example. This is a State Department that has redacted counterterrorism training manuals because they're Islamophobic, has redacted the word Islam and jihad from counterterrorism training manuals. Has fired FBI officials for being Islamophobic. This State Department does not have the*

---

260 "The Lawfare Project," *States News Service*, November 28, 2011

261 "Global Outpouring of Support for France; Twelve Killed in Paris Terror Attack," Fox News Network, January 7, 2015

262 "Lawfare Project Concerned with Hyatt's Decision to Host American Muslims for Palestine Conference," Lawfare Project website, December 2, 2014, http://www.thelawfareproject.org/Press-Releases/lawfare-project-concerned-with-hyatts-decision-to-host-american-muslims-for-palestine-conference.html

> *courage to designate a terror front organization in the United States. And it's a shame.*[263]

For years, Israel and affiliated lawyers working abroad have had to defend Israeli officials arrested in various countries from war crimes charges promoted by NGOs. Although The Lawfare Project publicly decries "the use of law as a weapon of war," it is not opposed if the "weapon" is being wielded on Israel's behalf. TLP encourages legal attempts to deny Title VI federal funding to universities that do not prevent Students for Justice in Palestine and similar groups from becoming more effective advocates on campus.

In 2014, TLP was at the head of a six-IAO-member coalition that sent letters to the presidents of NYU and UCLA. They warned that pro-Palestinian activities amounted to "harassment and intimidation of Jewish students" that exposed the universities to legal action. Northeastern University, in March of 2014, subsequently expelled members of Students for Justice in Palestine over their on-campus activities.

TLP was also a backer of *Zivotofsky v. Kerry*, a case that went to the Supreme Court. A law passed by Congress ordered the Secretary of State to record the birthplace of American citizens born in Jerusalem as having been born in "Israel." The United States does not recognize Jerusalem as Israel's capital, in line with the rest of the world. According to the Constitution such recognition is left to the president. This attempt to skirt presidential powers was ruled unconstitutional in that it "impermissibly infringes on the President's exercise of the recognition power reposing exclusively in him." In a setback to TLP and other backers such as the ADL, the Supreme Court ruled the law unconstitutional.

TLP could more accurately be described as an organization working to ensure, justifiably or not, "that international law is not turned against Israel."[264] As is the practice of most IAOs, TLP's leadership conflates dangers posed by Israel's enemies as threats to the United States:

> *We know Hamas does not care about the Palestinian people because they are using them as human shields. Hamas is attacking Israel because it sees Israel as the outpost of the west in the Middle East. And it knows if we abandon Israel, if we allow Israel to be destroyed, then we are next. And it can destroy us. And the only reason why Hamas has not been able to kill more Americans abroad, it has killed Americans in Israel, is because*

---

263 "Immigration and Executive Orders; American Muslim Groups Get Terror Label; ISIS Beheads U.S. Army Veteran," Fox News Network, November 17, 2014

264 "Released: The 'Official' List of Hamas Violations of Int'l Law," *Arutz Sheva*, September 18, 2014

> *the Israeli counter terror naval and air blockade and ground blockade of Hamas.*[265]

TLP has also attempted to have the IRS revoke[266] the American Studies Association's tax-exempt status after the group voted to boycott Israel's higher education institutions in protest of Israel's treatment of Palestinians. Filed under an IRS "whistleblower" program, the attempt which resembles a legal complaint has yet to produce IRS revocation or a whistleblower award.

An IRS revocation that did occur—and generated considerable controversy—swept up the Zionist Organization of America. As one of the "first wave" IAOs, and a member of the consortium American Zionist Council that led to the creation of AIPAC, the ZOA's loss of tax-exempt status resulted from the internal disarray behind its failure to file tax returns, revealing a great deal about an organization that was once at the epicenter of the Israel advocacy groundswell. The IRS has destroyed all applications for tax-exempt status of the older charitable corporations. This compelled the ZOA to state by precisely which modern-day social welfare standards its activities were to be considered worthy of exempt status.

Unlike B'nai B'rith, the organizations that coalesced into the ZOA were explicitly centered on the creation of a Jewish state in Palestine, and more anti-assimilationist at their core. *Hoveve Zion*—Lovers of Zion—societies were formed by Russian immigrants living in New York, Chicago and Baltimore. The founder of the New York Lovers of Zion group, Dr. Joseph Bluestone, believed that the Zionist movement's purpose was safeguarding American Jewry against assimilation. The Zion Society of Chicago was the only such organization to send a delegate to the First Zionist Congress in Basel. The Zionist Organization of America held its very first meeting in Pittsburgh in 1917, where it adopted its own "Pittsburgh program."[267]

The Zionist Organization of America is similar to other older IAOs such as the American Jewish Committee in that its incorporation on April 14, 1920 was officially promulgated inside a government body highly accommodating to Zionist activism—the legislature of the State of New York. Without citing why it was in the interest of New Yorkers to do so, the legislature chartered

---

265 "President Sticks to Fundraising Schedule Despite Crises in Ukraine, Gaza; Israel Launches Military Operation Against Hamas in the Gaza Strip; Investigation: 23 Americans May Have Been Murdered in Ukraine Crash," Fox News Network, July 17, 2014

266 Maya Shwayder, "American Studies Associations tax-exempt status challenged," January 8, 2014. The complaint profiled in the report may be consulted at: http://www.scribd.com/doc/290938513/American-Studies-Association-IRS-Whistleblower-w-Out-Exhibits-1

267 Mordecai Schreiber, Alvin I. Schiff, Leon Klenicki, *The Shengold Jewish Encyclopedia* [Rockville, MD, Schrieber Publishing, 2003] 297

the ZOA, declaring:

> *The object of said corporation shall be (a) to further the aim of the Basle program, to wit; To establish a publicly recognized and legally secured home for the Jewish people in Palestine, and (b) to do any and all things that may be necessary or incidental to the attainment of this object…*[268]

Some leaders within the ZOA, including Zalman Shapiro and Ivan Novick, would give meaning to the term "any and all things that may be necessary," as explored in the case of diverted weapons-grade uranium from NUMEC. The Basel program did not inherently have anything to do with the interests of the people of the State of New York or even the citizens of the United States. The first Zionist Congress, held in a concert hall of the Basel Municipal Casino on August 29, 1897, was called by Theodor Herzl for those who wanted to implement the Zionist goals outlined in his book, *The Jewish State.* The political program adopted by the First World Zionist Congress was very specific: "to create for the Jewish people a home in Palestine secured by public law." However, the Basel program did not have the power of a treaty, or recognition by any dominant world power, until it was encapsulated in the proclamation of the Balfour Declaration in 1917 and, later, Great Britain's receipt by the League of Nations of a Mandate for Palestine in 1920. At this point, Zionists across the globe—but most importantly in the United States—could shift from lobbying for governmental recognition and support of the aims of Zionism to actual state building.[269] By orchestrating its incorporation through the State of New York, the ZOA gained a quasi-official status through state-supported recognition of its objectives.

Perhaps realizing that such official recognition of its aims from the State of New York alone would look a bit dodgy, ZOA also lobbied for and secured passage of a joint resolution by both houses of Congress and signed by President Warren G. Harding on September 22, 1922. In hindsight, the resolution was even worse than the New York law bringing ZOA into existence because—in addition to again failing to justify why Americans would be served by the creation of a Jewish state in Palestine—it promised to uphold the rights of other communities living there, which clearly never happened. It reads:

> *JOINT RESOLUTION: favoring the establishment of a national home for the Jewish people…RESOLVED: By the*

---

[268] Laws of New York, 1920, chapter 205, 707 The Israel Lobby Archive http://israellobby.org/ZOA/DOJ-149-1603-ZOA/Chapt_205_Law_1920.pdf

[269] Samuel Halperin, "Ideology or Philanthropy? The Politics of Zionist Fund-Raising," *The Western Political Quarterly*, Vol. 13, No. 4, December, 1960, 951

> *Senate and House of Representatives of the United States of America in Congress assembled, that the United States of America favors the establishment in Palestine of a national home for the Jewish people, it being clearly understood that nothing shall be done which may prejudice the civil and religious rights of Christian and all other non-Jewish communities in Palestine, and that the holy places and religious buildings and sites in Palestine shall be adequately protected.*[270]

Use of the word "homeland" or "Jewish National Home" was a purposeful framing—or, less charitably, a "bait and switch"—useful, besides echoing the terms of the Balfour Declaration, in corralling reluctant donors and making them feel good about themselves by avoiding the most uncomfortable questions raised by the enterprise. Surveys of Zionist publications between 1930 and 1941 reveal the more specific term "Jewish State" had almost disappeared in favor of weaker and more ambiguous formulations.[271] This was purposeful, according to ZOA President (1947-1949) Emanuel Neumann, who said:

> *...for many years the "Jewish State" became taboo—not merely on grounds of expediency. The very word was banned from official Zionist use and driven underground. The State was not only impossible of achievement, but of questionable morality. The National Home, interpreted as a spiritual and cultural center, was deemed a nobler and loftier conception—and one which offered practical advantages. A "spiritual center" required little space, no Jewish majority and no political sovereignty...The accent of this "Spiritual Zionism" was upon patience, caution and restraint, and the avoidance of risk. Zionist statesmanship was made synonymous with moderation—carried at times to an immoderate extreme."*[272]

It is interesting to note that, in the 21st century United States, what has now become taboo is questioning the morality of the now real "Jewish State" and its treatment of Palestinians—or so organizations like ZOA would like it to be. At the forefront of the so-called "Zionist movement," ZOA dedicated itself to taking over the predominantly non-Zionist fundraising

---

[270] A joint resolution of both Houses of Congress of the United States, Congressional Record, June 30, 1922,

[271] Samuel Halperin, "Ideology or Philanthropy? The Politics of Zionist Fund-Raising," *The Western Political Quarterly*, Vol. 13, No. 4, December, 1960, 967

[272] Abba Hillel Silver, *Vision and Victory* [New York, Zionist Organization of America, 1949] 1-2

apparatus of Jewish social welfare organizations and harnessing it to the political objective of creating a Jewish state in Palestine. This was not an easy task. In 1935, ZOA set an objective in its "National Zionist Roll Call" to enlist 250,000 new members—paying ZOA the quite reasonable sum of $1 each—into its national chapter system. Its membership drive fell utterly flat, enlisting less than 20,000. Yet another campaign to raise $100,000 gathered only $13,500.[273]

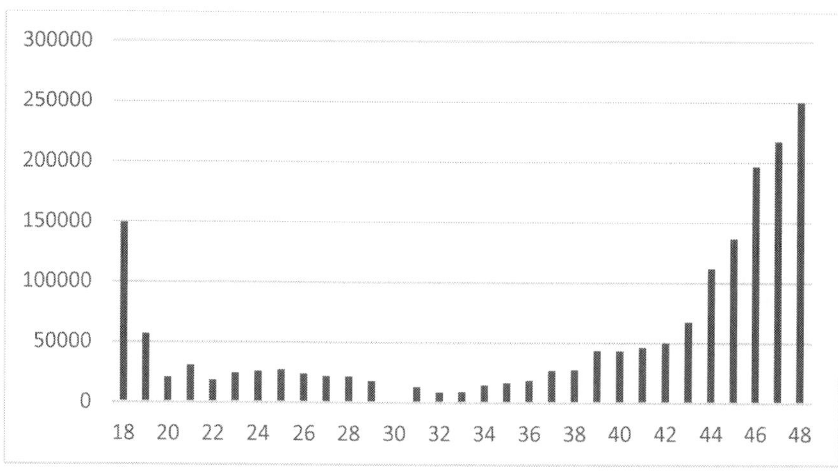

Figure 24 ZOA membership 1918-1948[274]

Zionist activists charged that an "interlocking directorate of anti-Zionist plutocrats" controlled the checkbooks of the influential organizations, such as the Joint Distribution Committee, the American Jewish Committee and National Refugee Service. This sometimes very public fight embarrassed Zionists and non-Zionists alike. Many were stunned by the ferocity of charges that the "grassroots" demands of Zionists were being ignored. According to one report:

> *The Lakeport Jewish community is not so much led as controlled by a moneyed oligarchy which is only vaguely responsive to the 'needs' and 'interests' of the individuals supposedly being 'served.'*[275]

Zionists building a state in Palestine and community-minded

---

[273] Zionist Organization of America, 38th Annual Report, 5-6

[274] Data from Samuel Halperin, *The Political World of American Zionism* [Detroit, Wayne State University, 1961]

[275] Norman Miller, "The Jewish Leadership of Lakeport," in *Studies in Leadership*, ed. Alvin Gouldner [New York, Harper, 1950] 195-227

philanthropists formed tenuous national joint fundraising campaigns, only to see them rupture into controversy. Zionists responded to non-Zionist efforts to diminish their share of jointly raised funds by exhorting followers to "conquer the local Jewish Federations" and "infiltrate the welfare funds!" The rise of the Nazi party in Germany, its takeover in Austria, and later successful Zionist transfer of Displaced Persons to Palestine, though challenged by British efforts to restrict emigration, caused the Zionist share of united charitable funding to grow steadily, from a low of only 29 percent in 1939 to 51.1 percent by 1950.[276]

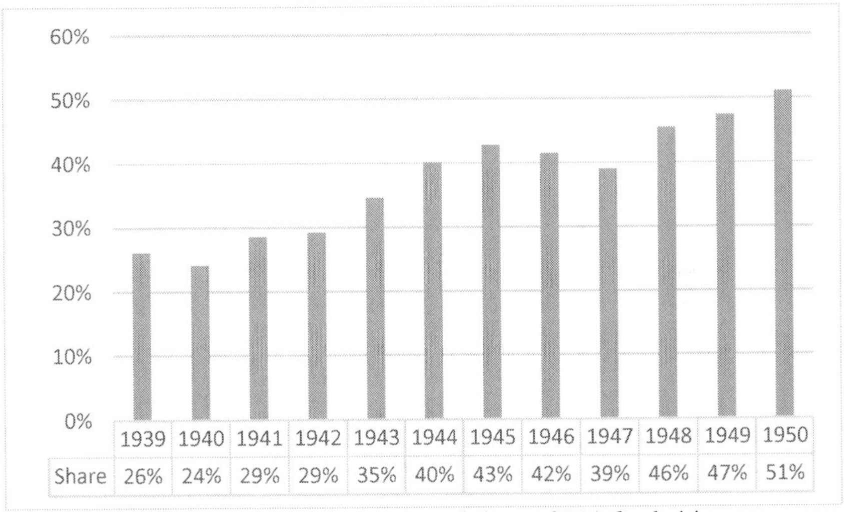

	1939	1940	1941	1942	1943	1944	1945	1946	1947	1948	1949	1950
Share	26%	24%	29%	29%	35%	40%	43%	42%	39%	46%	47%	51%

Figure 25 United Palestine Appeal share of UJA fundraising

On November 10, 1942, 818 American rabbis issued a news release that Zionism was an affirmation of Judaism. This was a response to a statement by ninety Reform rabbis who had formally proclaimed that Zionism was incompatible with the teachings of Judaism. Propaganda injected by Zionist leaders into the Jewish community discourse was seen as the key to success for changing the allocation of charitable funding flows, as reported in *New Palestine*:

> *...there is no reason why propaganda for Palestine cannot be conducted in the midst of a Welfare Fund campaign. ... It is the duty of Zionists...to find a constructive way to place Palestine and*

[276] Reports of the executives submitted to 23rd Zionist Congress at Jerusalem, 1951, 29

> *Zionist interests in the center of community life. The Welfare Chests may be that way.*[277]

After faltering in the Depression years, the ZOA and Zionist movement eventually succeeded—not due to the savviness of their leadership, the subject of much self-promotional material available from the key organizations, but to Hitler's decimation of European Jews. Only as word of the Nazi-driven Holocaust became widespread in America did the Zionist program of moving displaced persons to Palestine—rather than offering aid in place within Europe, or immigration to the U.S., truly take hold. Between 1940 and 1948, ZOA's membership grew rapidly, to 250,000. Funding for Israel/Palestine from the United Jewish Appeal amounted to an inflation-adjusted $2.7 billion during 1939-1948, an amount that does not include additional millions from direct personal and family donations, private and commercial investments, and other initiatives.[278]

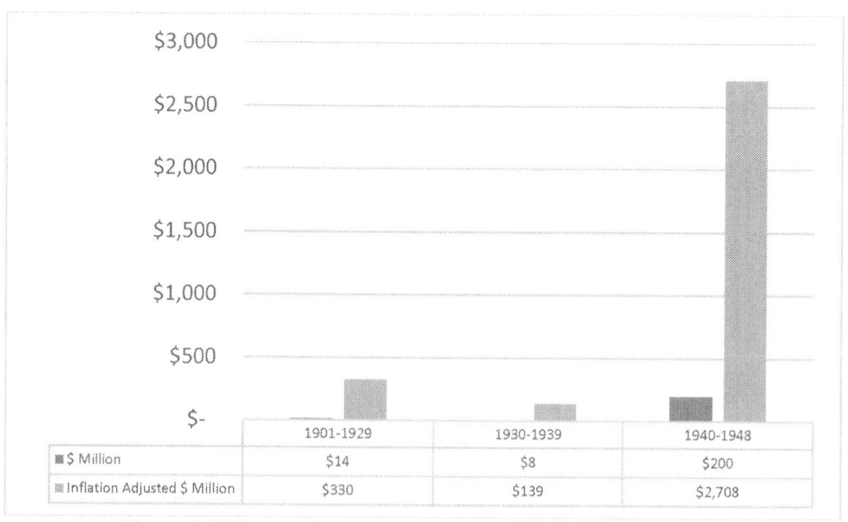

	1901-1929	1930-1939	1940-1948
$ Million	$14	$8	$200
Inflation Adjusted $ Million	$330	$139	$2,708

Figure 26 Zionist share of United Jewish Appeal fundraising

Zionists, having demanded and won an increasing share of Jewish philanthropic donations, saw how crisis and tragedy at last broke open the funding floodgates of donors both large and small. This allowed Zionists to credibly claim that donations to their long-term political program was, in fact, humanitarian-crisis-driven philanthropy. The lessons of how crisis could

277 *New Palestine*, January 14, 1938,4

278 Composite figures from original research contained in the Samuel Halperin doctoral dissertation "American Zionism: The Building of a Political Interest Group," Washington University, St. Louis, 1956, 491-493. Adjustment for inflation by the author.

motivate the base and open funding floodgates would never be forgotten by the ZOA or other Israel Affinity Organizations.

The 1973 Arab-Israeli conflict known as the Yom Kippur War triggered fresh demands for Israel: specifically, that the U.S. government ship massive resupplies of arms to Israel. "Israel in danger" emergency alerts to the IAO ecosystem portrayed Israel as being under an existential threat. In response, neoconservatives, "concerned that the United States might not be able to provide Israel with adequate military supplies in the event of another Arab-Israeli war," formed the Jewish Institute for National Security Affairs (JINSA) in 1976.[279]

When it first launched its website two decades later in 1996, JINSA boasted on its homepage that, "Only one think tank puts the U.S.-Israel strategic relationship FIRST—JINSA!"[280] JINSA's board of advisors has included numerous former high-ranking military and other government officials, many of whom became active lobbyists for military contractors:

> *...What JINSA represents can best be described as the Military-Industrial-Israeli complex.*
>
> *Sitting on its board, in addition, are such public figures as former UN ambassador Jean Kirkpatrick, former CIA chief James Woolsey, former Congressman Jack Kemp, Michael Ledeen, an un-indicted co-conspirator in the Iran-Contra affair, and former Congressman Stephen Solarz...and, of course, [Richard] Perle. Of all those recruited into the ranks of JINSA, none would prove to be more important than Dick Cheney, the former congressman who served as Secretary of Defense in the first Bush administration.*[281]

JINSA on its website has described its mission as twofold:

> *To educate the American public about the importance of an effective U.S. defense capability so that our vital interests as Americans can be safeguarded; and To inform the American defense and foreign affairs community about the important role Israel can and does play in bolstering democratic interests in the Mediterranean and the Middle East.*

The gravitational pull within JINSA's universe is an insistence that U.S. and Israeli interests are identical. Therefore, unconditional military aid and

---

279 Jason Vest, "The Men from JINSA and CSP," *The Nation*, August 15, 2002

280 JINSA website in 1996, via the Wayback Machine, consulted August 17, 2015 https://web.archive.org/web/19961221064616/http://jinsa.org/

281 Jeffrey Blankfort, "A War for Israel" *LeftCurve*, April, 2004. Issue No. 28

diplomatic support to Israel are, as promoted by JINSA, by default a U.S. national interest. JINSA had a major influence on the George W. Bush administration's policymaking, by insisting that the longstanding Israeli-Palestinian conflict could not be resolved until Iraq, Iran, Syria, Saudi Arabia, Libya and other countries in the region were confronted militarily.[282] Indeed, reflecting on the U.S. invasion of Iraq, former Secretary of State Colin Powell said, "I believe the JINSA crowd had a lot to say about it." referring to former Secretary of Defense Donald Rumsfeld's team of neoconservative appointees which included Richard Perle and Douglas Feith who along with Vice President Dick Cheney had served on JINSA's board.[283]

JINSA runs major programs dedicated to enhancing ties between the U.S. and Israeli military and law enforcement communities. Its Military Academies Programs works to place IDF officials as instructors in front of top military training school cadets. The Law Enforcement Exchange Program (LEEP) provides funding to bring groups of American law enforcement officials to Israel for training. In 2006, JINSA took forty U.S. law enforcement officials to Israel to "learn counter terrorism techniques" and claimed to have "trained" 6,000 American law enforcement officials.[284] JINSA's Generals and Admirals Program to Israel, established in 1981, takes recent retirees from top levels of the military to Israel for debriefing by senior Israeli military, intelligence and political leaders.

The organization's focus on law enforcement and military exchanges clearly raises questions. It is commonplace for both professions to seek out training and exchange opportunities with worthwhile partners. During the height of Irish Republic Army violence, law enforcement organizations, noting financial flows and political organizing to both sides of the Atlantic, set up information exchanges and counterterrorism exchanges with Scotland Yard and in Northern Ireland. After 2001, the FBI sent agents working on counterterrorism to work with law enforcement in Cairo, Riyadh, Amman and Abu Dhabi. However, Israel is the primary catalyst for joint programs training Americans.

If Israel really were such an exceptional exchange and training partner, of course, there would be no need for a third-party promoter. However, JINSA set up its law enforcement training program quickly after 9/11 and, in 2002, sent its first delegation for "training" in Israel. It is likely that, like the Anti-Defamation League's decades of efforts to insinuate itself into the FBI, and the Jewish Telegraphic Agency's similar offer to conduct intelligence gathering, the JINSA programs are of much greater value to Israel than to the United States.

---

[282] Blankfort, Jeffrey, "A War for Israel," *LeftCurve*, April, 2004. Issue No. 28

[283] Karen DeYoung, *Soldier, the Life of Colin Powell* [Knopf, New York, 2006]

[284] JINSA 2006 IRS form 990

Suicide bombings are not the challenge in the United States that they have been in Israel. Between 1982-2015, the total number of such attacks is four, with September 11, 2001 accounting for most of the casualties.[285] However, the training allows Israeli police to showcase their tactics (inevitably the subject of glowing newspaper reports back in the U.S.), such as quickly cleaning up attack scenes, shooting suspects in the head to avoid setting off chest explosives and how to surveil Muslim communities for extremism. It would make no sense for police in the United States to scrub crime scenes and potentially lose valuable evidence, such as was found in the Boston Marathon bombing. Since the handful of suicide bombers in the U.S. do not use chest explosives, it also makes no sense for law enforcement to be trained in the art of "head-shots." More recent policies announced in Israel to shoot Palestinian stone throwers raises the question of whether organizations like JINSA and the ADL will now attempt to train U.S. law enforcement in the use of deadly force against U.S. protesters and disenfranchised groups.

All JINSA training leaves out the most important question concerning suicide terrorism—the reason Israel continues to be a target. An honest assessment of the grievances underlying the attacks is not on the JINSA agenda.[286] Rather, close study of the tactics of "fundamentalist Islam" and transmitting the scare back into America is the real goal behind the programs, creating affinity where there should be none, as inappropriate law enforcement tactics are embedded in police units eagerly receiving free overseas trips.

The Israeli government and IAOs portray training programs for American law enforcement as goodwill gestures aimed at sharing Israeli expertise in counterterrorism with the United States. There being no centralized database of statistics, it is impossible to compile on a year-by-year basis how many American local, state and federal law enforcement officials have traveled to Israel on IAO subsidies for training. As one Israeli trainer told *The Washington Post*, "We are a little nation that has paid with blood for our experience…We don't want the American people or the American police to pay as we have."[287] However, it would be naïve to believe that such training is conducted for only the purest of motives. U.S. assistance programs for

---

[285] Chicago Project on Security and Terrorism (CPOST), 2015. Suicide Attack Database (July 24, 2015). Retrieved from http://cpostdata.uchicago.edu/ on August 17, 2015

[286] Professor Robert Pape has compiled the world's largest database of suicide terrorist attacks. His conclusion is that suicide terrorism is a disenfranchised population's asymmetric response to foreign occupation. See Robert Pape, *Dying to Win: The Strategic Logic of Suicide Terrorism* [Random House, New York, 2006]

[287] Sari Horwitz, "Israeli Experts Teach Police on Terrorism," *The Washington Post*, June 12, 2005 http://www.washingtonpost.com/wp-dyn/content/article/2005/06/11/AR2005061100648.html

foreign law enforcement are purposeful and designed from the ground up to serve U.S. national interests. They are sometimes designed in ways many Americans, and occasionally Congress, do not agree with.

U.S. assistance to foreign police began in earnest in the 1950s, with a single clear purpose: to suppress insurgent activities in key foreign countries during the Cold War. Annual aid grew to $60 million to foreign police organizations in thirty-four countries for counterinsurgency techniques, including interrogation, riot control, surveillance, weapons training and bomb disposal. In the American government view, it has kept countries on the edge from falling like dominos to communist guerillas. It also provided opportunities to U.S. contractors to sell weapons, telecom and transport equipment.

However, in 1973, when foreign police organizations were found to be abusive and corrupt, and some U.S. programs lacking clear missions and results, Congress banned assistance and terminated funding for such "public safety programs." Later, exceptions were made for counter-narcotics and counterterrorism programs with clear missions.

To implement policies aimed at stemming the supply of illegal narcotics into the United States (while doing much less about domestic demand fueling that supply), the Drug Enforcement Agency and Federal Bureau of Investigation worked with local police liaisons to combat international narcotics trafficking. In 1981, counterterrorism, investigative and police force development in Central America and the Caribbean were exempted from restrictions. In 1990, 125 countries were receiving U.S. police training assistance totaling $117 million, with most $45 million going to fight narcotics trafficking and a similar amount assisting national police forces through authorized programs.

Although spread across multiple agencies and lacking any focal point for coordination and decision making U.S. assistance and training programs to foreign police forces through the 1990s had at least three major objectives: stemming the spread of communism anti-narcotics and counter-terrorism to protect "U.S. citizens and interests."[288]

In contrast, according to a 1979 Central Intelligence Agency report, Israel's earliest "police training" assistance in African nations were in reality a cover for intelligence and covert action activities. Israel used Indonesian counterterrorism training programs as an "opportunity to collect information and engage in political action in another Moslem power."[289] A close review

[288] "Foreign Aid: Police Training and Assistance, Report to Congressional Requestors," U.S. General Accounting Office, March 1992 http://www.gao.gov/assets/220/215566.pdf

[289] "Israel: Foreign Intelligence and Security Services," March, 1979, Central Intelligence Agency

of Israeli police training funded by IAOs reveals the hidden Israeli national interests served by the sharp increase in such programs since 9/11.

Israel's 60-plus-year experience controlling, occupying and monitoring indigenous Arab populations is actively packaged and marketed by the Ministry of Commerce, public security organs and foreign affairs entities. Although some formal accords have been signed with the U.S., such as a 2007 memorandum of understanding between U.S. Director of Homeland Security Michael Chertoff and Israeli Minister Avi Dichter a great deal of the training arrangements are multi-level, promoted by IAOs and uncoordinated.

It has already been noted that the Jewish Institute for National Security Affairs is a major promoter of such programs. Given Israel's past use of training as a vehicle for intelligence gathering, the continued flow of high ranking former U.S. officials still holding security clearances and with ongoing access to classified information to Israel should raise concerns. In this light, it appears to be a free trip in exchange for Israelis debriefing U.S. military officials.

According to *Raw Story*, the Anti-Defamation League has provided Israeli-run "Extremist and Terrorist Threats" training to more than 700 U.S. police officers. Israeli perspectives likely permeate such training given to another 45,000 through the ADL's "Law Enforcement and Society" program, which is now required curriculum for all new FBI special agents.[290]

The New York Police Department imported some Israeli tactics when it set up "counterterrorism" monitoring of Muslim communities in the city, dubbed the "Demographics Unit."[291] Such "anti-terrorism" policies adopted from Israeli practices in occupied territories include the use of torture and treating common criminals as terrorists. The "Israelification" of policing in the United States "appears to have intensified police hostility towards the civilian population, blurring the lines between protesters, common criminals and terrorists."[292]

Common to any IAO training junket are well-publicized expressions of gratitude by U.S. law enforcement officials who applaud Israeli "expertise." Sometimes the timing of such training can serve Israeli narrative building,

---

http://www.serendipity.li/cia/counterspy/secret_cia_documents_on_mossad.htm#1

290 Muriel Kane, "Israeli model underlies militarization of U.S. police," *RawStory*, December 4, 2011 http://www.rawstory.com/2011/12/report-israeli-model-underlies-militarization-of-u-s-police/

291 "Are U.S. Police Training with the Israeli Military?" *Daily Kos*, December 12, 2011 http://www.dailykos.com/story/2011/12/12/1044508/-Are-U-S-Police-training-with-the-Israeli-Military#

292 Muriel Kane, "Israeli model underlies militarization of U.S. police," *RawStory*, December 4, 2011 http://www.rawstory.com/2011/12/report-israeli-model-underlies-militarization-of-u-s-police/

such as when NYPD Police Commissioner Ray Kelly embarked on his first trip to Israel just as Israel was engaged in a massive military assault on the Gaza Strip in 2009. Before she became Washington, DC's chief of police, Cathy Lanier told *The Washington Post* in 2005, "No experience in my life has had more of an impact on doing my job than going to Israel."[293]

Israeli training reinforces its self-proclaimed status as the "good guy" in a fight against unjustified Muslim, Arab, and particularly Palestinian resistance. By getting local, state and federal "buy in" to accept Israel's rivals as American enemies through professional ties with influential U.S. authorities, Israel also increases the likelihood that intense and ongoing Israeli espionage against the United States will be ignored, or if detected, treated with kid gloves. (See the author's book *Spy Trade* for more a detailed treatment of Israeli economic and national defense espionage against the United States). Today it is difficult to imagine that any major U.S. law enforcement official views taking a public stand against Israeli espionage as a career-enhancing move. Israel also boosts exports of goods (arms and related equipment) and services (training) by positioning itself as a law enforcement training center, according to a CIA report:

> *Other Israeli government organizations that provide support to the intelligence and security community are the Ministries of Finance (Customs and Excise, Investment and Securities) and Tourism, the national airline, El Al, and the national shipping line, Zim. Unofficial Zionist organizations based in Israel and Jewish communities throughout the world also give aid to Israeli operations when needed.*[294]

It is logical to assume that Israeli objectives to exert influence and gather intelligence remain the core purpose of training programs. History also confirms that IAOs, which concentrate Israel's most dedicated supporters, are under continual use by Israel to support Israeli covert operations in the United States.

Almost like a competing government, the Israel lobby also has its own diplomatic corps. Deputy Secretary of State Antony J. Blinken on June 8, 2015, made an extraordinary introductory remark to the American Jewish Committee's "Global Forum":

---

[293] Sari Horwitz, "Israeli Experts Teach Police on Terrorism," *The Washington Post*, June 12, 2005 http://www.washingtonpost.com/wp-dyn/content/article/2005/06/11/AR2005061100648.html

[294] "Israel: Foreign Intelligence and Security Services," March, 1979. Central Intelligence Agency http://www.serendipity.li/cia/counterspy/secret_cia_documents_on_mossad.htm#1

You've been called the State Department of the Jewish people, a title so apt I may start giving out some assignments today.[295]

A review of history reveals that the volume of "assignments" flowing from the American Jewish Committee to the U.S. State Department far exceeds any likely to flow in the opposite direction. More problematic is official recognition—even though made with levity—that the American Jewish Committee represents something more than its 294 employees, big donors (who gave $47.9 million in 2012[296] though its global revenue may be much more) and membership base, much less the entire "Jewish people."

The American Jewish Committee was founded in 1906 by 58 representatives of different Jewish communities as a district-based organization. Early on, the organization had designs on becoming quasi-governmental, through elections and a congress formed of delegates from various Jewish organizations. Nevertheless, noting the failure of an earlier attempt to create an American Jewish congress along similar representative lines, the American Jewish Committee settled on the non-representative, non-elective model most IAOs have today, according to internal reports:

...A third suggestion which was made was that a small committee be formed of persons who, while representative of American Jewry, need not necessarily be formally accredited representatives of any organization...this suggestion also met with opposition, but it was the only one upon which a majority of the conferees could agree...[297]

Like the Zionist Organization of America, the American Jewish Committee (AJC) was granted a charter of incorporation by the New York State Legislature in 1911, with a broad international mandate rather than a domestic social welfare function. That mandate states it exists:

1) To prevent the infraction of the civil and religious rights of Jews in any part of the world; 2) to render all lawful assistance and to take appropriate remedial action in the event of threatened or actual invasion or restriction of such rights or of unfavorable discrimination with respect thereto; 3) to secure for Jews equality of economic, social and educational opportunities; 4) to alleviate

---

[295] Antony J. Blinken, "Remarks at the American Jewish Committee's Global Forum 2015" at the Washington Hilton. U.S. Department of State, June 8, 2015 http://www.state.gov/s/d/2015/243266.htm

[296] An internal ADL PowerPoint presentation leaked in 2015 twice pegs total AJC 2013 revenue at $352,594,099, far more that the $55,699,731 reported to the IRS.

[297] Ninth Annual Report of the American Jewish Committee, *The American Jewish Year Book*, Vol. 18, September 28, 1916 to September 16, 1917, 328

the consequences of persecution and to afford relief from calamities affecting Jews wherever they may occur.[298]

AJC built on B'nai B'rith's early work on behalf of Jews throughout the world it felt were being marginalized—in the AJC's case, through influence on U.S. foreign policy. A particular emphasis was reacting to Russian pogroms, after fleeting organizations such as Relief of Sufferers by Russian Massacres hosted successful fundraisers but then quickly disbanded.

Founding executive member and financier Jacob Schiff, who was determined to strike back at Czarist Russia over its pogroms, worked diligently to raise funding for Imperial Japan's war against Russia. Japan sneak attacked Russian ships at Port Arthur on February 8-9 of 1904, in a bid to win hegemony over Manchuria and Korea. Schiff met with the Japanese official in charge of bond sales, Baron Korekiyo Takahashi, and became convinced that supporting Japan would strike a fatal blow against Russia. He then urged major U.S. banks and insurance companies to buy up Japanese bonds going on sale May 12, 1904. Ultimately, $180 million was raised in the U.S. to help Japan win its war. The Emperor of Japan bestowed upon Schiff an honor normally given only to foreign princes, a visit to his Palace.[299] Japan asked the U.S. to mediate a peace settlement that was conducted in Portsmouth, New Hampshire in 1905. President Theodore Roosevelt, like a subordinate left to write up meeting minutes, was less partisan than Schiff, and wanted to "end the war on terms that left both Russia and Japan a role to play in northeast China."[300]

In its 1916 annual report, the American Jewish Committee reported raising $3,760 to "undertake a thorough investigation of the Jews in belligerent countries, especially Russia." It fought congressional legislation on literacy tests for immigrants in order "to safeguard the rights of Jewish immigrants who are refugees from persecution." The AJC also tried to prevent the Federal Reserve from extending $25 million in trade credit to the Russian government. It pressured the Associated Press to include information about the plight of Jews whenever it wrote about Russia. The

---

[298] Ninth Annual Report of the American Jewish Committee, *The American Jewish Year Book*, Vol. 18, September 28, 1916 to September 16, 1917, 334

[299] Gary Dean Best, "Financing a Foreign War: Jacob H. Schiff and Japan, 1904-05," *American Jewish Historical Review* no. 61 1971/72: 2, Stephen Birmingham,. *Our Crowd: The Great Jewish Families of New York* [New York: Harper & Row, 1967]:3 Naomi Wiener Cohen, *Jacob H. Schiff: a Study in American Jewish Leadership.* [Brandeis University Press, Hanover, N.H. 1999]:4, Cyrus Adler, *Jacob H. Schiff* [Jewish Publication Society, Philadelphia: 1947]

[300] U.S. Department of State, "Office of the Historian, Milestones: 1899-1913, the Treaty of Portsmouth and the Russo-Japanese War 1904-1905" https://history.state.gov/milestones/1899-1913/portsmouth-treaty

AJC also successfully intervened to prevent the extradition to Russia under a Russia-U.S. extradition treaty of two Jews—Jan Pouren and Christian Rudovitz—who had been convicted of arson and murder during revolutionary uprisings in Russia in 1905. Later, the Committee saw an opportunity to shape the aftermath of WWI, according to internal reports:

> *In addition to being compelled to face the need for relief on a large scale of our coreligionists in the war zones, a war of such magnitude might present to the Jews of neutral countries, and especially to the Jews of the United States, opportunities for influencing changes in the political status of the Jews to reside in countries where they do not enjoy equal rights. Both aspects of the situation were closely studied.*[301]

The Committee expected to have a significant role in any future peace conference—almost like a nation-state—by organizing an elite gathering in Washington with delegates from other major Jewish organizations to consolidate a list of demands for the United States to incorporate in its negotiations. Cyrus Adler, chairman of the American Jewish Committee, wanted to call it this a conference, but Justice Louis Brandeis insisted on using the more government-like designation a "congress." Though Israel was not yet in existence the American Jewish Committee summed up its core mission in 1915 as the "accomplishment of Israel's work in America."

The transfer of Jewish populations from the Ottoman Empire "under whose tolerant sway the Jews had lived peacefully for several centuries," concerned the Committee. It urged the U.S. to get involved under obscure 1891 doctrines emitted by President Harrison to Congress that "banishment" of large populations was "not a local question" and "acting in the name and at the behest of humanity whether American interests are involved or not," even though internally the AJC assessed that "it [the United States] was supposed to have no standing."

Today the American Jewish Committee routinely meets with heads of state and foreign military leaders to press Israel's agenda, whether it is pushing for strict sanctions on Iran, or justifying Israel's treatment and ongoing occupation of Palestinian land. If there is a Jewish community in the host country, the AJC involves its leadership in these meetings. It also leverages the reputation of the Israel lobby in the U.S., which is well known throughout many foreign capitals. The AJC delegations usually find open doors. In that sense, the American Jewish Committee also acts to augment Israel's own diplomatic corps. In 1985, AJC President Howard Friedman met with the Pope, urging the Vatican to establish diplomatic ties with Israel,

---

[301] Ninth Annual Report of the American Jewish Committee, *The American Jewish Year Book*, Vol. 18, September 28, 1916 to September 16, 1917, 308

saying:

> *Such a move would reinforce the legitimization of Israel as a sovereign state and compel Arab rejectionist states to give up their illusion that Israel will somehow disappear.*[302]

In 1989, an AJC delegation traveled to Tokyo to meet with Japanese government, trade, labor and business group leaders to suppress the publication of books by Masami Uno, an author of popular books such as *If you understand Jews, you will come to understand the world.* In response, the Japanese foreign ministry issued a letter directed to the entire domestic publishing industry not to print any books that might "unintentionally offend the most sensitive areas of Jewish psychology."[303] Ironically, the positive reception accorded the AJC and the response to its demands may have been influenced by lingering memories of Schiff's powerful interventions on Japan's behalf—something the AJC delegation certainly realized and documented. "Perceptions that the U.S. Jews might be more powerful than they really are—controlling, as Uno charged, GM, IBM or other major companies—could make Japanese more willing to listen to their concerns."[304]

Two years later, the AJCs Pacific Rim Institute director announced that Japan was voting in the United Nations to rescind a 1975 resolution equating Zionism with racism. That same year, the AJC led another delegation, ostensibly to reward Japan—which had a rare trade deficit with Israel, due to Israel's heavy diamond exports—by opening up more direct trade with Israel—that is, if Japan stopped being too sympathetic to Palestinians or too vocally opposed to Israeli settlements in the occupied territories.[305]

In 1992, an AJC delegation met with Hungarian Foreign Minister Geza Jeszenszky about Hungarian Democratic Forum vice-president Istvan Csurka's observations that a Jewish plutocracy existed. Jeszenszky issued reassuring remarks to the delegation that, "It is well-known that international plutocracy is multinational and has nothing to do with racial or religious circles." In exchange, the AJC affirmed its view, without quoting any survey or other empirical evidence, that "anti-Semitism is least in Hungary for all of

---

302 American Jewish Committee letter to the editor printed in *The New York Times*, November 19, 1985

303 David Rosenfeld, "Anti-Semitic Books Spark U.S. Initiative," *The Daily Yomiuri*, December 13, 1989.

304 David Rosenfeld, "Anti-Semitic Books Spark U.S. Initiative," *The Daily Yomiuri*, December 13, 1989.

305 T.R. Reid, "Japan, Israel Improving Commercial Ties; New Trade Links Raise Prospects for Closer Political Cooperation," *The Washington Post, Foreign Service*, July 12, 1991

Europe."[306]

The same year, alarmed that so many Soviet Jews were applying to immigrate to Germany rather than Israel, a 60-member-strong task force of AJC members met with local Jewish leaders to press the German government on the issue, while urging Chancellor Helmut Kohl to speed up the processing of Jewish claims on properties in East Germany seized by the Nazis and kept by the Communist governments that they be returned to their rightful owners.[307] The AJC also proposed that Chancellor Kohl could tender loan guarantees for Israel to settle Soviet Jews because of "East Germany's lack of reparations for Nazi crimes."[308]

In 1993, the AJC formally called for U.S. airstrikes on Bosnian Serb targets and a lifting of all arms embargoes on Bosnia. In a position at odds with its concern about Palestinian victims of ethnic cleansing, AJC called for international action against those responsible for atrocities and ethnic cleansing in former Yugoslavia.

In Germany, the AJC advised the government not to try to influence Holocaust education in the U.S. The Konrad Adenauer Foundation, which received German government funding, had offered organizers of the U.S. Holocaust Museum "millions of dollars" to fund programs that would study post-war German democracy-building efforts in conjunction with Holocaust history courses in the United States.[309] German representatives approached George H. W. Bush administration officials and IAOs, suggesting that U.S. high schools add this study of post-war German democracy to the growing number of Holocaust history courses being offered around the country. The AJC reaction was swift, as reported by *The Washington Post*:

> *A U.S. diplomat in Bonn said the Germans were told that school curricula are controlled by the states, not the federal government. And a senior official of the American Jewish Committee said he advised the Germans that efforts to steer attention away from the Holocaust Museum would not help Germany's image.* [310]

The American diplomat apparently had no idea how JCRCs and the lobby maneuvered all sorts of initiatives on Israel's behalf, from bilateral economic

---

306 "Hungarian Foreign Minister Addresses the UN," *MTI Econews*, September 25, 1992

307 Mark Heinrich, "Germany tempts Soviet Jews," *The Independent*, February 7, 1992

308 "Bonn may help Israel over loans," *The Independent*, February 5, 1992

309 Marc Fisher, "Germany's Holocaust Fears; Museum Offered Millions to Update Image," *The Washington Post*, March 30, 1993

310 Marc Fisher, "Germany's Holocaust Fears; Museum Offered Millions to Update Image," *The Washington Post*, March 30, 1993

and trade programs to education and training initiatives, through state legislatures.

Publication of findings from surveys chartered by the AJC are meant to trigger action for residents of U.S. and foreign cities to mend their ways. Like ADL surveys and later The Israel Project, some AJC surveys appear to be "weaponized," through exposure and embarrassment, to punish or encourage changes in foreign countries and the United States—often through leading questions.

Like many other major IAOs, the American Jewish Committee's activities appeared on the screen of the FBI. However, in AJC's case the red flag was its survey activity. Perhaps without realizing that the Justice Department was only about a year away from the *de facto* termination of foreign agent enforcement attempts over IAOs, in 1969 the Special Agent in Command of the FBI's New York field office observed a change in AJC's survey bombsight. The agent addressed these concerns in a classified memo to the FBI director, which stated:

> *The enclosed LHM [Letterhead memo] reveals that the AJC has recently conducted a study of anti-Israeli propaganda as opposed to anti-Semitism. The AJC proposed definite steps to be taken to further the interest of the State of Israel…In view of the possibility that the AJC has incurred an obligation under the Foreign Agents Registration Act of 1938 as amended, it is recommended that this matter be referred to the Department of Justice for its opinion.*[311]

In 1991, a short AJC-chartered poll published in *The Wall Street Journal* was succinct about Austria. According to Gallup, one-third of Austrians disliked Jews, and one-fifth wanted them barred from top jobs and believed the country would be better off without them.[312]

In 1992, a Roper poll charted by the AJC found that forty-seven percent of New Yorkers felt Jews had "too much influence" in city life and politics, with sixty-three percent of blacks and sixty-six percent of Hispanics feeling the same. Rather than use the data to analyze underlying causes, build bridges, or discuss how to "grow and share the pie," David Singer of the AJC brushed it all off as sour grapes:

---

311 "FBI SAC, New York recommends FARA referral of AJC," The Israel Lobby Archive, http://IsraelLobby.org/AJC/07231969_AJC.pdf

312 "Austrians Dislike Jews," *The Wall Street Journal*, October 25, 1991

> *We are dealing here, unfortunately, with a zero-sum game in which groups that are less well-off manifest resentment, envy, jealousy and that is the focus of animosity toward Jews.*[313]

In Britain, the AJC surveyed Holocaust knowledge, then used the data to trumpet back home that Americans were comparatively lacking in adequate knowledge, while becoming increasingly infected with denial, reporting:

> *Adults in Britain have more knowledge about the Holocaust than do U.S. adults, according to a Gallup poll for London's Daily Telegraph. Survey questions were the same as those posed to U.S. adults in a survey last month by the American Jewish Committee. The polls show 41% of Britons, vs. 35% of Americans, know 6 million Jews were killed during the Holocaust; 76% of Britons, vs. 62% of Americans, know that Auschwitz, Dachau and Treblinka were Nazi concentration camps; 7% of Britons, vs. 22% of Americans, said it seems possible the Nazi extermination might not have happened.*[314]

Like a sovereign state, the AJC occasionally issues threats against other players in the international system, in one news report threatening to reveal tightly held UN information it had somehow obtained:

> *A leading American Jewish organization said today that it would publish a list of 40,000 names of possible World War II criminals contained in secret United Nations archives unless the archives are opened to inspection soon. The threat came from the American Jewish Committee on the eve of a meeting here of representatives of the 17 member countries of the United Nations War Crimes Commission to discuss opening the archives. Last month, several countries expressed fear that public inspection of the archives could lead to unfounded accusations against people still alive.*[315]

In the 1990s, the AJC began to insist that it was not—in fact—an organization primarily dedicated to advancing what it originally termed "Jewish interests" on the global stage, but was instead a "human rights" organization. In subsequent clarifications, it insisted that since Jews were the canary in the coalmine, or the first to suffer human rights abuses, they of

---

313 "47% in N.Y. Say Jews Are Too Influential," *The Washington Post*, October 17, 1992

314 Arlene Vigoda, "Holocaust Knowledge," *USA Today*, May 19, 1993

315 "Group Threatens to Publish List of War-Crime Suspects," Special to *The New York Times*, October 13, 1987

course, warranted special AJC monitoring and support—implying that the AJC did not really have to do anything differently than what it had done since 1906. The AJC claimed its office in Berlin, for example, is really a "sentinel against bias."

In politics, AJC issued judgements on foreign affairs that some presidents viewed as pivotal for the future. In 1991, President George H.W. Bush linked U.S. loan guarantees to Israel's halting settlement expansion and not using settlements as a destination for the huge influx of Soviet Jews. Bush even dared to call out the Israel lobby, a move which threatened to ignite anti-Semitism, retired AJC head Hyman Bookbinder, told *The Washington Post*:

> *Hyman Bookbinder, everyone's favorite Jewish lobbyist who recently retired from the American Jewish Committee, is an impassioned advocate of Israel. He deplores Bush's methods and tactics, but thinks that he has a point on substance. To Bookbinder, Bush's Sept. 12 attack on the Jewish lobby and his depiction of himself as "one lonely little guy" up against thousands of lobbyists, was "a political temper tantrum, a disgrace" and a clumsy and dangerous move that could ignite ever-menacing antisemitism.*[316]

The George H.W. Bush administration made a last-ditch effort to repair relations with the AJC by sending over a State Department official. Edward Djerejian, after speaking at the organization's 87th annual conference, was dubbed an "Arabist" pandering to Israel, sent by an administration unable to deliver anything of substance. That November, Bush lost his bid for reelection.

The American Jewish Committee provides positive reinforcement to friendly journalists through its "Mass Media Award," and there are many heads to pat. Recipients have included Walter Cronkite, *New York Times* reporters Tom Friedman and A.M. Rosenthal, Bill Moyers, the MacNeil/Lehrer Report, Martin Peretz of the *New Republic*, and *The Washington Post* publisher Katherine Graham.

Long considered one of the "big four" organizations, the AJC did not seek membership in the Conference of Presidents of Major American Jewish Organizations until 1991. It did so to even more heavily influence U.S. foreign policy on Israel according to news reports:

> *'I think this is the ultimate recognition that all parts of the organized American Jewish community now look to the Conference of Presidents as the spokesman for organized Jewry in*

---

[316] Mary McGrory, "Hardly a Lonely Stand on Israel," *The Washington Post*, October 1, 1991

> *areas involving Israel and foreign policy,' said Julius Berman, a former Presidents Conference chairman. Said American Jewish Committee deputy director Shula Bahat: 'We had the sense that the kinds of challenges the American Jewish community is going to face in the near future, particularly where Israel and Soviet Jewry are involved, will require as much unity as possible.'*[317]

Similarly, upon reopening its office in Berlin in 1998, the American Jewish Committee's official announcement sounded more like the proclamation of a foreign government reestablishing diplomatic relations through opening a long-shuttered embassy, according to yet another *Washington Post* article:

> *With Germany now playing host to the fastest-growing Jewish population in the world, leaders of the American Jewish Committee today opened their first office here since the Nazi era, vowing to sustain the memory of the Holocaust and to fight any revival of right-wing extremism… 'The U.S. lags far behind Israel in understanding developments in Germany over the past 50 years,' [David] Harris said in an interview. 'This must change because Germany remains important to the Jewish future in more ways than we can imagine.' 'Before the Nazis rose to power in 1933, Berlin was a flourishing financial and cultural metropolis that owed much of its dynamism to a lively and prosperous Jewish community…'*[318]

No Israeli claim has seemingly been too small for a formal AJC inquiry seeking active involvement of the top officials from U.S. federal agencies (particularly the Treasury Department) and top foreign governments: unpaid insurance policies on Holocaust victims; gold stolen by Nazis and hidden in Swiss banks; property that went behind the Iron Curtain. Utterly lost on the AJC is the irony of all its insistence on reparations even as Israel continues to appropriate and annex lands and property that do not belong to it.

The advocacy segment of the Israel lobby, when added together, claimed to have 2,082 employees, 6,633 volunteers and a total budget of $403.5 million in 2012. These numbers do not fully reveal their power and ability to move America, however, by working with federations and JCRCs, coordinating with the Israeli government, either through its embassy or consulates, through programs fielded from its own offices around the world, and by signaling how large donors should contribute to politicians, advocacy IAOs form the tip of the Israel lobby's spear in the United States.

---

[317] J.J. Goldberg, "Joining the Pack," *The Jerusalem Report*, April 4, 1991

[318] William Drosdiak, "Jewish Group Returns to Berlin-U.S. Organization Aims to Improve Understanding," *The Washington Post*, February 10, 1998

7 EDUCATION

Until 2010, automatic IRS recognition that promoting Zionism in the United States has "educational" and other social welfare functions rarely hit a speed bump. That year, however, a prospective IAO called "Z Street" ran into trouble. Z Street was apparently named as a confrontational play off "J Street, "an IAO that due to some "moderate" positions such as opposing settlement expansion, was considered to be anti-Israel by the Conference of Presidents of Major American Jewish Organizations and some other IAOs. After Z Street applied for tax-exempt status, it received IRS requests for more information. The IAO's stated mission was "educating the public about Zionism; about the facts relating to the Middle East and to the existence of Israel as a Jewish State; and about Israel's right to refuse to negotiate with, make concessions to, or appease terrorists."

Z Street sued the IRS in October 2010, claiming that an IRS official communicated to the group that its application for tax-exempt status was delayed because it had been assigned to a "special unit." Z Street decried it had been targeted solely for being connected to Israel. The IRS was concerned that the organization intended to engage mostly in activities not permitted under Section 501(c)(3). Its particular concerns were about "applications from organizations whose activities relate to Israel, and whose positions with respect to Israel contradict the current policies of the U.S." After decades of rubber-stamping IAO applications—although most did not have such confrontational mission statements—the move was clearly a departure. As previously mentioned, the United Israel Appeal's leadership believed it had a blank check to do anything, including fund illegal settlements, without worrying about enforcement from the United States. Senator J.W. Fulbright's written inquiries and complaints to the IRS during formal hearings were met with a stone wall of delay and terse IRS responses.

Z Street's lawsuit, based on claims that its First Amendment rights had been denied, also sought public disclosure about an IRS "special Israel unit" and its screening activities. The question of whether or not the IRS improperly applied a more "stringent" standard to Z Street remained open in mid-2015, despite repeated IRS attempts to get the case dismissed. However, the case may have been evidence that after decades of tacit acceptance that any and all types of Israel advocacy activity was automatically entitled to operate with the benefits of tax-exempt status, a long and overdue review process for applications was finally implemented by the Obama administration's IRS tax-exempt organization unit.

One of the oldest "educational" IAOs is the Jewish Telegraphic Agency (JTA). The JTA traces its roots to the Jewish Correspondence Bureau founded in The Hague in 1917 by Jacob Landau. It sought to disseminate news to Jewish communities worldwide, especially from European theatres of war. By 1925, the Jewish Telegraphic Agency claimed its cable subscription news feed was serving over 400 newspapers. Today, the news organization uses the World Wide Web and claims global leadership on broadly defined "issues of Jewish interest and concern" and journalistic independence—due to funding from fifty Jewish federations in North America and eighteen Jewish foundations.

Officials inside the U.S. federal government initially viewed the Jewish Telegraphic Agency as either an organized Jewish interest group, or, after the founding of Israel, an Israeli foreign agent that used news coverage as a pretext to get inside such sensitive agencies as the U.S. State Department to then relay information directly back to Tel Aviv. With the declassification of critical FBI and Justice Department files released in July of 2015[319] and referenced below it has become clearer why this was so. Unless otherwise noted, the following references and quotes about JTA are from these files.

In 1939, citing changes in media access policies announced by the attorney general, Jewish Telegraphic Agency reporter Pat Frank, who ran the Washington Bureau from the National Press Club, wrote FBI Director J. Edgar Hoover asking for an interview on "Nazi and anti-Semitic organizations, which have become prominent within the last year." Hoover rebuffed him, stating FBI policies on interviews had not changed.

In 1940, the editor of the Jewish Telegraphic Agency, H. Wishengrad, complained to the FBI that it had been scooped because the FBI failed to notify JTA, as it had other news organizations in New York City, of the arrest of seventeen alleged plotters of the Christian Front. The FBI grudgingly added the Jewish Telegraphic Agency to its distribution list. The Christian

---

319 "The Jewish Telegraphic Agency offers to spy for the FBI," Israel Lobby Archive http://israellobby.org/jta/

Front was an organization founded in 1938 after radio priest Father Charles Coughlin urged activists to launch a "crusade against the anti-Christian forces of the Red Revolution." The group organized anti-war rallies and boycotted Jewish businesses. The law-enforcement raid seized only a 1873 Springfield rifle and an old saber. Charges were dropped in 1941.

Like the ADL, the Jewish Telegraphic Agency was interested in a close, insider relationship with the FBI. Founder Jacob Landau secretly offered the FBI an attractive partnership at a time the bureau was struggling to have an effective presence in Latin America. The FBI typically rotated in agents lacking in language skills or cultural experience, who then failed to provide any intelligence or law enforcement value.[320] In a signed proposal to the FBI dated April 23, 1942, Landau offered to cover Latin America for the FBI as a plausibly deniable intelligence service leveraging Jewish correspondents in key countries for $540 per week. Landau emphasized in his proposal that:

> *Particularly intimate contacts have been established with the Jewish Groups and Leaders in South America. While the Germans and Italians in South American number in the millions, the American and British Population in South America is numerically insignificant. On the other hand, there are 600,000 Jews living in South America, many of whom occupy important positions in commerce, industry and the free professions. They are an important source of information, possessing many intimate contacts with politicians, government officials, etc. etc. It is suggested that a special effort be made to utilize this important source of information. It is needless to point out that the Jews in South America are anti-Nazi and are vitally interested in the victory of the United Nations. Special representatives should be appointed in each of the countries, not only in the capitals, but in the various provincial centers…In the two largest countries, Argentina and Brazil, a weekly budget of $400 to $500 would be required in order to cover adequately the most important cities as well as the various provincial centers.*

Landau further proposed to spy on U.S.-based foreign language speaking groups of interest, such as Ukrainians. The weekly costs quoted were not insignificant, amounting to over $7,500 in 2015 dollars. By 1946, Landau claimed the Office of Strategic Services, precursor to the CIA, "paid $300 per month for the news service," and that "the Office of War Information and other organizations receive the service at varying rates or free of charge."

The Jewish Telegraphic Agency proposal both tempted and angered the FBI. It refused to pay for any specialty services, but nevertheless sought out

[320] Tim Weiner, *Enemies: A History of the FBI*, [New York, Random House, 2012]

Jewish Telegraphic Agency news free of charge by other means, internally noting, "The bulletins are available through confidential informants." It rebuffed another solicitation in 1946—in part to avoid any potential Jewish Telegraphic Agency claims that the FBI was a client. An FBI file memo read:

> *Jacob Landau, a subject in the Alto case, is Secretary and Managing Director of the JTA. He at one time tried to sell the Bureau the service of this agency and of the Overseas News Agency with which he is also connected but was refused…recommend deletion of his [New York Field Office agent] name from the [Jewish Telegraphic Agency] mailing list.*

The Foreign Agents Registration Section felt information in possession of the Bureau revealed "a possible violation of Federal law on the part of the Overseas News Agency, the Jewish Telegraphic Agency and Jacob Landau for failure to properly register as agents of a foreign principal." The FBI also became concerned that the Jewish Telegraphic Agency was operating a branch in the Soviet Union.

A conflict between JTA and the FBI arose after the Jewish Telegraphic Agency distributed an erroneous story written by correspondent Milton Friedman (not the famous economist) that the FBI had begun to use "Jewish" as an ethnicity in criminal activity reports, rather than "white." An internal FBI memo recorded, "It is not believed that the Jewish Telegraphic Agency can be considered reputable enough to warranting your contacting them…" over the mistake. The FBI further charged that:

> *The Jewish Telegraphic Agency is not of the best reputation. You recall that Beatrice Heinman, who has been named as a Community Courier, is connected with Jacob Landau, who had contacts with Soviet representatives and Communist Party members and was formerly head of the Jewish Telegraphic Agency…In 1944 the Jewish Telegraphic Agency inaugurated a news service with the Soviet Union by arrangement with the Jewish press of Moscow and with the permission of the Soviet Union.*

FBI Assistant Director Louis Nichols nevertheless met with Friedman to receive a formal apology in early 1950. Friedman suddenly offered to spy on the Soviet Union for the FBI using his access as a reporter, claims the FBI:

> *Friedman then got down to the purpose of his coming to the Bureau. He wanted to know if he could be used in any way to penetrate the Russian Embassy, Tass News Agency or the Daily*

> *Worker for the purpose of security information. I told him, of course, we would not be interested in having anybody do anything like this. He wondered what he should do and I told him as long as he was a reporter he should be a good reporter and not permit himself to be used. I advised him that any time he ran across anything he felt we should know about we would be glad to receive it as we would from any reporter. Friedman is a fast talker and he appeared sincere although I could not help but wonder if he was telling the truth as to the real reason for coming in. He apologized again for the St Louis [FBI using "Jewish" designation on criminal reports] story and for the subsequent involvement of the Bureau. He stated that since that, he is very sensitive when he mentions the FBI.*

The FBI kept careful records that it consulted whenever dealing with the Jewish Telegraphic Agency noting, "there are over 120 miscellaneous references to the Agency scattered throughout Security files on various subjects." Whether it viewed the organization as a for-hire private intelligence service that offered news services, or a news service organization that offered for-hire private intelligence services is uncertain. In 1950, as Landau stepped down from management, the FBI became convinced that not only was the Jewish Telegraphic Agency receiving funding from the Israeli government—but also, through its tight coordination, it was rewriting Israeli government communiqués for distribution as news. The FBI reported internally:

> *...Landau made a deal with Gershon Agronsky, head of the Israeli Ministry of Press, whereby the Israel government would transmit routine instructions and directions to its consuls and embassies abroad through the wire facilities of the JTA. Such items would be given a dateline and would be written to some extent in ordinary journalistic terminology to give the appearance of bona fide news dispatches...arrangements at New York are handled by Dr. Nahum Goldman, head of the Jewish Agency for Palestine in New York City.*
>
> *The Israeli Government, which is seriously short of dollar credits, is supposed to be underwriting the operations of JTA to the extent of $5,000 per month...*

The FBI investigated the Jewish Telegraphic Agency's new editor in chief, Boris Smolar, for espionage in the 1950s for handing "to the Russian Embassy confidential information." Under the JTA's reorganization, the incoming chairman of the board was Rudolph Sonneborn. Herman Edelsberg of the Anti-Defamation League sent one of the FBI's top officials,

L.B. Nichols, a *National Jewish Post* clipping from April 7, 1950, announcing the change, with a cover note saying, "This means more responsibility in JTA news handling," over which Nichols scrawled, "It is about time." However, the FBI was steadily compiling a 6,000-page file about smuggling fronts including photostats of internal documents on one of the very first, called the "Sonneborn Institute." In 1945 Rudolph Sonneborn had, after a visit by Jewish Agency executive David Ben-Gurion, founded a massive weapons and supply smuggling network in the United States funded by wealthy Zionists and IAO leaders, according to researcher Ricky Dale Calhoun:

> *...the conspiracy began with a meeting on 1 July 1945 in the New York penthouse apartment of Rudolf Sonneborn, scion of a wealthy American Jewish family that had made its fortune in the oil and chemical business. Besides Sonneborn, those present at the meeting were Henry Montor, director of United Jewish Appeal, the fundraising arm of the Jewish Agency in the United States; David Ben-Gurion, chairman of the Executive of the Jewish Agency... Sonneborn and his associates eventually adopted the legal cover of a charity, the Sonneborn Institute, dedicated to the relief of European Jews. In fact, the group became the fundraisers, facilitators, and behind-the-scenes masterminds of the Haganah's illegal armaments procurement effort in the United States.*[321]

The JTA's next major run-ins over whether it was an intelligence organization or a legitimate, though noncommercial, foreign-funded news service, was with the U.S. Department of State and Senator J.W. Fulbright's investigation of foreign agents active in U.S. politics and media.

On January 28, 1963, the U.S. State Department refused to allow the previously mentioned Milton Friedman to attend a briefing about the resignation of the Special Representative of the Palestine Conciliation Commission, Dr. Joseph E. Johnson. When Friedman had requested access, the Director of the Office of Near Eastern Affairs used the opportunity to question the accuracy of Friedman's reporting. The State Department later disavowed any linkage between that discussion and his not being invited.

The JTA came under scrutiny from the Senate Foreign Relations Committee hearings in May and August of 1963 about the activities of foreign agents in the United States. Under the 1938 Foreign Agents Registration Act, foreign funding for propaganda and lobbying had to be declared and kept on file at a special office in the U.S. Department of Justice. Letters seized under subpoena from the Jewish Agency's New York-based American Section

---

321 Ricky Dale Calhoun, "Arming David: The Haganah's illegal arms procurement network in the United States 1945-1949," *Journal of Palestine Studies* Vol. XXXVI, No. 4 (Summer 2007), 22–32

revealed the Jewish Agency had not only secretly acquired and owned the Jewish Telegraphic Agency since June 28, 1951, but was then paying $1,750 per week to make up for shortfalls from American sources such as the United Israel Appeal.[322] In 2015 dollars, the Jewish Agency pumped, on average, $770,000 per year into the Jewish Telegraphic Agency.[323]

It was all a result of "acute financial difficulties" which "jeopardized its continued existence," according to a letter to Fulbright by JTA president Eleazar Lipsky. Nevertheless, Lipsky was frank about the role of the Jewish Telegraphic Agency scouring the globe for information that would be analyzed and brought forth for action, writing to Fulbright that:

> *It[s] sole purpose and its sole function has been to report as accurately and objectively as human frailties permit those developments anywhere in the world of special concern or interest to the Jewish people, to bring to light information which their well-being required had [and] to provide the information on which Jewish Leadership could take informed action.*[324]

Since the mid-1950s, the Jewish Agency hid funding to the JTA. Funds were hidden within larger "grants and subventions" line item inside its reports to the Justice Department. The Jewish Agency formed a holding company called the Jewish Telegraphic News Agency to own the organization's stock, it claimed, so it could easily be spun off as soon as American funders and owners could reassume ownership. It was clear at the time by its heavy investment that Israel highly valued the abilities of the Jewish Telegraphic Organization to collect, agitate and influence even more than other American IAOs.

The Jewish Agency's legal counsel claimed it never "attempted to influence the editorial policy" of the Jewish Telegraphic Agency.[325] However, Senator J.W. Fulbright questioned the independence of the Jewish Telegraphic Agency from the quasi-governmental Jewish Agency, given its ownership and purpose. The Jewish Agency's representative, Isadore Hamlin claimed, unconvincingly, "We owned it, but we did not control in any way at

---

[322] "Activities of Agents of Foreign Principals in the U.S.," *Congressional Record*, May 23, 1963 1237, 1284

[323] "Activities of Agents of Foreign Principals in the U.S.," *Congressional Record*, May 23, 1963 1411

[324] "Activities of Agents of Foreign Principals in the U.S.," *Congressional Record*, August 1, 1963 1773

[325] "Activities of Agents of Foreign Principals in the U.S.," *Congressional Record*, May 23, 1963 1286, 1284

all the affairs of this Agency."[326] Fulbright later pointed to an internal Jewish Agency directive designed to hide its ownership of the Jewish Telegraphic Agency. "I must ask JTA to check with the Jewish Agency all texts and general communications which refer to JTA's relationship to the Jewish Agency, as they must be cleared with us before being sent out." Fulbright asked, "Don't you think that speaks for itself as to your relationship to the Jewish Telegraphic Agency?"[327]

Today, as in the past, influencing opinion makers and focusing on Israel is the major role of the Jewish Telegraphic Agency. Much of this burden is shared with weekly Jewish publications in American cities with a substantial Jewish population that redistribute JTA news, and make other good use of JTA's content when the need arises to present a monolithic Jewish "viewpoint." It claims to the IRS that:

> *JTA's Mission is to be an indispensable independent resource to the Jewish people, with special emphasis on current and potential Jewish leaders, activists and opinion makers—by providing compelling news and analysis about Israel and the global Jewish community in a format that is timely, meaningful and relevant JTA will also be the Jewish reference point for non-Jewish press and opinion makers—a respected, reliable source for the Jewish perspective on issues that matter.*[328]

The Jewish Telegraphic Agency would have any reader who took its mission seriously believe that anti-Semitism was the motive behind espionage prosecutions of two AIPAC officials caught passing classified information to the Israeli government; that the U.S. invasion of Iraq was a smart policy, backed by most American Jews; that the pursuit of confessed Israel spy Ben-Ami Kadish was a vindictive attempt by U.S. counter-intelligence to find the highly placed mole who helped task convicted spy Jonathan Pollard, and simultaneously tarnish Israel's image.[329] The claimed independence gained by obtaining funding from Jewish federations rather than the Jewish Agency exists only on paper. JTA continues to be a voice following Israel government cues for Israel advocacy in America.

Questioning the amount of resources devoted to raising American public consciousness of the Jewish Holocaust and its underlying purposes is a taboo

---

326 "Activities of Agents of Foreign Principals in the U.S.," *Congressional Record*, May 23, 1963 1393

327 1395 Activities of Agents of Foreign Principals in the U.S., Congressional Record, May 23, 1963

328 Jewish Telegraphic Agency 2013 IRS form 990

329 Leslie Susser, "Kadish affair: bid to find 'super mole?'" *The Jewish Telegraphic Agency*, April 28, 2008.

some IAO leaders conflate with questioning facts about the Holocaust itself. However, it is valuable to examine what role IAOs believe promoting Holocaust memorialization has in modern-day America without questioning the generally accepted historical Holocaust narrative.

According to historian Peter Novick, in the aftermath of WWII the Holocaust was not characterized as such by American Jews working either in the American government or Hollywood. Both sought to de-emphasize the victimhood of Jews during the war in order to avoid charges that Jews had dragged America into war with Nazi Germany.[330] In the early 1960s, only two new research books about the Holocaust were available, according to scholar Norman Finkelstein. Until then there were no commemorative Holocaust monuments or interpretive centers in the United States.[331] So what led to the sudden and sharp rise of IAO promotion of Holocaust remembrance?

Statistical analysis of Holocaust-themed books listed in a popular online database by publication date[332] reveals publication growth may have peaked in the 1990s at 93 percent (108 books published) over the previous decade. Growth slowed to 164 books published in the first decade of the millennia (52 percent decade-over-decade growth). This snapshot broadly includes biographies, historical accounts, books for children and young adults, as well as a huge boom in independently published historical fiction output.

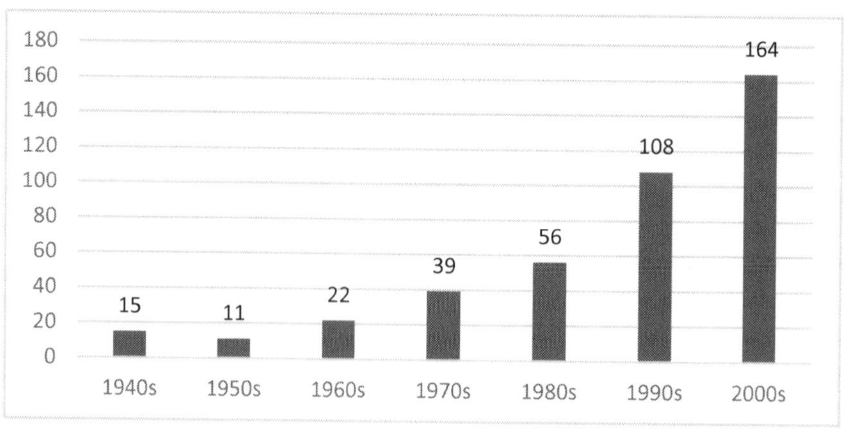

Figure 27 Holocaust-themed books by decade

330 Peter Novick, *The Holocaust in American Life* [Boston, Mariner Books, 2000] p 28

331 Norman Finkelstein, *The Holocaust Industry: Reflections on the Exploitations of Jewish Suffering* [Verso, New York, 2003] 3

332Data source: Well Written Holocaust Books, Goodreads website, consulted November 21, 2015 http://www.goodreads.com/list/show/1720.Well_Written_Holocaust_Books

A similar review of Holocaust-themed major motion pictures also reveals a fall-off in production growth rate after the 1990s.[333]

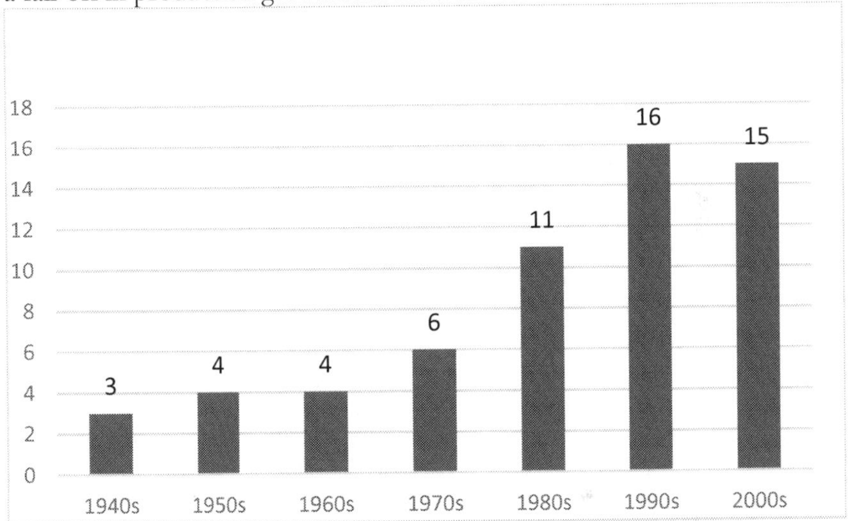

Figure 28 Holocaust-themed major motion pictures by decade

The impetus behind more Holocaust memorialization was the intractability of the Israeli-Palestinian conflict, according to Novick. Israeli military victories in 1956, 1967 and 1973 diminished the mistaken view held by many American Jews and others that the state was vulnerable, while the intifada cast Israeli actions in an increasingly unfavorable light. Remembering the Holocaust "therefore offered a substitute symbol of infinitely greater moral clarity" than the Arab-Israeli conflict and growing global sympathy toward Palestinian resistance.[334] The use of portrayals of Jewish victimization in the Holocaust advanced the Zionist agenda by allowing unfavorable comparisons to be made with relatively more mild Soviet discriminatory policies, in reframing Arabs as new hordes of anti-Semites, and even by countering growing criticism of American Jewish support for Zionism as "anti-Semitic."[335]

According to Novick, when the flows of unassimilated Jews to America and American anti-Semitism simultaneously declined, IAOs were left scrambling to answer the question of how to shore up group identity. Mobilization on behalf of Israel was only a *purpose.* Only the Holocaust could provide a binding identity.[336] Jewish Zionist presence in major media enabled

---

333 For the list compiled by the author see http://IsraelLobby.org/movies

334 Peter Novick, *The Holocaust in American Life* [Mariner Books, Boston, 2000] 169

335 Joseph Massad, "Deconstructing Holocaust Consciousness," *Journal of Palestine Studies*, Vol. 32, No. 1 (Autumn 2002), 78-89

336 Peter Novick, *The Holocaust in American Life* [Mariner Books, Boston, 2000] 186

a massive campaign to make the Holocaust not only a binding glue of Jewish identity, but the inception of an American "memory" as well. An IAO campaign was thus born as Columbia scholar Joseph Massad wrote:

> *... Jews play an important and influential role in Hollywood, the television industry, and the newspaper, magazine, and book publishing worlds. Anyone who would explain the massive attention the Holocaust has received in these media in recent years without reference to that fact is being naive or disingenuous" Programs like NBC's April 1978 miniseries the Holocaust constitute a major example. With 100 million Americans watching the program, 'more information about the Holocaust was imparted to more Americans over those four nights than over all the preceding thirty years...'*[337]

Such broadcasts were so successful they soon attracted formal IAO support. In 1987, PBS in collaboration with the American Jewish Committee sponsored a primetime four-night broadcast the series "Shoah."[338] According to Novick, the mass revival of "Holocaust memory" has been principally due to the priorities of IAO leaders and their constituents. Finkelstein also finds that the reason for reviving Holocaust memory in the 1970s was to build Jewish power through identity, claiming:

> *[t]he Holocaust performed for American Jews the same function as Israel: another valuable chip in a high-stakes power game. The avowed concern for Holocaust memory was as contrived as the avowed concern for Israel's fate. . . It was not Israel's alleged weakness and isolation, not the fear of a 'second holocaust,' but rather its proven strength and strategic alliance with the United States that led Jewish elites to gear up the Holocaust industry after June 1967.*[339]

Like Novick, Finkelstein's analysis reveals the incredible spread of Holocaust awareness. The movies, fiction and nonfiction books, commemorations, conferences, and museums are a reflection of IAOs need to deflect warranted opposition to Israeli policies and reclaim moral high ground. The Holocaust has become the check that organizations such as the ADL, Simon Wiesenthal Center, and Holocaust Museum never stop cashing:

---

[337] Joseph Massad, "Deconstructing Holocaust Consciousness," *Journal of Palestine Studies*, Vol. 32, No. 1 (Autumn 2002) 82

[338] "Holocaust Documentary on WEDU," *St. Petersburg Times*, April 25, 1987, city edition

[339] Norman Finkelstein, *The Holocaust Industry: Reflections on the Exploitations of Jewish Suffering* [Verso, New York, 2003] 30-31

> *Organized American Jewry has exploited the Nazi Holocaust to deflect criticism of Israel's and its own morally indefensible policies.*[340]

The prevalence of Holocaust memorial resources in the United States as a politically useful venture is made suspiciously prominent in the absence of memorials and mass media about more closely related and relevant events that occurred in the Americas. Those include the death by disease and violence of multitudes of Native Americans as a result of European colonization and epidemics as well as hundreds of years of black enslavement and oppression. No similar effort to memorialize or educate about these tragedies that have far more relevance to the American experience have anywhere near the funding trajectory of Holocaust memorialization. Due to the extreme and lasting nature of Israeli suppression of Palestinians, the Israel lobby's need for Holocaust memorialization in places of learning and other venues is ongoing. Because there are so many tragedies in competition for "most brutal of all" status, the Holocaust is also framed and defended by IAOs and memorialization advocates as "unparalleled" and therefore "unique" and "beyond comparison."

The United States Holocaust Memorial Museum opened its doors in 1993 and received more than a million visitors during its first year. It generated a great deal of descriptive press about both its permanent and rotating exhibits but little examination of the controversial nature of some of the framing it applied to both historical and current events. A core objective of the museum is to generate identification with and empathy for Holocaust victims. When it first opened, the museum delivered an identity card to each visitor that would communicate the status of a particular victim through various stages while communicating what ultimately happened to them (most perished). The goal was to provide a bridge from past to present, and was a conscious effort to overcome what a non-empathetic approach might have achieved: visitor identification with the principal American historical engagement—the liberation of Nazi concentration camps.

Today, the museum attempts to create even more bridges, some long before the footings have solidified. It does not conduct itself like any ordinary museum. In 2014, the museum announced it had obtained 55,000 photos of atrocities it alleges were committed by the Syrian government of Bashar Al-Assad that could serve future war crimes prosecutions. Chairman of the United States Holocaust Memorial Council Tom Bernstein immediately laid blame on the Syrian government for chemical weapons attacks on civilians in 2013, although there is still a great deal of international (though not White

---

340 Norman Finkelstein *The Holocaust Industry: Reflections on the Exploitations of Jewish Suffering* [Verso, New York, 2003] p 149

House or establishment American press) uncertainty about whether rebels or Syrian government forces had deployed the banned weapons. In March of 2015, the United Nations resolution condemning the attacks did not lay blame with either rebels or the Syrian government. The United Nations was still working to assemble a mechanism for finally assessing parties at fault, even as hipshot interpretive exhibits were being mounted at the Holocaust Museum to place the incidents in the most effective perspective, at least from the Israeli standpoint.

Like the ADL, the Holocaust Museum provides proprietary training programs to federal law enforcement which it refuses to make public. Though a recipient of generous taxpayer and charitable donations, when asked to provide a review copy of its "Law Enforcement and Society: Lessons of the Holocaust" program, Marcus Appelbaum, director of Law, Justice and Society, responded, "Our educational programs are supported by private donations and our training materials have international copyright restrictions that prevents its open disbursement."[341] Given the Museum's leap into Syria editorializing and the way other major promoters, such as ADL national director Abraham Foxman, exploited the Holocaust as grounds for opposing a Muslim community center to be located near "ground zero" in New York, it is likely that such training is similarly misused to unduly influence law enforcement. The ADL leader told *The New York Times*:

> *It's the wrong place, Mr. Foxman said. Find another place. Asked why the opposition of the families was so pivotal in the decision, Mr. Foxman, a Holocaust survivor, said they were entitled to their emotions.*
>
> *Survivors of the Holocaust are entitled to feelings that are irrational, he said. Referring to the loved ones of Sept. 11 victims, he said, Their anguish entitles them to positions that others would categorize as irrational or bigoted.*[342]

Within the Israel affinity movement, Holocaust memorials and the Holocaust as a justification for the creation of Israel can complicate the framing and messaging of other issues. Palestinians argue in the United Nations and other venues that they should not have to provide compensation for Europe's treatment of Jews before and during WWII. President Barak Obama's citing the Holocaust as the justification for Israel's existence just after taking office set off alarm bells within Israel's Foreign Ministry. This was only laid to rest during Obama's highly choreographed March 2013, visit

[341] Email exchange with author, July 29, 2014

[342] "Debate heats up about mosque near ground zero," *The New York Times*, July 30, 2010, 2

to Israel, which seemed mostly designed to walk back that framework, to the delight of IAOs and Israeli government officials. The president visited the Shrine of the Book to view the work of Judean scholars written two thousand years before. He laid a wreath on Theodore Herzl's grave. Then the president recanted his 2009 words by quoting an American Israeli journalist. "The State of Israel does not exist because of the Holocaust, but with the survival of the State of Israel there will never be a Holocaust again." This retraction excited then-Ambassador Michael Oren, an American historian who had renounced his U.S. citizenship to become Israel's ambassador to the U.S.

> *I recognized the phrase from an article written by Yossi Klein Halevi, and excitedly tried to phone him.*[343]

By 2015, six states (California, Florida, Illinois, Indiana, New Jersey and New York) mandated that the Holocaust be taught in the educational curriculum. Eleven states (Alabama, Connecticut, Georgia, Mississippi, Missouri, Nevada, North Carolina, South Carolina, Tennessee, Washington and West Virginia) recommend teaching the Holocaust in their educational curricula.[344] Every year, millions of dollars in federal and state appropriations are sought to fund the expansion of Holocaust curriculum in American schools.

Holocaust survivor Simon Wiesenthal founded the Simon Wiesenthal Center in 1977, and claims its purpose is educating the public about anti-Semitism while attempting to expose Nazis in hiding and pressure governments to prosecute them for war crimes. It also seeks to preserve the memory of the Holocaust via the "Museum of Tolerance" in Los Angeles. The IAO is building an even larger facility in Jerusalem after winning a multi-year battle against Muslim organizations upset about the museum being built over the site of a Muslim cemetery.

Yet another "educational" program stretches the concept of tax-deductible social welfare activity. In 1998, Benjamin Netanyahu announced a new initiative directed against Jewish assimilation and intermarriage with non-Jews that he viewed as a "demographic threat," through a jointly funded Israeli government–Jewish Federations program called Birthright Israel. The Associated Press reported:

---

343 Michael Oren, *Ally: My Journey Across the American-Israeli Divide* [New York, Random House, 2015]

344 Text of H.R.2545 — 114th Congress (2015-2016) https://www.congress.gov/bill/114th-congress/house-bill/2545/text?q=%7B%22search%22%3A%5B%22wiesenthal%22%5D%7D&resultIndex=1

> *The 1990 Council of Jewish Federations survey found that more than half of all American Jews intermarried and that 38 percent of Jews under 18—and 72 percent of the children of intermarried parents—are being raised in other faiths.*
>
> *Before 1965, only 9 percent of American Jews intermarried. The 1990 study found an intermarriage rate of 57 percent.*[345]

Birthright's donor base in 2001 was narrow, with just seven big donors providing 91 percent of its $14.6 million in revenues.[346] Canadian-American billionaire Charles Bronfman and hedge fund manager Michael Steinhardt were two important founding members. Another donors and board members was Marc Rich, the international financier, commodities trader and hedge fund manager who was indicted in the United States for tax evasion and making illegal oil deals with Iran during the hostage crisis. Rich remained in Switzerland at the time of the indictment until he received a presidential pardon from U.S. President Bill Clinton on January 20, 2001, as he was about to leave office. This had been the recommendation of Deputy Attorney General Eric Holder. In 2005, Rich left Birthright's board and was replaced by AIPAC's former *Near East Report* newsletter editor and CNN's situation room host, Wolf Blitzer.[347]

Birthright's annual revenue growth curve has been steep and is on track to reach $150 million by year 2020, with billionaire casino magnate Sheldon Adelson standing out as a key funder. By far the biggest donor to Birthright, Adelson increased his total donations to the organization to $160 million with a year 2015 donation of $40 million.[348] The program's free ten-day trips to Israel for teenage Jews from American colleges and universities are nicknamed "birthrate Israel." Participants who note the non-rigorous schedule and fact that the purpose is to build affinity with, as opposed to encourage *Aliya* to, Israel, coined this label. "Hooking up" and bonding with other American Jews to become future affinity leaders and reduce the dreaded "intermarriage" rate is really what the trips are all about. Unknowingly ripping a page out of "Buckeye's" ADL playbook, Palestinian Arabs have tried to sign up for Birthright trips during its on-campus promotions. Unsurprisingly, the insular anti-assimilation at the core of the Birthright program goes unnoticed by the self-appointed champion of anti-bigotry in America, the leader of the ADL, who cheered the results:

---

[345] Jon Marcus, "American Jews Seek to Reverse Decline," The Associated Press, December 8, 1993

[346] Birthright 2001 IRS form 990, schedule of contributors

[347] Birthright 2005 IRS form 990

[348] Stephanie Butnick, "Sheldon Adelson Doubles Down on Birthright" *The Tablet*, February 12, 2015

> *[Abraham] Foxman: We lost two generations, ok? Up until Taglit-Birthright, because what we did was truncate Jewish education of our children at the age of 12 and 13 when they began to think as adolescents. Then the message to the overwhelming majority of American Jewish kids was: "Your Jewish education is finished." They then, five years later, came onto campus and all of a sudden we expected them to be Jewish and defend Israel. They didn't know how! They didn't understand.*
>
> *It has changed. Taglit has now delivered. A hundred thousand, 150,000 kids who now understand. I came to Israel when I was 18, on a summer program with 400 kids. In the last 40 years, I find these kids who are now grandparents, leaders in Jewish communities, in synagogues and so on. But the majority were not educated, they were not exposed. Today, things have changed. I don't think it's a calamity, I don't think it's a crisis. It's a question of perspective.*[349]

Birthright has come under scrutiny by Palestinian on-campus activists crowding registration tables asking for their opportunity for a free trip to the very places from which many of their parents or grandparents were forcibly removed during Israel's creation. These requests have gone unfulfilled. Boards of regents have not taken any interest in determining whether, given the religious filters on applying, the program violates applicable discrimination policies. The program has also backfired with some Jewish students who find the tour to be a catalyst for joining the pro-Palestinian movement in the U.S. One student provided eyewitness testimony:

> *During my Birthright trip we stayed in a settlement. When I asked about it, I was told that it was not a settlement, because under Israeli law the settlement was legal, and the word settlement implies illegality. In reality, any settlement in the West Bank is illegal under international law. To get to Jerusalem from the illegal settlement, we had to pass through a checkpoint. We were told it was a tollbooth. When I asked why we did not pay the toll, I was told we had an E-ZPass. We did in fact have an E-ZPass, but not like the one we have on cars in Boston. Instead, it was our Jewish privilege, embodied by the Taglit-Birthright sign on the front of our bus. As Jewish tourists, we passed right through the checkpoint, while Palestinians*

---

349 Ricky Ben-David, "On delegitimization –A 'Jerusalem Post' roundtable" June 27, 2011

> *attempting to cross it to get to work or the hospital were stuck in hours long queues. In five years, sixty-seven Palestinian babies were born at checkpoints. Thirty-six of them died. That doesn't happen at toll booths.*[350]

The situation on campuses has become so tense that Hillel houses have become an epicenter for asserting IAO influence over campus publications, threatening funding cutoffs over professorial appointments or program funding deemed to be insufficiently deferential to Israel. None of this activity was originally contemplated as core functions of the IAO. The Hillel network on campus across American colleges and universities began with a simple premise that embraced Jewish Zionists, anti-Zionists, the ardently religious, the secular and the assimilationists, according to a 1924 speech given by its founder Rabbi Benjamin Frankel who said:

> *...the Jewish university student presented a unique problem in American life. As a rule he was passively Jewish, and when he entered the university and found what he interpreted as anti-Semitism, he stuck his head in the sand. If American Jews were to produce a generation of leaders, that attitude must be overcome. Hillel integrated the Jewish student socially by bringing him into an organization that represented him on the campus. By affiliating with Hillel, a student openly declared, 'I am a Jew' and as time went on, if he made a name for himself with his classmates, the respect he received was reflected on all of his coreligionists.* [351]

Like many other IAOs, Hillel's mission has been transforming radically over time. As noted in the analysis of Jewish federation giving, Jewish students are now vastly over-represented on elite campuses as a percentage of the student body. The original mission of fighting discrimination against Jewish students now accomplished, many Hillels have now embraced a broader definition of anti-Semitism that includes targeting pro-Palestinian movements on campus as purpose-built to make Jewish students "feel uncomfortable" or "unsafe," while Hillel's professional staff carefully tracks

---

[350] Julia Wedgle and Chase Carter, "On 'Birthright' a checkpoint is called a tollbooth, and Jews have E-ZPass," *Mondoweiss*, March 8, 2015 http://mondoweiss.net/2015/03/birthright-checkpoint-tollbooth#sthash.PpSdy1pv.dpuf

[351] Winton U. Solberg, "The Early Years of the Jewish Presence at the University of Illinois," *Religion and American Culture: A Journal of Interpretation*, Vol 2, No. 2 (Summer, 1992) 232

the composition of campus media and student government.[352] At Rutgers University, under pressure by the campus Hillel, the administration ordered the campus newspaper's editorial staff to submit any letter to the editor or article dealing with Israel or Palestine to the board of trustees for approval prior to publication.[353] The Zionist Organization of America uses Hillel chapters as lily pads for events and its own efforts to cut off federal higher education funds.[354]

Hillel has implemented an internal ban on branches hosting speakers who advocate for BDS, dubbed the "standards of Partnership." The organization in particular strives on some campuses to take control of student bodies that are engaged in the boycott, divestment and sanctions battles. At UCLA, the campus Hillel solicited advice from IAO-connected public relations firm 30 Point for advice on how to confront a divestment campaign. The Hillel decided to attempt to "isolate" the group, Students for Justice in Palestine, claiming they were:

> *Unrepresentative, a groups [sic] of isolated graduate students, part of Nationwide Agenda that has nothing to do with Student Life at UCLA and is an issue which our student government shouldn't even be considering.*

The UCLA Hillel proposed "a counter offensive" that would be "launched against Qatar, ISIS and Hamas to focus our concerns on terrorists who seek to kill our People around the world," as if the targets were at the center of—or had any connection with—the BDS movement. According to leaked emails, 30 Point appears to now have a contract with Hillel International to counter BDS on a case-by-case basis by sending targeted communications to "UCLA Hillel stakeholders, students, donors, etc…"[355] In the mid-2000s, Hillel began deploying a slogan that revealed it to be much more than an average on-campus religious organization: "Wherever we stand, we stand with Israel." However, Hillel is not alone standing with Israel as an "educational" organization.

---

352 Holly Bicerano, "Safe Hillel Exposed: Undermining open dialogue in the Jewish Community," *Mondoweiss*, February 26, 2014 http://mondoweiss.net/2014/02/undermining-dialogue-community

353 Amani Al-Khatahtbeh,"Daring to Speak Out on Campus," speech at the National Press Club, *The Israel Lobby, Is It Good for the U.S.? Is It Good for Israel?* April 10, 2015 http://israellobbyus.org/transcripts/3.1Amani_Al-khatahtbehT.htm

354 Zionist Organization of America application for reinstatement of tax-exempt status. The Israel Lobby Archive. http://IsraelLobby.org/ZOA/ZOA_taxexempt.pdf

355 Alex Kane, "UCLA Hillel partners with PR firm to fight BDS movement" http://mondoweiss.net/2014/10/hillel-partners-movement

Alpha Epsilon Pi is a historically Jewish fraternity. Although its pro-Israel advocacy varies across campuses, the fraternity took up Israel advocacy institutionally only after the second intifada which began in 2000. "We knew then that if being the last remaining Jewish fraternity means anything at all, it must mean that we are going to stand and support the Jewish people, which is the Jewish State," said international president Elan Carr in 2013. The organization has 9,000 undergraduates and a total alumni network of 80,000 men.[356] The fraternity's foundation now provides chapter grants for Israel advocacy training as a priority within its Jewish identity programs. Fraternity chapters organize black t-shirt "never forget" marches on campus as part of a "walk to remember" program in conjunction with local federations. Up to 110 chapters participate in the program as a means to "combat anti-Semitism by spreading positive messages and education."[357]

The Jewish Community Centers Association of North America–JCC Foundation runs a number of education, summer camp and athletic programs designed to instill a sense of being "part of K'lal Israel, the greater Jewish people" in its U.S. programs.

The Women's International Zionist Organization seeks to enhance "the bond between American Jewry and the State of Israel through efforts to improve social service programs and educational facilities for babies, youth, women and the elderly in Israel."

Other education IAOs have major initiatives to promote Israel in the United States. Aish International Hasbara Fellowships sends 700 students for two to three-week activism programs in Israel. "A key component of the program is training students to run successful propaganda campaigns upon their return to campus. Participants receive support from professional Hasbara Fellowships staff to help facilitate pro-Israel programs back at their university."[358]

Education IAOs amassed $317.7 million in revenues in 2012, on track to reach $762 million by the year 2020. Their impact can increasingly be seen flipping through a junior or senior high-school student's class syllabus and

---

[356] Richard Cohen, "Jewish Fraternity Alpha Epsilon Pi marks 100 years amid sweeping culture changes," *The Jewish Daily Forward*, September 1, 2003 http://forward.com/news/183219/jewish-fraternity-alpha-epsilon-pi-marks-100-years/

[357] "A Vanderbilt Chapter of Alpha Epsilon Pi Combats Anti-Semitism by Spreading Positive Messages And Education," *AEPI News*, April 2, 2015 http://www.aepi.org/news/vanderbilt-chapter-of-aepi-combats-anti-semitism-by-spreading-positive-messages-and-education/

[358] "Hasbara Fellowships training 700 students for pro-Israel advocacy in Israel this summer," AISH website. http://www.aish.com/ai/bn/ji/Hasbara_Fellowships_700_students_Israel_summer.html

recommended reading. As concerns grow about creating empathy for Israel through socializing younger Americans, so too will the pressures to create ever more teaching guides, attractive suggested reading lists, visits to Holocaust memorial museums and other highly effective school programming.

8 COORDINATION & SUPPRESSION

The lobbying priorities, tight connections to the Israeli government, and unified messaging campaigns across major IAOs suggest intense ongoing behind-the-scenes coordination. At the heart of much of this coordination is the Conference of Presidents of Major American Jewish Organizations (CPMJO). What it lacks in terms of reported revenue—only $4.5 million in 2013—it makes up for in the number of member organizations and connections in its highly strategic location. The combined power of these member organizations means there are few White House gatherings on issues of interest to Israel the conference does not attend. In many ways, the Conference of Presidents has reassembled and wields the organizational consortium power the Jewish Agency originally sought for the American Zionist Council. AIPAC is the IAO in charge of lobbying Congress. According to AIPAC's bylaws, the chairperson of the CPMJO is automatically a director of AIPAC, and all constituent organization heads are given AIPAC membership at no cost.[359] This creates an institutionalized linkage allowing AIPAC lobbyists to claim they represent the official position of the organized Jewish community in America.

Housed within CPMAJO's own offices are a number of other IAOs, including the American Zionist Movement, the Lawfare Project, the Feinberg Graduate School of the Weizmann Institute of Science, the American Committee for the Weizmann Institute and the Jewish Agency for Israel—North American Council. The latter organization continues to

[359] Bylaws of the American Israel Public Affairs Committee, January 28, 2003. The Israel Lobby Archive http://www.irmep.org/ila/aipac/2003AIPAC_bylaws.pdf

"intermediate"[360] between the Jewish Agency for Israel and American federations despite the Jewish Agency's rocky history of run-ins with the Senate and Justice Department.

Also located in the same building (633 Third Avenue in New York City), the World Zionist Organization occupies 27,000 square feet of office space for its U.S. foreign agent, the "American Section." Since 2010, the Bank of Israel has also maintained a U.S. branch. Why CPMAJO is co-located with the WZO, a foreign agent that is also a CPMAJO member organization, is a story that begins in the 1960s.

It was then that the Jewish Agency's American Section was finally forced by the Justice Department to file more revealing foreign agent registrations. The Jewish Agency at last coughed up its secret 1953 covenant with the Israeli government, which formalizes access to Israeli government funding and bestows Jewish Agency legislative powers in the Knesset. However, like the American Zionist Council, the Jewish Agency American Section also dodged open and transparent regulation under the 1938 Foreign Agents Registration Act.

In 1971, the Jewish Agency American Section counsel told the Justice Department it was not an agent of the Jewish Agency in Israel after all, but rather part of another foreign sister organization, the World Zionist Organization. The Justice Department wrote that the sudden paper reorganization, with no resultant change of staff, executives, or even office space, was "sketchy."[361] But as in the AZC-to-AIPAC reconstitution, the operations of a major foreign agent active in promoting Israel's interests in the United States continued without interruption.

World Zionist Organization operatives, through their presence in New York and other locations, communicate Israel's needs to Jewish federations on whirlwind briefing tours. They advocate for the inclusion of more Israel-centric Jewish education programs in Jewish day schools and synagogues through WZO's "Department for Jewish Zionist Education," while working to make Israel a preferred "study abroad" destination in American universities. WZO also spends up to $1.5 million a year sending sixty lecturers and instructors on Zionism to Jewish youth groups. The WZO also reimburses many political programs that take place in Hillels across the American university system.[362] However, the Jewish Agency has now relinquished its overt role as supreme coordinator to the American IAO, the

---

[360] Jewish Agency for Israel—North American Council 2005 IRS Form 990

[361] American Section - Jewish Agency for Israel, Inc. Deregisters as a Foreign Agent after the DOJ orders it to file secret 1953 Covenant Agreement with the Israeli Government, The Israel Lobby Archive http://www.irmep.org/ila/JA/

[362] World Zionist Organization—supplemental filing with the Department of Justice Foreign Agents Registration Act office. http://www.fara.gov/docs/2278-Supplemental-Statement-20100729-11.pdf

Conference of Presidents of Major American Jewish Organizations.

The CPMAJO makes the news mostly while lobbying American presidents on behalf of the Israeli government and pumping messages bearing the government's position into the ecosystem of IAOs. President and CEO Malcolm Hoenlein's frequent travels to Israel to meet with top government officials, particularly the prime minister, and to preside over various Jerusalem conferences and gatherings leave no daylight between Conference of Presidents member organization demands as "U.S. citizens" and the agenda of the current Israeli government. Hoenlein's meetings with Benjamin Netanyahu likely take place in a secure communications unit at Mossad headquarters, given Netanyahu's documented paranoia about spying and American IAOs fear of being overheard and labeled as foreign agents. Middle East Forum's Daniel Pipes commented on Netanyahu in 2015:

> *Prime Minister Netanyahu is also being personally targeted. Knowing this, he intentionally makes himself obscure. He has no private phone, doesn't send e-mails, and has no computer in his office. His most sensitive conversations take place in Mossad offices and even then he's prone to using hand gestures, writing down commands, and speaking in code. He won't even clarify what the code means, much to the dismay of Israeli officials.*[363]

From Monday to Friday, the CPMJO produces a bulletin called "Daily News Alert from Israel." In conjunction with driving the transmission belt to the most influential IAO cogs, the CPMJO itself is a well-oiled machine. Yet if Israel Affinity Organizations simply marched around supporting benevolent charities or issuing dry policy studies about what the United States should do in the Middle East, no politician would probably pay much attention to them. The White House and Congress must listen to the Conference of Presidents of Major American Jewish Organizations and the American Israel Public Affairs Committee because they can be counted on to influence the massive war chest of campaign contributions awaiting those who will do their bidding.

As mentioned, AIPAC has distributed guides on how to create stealth "political action committees," the campaign funding entities that are coordinated and intentionally hide their pro-Israel agenda through innocuous names. AIPAC directs these stealth PACs on how much to give to particular candidates.[364] It also issues politician "score cards" that leave no doubt who should be supported, and who should be opposed, based on their support

---

[363] Machla Abramovitz interview of Daniel Pipes, "Spying on Friends," *Mishpacha*, August 5, 2015

[364] "AIPAC coordinates PACs," The Israel Lobby Archive, http://israellobby.org/AIPAC/PAC_Coordination/

for Israel. It bundles contributor checks for candidates. It all adds up.

Jewish donors to the Democratic Party make up 25 to 50 percent of those who individually give $25,000 or more, the so-called "major contributors."[365] According to studies, Democrats typically receive about 66 percent of total "Pro-Israel" campaign support, with Republicans harvesting the other 34 percent.[366] According to former AIPAC and congressional staffer MJ Rosenberg, AIPAC's role directing stealth PAC money to candidates pales only in comparison to its direction of large individual contributions.[367] Analyst Jeffrey Blankfort examined the "Top 400 Campaign Donors in 2000," listed in *Mother Jones* magazine. Blankfort discovered that:

> *... on its [year] 2000 list, seven of the top 10, 12 of the top 20 and at least 125 of the top 250 were Jewish, which is where I stopped counting. Seventy-five percent of their money went to the Democrats and the remainder to the Republicans. The donors came from every major sector of U.S. society, Wall Street, insurance, banking, real estate, the communications industry, which includes movies, TV, and the press, sports, etc.*[368]

There being no relevant opposition, party candidates strive to "out-Israel" each other to chase support, or at the very least avoid being tarred as insufficiently supportive of Israel. The dynamics of the two-party system keep everyone in line. Conservative pundits never stop predicting a "seismic shift" of pro-Israel money to Republicans as the result of even the slightest deviation in Democratic Party support for Israel, or if public disagreements with its prime minister become too noisy. In October of 2012, Mitt Romney's top supporter, through bundling, contributions and "outside" group support, was casino mogul Sheldon Adelson, at $34.2 million. At the number one and two spots in the Obama fundraising machine were movie mogul Jeffrey Katzenberg, $2.6 million, and Irwin Jacobs, giving $2.1 million.[369]

Being a politician's top donor has long been a well-traveled path for Israel

---

365 Alexander Bolton, "Jewish Donors may be chilled by Israel policy," *The Hill*, March 3, 2010 http://thehill.com/homenews/campaign/89941-jewish-donors-may-be-chilled-by-israel-policy

366 "U.S. Campaign Contributions, Pro-Israel PACs, Individuals & Soft Money 1990-2012," Jewish Virtual Library http://www.jewishvirtuallibrary.org/jsource/U.S.-Israel/israelpacs.html

367 MJ Rosenberg, "Is it all about the Money?" Speech at the conference *The Israel Lobby: Is It Good for the U.S.? Is It Good for Israel?* at the National Press Club on April 10, 2015 http://israellobbyus.org/transcripts/5.1MJ_Rosenberg.htm

368 Jeffrey Blankfort, "JTA reports that as much as 2/3 of Democratic money comes from Jewish donors," *Mondoweiss*, June 8, 2011

369 Ilan Ben Zion, "Jewish Donors prominent in presidential campaign contributions," *The Times of Israel*, October 20, 2012

advocates. Legendary bundler Abraham Feinberg was best known for funding President Harry S Truman's "whistle stop" campaign, saving Truman's 1948 election campaign from almost certain defeat. In an interview, Feinberg summarized his long success in Democratic Party politics. "My path to power was cooperation in terms of what they needed—campaign money."[370] Feinberg was a major figure in Democratic politics through the reign of LBJ.

The major Advocacy IAOs have been heavily involved in promoting economic warfare against Iran, unconditional support for Israel, and measures to combat "assimilation." Their financial might (and self-promotion) would also have politicians believe this is the undistilled view of the entire Jewish community. Yet most Jewish adults in America have never been to Israel (57 percent), think the building of settlements is detrimental to Israel's security (44 percent), and are either only "somewhat" or not at all "attached" to Israel (70 percent).[371]

The major 2015 lobbying drive by IAOs such as the Republican Jewish Coalition, the Emergency Committee for Israel, the Zionist Organization of America and Christians United for Israel, was an attempt to thwart any nuclear deal with Iran. This drive generated a boost in revenue for IAOs and Obama administration promises to "compensate" Israel. From this perspective, it was not a defeat; despite the embarrassing polling that revealed how particularly unrepresentative of the "Jewish community" were such IAO positions. A June 2015 nationwide poll of U.S. Jews found that 59 percent supported a final agreement for easing sanctions, in return for inspections, and a cap on Iran's nuclear program. This exceeded the 53 percent general public support for an Iran deal found by a CNN poll in April.[372] However, other coordinated IAO campaigns, some on the fringes of the Israel lobby, are succeeding. One of the most successful to date—ironic given the ADL's own launch as an organization dedicated to fighting anti-Semitism—is a coordinated IAO campaign seeking to negatively brand and disenfranchise adherents of an entire religion.

The Center for Security Policy, led by Frank Gaffney, Daniel Pipes at the Middle East Forum, Steven Emerson of the Investigative Project on Terrorism/Counterterrorism & Security Research Foundation, the Clarion Fund, the David Horowitz Freedom Center and the American Congress for Truth comprise a network of anti-Muslim/anti-Islam IAOs. Through

---

370 Seymour M. Hersh, *The Samson Option: Israel's Nuclear Arsenal and American Foreign Policy* [New York, Random House, 1991] Chapter 8

371 "A Portrait of Jewish Americans" Pew Research Center, October 1, 2013 http://www.pewforum.org/2013/10/01/jewish-american-beliefs-attitudes-culture-survey/

372 Jim Lobe, "Support for Iran Deal Stronger among U.S. Jews than General Public," *LobeLog Foreign Policy*, June 11, 2015

constant cross-promotion of "experts" and analysis, these organizations effectively portray Islam as an inherently violent religious movement intent on dominating the United States and replacing constitutional protections with religious doctrines. They produce a constant flow of books, documentary videos, reports and bulletins depicting the infiltration of Muslims into powerful political, educational and civic leadership positions. Mosques, according to this theme, are strategically positioned assets for spreading radical and violent theology. One was even intended to be located a few blocks from the destroyed World Trade Center as a defiant display of "victory" following the 9/11 terrorist attacks, according to these "experts."

Frank Gaffney, a former Department of Defense appointee in the Reagan administration, labeled the proposed Park51 community center in New York as a place for spreading "sedition" in the form of "*Sharia* law." He has gone on roadshows to various states to testify against mosque construction on this basis, though he admits he is not an expert in the subject. A Gaffney report on *Sharia* suggests that all practicing Muslims engage in religiously mandated lying, or *taqiyya*. In reality, *taqiyya* is the practice of concealing one's faith when in fear of death, and is only practiced by a minority of Muslims.

Gaffney characterizes individual or organized attempts by Muslims to exercise their civil rights as part of a looming threat:

> *...most of the Muslim-American groups of any prominence in America are now known to be, as a matter of fact, hostile to the United States and its Constitution.*[373]

Gaffney and his Center for Security Policy are broadly supportive of expanding U.S. military expenditures and military interventions. His daily broadcast/podcast from Washington, DC is "Secure Freedom Radio," and hosts a rotation of conservative guests from former Republican administrations such as former Attorney General Michael Mukasey, reporters from the *Washington Times* and *Washington Examiner*, retired military officers and other pundits. Freedom Radio commercial slots are dominated by advertisers that are mostly nonprofit groups raising money to support veterans and promoting webinars, videos and books about the dangers of Muslim immigration to the U.S. and *Sharia* law. One book's commercial spot from the "Civilization Jihad Reader Series" that aired in 2015 revealed an alleged Muslim plot, abetted by the federal government, quietly targeting rural America, the narrator ominously drones;

> *It's been a few years since a church group from another state brought a couple hundred refugees to the rural county where I live.*

---

[373] Sheila Musaji, "Steven Emerson and the Investigative Project," *The American Muslim*, March 26, 2011

> *I wanted to know, "how could they do this?" What was the governmental process that allowed the resettlement of refugees to a county ill-prepared to assimilate them? Employment opportunities were scarce. The health department has no familiarity with illnesses and mental health problems of people who came from parts of the third world. The school system was not prepared to teach large numbers of students who didn't speak English.*
>
> *VOICE OVER "That's author Anne Corcoran discussing her new book, Federal Immigration Policy, Resettlement and the Hijra*[374] *to America. She explains how Muslim immigrants are being quietly resettled into American towns without vetting them even for terrorist links. Corcoran also explains how the global Jihad movement is using immigration as a stealth campaign to spread its influence in America. You can read Federal Immigration Policy, Resettlement and the Hijra to America at SecureFreedom.org or purchase a copy on Amazon.com.*

The location of the offending migration documented by Corcoran in her book and blog, "Refugee Resettlement Watch," was Hagerstown in western Maryland. This was one site of a federal refugee resettlement program in partnership with the Virginia Council of Churches that tried to lawfully place Russian refugees into areas where they could resume normal lives. The Center for Security Policy, as part of the Israel lobby, is part of a movement that launched in the 1800s in order to address the assimilation of German Jews in America, while later confronting Czarist Russia's pogroms and working to resettle Soviet Jews in Israel and other Western countries. Viewed from this perspective, the Center for Security Policy's opposition to the latest wave of refugees seems out of sync, if not xenophobic—until one understands that these particular Russian immigrants are Muslims, not Jews.

Daniel Pipes founded the Middle East Forum in 1990. Pipes leverages a 1973 Harvard doctoral degree in medieval Islamic history to portray himself as an expert in modern-day movements threatening the United States. In 2002, Pipes launched the Campus Watch web platform to "out" college instructors who he felt were insufficiently pro-Israel, and to encourage students to "report" instances of professorial bias. In 2003, Pipes published the pioneering book, *Militant Islam Reaches America,* and, in 2006, launched another web platform, Islamist Watch, combatting "ideas and institutions of lawful Islamism in the United States." This culminated in an attack on the Council on American-Islamic Relations (CAIR), an organization designed to

[374] "*Hijra*" is an Arabic word for "migration," referring to the *Hegira* or *Hijra* of Muhammad, or the migration of Muhammad and his followers from Mecca to Yathrib (later renamed Medina) in 622 CE.

empower Muslims and combat stereotypes of Islam. In 2007, Pipes created a subsidiary, the Legal Project, in response to defamation lawsuits brought by an Islamic organization in Boston against many Pipes confederates. The preferred Pipes label for many such individuals and groups attempting to use law, speech and other constitutionally protected rights is "Islamists." This charge is also leveled at higher-ups. Pipes has frequently written that Barack Obama is a former Muslim who practiced Islam.

In 2015, the Middle East Forum announced a search for a lobbyist who will work to redefine who counts as a Palestinian refugee (only those who fled during the creation of Israel, but not their descendants languishing in camps, according to Pipes). The IAO hosts forums on how to further marginalize an already highly marginalized group. This program is combatting "Palestinian Refugee Proliferation."

Robert Spencer runs the Jihad Watch website for the David Horowitz Freedom Center to "track the attempts of radical Islam to subvert Western culture." Spencer has trained U.S. Central Command, the U.S. Army Command and General Staff College, the U.S. Army Asymmetric Warfare Group, the Joint Terrorism Task Force and entities in the U.S. intelligence community. He has trained FBI special agents in "interrogations with individuals from the M.E. [Middle East]." The FBI listed one of his books, published in 2007, *The Truth About Muhammad: Founder of the World's Most Intolerant Religion,* as "recommended reading."

Steven Emerson's Investigative Project on Terrorism also focuses on the alleged threat of Islamist infiltration of America. Emerson is a former U.S. Senate Foreign Relations Committee investigator and journalist. His 1994 film, *Jihad in America,* received a George Polk award for documentary television. The Investigative Project positions itself as "one of the world's largest storehouses of archival data and intelligence on Islamic and Middle Eastern terrorist groups."

A related organization, the Counterterrorism & Security Education and Research Foundation (CTSERF), like the Investigative Project, acts as a tax-exempt nonprofit conduit for transferring funds to private, for-profit entities, in this case the International Association of Counterterrorism and Security Professionals. In January of 2015, Emerson made the claim that non-Muslims dared not go to the British city of Birmingham, which had undergone a transformation into a "totally Muslim" city. Emerson also claimed gangs of religious police in portions of London were beating up people not wearing Islamic clothes. Emerson later apologized for his comments. The U.S. news network that aired Emerson was Fox News, an amplifier and echo chamber that hosts the above-referenced analysts. Other outlets include the *National Review*, *Washington Times*, and Christian Broadcasting Network (CBN).

In August of 2011, the Center for American Progress—a Democratic

Party-leaning think tank—published a groundbreaking report on anti-Islam organizations titled *Fear Inc. The Roots of the Islamophobia Network in America,*[375] The document footer that appears in chapter 3 of the online report suggests the original title may even have been much harsher *Hate, Inc.* The explosive report identified many conservative and conduit foundations that hide names of donors that had given $42.5 million to the "Islamophobia network."[376]

Former AIPAC spokesperson, Josh Block, now the director of The Israel Project, immediately launched a campaign to brand the authors as "anti-Semites," compiling CAP writer statements into a dossier he circulated as proof of an "outrageous vilification of pro-Israel Americans." Ben Smith of *Politico* faithfully joined the fray and charged that CAP was advancing "a heretical and often critical stance on Israel heretofore confined to the political margins" and that "warm words for Israel can be hard to find on [CAP's] blogs." In January, 2012, CAP scrubbed already-published references to Alexa Traiman, "an Israeli-American resident of an ideological settlement in the Occupied Palestinian Territories," and three others, exposing Israeli funding sources, from a CAP exposé by Eli Clifton and Ali Gharib about the latest video, *Third Jihad*, produced by the shadowy Clarion Fund. Clarion also produced the video *Obsession*, which was distributed as a free newspaper insert to hundreds of thousands of swing voters in 2008. This was intended to scare voters away from the Obama campaign. Clarion's *Iranium* video similarly delivered disinformation about Iran as part of the nuclear scare.

Internal emails leaked in 2015 revealed how concerns about placating AIPAC and Israel advocates within CAP lead to the ouster of these troublesome investigators. A review of their data also suggests they did not fully realize how broadly popular Islamophobia promotion is with largely mainstream IAO funders and organizations not easily characterized as "right wing."

In January 2012, CAP President Neera Tanden warned she had received an email from Hillary Clinton's 2008 "advisor on Jewish matters," that CAP was going to have a problem until its writing "seems like it's not anti-Israel," and recommended Tanden consult with the ADL and AJC on these matters. On January 19, 2012, *The Washington Post* weighed in with a hit piece titled "Center for American Progress, group tied to Obama, under fire from Israel advocates," quoting ADL chief Abraham Foxman:

---

[375] "Fear, Inc. The Roots of the Islamophobia Network in America," Center for American Progress, August, 2011
https://www.americanprogress.org/issues/religion/report/2011/08/26/10165/fear-inc/

[376] Donors Capital Fund, Richard Mellon Scaife Foundation, Lynde and Harry Bradley Foundation, The Russell Berrie Foundation, Becker Foundations, Anchorage Foundation/William Rosenwald Family Fund and the Fairbrook Foundation.

> *Abraham Foxman, national director of the Anti-Defamation League, said some of the statements from CAP staffers "are anti-Semitic and borderline anti-Semitic."*

CAP soon threw its investigators under the bus, denouncing their language as "inappropriate" and telling the *Post* that offensive tweets had now all been deleted. CAP's then chief-of-staff, now senior national security fellow, Ken Gude had a "very positive" meeting with AIPACs Deputy Director of Policy and Government Affairs, Jeff Colman. CAP was soon returning to the good graces of AIPAC, and Gude was even promised a slot on an upcoming trip to Israel with AIPAC. Like many college regents concerned about content in student newspapers, Tanden set up a special editor to review before publication all of CAP's written output mentioning Israel. Tanden's original 2010 demand that CAP put "Israel Palestine" along with "trade and guns" as topics that were "off the table"[377] was restored, as the offending writers—Wajahat Ali, Ali Gharib, Eli Clifton, Lee Fang and Zaid Jilani—left the organization. Another AIPAC target, MJ Rosenberg (a former AIPAC employee pilloried for his blogging at Media Matters, using the term "Israel-firster" to describe pandering politicians, while dishing inside info on AIPAC) was also a casualty of the purge.

In November of 2015, Neera Tanden warmly received Israeli Prime Minister Benjamin Netanyahu at CAP before a handpicked audience and reporters. Widely depicted in the alternative press as an almost Soviet-style "show" gathering, the attempt at "progressive hospitality" to one of the most controversial leaders of the Middle East instead backfired, again revealing the deepening divide depicted as between "the Left" and "the Right." However, the rift is more accurately described as between an ensconced IAO elite and giant donors versus multitudes of informed opposition. Given the actual, relatively tiny, number of IAO members, it cannot be credibly characterized as excess by the "one percent." According to the previous analysis of Pew research data, "the 0.3 percent" is a far more likely number.

---

[377] Glenn Greenwald, "Leaked Emails from Pro-Clinton Group Reveal Censorship of Staff on Israel, AIPAC Pandering, Warped Militarism," *The Intercept*, November 5, 2015

Israel Affinity Organization	"Right-wing" 2001-2009 donations identified in 2011 CAP Report "Fear, Inc." Million	Total IAO 2001-2009 Revenue Million	"Right wing" donations percentage of total IAO revenue
Middle East Forum	$5.96	$21.83	27%
Center for Security Policy	$4.62	$21.85	21%
Investigative Project on Terrorism	$0.56	$6.90	8%
CTSERF	$4.53	$19.92	23%
Clarion Fund	$18.09	$20.45	88%
David Horowitz Freedom Center	$8.63	$39.11	22%
American Congress for Truth	$0.18	$2.03	9%
	$42.58	$132.09	32%

Figure 29 Islamophobia funding from major IAO donors

Fear, Inc's key financial finding—that support from the identified "right wing" foundations funding anti-Muslim programs can be put into perspective as an Israel lobby phenomenon. When compared to total IAO revenue during the period studied (2001-2009), the total funding from "right-wing" foundations was less than a third of available resources. The numbers reveal that the Investigative Project on Terrorism was getting 92 percent of its funding elsewhere (with the Center for Security Policy "other" funding at 70 percent, and Middle East Forum at 73 percent). A wider review of the giving patterns of Jewish federations reveals healthy support for organizations such as the Middle East Forum, as well as from many smaller private foundations.[378]

Identifying support from the Charles and Lynn Shusterman Foundation as an Islamophobia funder was likely critical to backlash against some *Fear, Inc.* writers. Charles and Lynn Shusterman Foundation gives hundreds of thousands to AIPAC's travel agency—the American Israel Education Foundation—where Lynn Shusterman is a board member. The Charles and

---

[378] The Abramowitz family foundation, The Steinberg Family Fund, Inc., Abraham Kamber Foundation, Mark and Anla Cheng Kingdon Foundation, The Ginsberg Family Foundation, The William P. Goldman and Brothers Foundation Inc., Rind Family Foundation, Norman D. Cohen Family Foundation

Lynn Shusterman Foundation is also an important longtime Middle East Forum funder, undoubtedly in the good company of many individual "progressive except for Palestine" Jewish donors. In exposing funding for Islamophobia, *Fear Inc.,* authors were exposing core Israel lobby funders. This exposure was a threat to funding that the Israel lobby had to nullify.

Fear, Inc. report authors also perhaps thought they would be inoculated from backlash by quoting Anti-Defamation League findings about bigotry in their *Fear, Inc.* report—undoubtedly without realizing that the ADL itself has long dabbled in the business since it first began targeting Arab embassies and infiltrating Arab student organizations with the intent to discredit and destroy them. Alternatively, a better example is the ADL's willingness to abandon all of its pretenses when it secretly began agitating against Japanese Americans in order to protect Hollywood funding. The authors of *Fear, Inc.* had to be jettisoned from CAP at all costs. Similarly, for the Israel Lobby and The Israel Project, journalist Rula Jebreal had to be banished from the airwaves at all costs.

The Israel Project, as a *de facto* press agency for the Israeli government, exerts its substantial and mostly behind-the-scenes influence on mainstream media organizations by threatening to withhold a relatively scarce and valuable resource that is in constant demand: access to high Israeli government officials and famous pro-Israel pundits. Given the abundance and growing ranks of credible, experienced and eloquent analysts critical of Israeli government policies, it seems increasingly suspicious that greater numbers do not appear on major network broadcasts. Until, that is, the works of IAOs like The Israel Project are exposed to daylight. The recent case of Rula Jebreal explicitly illustrates this, as well as the age-and-time-tested nature of IAO suppression tactics.

In July of 2014, journalist and author Rula Jebreal appeared on MSNBC and was asked by the host to respond to a statement made in the year 2000 by former Secretary of Defense Robert Gates, who claimed:

> *Every president I worked for, at some point in his presidency, would get so pissed off at the Israelis that he couldn't speak. It didn't matter whether it was Jimmy Carter or Gerry Ford or Ronald Reagan or George Bush. Something would happen and they would just absolutely go screw themselves right into the ceiling they were so angry, and they'd sort of rant and rave around the Oval Office. I think it was their frustration about knowing that there was so little they could do about it because of domestic politics and everything else that was so frustrating to them.*

Host Ronan Farrow finished reading the quote. This was not spontaneous. It appeared onscreen in text blocs as he read it. He asked his guest for a response. Jebreal, who had worked under contract with MSNBC as an analyst, responded powerfully:

> *Well, because of AIPAC [the American Israel Public Affairs Committee]. Because of the money behind it. And because of Sheldon Adelson. And because of all of us in the media. We are ridiculous. We are disgustingly bias [sic] when it comes to this issue. Look at how many [sic] air time Netanyahu and his folks have on air on [a] daily basis, on Andrea Mitchell and others. I never see one Palestinian being interviewed on these same issues…Maybe for 30 seconds. And then you have 25 minutes for Bibi Netanyahu and half an hour for Naftali Bennett and many others…One-tenth is given to the Palestinian voice, and ninety-nine to the Israeli voice, and that's why the public opinion is pro-Israeli, which is the opposite in the rest of the world.*[379]

When Farrow countered that MSNBC had Palestinians on before, Jebreal insisted there was a structural imbalance. Farrow then asked the ubiquitous pro-Israel pundit Eli Lake whether U.S. media was biased in favor of Israel. Lake appeared flustered at even being asked such a question and stammered for several seconds. Then, just as the Frank Luntz handbook suggests, Lake began talking about civilian casualties of the conflict, without assigning responsibility:

> *I'd say I'm baffled by what Rula was just saying there. Israel has experienced terrible press, when you have these pictures of dead Gazans and you see these casualties, I think the media has been covering that for what it is, which is a terrible human tragedy, and the response is often from Israeli officials in U.S. and Western media in general has often been very defensive. And the notion that AIPAC is a very powerful lobby on Capitol Hill, I think that Israel has a lot of support because there is a kind of cultural affinity between Americans and Israelis, and they see them as less foreign in a lot of ways, than they do with Palestinians. But that's a much deeper question and I don't think it can be explained by lobbyists or the political process…*

This exchange was the final phase of Jebreal's work with MSNBC. Jebreal stepped up her criticism after MSNBC suddenly began labeling her on air as a "Palestinian journalist." She revealed on CNN's Reliable Sources program that, "I felt terrible because I was hired by MSNBC and for two years I was

---

[379] Egberto Wilies, "Palestinian commentator Rula Jebreal explodes on MSNBC," Dailykos, July 21, 2014 http://www.dailykos.com/story/2014/7/21/1315570/-Palestinian-commentator-Rula-Jebreal-explodes-on-MSNBC

labeled as analyst, journalist, foreign policy expert, contributor. I was never labeled a Palestinian journalist."

Jebreal is a highly experienced, award-winning journalist, author, and foreign policy analyst. The multi-lingual Jebreal had broken glass ceilings by anchoring multiple television programs in both Italy and Egypt, and reported extensively from across the Middle East, Europe, and the U.S. Her first novel, *Miral*, sold two million copies and was made into a major motion picture. She frequently appeared on CNN, HBO and Bloomberg News, and contributed op-eds to *The New York Times*, *The Washington Post*, *Foreign Policy*, *The Guardian*, *Newsweek*, *The Nation*, and *San Jose Mercury News.* Jebreal told CNN that there was no reason to suddenly begin typecasting her by ethnicity when she had been hired to report important Middle East issues as a journalist and expert:

> *Is this how we label people? I think whoever is doing this PR campaign for MSNBC needs to rethink these issues...Did I become Palestinian because this way you can describe me as emotional and as biased, and this way can avoid debate as to who is really biased on this [sic] issues?*[380]

Jebreal's contract at MSNBC was over, but the campaign she suspected was being waged against her did not end. She only momentarily won the trifecta: revealing media bias, broadcasting it over mainstream media, and accurately identifying the forces working behind it.

It is impossible to obtain records from the producers and bookers working within networks such as MSNBC, Fox and CNN. However, a 2015 Freedom of Information Act request for the records of a large taxpayer-funded U.S. government global news organization, Voice of America, which is subject to such records requests, revealed the Israel Lobby's pressure tactics.

Josh Block, as a former AIPAC spokesperson, is often tasked by AIPAC to undertake public relations and other initiatives where AIPAC does not want, in its own words, "to leave fingerprints." One of Block's roles as CEO and President at The Israel Project is gatekeeper of pro-Israel pundits that producers book on various broadcast programs, and using that influence to shape the final output. This involves courting producers and turning them into part of the Israel affinity choir. It is a no-holds-barred endeavor, with Block even portraying successful interventions as mafia-style "hits."

Hooman Bakhtiar is Voice of America's television producer for Persian-

---

[380] Caitlin MacNeal, "Rula Jebreal Rails Against MSNBC for labeling her 'Palestinian Journalist'" *TPM Livewire,* July 27, 2014 http://talkingpointsmemo.com/livewire/rula-jebreal-critical-msnbc-palestinian-journalist

language broadcasts. His close relationship to The Israel Project and to Block is revealed in a series of clubby emails, as is the sexist and bigoted nature of their campaign against Rula Jebreal. On October 21, 2015, Bakhtiar reached out to Block via email soliciting somebody to appear on a program opposite Jebreal, writing:

> *Hi Josh, I have been tasked to put together a debate between a Palestinian advocate and one from the Israeli side. The debate will center on the root causes of this latest wave of violence and how to tamp it down. Unfortunately, this Israeli perspective has to come from the Holy Land. Otherwise, I would have asked you, Noah Pollak or Omri Ceren. Is there any way you can help me find an articulate expert who can go toe-to-toe with this Rula Jebreal on Tuesday…I have put in a call to David Weinberg in Israel and he was supposed to book either Dore Gold or Mark Regev, but they took a pass. You need to save my bacon here. I cannot have this lady Rula all by herself.*[381]

An hour later, Block responded to Bakhtiar:

> *…I understand why Dore and Regev wouldn't do it. Rula Jebreal is a crazy person will [sic] not [sic] real legitimacy, and Dore like their Undersecretary of State and Mark Regev is on his way to be the Ambassador in London. The challenge here is to find someone not strident who want [sic] to fight with a slanderous anti-Semite and doesn't worry about imparting their credibility to a non-entity like her, or is more at her level. I think it is doable though, and our guys will get to work.*
>
> *I don't know who booked Rula Jebreel [sic] but she may be hard to pair up! You would be better off with someone like Ghaith al-Omari,*[382] *who is a former PLO official and Palestinian peace process negotiator. That would be a more productive debate and discussion for listeners, and a lot easier to book. I know this is preaching to the quire [sic], but she is so inflammatory—its [sic]*

---

[381] "The Israel Project and Voice of America negotiate guest media appearances" The Israel Lobby Archive, http://IsraelLobby.org/TIP/VOA.pdf

[382] Ghaith al-Omari was at the time and remains a senior fellow at the Washington Institute for Near East Policy running "The Irwin Levy Family Program on the U.S.-Israel Strategic Relationship" http://www.washingtoninstitute.org/experts/view/ghaith-al-omari

> *like hand [sic] U.S. government paid for matches to a pyromaniac…The hit is next Tuesday at 12:30 pm EST…*

Block was suggesting that Ghaith al-Oamari, who was working at AIPAC's think tank spinoff the Washington Institute for Near East Policy as a specialist on U.S.-Israeli relations, would be a credible "opponent" to yet another pro-Israel pundit. However, five hours later Bakhtiar reported that David Weinberg, the self-described "spokesman, speechwriter, columnist and lobbyist who is a sharp critic of Israel's detractors and of post-Zionist trends in Israel"[383] had finally located someone to appear with Jebreal, Emmanuel Navon, author of the book, *The Victory of Zionism.*

> *David Weinberg in Israel has booked a gentleman by the name of Emanuel Navon for us. I have no idea who he is, but he has apparently accepted the challenge of taking on Lady Rula. I know that Rula's bona fides and credentials as a Middle East analyst are quite questionable, but my editor was keen on having her on because of her looks (although she is hardly my type).*

Block approved of the choice. "Now that makes sense! Emanuel will be a good guest—and he goes into a third category—one who probably has no idea who she is! Excellent." But in the end, Navon never had to face "Lady Rula," who did not appear on the program. Instead, on October 27, 2015 he debated Omar Baddar, a Washington-based political scientist and human rights activists serving as the executive director of an organization called the Palestinian Freedom Project.[384]

In historical context, the offensive strategy of The Israel Project's spelling-challenged president syncs with the Israel lobby's standard playbook. Even before AIPAC split off from the American Zionist Council in 1963, it had a number of practices designed to detect and eliminate when possible—or counteract when not—credible voices for Arab or Palestinian causes being delivered to relevant audiences:

> *For obvious reasons our activities in this area cannot be minutely described, nor can we give names, dates, or places. We are, however, fighting hostile propagandists as one of our major activities throughout the year by: a. a careful check of newspapers, bulletins and confidential sources of our own, who can give us reliable*

---

383 Website, "David M. Weinberg: A Citadel Defending Zion," http://www.davidmweinberg.com

384 Voice of America, October 27, 2015, https://www.youtube.com/watch?v=QNOJd68TgU4

> *information on the movements or itineraries of these propagandists. b. alerting our community contacts...c. requesting that all known meetings be monitored....furnishing speakers and arranging for them to address the forums...*[385]

In those days, if AIPAC/AZC could not detect and get an event canceled from behind the scenes, the next step was to demand that the organizers allow one of its own hand-picked speakers to address the audience from the same platform. This self-serving lobby courtesy is rarely—if ever—extended to opponents of the lobby's own public events, where pro-Israel speakers mostly speak alone or in groups, and go entirely unchallenged.

Today, rather than public meetings, the major arena for such suppression efforts is broadcast and cable television as well as radio. Major broadcast news outlets operate under constant pressure from media watch IAOs and internal watchdogs enforcing these practices. This is why so few eloquent or effective Arab, Muslim or Palestinian voices—let alone other critics—are allowed to appear. When they do, they are seldom alone. This is in contrast to Israeli government officials and pro-Israel pundits, who frequently appear alone and unchallenged.

Once Jebreal and others are effectively labeled as "Palestinian journalists," or given other such titles that lower their broader credibility and explicitly tie them to an Arab, Muslim or Palestinian cause, they begin to disappear from U.S. airwaves. There is no countervailing pressure on big media—external or internal—to apply the same standards by dubbing as "Israeli or Pro-Israel" Eli Lake, Dore Gold, Emmanuel Navon, or, most especially, pundits from the Washington Institute for Near East Policy such as Dennis Ross or Ghaith al-Omari. All could accurately be categorically dubbed "Zionist journalists" or "Pro-Israel advocates" as a form of warranted public disclosure to viewers. However, such warnings are never permitted to appear on the bright graphic overlay of television screens known within the industry as the "lower third."

---

385 "The AZC's internal 'Information and Public Relations Department' reports," The Israel Lobby Archive http://www.israellobby.org/AZC/

9 AMERICAN PUBLIC OPINION

Despite all of the IAO programs and billions of dollars spent, and a great deal of one-sided coverage of Israel in the national media, overall American public support for Israel is low. That fact is generally little reported, little known and only spreading slowly. Mainstream public opinion polls, possibly sensitive to putting increasingly scarce advertising dollars at risk, generally avoid asking Americans key questions about their level of support for massive and unconditional U.S. foreign aid to Israel. This aid is an observable product of IAO advocacy, yet it is hidden in plain sight because it is not placed into perspective. A great deal of specialty polling about the Middle East in America is highly compromised. Those reporting key findings at times offer conclusions that directly contradict their own survey data, but they are seldom called out over this. Investigation into the organizations conducting the surveys reveals institutional and donor pressures are the most likely reason.

Top IAOs certainly know that not all Americans support Israel, even without revealing the true picture. According to the Conference of Presidents of Major American Jewish Organizations leader Malcolm Hoenlein, in 2011:

> *Our polls indicate that 25% of Americans are hard-core supporters and 10% are hard-core opposers. We have to focus our efforts on that middle, with positive messaging, telling the story of Israel.'*[386]

[386] David Brinn, "Deconstructing an 'eroticized hatred'" *The Jerusalem Post*, May 4, 2012, report from The Jerusalem Post Conference in New York

Since the industry of public opinion polling first began in the 1930s, polls have become indispensable measurement tools, even though they are often misused. All democracies are theoretically concerned about public opinion since governments are supposed to be reflections of public will. Israel lobbying organizations encourage polls favorable to Israel, censure and ignore those that are not, and charter and publish their own public opinion surveys for similar reasons, to "prove" that Israel is a highly popular cause in the United States and that Americans favor extraordinary foreign aid and other support, all delivered without conditions. As noted, the American Jewish Committee and ADL use polls as a bludgeon both to chastise the U.S. public and influence other nations.

At the front end, all polling is fraught with possibilities for pre-determining or rigging the response to be most favorable to a particular cause or partisan position. "Tailoring" the sample to include only individuals who will respond reliably is one method, and seems to be the only explanation for The Israel Project polling results that are usually wildly at odds with mainstream pollsters. In the Internet age, allowing those surveyed to respond multiple times in online polls in order to tip the results is the simplest way to do that. Asking "leading" or "suggestive" questions designed to elicit a particular response from a broader audience—often done in the run-up to an election—is yet another technique, called "push polling."

Though often better than The Israel Project's polls, mainstream organizations like Gallup devote a great deal of effort fielding highly suspect polls where the outcome is all but certain—only to then trumpet the result as proof Americans "view Israel favorably." Unfavorable findings receive no noisy splash. One example is a polling report on American favorability comparing only three entities, Israel, Iran and the Palestinian Authority. With little variation, year after year, the poll report painstakingly reveals that about 65 percent of that Americans view Israel "very/mostly favorable" over the Palestinian Authority (17 percent) and Iran (11 percent). Perhaps Gallup's unsubtle headline, "Americans Continue to Tilt Pro-Israel," is the purpose of the poll.[387] Presumably, such findings keep in check politicians thinking of any innovative peace initiatives. Or perhaps they reassure pro-Israel voters while de-motivating those who think Israel has too much influence. Clearly, the results further marginalized Iran and the Palestinian Authority during an intense period of Israel lobbying against Iran's civilian nuclear program and Palestinian bids for United Nations recognition. Nevertheless, such polls do

---

[387] Elizabeth Mendes, "Americans Continue to Tilt Pro-Israel," Gallup, March 2, 2012. Gallup did not respond to an inquiry whether any organization had chartered, sponsored, or in any way financially supported a decade-long fielding of the survey. http://www.gallup.com/poll/153092/americans-continue-tilt-pro-israel.aspx

little to reveal why Americans think the way they do, through more probing and relevant questions or providing opportunities for more informed choices.

Middle East analysts eagerly await the biennial Chicago Council on Global Affairs survey results for its frank reflection of American views about foreign policy toward the region. Many in 2014 were surprised by the Chicago Council's conclusions that 64 percent of Americans prefer not to take sides in the Israel-Palestine conflict and that 55 percent would oppose sending U.S. troops to protect Israel if it attacked Iran. But these results are confirmed by other surveys. This seems to be a refreshing break from mind-numbing reports of blanket American support from organizations like The American Jewish Committee. Yet even the vaunted Chicago survey had insurmountable and highly suspicious flaws.

The Chicago Council poll analysis concluded that the majority of Americans would keep economic and military aid to Israel, Mexico, Taiwan, Afghanistan, Iraq, Egypt and Pakistan "about the same." Only a small percentage of Americans —claimed the survey—would increase aid, while most of the rest would prefer to decrease or stop aid altogether. One problem identified by the Chicago Council was that most Americans think such U.S. foreign aid is far more than it actually is. A second issue was timing, and that "this question was asked before August [2014] violence between Israel and Palestinians…" Despite these factors, the Council confidently concluded:

> *Americans tend to support maintaining or increasing military aid to Israel, Taiwan and Mexico. In a pattern similar to preferences for economic aid, the public tends to favor decreasing or stopping military aid to Egypt, Pakistan, Afghanistan and Iraq.*[388]

The Chicago Council could easily have provided relevant comparative data to respondents within its survey questions, but chose not to. In this case, one could argue it that was required, since the 2014 U.S. foreign aid budget for Mexico was $206 million; Afghanistan was $749 million, while Pakistan was $881 million, with Iraq getting only $73 million. Meanwhile Israel and Egypt received the lions' shares, with a whopping $3.1 billion for Israel and $1.6 billion to Egypt. Furthermore, aid to Israel increased on average 30 percent annually since 1970, to the point that Israel received nine percent of the entire U.S. foreign aid budget, while benefiting from Egypt's five percent share, which is justified as maintaining the 1979 Egypt-Israel peace agreement. In Israel's case, the figure understates actual aid levels, since Congress is regularly tapped by the American Israel Public Affairs Committee and member IAOs for additional military aid and joint program funding

388 "Foreign Policy in the Age of Retrenchment," The Chicago Council on Global Affairs http://survey.thechicagocouncil.org/survey/2014/index.html

during the year. It excludes additional support lobbied for by JCRCs and passed in state legislatures. Official figures also omit the secret intelligence budgets and dollar value of the massive flows of raw intelligence on Americans approved by President Obama in 2009 and later revealed by NSA whistleblower Edward Snowden. How do Americans really feel about aid to Israel when it is put in perspective?

It used to be impossible for small accountability organizations or individuals to "fact check" large public opinion polls. With the advent of Google Consumer Surveys, that is happily no longer the case. The Google Consumer Survey samples the American adult population of Internet users, selecting visitors with known demographics to websites and through mobile apps that have agreed to allow Google to administer surveys that are usually one or two questions. In 2012, there were about 80 sites in the survey network, including a mix of large and small publishers (such as *New York Daily News*, *Christian Science Monitor*, *Reader's Digest*, *Lima, Ohio News* and the *Texas Tribune*). Google Consumer Surveys also appear on major sites such as YouTube and Pandora, among others. During the 2012 presidential race Google was the number two polling service for accuracy, according to a much-cited ranking by Nate Silver. The oft-cited and highly regarded Gallup ranked last place as the least accurate pollster. [389]

The author surveyed a statistically significant number of American adults on the topic of foreign aid in order to fact-check the Chicago Council. (See following figure) The Google Consumer Survey was fielded after the brutal Israeli invasion of Gaza—a significant difference. The survey question, however, included the necessary context that the Chicago Council omitted, asking, "The U.S. gives Israel over $3 billion annually (9 percent of the foreign aid budget and more than any other country). The amount is." Respondents could choose between "much too much, too much, about right, too little, and much too little." The order of those response choices was randomly reversed to avoid bias.

[389] Nate Silver, "Which Polls Fared Best (and Worst) in the 2012 Presidential Race?" *The New York Times*, November 10, 2012 http://fivethirtyeight.com/features/which-polls-fared-best-and-worst-in-the-2012-presidential-race/

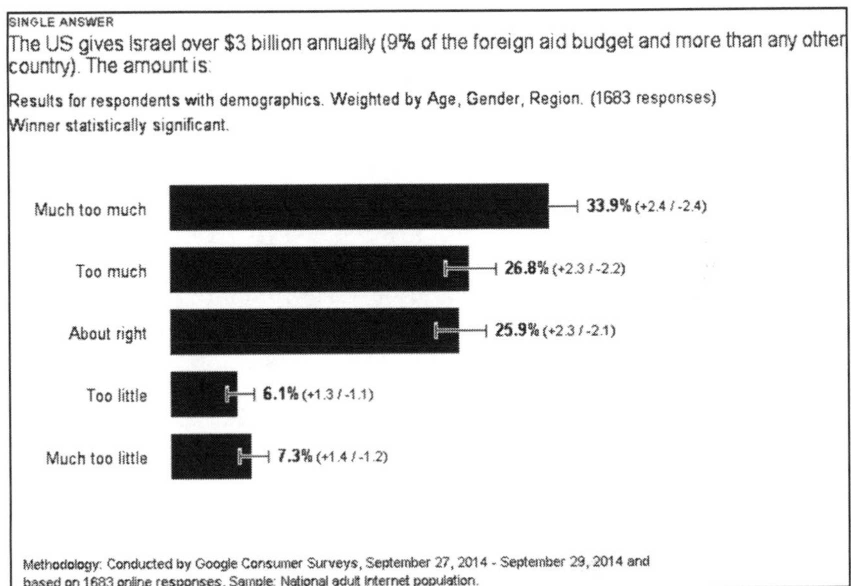

Figure 30 Survey: American public opinion about aid to Israel

Almost 61 percent of Americans said the U.S. was giving too much aid to Israel. 33.9 percent said the U.S. gives "much too much," while 26.8 percent described it was "too much." Some 25.9 percent felt aid to Israel was "about right," but only 6.1 percent said it was "too little" and 7.3 percent said "much too little."[390]

That such an overwhelming majority of Americans believe the U.S. is giving too much aid to Israel may surprise many who are accustomed to seeing mainstream pollster surveys (including Chicago's) incorrectly claiming overwhelming U.S. support for Israel. It simply should not be this way. The fault lies in flawed questions and lack of relevant context. Comparing American favorability rankings of Israel, the Palestinian Authority and Iran is about as useful as comparing U.S. aid to Mexico and Israel, though such approaches may comfort IAOs which do a lot of their own proprietary polling for internal use without publicizing results. Many important questions about Israel are simply never asked in U.S. surveys. Where results would likely produce a very "bad" outcome, entire categories of polls—particularly the World Values Survey, as previously discussed—are never conducted.

The Chicago Council confidently noted that Americans uniformly despise Iran, citing the 1979 hostage crisis and Iran's nuclear program as self-evident reasons. According to the Chicago Council survey analysis, "They [Americans] are also prepared to use force if necessary to prevent Iran from

---

[390] Grant F. Smith and Jeffrey Blankfort, "American Public Opinion on U.S. Aid to Israel," IRmep, September, 2014 http://www.irmep.org/09302014_usfati.pdf

obtaining a nuclear weapon." The Council claims that the third highest perceived threat to U.S. vital interests is "the possibility of unfriendly countries becoming nuclear powers," followed by the even more specific number four, "Iran's nuclear program."

Before making such broad claims, it would again be useful to insert the type of control questions that not only would improve survey quality (which Chicago Council sometimes does at a basic level), but also ascertain whether respondents have already been subjected to propaganda or scare campaigns that explains their most elevated but unfounded worries. In the case of Iran, the Israel lobby has been relentless in its campaign to pit Americans against Iran, and it paid off. Although no Western intelligence agency or, indeed, Israel's own, plainly asserted Iran had nuclear weapons, a majority (58.5 percent of Americans) believed Iran had nuclear weapons in 2014.[391]

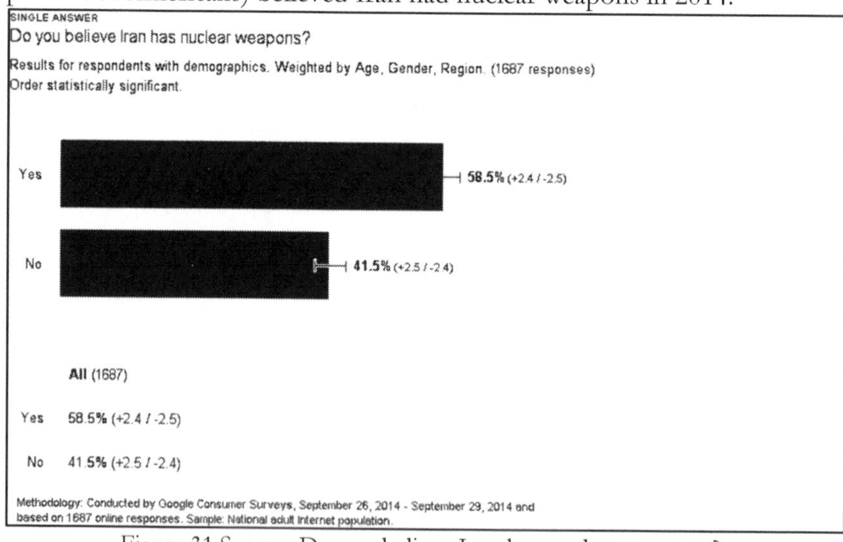

Figure 31 Survey: Do you believe Iran has nuclear weapons?

Most polls dealing with Middle East policy—where disinformation created and fielded by IAOs is overwhelming—would produce different results if they gave American respondents some key facts and relevant data before asking the questions. In the end, what many such polls most reveal is the sorry state of American news reporting and the stunning success of propaganda and disinformation campaigns. This is starkly revealed in the author's March 2016 four-country survey asking whether Israelis occupied Palestinian territory, or Palestinians occupied Israeli territory. The majority

---

[391] IRmep Google consumer survey. "Do you believe Israel has nuclear weapons?" September 26, 2014 https://www.google.com/insights/consumersurveys/view?survey=7gfftskexqbf4&question=1&filter=&rw=1

of the citizens of the United Kingdom, Canada and Mexico answered correctly that Israel occupies Palestinian territories. A plurality of the citizens of the United States believed that Palestinians—in fact—occupy Israeli territory.[392]

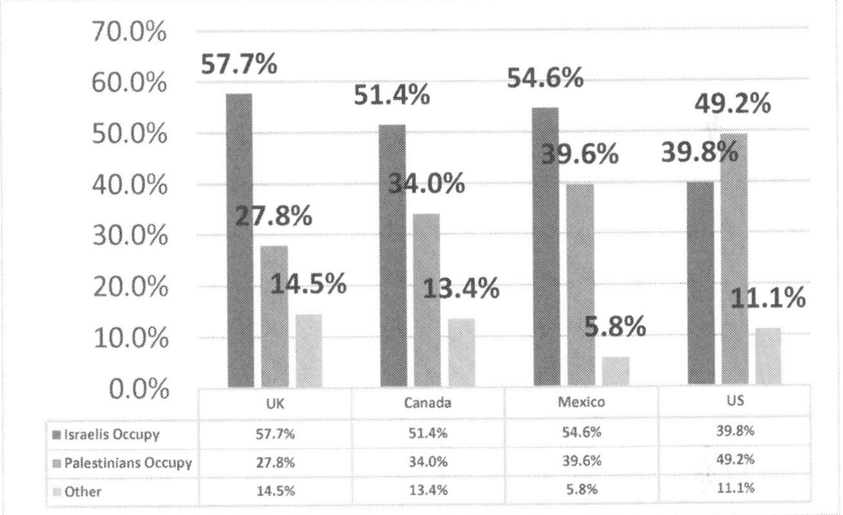

	UK	Canada	Mexico	US
Israelis Occupy	57.7%	51.4%	54.6%	39.8%
Palestinians Occupy	27.8%	34.0%	39.6%	49.2%
Other	14.5%	13.4%	5.8%	11.1%

Figure 32 Survey: Do Israelis occupy Palestinian land or the reverse?

Yet when asked, Americans are also not overwhelmingly supportive of another major program of both AIPAC and Jewish Community Relations Council "grassroots" Astroturf lobbying: legislative resolutions expressing unconditional support for Israel. An April 2014, Google Consumer Survey reveals 68.3 percent of Americans saying such resolutions "do not represent my views."

---

392 Eric Schuler, "Who Occupies Whom in Israel-Palestine? Don't Ask an American" *Antiwar.com*, April 2, 2016

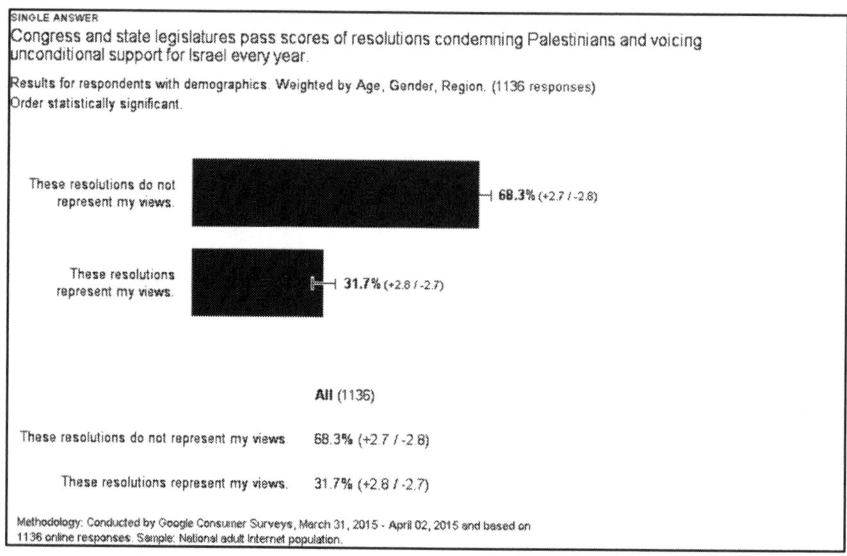

Figure 33 Survey: Do you support pro-Israel resolutions?

A final survey asking an unprecedented question about Israel's own secret nuclear weapons program produced stunning results in May of 2015. Nearly 65 percent of Americans believe Israel's clandestine nuclear weapons program should be officially acknowledged. Almost 55 percent believe the program should be subject to international inspections. This reflects a direct, majority opposition on the part of the public toward the U.S. and Israeli policy of "ambiguity" about Israel's nuclear arsenal.

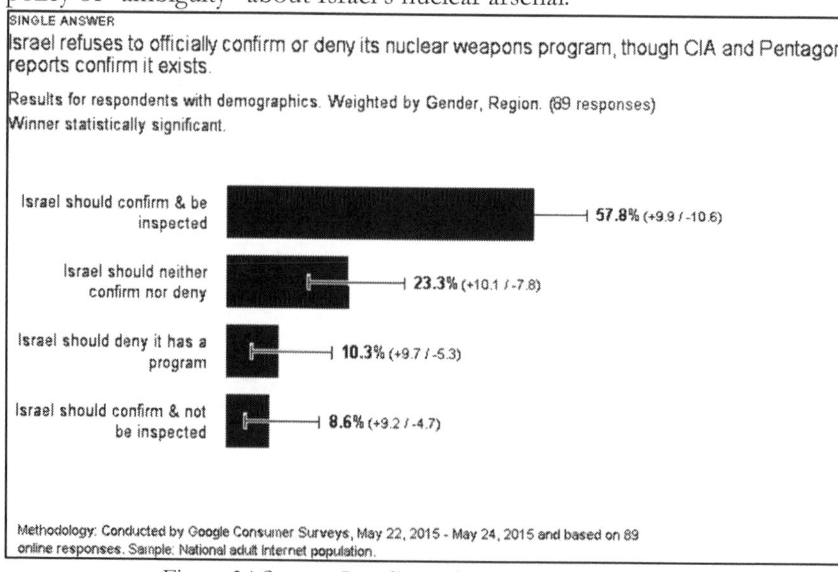

Figure 34 Survey: Israel's nuclear weapons program

IAOs floated proposals for presenting Israel with yet more U.S. aid upon the successful conclusion of negotiations to limit Nuclear Non-Proliferation treaty signatory Iran's nuclear program in 2015. Yet Americans responded mostly negatively to each specific proposal circulated for increased aid to Israel. They opposed paying "compensation" for a highly beneficial international agreement that both the Israeli government and its U.S. lobby—in tight coordination—fought against and lost.

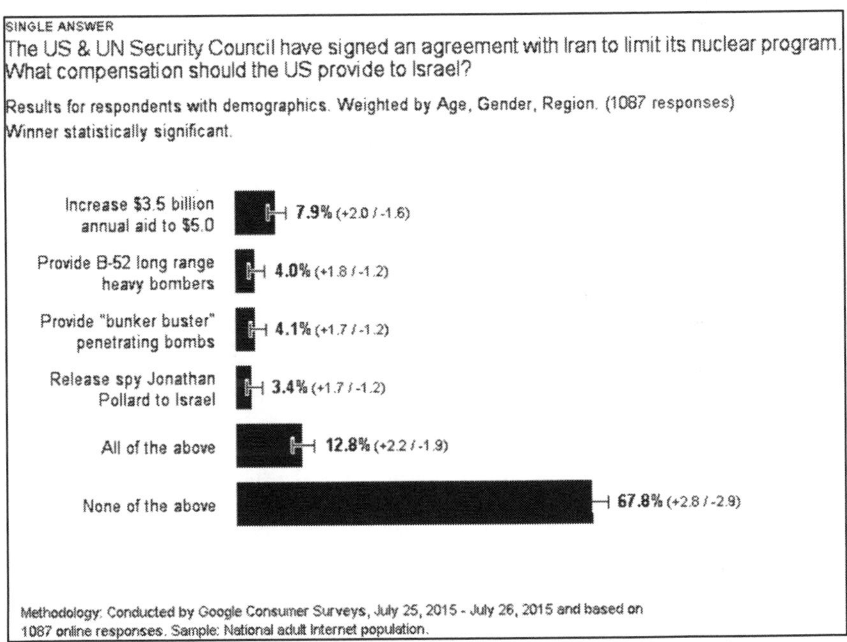

Figure 35 Survey: Compensating Israel over Iran nuclear deal

A January 2016 poll conducted by the author measured how the public wants the government to act when it comes to sensitive disclosures. Decontextualizing the diversion site and destination of stolen U.S. weapons-grade uranium during the so-called NUMEC affair (discussed in more depth later), a statistically significant poll found 58 percent of Americans wanted full disclosure.

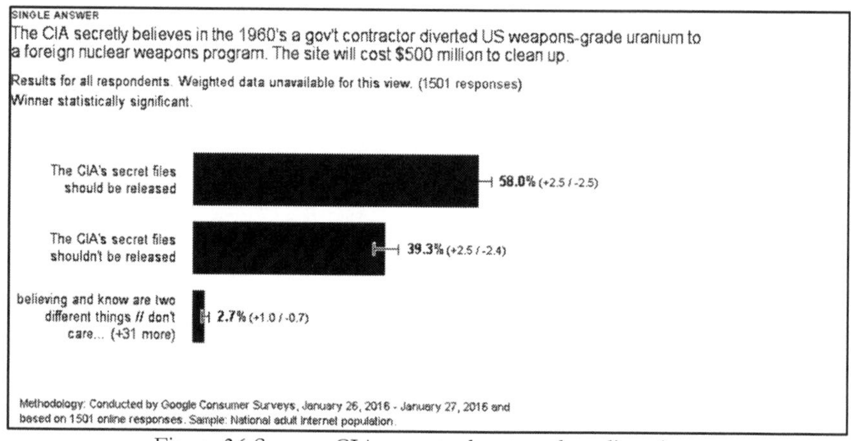

Figure 36 Survey: CIA secrets about nuclear diversion

Generally speaking, public opinion polls taken and made available to a general audience that explore American attitudes toward aid to Israel by providing relevant comparative information are few and far between. That was not always true, according to Middle East analyst Jeffrey Blankfort. *The Washington Post* and ABC News in March, 1989, during the first Palestinian intifada, fielded a poll revealing that "support for cutting aid [to Israel] increased significantly when respondents were first informed about the amount of assistance that Israel now receives, suggesting that some who favor present aid levels might change their minds if they knew how much aid Israel actually receives compared to other countries." Half of those polled in 1989 were asked if they thought U.S. aid to Israel should increase or decrease or remain the same. Six percent favored an increase, 26 percent a decrease and 66 percent preferred that aid remain "about the same." The second half, informed about the actual amount of aid, showed a noticeable difference. While those supporting an increase declined a negligible two percentage points to four percent, the number approving a decrease in aid jumped to 43 percent, while those believing it should remain the same dropped to 51 percent. There is no evidence that a similar dual-poll has been taken since by any mainstream news organization.[393]

What accounts for the Chicago Council's particular failure to field a reasonable survey and correctly interpret its data? Probably funding. Chicago Council Chairman Lester Crown, listed as a major financial supporter of the survey, is also a major supporter of Israel. A member of an IAO called the "Jewish Funders Network," Crown served as Deputy Chair of the International Board of the Weizmann Institute of Science in Israel, and as a

[393] Grant F. Smith and Jeffrey Blankfort, "American Public Opinion on U.S. Aid to Israel," IRmep, September, 2014 http://www.irmep.org/09302014_usfati.pdf

member of Tel Aviv University's Board of Governors. Crown donated the initial $10 million gift that started The Crown Center for Middle East Studies at Brandeis University. Crown and family are also funders of the Crown Fellows program in American History at Brandeis University.

The overreliance of the Chicago Council on Crown for survey funding makes the possibility of fielding better questions or honestly interpreting data unlikely. The same exposure is caused, on an immensely larger scale, by federation donations to universities and institutes of higher learning across the country that might also be interested in conducting such polling. Upon cashing large federation checks, the leadership of such institutions has a vested interest in avoiding anything likely to upset their pro-Israel donors.

Any polling tool can be twisted, fielded and then used for purely propagandistic purposes. On the other hand, polls can be carefully formulated and fielded to derive bona fide answers and educate the public. But unless the results of better polls are broadly distributed, analyzed, referenced and acted upon, the findings will not have any impact.

At present, it is the Chicago Council poll that is widely cited as a "go-to" source for foreign policy insights and policymaking. Nevertheless, no auditable data is released for independent verification of the results and analysis. The Global Values Survey data is available in digital format, but since it has rarely been fielded in Israel, and even then avoided the most relevant question, it is of no value. The author's own poll users can go directly to the Google Website and perform their own data cuts, raw data downloads and analysis and otherwise verify the results. No mainstream news outlets have yet attempted to debunk or replicate these stunning findings. As most already know, to do so would be to invite an immediate IAO pressure group reaction.

However, these poll results have spread virally through the Internet, "end-running" the gatekeepers and finding their way to users who appreciate what hidden truths such low-cost, rapid and accurate polling can reveal. Still, there is resistance in captured areas of government. Although the Congressional Research Office was given the data in 2014, in 2015 it continues to incorrectly report to Congress that Americans favor U.S. aid to Israel.[394] At least, with only a few clicks of a mouse, Internet users who care can now see that is not necessarily so. However, some groups which receive a great deal of media attention, such as Christians United For Israel (CUFI), by spending large percentages of their budgets on outsourced public relations services, make it their mission to show that far more Americans are pro-Israel than is actually the case.

IAOs have long heavily solicited inter-denominational support from

394 Sharp, Jeremy "U.S. Foreign Aid to Israel" June 10, 2015. This annual report goes to great lengths to find public support for U.S. aid for Israel, and its author refuses to engage public watchdogs with data contrary to its findings.

religious groups far beyond the Jewish community's walls. In its 1962-1963 budget, the Jewish Agency-funded American Zionist Council (the parent organization of AIPAC) listed Christian groups as the third most important target of its "Information and Public Relations" campaign.

> *3. Christian Religious Groups*
> *Cultivation of key religious leaders and groups*
> *Setting up Seminars on Israel for Christian clergy*
> *Stimulating of positive articles in the Protestant & Catholic press*
> *Counteraction of hostile material in that press*
> *Reprints and distribution of favorable materials from church press*
> *Stimulation of suitable articles in the journals of the Jewish religious groups.*[395]

The investment paid off handsomely. According to a 2014 poll by *Bloomberg Politics*, 45 percent of Americans would support Israel even if "our interests diverged," 47 percent would pursue America's interests "when we disagree with them," while eight percent were unsure. Religiosity is the main engine behind such blind support, according to Bloomberg:

> *Born-again Christians are more likely than overall poll respondents, 58 percent to 35 percent, to back Israel regardless of U.S. interests. Americans with no religious affiliation were the least likely to feel this way, at 26 percent.*[396]

Unfortunately for the IAOs long working to spread, then maintain, this religious support (including groups whose sole mission is strengthening that bond, such as International Fellowship of Christians and Jews, Christians United for Israel, Christian Friends of Israel America and Christian Friends of Israeli Communities), Americans are rapidly disaffiliating themselves from the largest denominations—predominately Christian—in favor of the "no religious affiliation" category. This category is going to be unwilling to prioritize Israel's interests over those of the United States.

According to a 2014 Pew Research Center poll on religion and public life, over a seven-year period the Christian segment of the overall U.S. population declined nearly eight percent, while the "unaffiliated" segment shot up nearly

---

[395] "Committee on Information and Public Relations," American Zionist Council, internal report seized under subpoena of the Senate Foreign Relations Committee for its 1963 hearings on foreign agents. Senate records available at http://www.irmep.org/ila/AZC2/

[396] Margaret Talev, "Bloomberg Politics National Poll Finds Deep Partisan Split on Israel and Iran," Bloomberg Politics, April13, 2015 http://www.bloomberg.com/politics/articles/2015-04-15/bloomberg-politics-national-poll-finds-deep-partisan-split-on-israel-and-iran

the same, at about seven percent. The importance this seismic shift will have on the Israel affinity ecosystem cannot be overemphasized. Christians made up 70.6 percent of the U.S. population in 2014, while the unaffiliated were 22.8 percent (the two totaling 93.4 percent of the combined population).

	2007	2014	Change
Christian	**78.4**	**70.6**	**-7.80**
Protestant	51.3	46.5	-4.80
Evangelical	26.3	25.4	-0.90
Mainline	18.1	14.7	-3.40
Historically black	6.9	6.5	-
Catholic	23.9	20.8	-3.10
Orthodox	0.6	0.5	-
Mormon	1.7	1.6	-
Jehovah's Witness	0.7	0.8	-
Other	0.3	0.4	-
Non-Christian	**4.7**	**5.9**	**1.20**
Jewish	1.7	1.9	-
Muslim	0.04	0.9	0.50
Buddhist	0.7	0.7	-
Hindu	0.4	0.7	0.30
Other world religion	0.3	0.3	-
Other Faiths	1.2	1.5	0.30
Unaffiliated	**16.1**	**22.8**	**6.70**
Atheist	1.6	3.1	1.50
Agnostic	2.4	4	1.60
Nothing in particular	12.1	15.8	3.70
Don't Know/Refused	0.8	0.6	-0.20

Figure 37 2014 Pew Research Center poll on religion & public life

An important factor behind the trend is that disaffiliated Americans are comparatively young (median age 36) compared to the overall adult population (age 46), and the segment is getting younger over time. Religious affiliation is therefore an "older person's thing" that is likely to decline faster as older adherents die and the younger disaffiliated population, forming families, do not indoctrinate new family members into religion of any type during a key formative period.

Even discarding these important growth factors, which would tend to accelerate the Christian decline and the growth rate of the unaffiliated, a forecast by the author suggests that by 2035, Christians and the unaffiliated will be nearing parity. Seven years later, absent some unforeseen religious revival, unaffiliated Americans will represent the overwhelming majority of the population. They will be increasingly unresponsive to appeals that "Judeo-Christian" principles underlie the so-called "special relationship" with Israel. They will stare blankly or even suspiciously at references to the importance of "the holy land," and emotional appeals to maintain a "Jewish State's" custodianship over Jewish, Muslim and Christian religious sites. They will similarly be unimpressed by references to Judea in the New Testament and other such selective 3,000-year-old Bible-based territorial claims.

	2021	2028	2035	2042
Christian	**62.80**	**55.00**	**47.20**	**39.40**
Protestant	41.70	36.90	32.10	27.30
Evangelical	24.50	23.60	22.70	21.80
Mainline	11.30	7.90	4.50	1.10
Historically black	-	-	-	-
Catholic	17.70	14.60	11.50	8.40
Orthodox	-	-	-	-
Mormon	-	-	-	-
Jehovah's Witness	-	-	-	-
Other	-	-	-	-
Non-Christian	**7.10**	**8.30**	**9.50**	**10.70**
Jewish				
Muslim	1.40	1.90	2.40	2.90
Buddhist				
Hindu	1.00	1.30	1.60	1.90
Other world religion				
Other Faiths	1.80	2.10	2.40	2.70
Unaffiliated	**29.50**	**36.20**	**42.90**	**49.60**
Atheist	4.60	6.10	7.60	9.10
Agnostic	5.60	7.20	8.80	10.40
Nothing in particular	19.50	23.20	26.90	30.60
Don't Know/Refused	0.40	0.20	0.00	0.00

Figure 38 Forecast rise of Americans unaffiliated with religion

By 2042, if the trend continues, unaffiliated Americans will be in the majority, and America will be a very different place.[397] The coming abandonment of organized religion by the majority of Americans, and the vanishing inclination to be spiritually harnessed into supporting Israel, of course do not guarantee popular opinion will be immediately well-represented in Congress, since its members may quite likely still be elected on the strength of IAO-coordinated campaign contributions. In 2014, there was only one religiously unaffiliated member of Congress, while Christians and Jewish representatives were vastly overrepresented, at 91.8 percent and 5.2 respectively.[398] The utter lack of Congressional mirror imaging of society at large is nothing particularly newsworthy. In 2015, four out of five members of Congress were also white males, with only 17 percent non-white and only 20 percent female.[399] In America, twenty percent of the population is non-white and females outnumber males by three percentage points.

Nevertheless, the coming wave of an unaffiliated American majority will not likely react positively to IAO religious appeals. The largest sub-category quantified by Pew was "nothing in particular (15.8 percent)," as opposed to Atheist (3.1 percent) or Agnostic (four percent). This reveals not an anti-religious bent, but rather that religion simply played no role in the respondent's identity or day-to-day life. Politicians will undoubtedly still pander behind closed doors to dwindling minority religious institutions and interest groups that are organized and demand a set of commitments in exchange for member support. Unaffiliated Americans, as is currently the case, will probably not be "joiners" flocking to organizations promoting secularism, such as the American Atheists, the Humanist Institute or Freedom From Religion Foundation. Although some such organizations are attempting to attract and organize unaffiliated Americans into a powerful voting bloc, most of these have not yet taken any formal position opposing IAO activities in the United States on religious grounds. However, even that could change.

David Silverman, president of the American Atheists, boasts of the large number of members who are culturally Jewish but nevertheless atheists and active in the organization. The driving priorities within such organizations overwhelmingly involve de-stigmatizing atheism and building a politically

[397] The author is aware of the "fallacy of extrapolation," or assumption that any trend will continue, at the same rate, over long periods of time. However, the factors driving this trend are strong enough to last several decades.

[398] Antonia Blumberg "A Look at the Religious Make-Up of the 114th Congress," *The Huffington Post*, January 5, 2015 http://www.huffingtonpost.com/2015/01/05/congress-religious-affiliation_n_6417074.html

[399] Philip Bump, "The new Congress is 80 percent white, 80 percent male, and 92 percent Christian," *The Washington Post*, January 5, 2015

empowered movement before attempting to change religiously driven foreign policies although, according to statements by Silverman, religion in policymaking in general and Israel in particular are important issues that will have to be dealt with. Silverman writes:

> *The idea that Israel is a home for all Jews is nothing more than a marketing scheme at this point, Silverman said, it's a great way to lure legal, loyal immigrants. It makes no more sense for a Jew, let alone a former Jew, to have religion-based allegiance to Israel than it does for a non-Italian Catholic to have allegiance to Italy.*[400]

The Israel lobby will likely need to redouble efforts in other major programs originally identified in the "Information and Public Relations" campaign. Top priorities, then and now, include mass media, academia, visits to Israel, and both public and secret campaigns focused on "counteracting the opposition."[401] Creating more empathy and support among youth is already receiving concentrated IAO funding and for good reason, from the Israel lobby's standpoint.

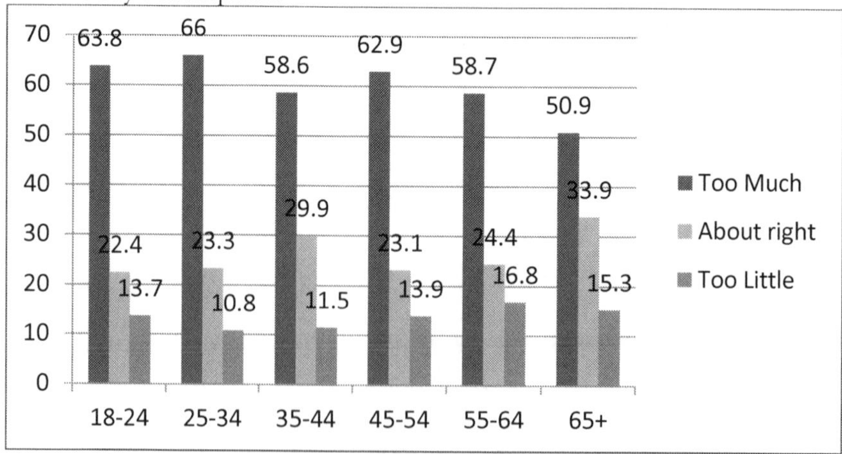

Figure 39 Survey: Opposition to U.S. aid for Israel by age category

The author's fall 2014 survey reveals that younger Americans were more

---

[400] Nathan Guttman, "America's Top Atheist Aims to Build Jewish Support for Ungodly Agenda," *The Jewish Daily Forward*, March 20, 2014 http://forward.com/news/194890/americas-top-atheist-aims-to-build-jewish-support/

[401] "Committee on Information and Public Relations," American Zionist Council, internal report seized under subpoena of the Senate Foreign Relations Committee for its 1963 hearings on foreign agents. Copy from Senate archives at http://www.irmep.org/ila/AZC2/

opposed to U.S. aid to Israel than older Americans, with nearly 64 percent in the 18-24 category believing aid was "too much," along with 66 percent in the 25-34 age category. Even among those aged 65+, less than half thought it was "about right" or "too little."

It may be tempting for some to think that the high levels of informed opposition to U.S. aid for Israel in the 2014 polling results were a fluke. However, when the same poll question, "the US gives Israel over $3 billion annually (9 percent of the foreign aid budget and more than any other country). The amount is:" was again fielded in March of 2016. The results were largely unchanged:[402]

ISRAEL AID POLL	SEP-2014	MAR-2016	DIFFERENCE
Much too much	33.9%	32.5%	-1.4
Too much	26.8%	29.4%	2.6
About right	25.9%	23.3%	-2.6
Too little	6.1%	6.5%	0.4
Much too little	7.3%	8.4%	1.1
Total	**100%**	**100%**	

Figure 40 US aid to Israel survey: 2014 v. 2016

In conclusion, popular U.S. support for Israel is nothing like what is commonly portrayed in mainstream media and trumpeted by the Israel Affinity Organizations that have a big hand in chartering polls and carefully spinning the findings. A demographic inundation is quietly eroding a core foundation of affinity—religious affiliation—as Americans float away from organized religion and Israel.

---

[402] Grant F. Smith, "US aid to Israel is 'too much' say 61.9% of Americans" *Antiwar.com*, April 6, 2016 http://original.antiwar.com/smith-grant/2016/04/05/us-aid-israel-much-say-61-9-americans/

10 CAPTURE

Capture occurs when regulators favor specific vested interests instead of serving the public interest.[403] IAOs, which together act as a kind of industry, have three close regulators and a more distant one. The Internal Revenue Service mandate is to ensure that all organizations granted charitable tax-exempt status have a recognizable social welfare purpose that relieves some burden otherwise incumbent upon the state. The Foreign Agents Registration Act enforcement section of the Justice Department constantly monitors individuals and organizations in the United States with foreign ties in order to ensure they are not acting as stealth agents of foreign principals by conducting lobbying and public relations campaigns without proper disclosure. The Department of Justice is also responsible for enforcing espionage laws and conducting warranted counterespionage activities through the FBI.

After the savings and loan debacle and the more recent financial crisis, Americans came to understand how the financial sector's contributions to the electoral campaigns of politicians could gradually strip away sensible regulatory oversight and small investor protections. The timing and design of bank branch deregulation in the 1970s and 1980s and overall systemic resistance to regulatory supervision in the 1990s, leading to the weakening of banks and the financial crisis, can be directly traced to politicians striking down protective laws in response to financial incentives and industry

[403] George Stigler, "The theory of economic regulation," *Bell Journal of Economics and Management Science*, Spring 1971

lobbying.[404] The "revolving door" between financial regulators who identify with and seek to curry favor with industry in hopes of someday rejoining it is a well-documented case study of regulatory capture. Innovation also creates a constant challenge to regulators.

Less widespread is the understanding about how individuals in government with an affinity for Israel or who were cultivated under pressure from IAOs, impact regulation. Individuals who grew up socialized to be sympathetic with the concerns of Israel and who view it as more vulnerable than the United States, are well represented across key agencies. In balancing their identification with Israel against their supervisory duties to regulate when warranted, too many have erred in Israel's favor. The most serious problems exist at the U.S. Department of Treasury.

The U.S. Department of Treasury in 2015 requested a budget of $16 billion to administer its programs with $12 billion provided to the Internal Revenue Service.[405] The IRS, as a regulator, has failed miserably when it comes to IAOs. It has never revoked IAO tax-exempt status except for the most flagrant failure to file, as was the recent case with the Zionist Organization of America and large numbers of defunct Hadassah chapters. Many IAOs won approval of their status from the Bureau of Internal Revenue, renamed the Internal Revenue Service in 1953, but it is impossible to know on what basis. The IRS gave the American Israel Public Affairs Committee backdated tax-exempt status in 1968, after earlier receiving letters of concern from Senate Foreign Relations Committee Chair J.W. Fulbright. More gravely, it has allowed an entire industry of "friends of" charities that export tax-exempt donations and externalize the burden on other taxpayers, despite their failure to reduce any identifiable burden on the U.S. government. To add insult to injury, the IRS has outsourced back onto the subsidy IAOs oversight into how the billions they transfer to Israel are spent. Even when presented with evidence that some funds are used for non-exempt purposes, the IRS has run away rather than investigate. FARA and counterespionage enforcement is no better. Moreover, no known citizen complaint has ever had the slightest impact on generating due IAO oversight.

General IRS practices also make what are supposed to be easy citizen audits of nonprofit tax-exempt organizations difficult. The IRS does not provide structured data (Extensible Markup Language, or XML, for example)

---

404 Dennis Veltrop and Jacob de Hann, "I just cannot get you out of my head: Regulatory capture of financial sector supervisors," *DNB Working Paper No 410*, January 2014 http://www.researchgate.net/publication/5216325_Regulatory_Capture_A_Review

405 "The Budget in Brief FY 2015," U.S. Department of the Treasury https://www.treasury.gov/about/budget-performance/budget-in-brief/Documents/Treasury_FY_2015_BIB.pdf

of IRS form 990s to the most commonly consulted public websites, such as Guidestar.org or CitizenAudit.org. Instead paper or portable document file (PDF) images of scanned paper forms, without any optical character recognition, are provided to individual requesters and these organizations that present the data to the public.

The IRS routinely excludes Schedule B (the schedule of contributors), which is the single most important part of a filing in terms of assessing donor support. Although the IRS must redact the names and addresses of contributors from the form, the remaining data (number and amount of contributions of greater than $5,000 from each donor) reveals a great deal about an organization's true level of public support. For IAOs, they mostly reveal extreme donor concentration and reliance on a small handful of donors for the majority of contributions.

Moreover, individual requests to the IRS for complete, redacted returns can take more than a year to process. The same is true for an organization's ostensibly publicly available IRS form 1023 request for tax-exempt status and IRS determination letter. The IRS routinely responds to requests for information with boilerplate letters about the confidentiality of filed tax returns—which is inapplicable to the tax-exempt charity domain. Failing to respond to such requests adds to the overall lack of serious enforcement, oversight and public accountability.

The Israel lobby has been keenly aware for decades that having friends in the U.S. Department of Treasury would be vital for Israel's long-term success. During WWII, Treasury Secretary Henry Morgenthau Jr. became infatuated with the efforts of Peter H. Bergson (aka Hillel Kook, born in Lithuania, 1915-2001) and his efforts to form a "Jewish Army" in the Middle East. Bergson's "Committee for a Jewish Army" circulated an early plan to the U.S. Congress calling for financing the proposed army of 100,000 Jews in Palestine to fight Nazis and "fifth columnists" from Syria, Iraq and Egypt. The request was politely turned down. Bergson was, in reality, leading an American front organization for Menachem Begin's Irgun Z'vai Leumi organization. Irgun also lobbied Nazi Germany for a Jewish Army, as well as a formal alliance between 1940 and 1941 during a time when Hitler appeared to have the upper hand in Europe.[406]

While Treasury Secretary Morgenthau supported Bergson's later rescue efforts to save Jews from Nazi barbarity by attempting to find refugee havens in Western host countries. He sought to remove entirely the "displaced

---

[406] Klaus Polkehn, "The Secret Contacts: Zionism and Nazi Germany, 1933-1941," *Journal of Palestine Studies*, Vol. 5, No. 3/4 (Spring–Summer, 1976), 54-82

person" policy from the jurisdiction of the U.S. State Department by commissioning his own Treasury Department assistants, Josiah Dubois, John Pehle and Randolph Paul, to compile a report on rescue opportunities and failures. Morgenthau presented the report to President Roosevelt on January 16, 1944. It roundly castigated the State Department and recommended that Roosevelt "remove the hands of men who are indifferent, callous and perhaps even hostile." He also threatened to launch a public relations attack on the State Department as a bastion of anti-Semitism. It was a charge, he said, that "will require little more in the way of proof for this suspicion to explode into a nasty scandal."[407]

Not wishing to face such a scandal in an election year, Roosevelt issued Executive Order 9417 establishing the War Refugee Board (WRB). He named Morgenthau, Secretary of State Cordell Hull and War Secretary Henry Stimson to head the board. John W. Pehle, who as assistant treasury secretary had spent much of his time working to produce evidence of State Department procrastination on refugee efforts, became director of the WRB. Earlier, Pehle had ordered that Bergson be allowed to utilize State Department cables to communicate with Irgun leader Vladimir Jabotinsky and facilitate his movements to Turkey.[408] Another Treasury Department official, Josiah Dubois, affirmed that Bergson's work was effective in "generating an atmosphere conducive to its [the WRB's] formation…we were seeking the same goals."

The WRB was authorized to establish refugee absorption centers in neutral countries. By late July of 1944, the WRB had only been able to secure infrastructure for 1,000 refugees at Fort Ontario, overlooking Oswego, New York. This number was unimpressive to other countries being simultaneously lobbied to absorb refugees, and the entire effort was largely a failure. In hindsight, this was more than just a failure to rescue innocent victims of the Holocaust or a diversion of wartime assets—with no referendum or act of Congress on the matter, Morgenthau had quietly allied a key U.S. government agency to terrorists.

Even before Bergson began receiving support from the Treasury, Irgun had plenty of blood on its hands. Jabotinsky was a major figure in the World Zionist Organization and put together a force of 5,000 soldiers as the organization's contribution to the British conquest of Palestine during WWI. In 1920, he organized the Haganah, the precursor to the Israeli Army, and

---

407 Sarah E. Peck, "The Campaign for an American Response to the Nazi Holocaust: 1943-1945," *Journal of Contemporary History*, Vol. 15, No. 2 (April 1980), 367-400

408 Sarah E. Peck, "The Campaign for an American Response to the Nazi Holocaust: 1943-1945," *Journal of Contemporary History*, Vol. 15, No. 2 (April 1980), 367-400

held a position in the WZO World Executive in recognition of his leadership role. The Haganah worked jointly with the British to quell the uprising as their "settlement police." He resigned to build his own far-right-wing Zionist-Revisionist World Union in 1925, which opposed World Zionist Organization president Chaim Weizmann's vision. Jabotinsky's was to "revise" the British decision to separate Trans-Jordan from territory allotted to become the "Jewish National Home" after WWI in the Balfour declaration. Jabotinsky also wanted to "revise" the British decision to disband the Jewish legion. His views evolved over time toward supporting the absolute necessity of violent armed displacement of Arabs in Palestine. This was frankly encapsulated in his 1923 "Iron Wall" manifesto, which bears striking resemblances to the utterances of many present-day Israeli leaders:

> *There can be no kind of discussion of a voluntary reconciliation between us and the Arabs…Any native people…view their country as their national home. They will not voluntarily allow, not only a new master, but even a new partner…Colonization can have only one goal. For the Palestinian Arabs this goal is inadmissible. This is in the nature of things. To change that nature is impossible…colonization can therefore, continue and develop only under the protection of a force independent of the local population—an iron wall which the native population cannot break through. This is, in toto, our policy toward the Arabs. To formulate it any other way would only be hypocrisy.*

Jabotinsky established his paramilitary Betar youth group in 1923 in Palestine and other countries. Menachem Begin joined in 1929 in Poland, rising to head the national unit that became Betar's largest branch. Arab Palestinians, sensing their own eventual violent displacement, had begun revolting against Jewish immigration in 1936. A Revisionist paramilitary split from the Haganah in 1931 and was placed under the command of Jabotinsky in December of 1936. Although they were originally committed to "self-restraint," by November the Irgun forces were actively engaging in terrorism, including the use of milk-can bombs that would be famously deployed a decade later against the British in the attack on the King David Hotel.

Early in September of 1936, 13 Arabs were killed, supposedly in retaliation for the death of three Jews. Several Irgunists were determined to act on their own, but the Irgun Command headed them off by organizing a wave of operations, beginning on November 14, that resulted in 10 dead and numerous wounded. The Irgun's campaign of attacks on purely civilian targets reached its zenith in the summer of 1938. On July 6, a bomb in a milk can went off in the Arab market in Haifa, leaving 21 dead and 52 injured. On July 15, an electric mine in David Street in the Old City of Jerusalem killed 10 and wounded 30. On July 25, another bomb in the Haifa market left 35 dead and 70 wounded. On July 26, a bomb in Jaffa's market killed 24 and injured 35.[409] Historian Paul Johnson claims that Israel owes its existence largely to the timely deployment of such terrorist attacks.[410] Still, in these days long predating the so-called "war on terror," the architect of many of these bloodbaths had no problem entering the U.S. with full Treasury Department support under Morgenthau.

In America, Irgun leader Jabotinsky roamed freely for a short time. On August 2, 1940, he was examined by a doctor who suspected he had heart trouble. Jabotinsky then made his way to a Betar training camp in Greene County in the Catskill Mountains, 130 miles from New York City. After reviewing an honor guard, he collapsed and died. Nevertheless, the Israel lobby's focus on the Treasury Department and attempts to capture it in pursuit of long-term initiatives that benefit Israel has never ceased.

The U.S. Treasury Department is seen as key to success in the Israel lobby drive for and ultimate confrontation with Iran over its nuclear program. AIPAC and its think tank, the Washington Institute for Near East Policy (WINEP), were instrumental in lobbying the president for the creation of the Office of Terrorism and Financial Intelligence unit in early 2004. The Israel lobby also supported candidate Stuart Levey as leader of TFI and President George W. Bush subsequently approved him to lead the new unit. Levey trumpeted his joy at having such a position to AIPAC's annual conference in Washington in 2005:

> *We all remember the Munich Olympics and Leon Klinghoffer and Pan Am 103 and Entebbe and Maalot and so many more. We all knew all along that terrorist groups could not be reasoned with or negotiated with, and that they sought nothing but destruction. As President Bush articulated in his address to you last year, '[Terrorists] kill without mercy. They kill without shame. And they count their victories in the death of the innocent.'*
>
> *You can imagine, then, how meaningful it is for me to play a role in this Administration's efforts to combat terrorism. I start off every morning reading the daily intelligence book, and then spend my day working to undercut the supply-lines of terrorist groups. It is, quite honestly, exhilarating. I often feel like the baseball players I used to watch growing up who, when asked about salary*

---

409 Lenni Brenner, "Zionist-Revisionism: The Years of Fascism and Terror," *Journal of Palestine Studies*, Vol. 13, No. 1 (Autumn 1983), 66-92

410 Paul Johnson, *A History of the Jews* [New York, Harper and Row, 1987] 526

> *issues, would say 'Are you kidding?? I get paid to do something that I love. I would do this for free.'...*[411]

Levey's primary qualification for the job was his knowledge about and dedication to Israel. Levey wrote his Fulbright-grant-funded undergraduate thesis under the guidance of another key Israel supporter, *The New Republic* editor Martin Peretz. It was about Meir Kahane.[412] Kahane was the Brooklyn-born rabbi who founded the Israeli group Kach (Chai). Kahane's Chai (or Kach) occupied slot number 20 on the State Department's list of terrorist organizations and was also pursued by the FBI. Though dense, the lesson of Levy's thesis appears to be that moderate, overwhelming nonviolent agitation for Israel can accomplish more than can violent outliers working for largely the same goals. Push, and push some more, but do not go overboard.

TFI originally claimed to be "safeguarding the financial system against illicit use and combating rogue nations, terrorist facilitators, weapons of mass destruction (WMD) proliferators, money launderers, drug kingpins, and other national security threats." However, its actions—and, more important, inactions—revealed it to be mostly a sharp-edged tool forged principally to serve Israel, especially in the Iran nuclear scare.

For example, the *Jerusalem Post* reported that TFI went after the Islamic Republic of Iran Shipping Lines, targeting the company and eighteen affiliates for their alleged effort to "facilitate the transport of cargo for UN Designated proliferators." TFI further charged that the shipping company "falsifies documents and uses deceptive schemes to shroud its involvement in illicit commerce." Later in the same article, AIPAC trumpeted this as yet another victory in the drive to confront the Islamic Republic of Iran:

> *AIPAC strongly supports these steps which are part of a coordinated effort by the United States and the international community to ratchet up the pressure on Iran and convince it to suspend its illicit nuclear activities. These steps send an important signal that America continues to lead the effort to confront and stop Iran's nuclear pursuit.*

TFI is most clearly revealed as an Israel lobby-captured unit of the U.S. Department of Treasury for two attributes. It mainly responds to public inquiries only within Israel lobby forums and does not pursue Israel for the

---

411 Jeffrey Blankfort and Philip Weiss, "Treasury officials are sure cozy with Israel lobby," *Mondoweiss*, April 21, 2010 http://mondoweiss.net/2010/04/treasury-officials-are-sure-cozy-with-israel-lobby

412 Stuart Alan Levey, U.S. Treasury Appointee, Thesis *Meir Kahane: The Development of a Religious Totalitarian and his Challenge to Israeli Democracy*, Harvard College, 1985 The Israel Lobby Archive http://www.israellobby.org/treas/

same kinds of violations it vigorously pursues against Iran. For example, TFI has never taken actions to undercut the largest likely nexus of money laundering between the U.S. and the Middle East, unveiled in 2005 by Israeli prosecutor Talia Sasson and exposed by *USA Today*.[413] Although Levey made multiple official visits to Jerusalem to liaise with Israeli government officials, when formally asked under a Freedom of Information Act request to reveal how TFI was tackling the reported $50-$60 billion laundered from the U.S. through Israel and into illegal West Bank settlements, TFI claimed that Levey's U.S.-taxpayer-funded missions to Israel had to be kept secret from the American public in order to comply with the Bank Secrecy Act, which ironically is an anti-money-laundering law.[414] When ambushed by alternative media reporters to answer tough questions, the TFI head who had taken over from Levey, David Cohen, fled according to a report in *Mondoweiss*:

> *Then–well ahead of the advertised 8 o'clock ending for the event–Cohen announced that he had to run. At least three reporters accompanied him up the stairs from the hall and out on to W. 3rd Street. Ali Gharib of Daily Beast asked Cohen about the human cost of the sanctions. I asked Cohen, Does Israel have nukes – and is our double standard here an issue when he seeks international partners to turn up the heat on Iran? Chase Madar, author of the recent book on Bradley Manning and a frequent contributor to this site and the American Conservative, pulled up the rear. He wanted to ask Cohen how the sanctions compare to what we did to Iraq, where the punitive measures were said to have killed hundreds of thousands.*
>
> *Cohen ignored the questions, but he obviously felt queasy about doing so, or maybe he felt rude. When we got out to the sidewalk, he turned to us and told us to call his spokesman, and gave Gharib the telephone number for the Treasury Department press department.*

---

413 "No one knows the full cost of Israel's settlement ambitions" *USA Today*, August 14, 2008 http://usatoday30.usatoday.com/news/world/2005-08-14-israelsettlercosts_x.htm

414 Grant F Smith, *America's Defense Line: The Justice Department's Battle to Register the Israel Lobby as Agents of a Foreign Government* [Washington, Institute for Research, 2008] 197-198

I did not have the presence of mind to say to him what I am saying now: You don't seem to feel any sense of public accountability for your actions.[415]

TFI is not a black box to its Israel lobby backers. Invited guests and members of WINEP have received many intimate briefings from TFI officials and consultants. No tough questions are ever asked. Another key Treasury unit, the Internal Revenue Service, also shuns tough questions and, when pinned down, runs down the clock with generalities. This is what happened when the author ambushed IRS Commissioner Douglas Shulman during a live NPR broadcast in 2010. The transcript follows:

Susan Paige, USA Today: Welcome back, I'm Susan Paige of USA Today sitting in for Diane Rehm. We're talking with Doug Shulman. He's the Commissioner of the IRS-the 47th Commissioner of the IRS. The IRS collects $2.4 trillion in tax revenue every year. It has 100,000 employees.

Grant F. Smith: I'd really like to take issue with this idea that IRS goes after powerful violators. In 2005, USA Today quoted Vice-premier Shimon Peres estimating $50 billion had been raised since 1977 in the U.S. and used to build illegal settlements in Israeli-occupied West Bank territories. And many U.S. charities like the One Israel Fund, American Friends of [the College of] Judea and Samaria, Christian Friends of Israel and even Jack Abramoff openly and illegally raise tax-deductible funds in the U.S. for illegal settlements. But while fellow Treasury officials like Stewart Levey and other political appointees supported by AIPAC [the American Israel Public Affairs Committee] aggressively go after many Muslim charities suspected of any criminal ties, none of these charities have ever lost a tax exemption and the IRS just doesn't go after any of these violators in spite of Obama administration policy against settlements.

Susan Paige: Alright Grant, thank you for your call. What about Grant's question in terms of 'does the IRS go after charities that get tax-deductible contributions if their actions violate U.S. policy?

[415] Philip Weiss, "Treasury official who cranks up the heat on Iran can't take the heat in New York," *Mondoweiss*, September 13, 2012

> *Doug Shulman, IRS: One of the interesting things about the agency, Susan, is that we actually reach into every nook and cranny of the country, so we focus on individuals, serving them and have an enforcement program, and have an enforcement program servicing business. We also have a tax exempt and government entities section of the IRS that focuses on charities and other nonprofits. They get the benefit of tax exemption, making sure that they're complying with the tax rules. We've, over the last ten years, beefed up that area, focused on everything from small nonprofits, international charities, hospitals, as well as education institutions, and we run a pretty robust program to make sure people are complying with the tax laws.*

Like TFI, which normally only meets with Israel lobbying organizations in friendly gatherings, the IRS will not meet with individuals or organizations wanting face-to-face meetings to discuss how Israel lobbying organizations function in the U.S. and overseas. This finally led in 2015 to a lawsuit filed against the U.S. Treasury Department for ignoring the issue of tax-exempt donations being used to fund illegal settlements. The lawsuit charges:

> *For at least 30 years, perhaps more, Treasury officials have turned a blind eye toward the criminal conduct that approximately 100 U.S. pro-Israeli-settlement 501(c)(3)s have either funded or engaged in as the primary source of funding to expand settlements in the occupied Palestinian territories and East Jerusalem. Plaintiffs seek an order requiring Treasury to initiate an investigation into any and all tax-exempt entities based in America which transmit $20,000 or more on an annual basis to any country in the world and, where appropriate, revoke the entity's tax-exempt status.*[416]

The U.S. Department of Treasury is an agency of particular interest to the Israel lobby, but not the only involved in regulating finance. The campaign in 2014 to insert Stanley Fischer straight from his position leading Israel's central bank into the number two spot at the Federal Reserve (America's central bank) generated almost no reporting on the appointee's career serving the Israel lobby or informed public debate about his record. At the time, coverage was focused on Fischer's co-authorship of a seminal textbook on macroeconomics and his handling an economic crisis at the International Monetary Fund. His work bending U.S. aid and trade packages to Israel's

---

416 Mohamed Abdel Aziz, Susan Abulhawa, Michael Several v. United States Department of the Treasury, 1:15-cv-02186, U.S. District Court for the District of Columbia, December 15, 2015

benefit was entirely ignored.

Fischer became a dual Israeli-American citizen in order to lead the Bank of Israel. Inserting such a figure into a top position in the most important central bank in the world could be a test case to assess public reaction as a precursor to more openly dual citizens working at the top level of agencies like the Department of Defense or U.S. State Department. While the doors of federal government have long swung open for Israel-lobby appointees focusing most if not all of their energies on advancing the interests of a foreign state, any who were actually Israeli dual citizens have traditionally kept that a closely guarded secret. That Fischer is just such an appointee requires only a search for information about him from his long-term boosters, most prominently the American Israel Public Affairs Committee.

Stanley Fischer was born in Northern Rhodesia in 1943. He studied at The London School of Economics and received a PhD in economics from the Massachusetts Institute of Technology. He taught at and chaired the MIT economics department and co-authored a leading macroeconomics textbook with Rudiger Dornbusch. Fischer joined the World Bank in 1988, and in 1994 became the first deputy-managing director of the International Monetary Fund (IMF). He oversaw emergency bailout lending and austerity programs over Mexico, Thailand, Indonesia, Russia, Brazil and Argentina. Citigroup—under the helm of Sanford "Sandy" Weill—recruited Fischer in 2002. There he rose to become vice president, with a seven-figure pay package.

Fischer has not only been an ardent supporter of Israel, his professional efforts began when he took sabbatical leave to Israel in 1972 and 1976-1977. He was a visiting scholar at the Bank of Israel in 1980. More importantly for Israel, shortly thereafter Fischer won an appointment to the Reagan administration's U.S.-Israel Joint Economic Discussion Group that dealt with Israel's 1984-1985 economic crisis. In October of 1984, Israeli Prime Minister Shimon Peres arrived in Washington asking an initially reluctant Reagan Administration for an additional $1.5 billion in U.S. emergency funding—over and above the already-promised enormous $5.6 billion aid package.[417] The help amounted to U.S. taxpayers funding each Israeli citizen $1,650. Another key component of the plan—as discussed elsewhere in this book—called for a largely unilateral lowering of U.S. tariffs and trade barriers to Israel, a program initially called "Duty Free Treatment for U.S. Imports from Israel," but later repackaged and sold as America's first "free trade" agreement. Over time, the FTA reversed a previously balanced U.S.-Israel trading relationship into one that has produced a growing cumulative deficit to the U.S.

The U.S.-Israel Joint Economic Discussion Group fundamentally

[417] Don Oberdorfer, "Will U.S. Dollars Fix Israel's Economy?" *The Washington Post*, June 9, 1985

transformed U.S. aid to Israel forever. Before the Reagan administration, most U.S. aid to Israel took the form of loans that had to be repaid with interest. After the input from Fischer's team, subsequent U.S. aid was delivered in the form of outright grants paid directly from the U.S. Treasury—never to be repaid or conditioned on good behavior—even when Israel took actions the U.S. opposed.

Like many of Fischer's later IMF austerity programs, the Joint Discussion Group initially announced that some of the strings attached to the aid would make it temporary. Secretary of State George Shultz insisted during a 1985 address to AIPAC that "Israel must pull itself out of its present economic trauma…No one can do it for them…our help will be of little avail if Israel does not take the necessary steps to cut government spending, improve productivity, open up its economy and strengthen the mechanisms of economic policy. Israel and its government must make the hard decisions."[418]

Shultz wanted to make the huge American cash transfer conditional on major Israeli economic reforms, but intense AIPAC lobbying in Congress threatened to make the State Department influence irrelevant. In the end, Congress delivered aid without requiring many Israeli sacrifices, such as selling off bloated state-owned industries and spending belt-tightening. The proposed privatization of $5 billion in state enterprises threatened too much bureaucratic "turf" and too many jobs, so Israel put them on hold. Fischer apologetically characterized the Likud years as a "wasted opportunity by a government that should have known better."[419] Not until 1996 were Fischer's proscribed economic remedies adopted by American neoconservative consultants to Benjamin Netanyahu as minor points in the "Clean Break" manifesto for Israeli regional hegemony. But they remain among the sole unimplemented tasks in an ambitious plan that called for military action against Iraq, Syria, and Lebanon.

Despite the absence of any real economic reforms that would take Israel off the American taxpayer dole, Fischer co-wrote a blustering 1986 article for *The Wall Street Journal* called "Israel Has Made Aid Work" that AIPAC circulated widely as an official memorandum of its achievements. In it, Fischer boasted:

> *Israel is the largest single recipient of economic aid from the U.S. This is partly because the economic stability of Israel is uncertain and is important to U.S. national interests. Therefore a report on*

---

[418] Don Oberdorfer, "Will U.S. Dollars Fix Israel's Economy?" *The Washington Post*, June 9, 1985

[419] Peter Passell, "Need Zionism Equal Socialism?" *The New York Times*, July 2, 1992

> *the progress of the Israeli economy is relevant to policy decisions to be made here.*

Fischer never bothered to substantiate his premise that U.S. national interests were somehow served by the bailout, or that any aid given to Israel produced tangible benefits. Instead, he delivered a fusillade of dry and all but unreadable statistics about Israel's temporary economic performance. Issues of long-term importance to most Americans, such as returning U.S. aid to the traditional structure of loans to be repaid and the likely impact of the FTA on U.S. jobs, went unaddressed by Fischer. Fischer's core achievement—the transformation of aid from loans to outright taxpayer giveaways—has remained unchanged since 1986. The premises behind this ever-increasing entitlement and one-sided trade agreement performance are likewise never reexamined by Congress—despite the fact that a majority of Americans polled have come to oppose aid increases to Israel. Fischer's rare admonitions that Israel be held to account, unlike like the economies he transformed through biting IMF austerity programs, have remained unimplemented.

At the end of 2004, Israel's UN ambassador recruited Fischer to become the head of Israel's central bank, asking, "Why not be our governor?"[420] Fischer accepted, and initially provided endless amusement to reporters by insisting on speaking Hebrew during press conferences and refusing to speak English. Initial concerns that Fischer's global stature and experience would overshadow and chafe the relevant players in Israel proved unfounded as Fischer moved energetically into his new role. In the United States, AIPAC continued to trumpet Fischer's accomplishments steering Israel through the global financial crisis, though beneath the surface he was performing far more serious tasks for Israel and its lobby.

As Bank of Israel governor, Fischer played a central role in coordinating the implementation of AIPAC-generated sanctions against Iran over its nuclear program. Stuart Levey, the aforementioned head of the U.S. Treasury Department's division for "Terrorism and Financial Intelligence," met often with Fischer in Israel alongside the Prime Minister, Foreign Minister and chiefs of both the Mossad and Shin Bet to explore how to "supplement" UN sanctions and end-run Russian and Chinese opposition.[421] The Levey-Fischer strategy was "to work outside the context of the Security Council to engage the private sector and let it know about the risks of doing business with Tehran," particularly to use the U.S. Treasury Department against European banks that had only partially drawn back their business dealings with Iran by threatening to cut them off from access to the U.S. financial system. In 2010,

[420] Shlomo Maital, "Stanley Fischer: the man and the plan," *Jerusalem Report*, February 7, 2005

[421] BBC Monitoring Middle East, March 5, 2007

Israel dispatched Fischer to meet with Chinese and Russian "counterparts" in order to financially isolate Iran.[422]

Fischer's final official duties for the Israeli government included drills and exercises for "big crisis" scenarios—specifically, Fischer told an Israeli television station, the unavoidable financial fallout of a military attack on Iran. "We do plans, we do scenarios, we do exercises about how the central [bank] will work in various situations."[423] After years targeting Iran, Fischer became convinced in his final months in Israel that sanctions alone were not enough to collapse its economy. He reluctantly concluded that even as Iranian economic prospects "continue to go down," the country would likely "find a way to continue to keep economic life going."[424] Fischer then suddenly resigned and left the Bank of Israel on June 30, 2013 before completing his second five-year term.

Before Fischer's name was floated to lead the Fed, he was considered for another position during a rushed George W. Bush administration attempt at damage control. In 2007, the controversial architect of the Iraq invasion and later World Bank President Paul Wolfowitz was engulfed in an ethics scandal over compensation and promotion for his girlfriend, Shaha Ali Riza. In just two short years leading the institution, Wolfowitz had catalyzed the insubordination of most divisions within the bank and the distrust of economics ministries around the world. Fischer, along with Robert Zoellick and Robert Kimmitt, were among a shortlist considered as emergency replacements while the administration and stakeholders strategized on how to ease Wolfowitz out with a minimum of scandal.[425] In the end, Zoellick took over and Fischer stayed put in Israel.

It therefore came as a surprise to many when *The Wall Street Journal* and Israel's Channel 2 news simultaneously reported in early December 2013 that the White House was "close to nominating" Fischer to be appointee Janet Yellen's second-in-command at the U.S. central bank.[426] Media reports initially indicated that Fischer's candidacy-to-Senate-confirmation would proceed on greased skids with no Senate debate allowed taking only a week so that the pair could quickly take over the Fed in January. However, the

---

[422] Herb Keinon, "Russia won't back crippling sanctions. Comment comes day before high-level U.S.-Israel meeting on Iran," *Jerusalem Post*, February 25, 2010

[423] Dan Williams, "Iran Stepping Up Its Atomic Efforts," *The Gazette*, August 13, 2012

[424] "Bank of Israel governor: Sanctions won't collapse Iran economy." Islamic Republic will likely find way to 'keep economic life going,' says Fischer in interview with CNBC," *Jerusalem Post*, October 24, 2012.

[425] Steven R Weisman, "Wolfowitz Said to Push for Deal to Let Him Quit," *The New York Times*, May 17, 2007

[426] "Fischer set to be tapped as vice chair of U.S. Federal Reserve," *Times of Israel*, December 11, 2013

Senate concluded its 2013 business without taking up the matter, and Fischer was not appointed until May 28, 2014.

Though the drive to maintain Iran sanctions appear to have foundered in 2015, the infrastructure for resuming it remains in place. The Fed was a key player and did a great deal of damage, levying hundreds of millions in fines against foreign banks such as R.B.S, Barclays, Standard and Chartered and H.S.B.C. which were charged with violating the Iran sanctions regime. Although AIPAC never mentioned it, American exporters were also seriously hurt by sanctions and secondary boycotts on Iran. A coalition representing the U.S. Chamber of Commerce, the Business Roundtable, Coalition for American Trade, the National Foreign Trade Council and others urged Congress not to enact sanctions provisions they estimated would cost $25 billion and 210,000 American jobs. However, any incoming administration will find Fischer and the Israel lobby's sanction program ready to "snap back" into place—since Fischer's appointment will last until 2018.

Until then, an equally important target for Fischer and Israel are anti-boycott activities with Israel in the crosshairs. The organization Fischer helps lead has experience in this. In the 1970s and 1980s, the Federal Reserve played an active "moral suasion" role chastising and corralling U.S. banks away from any activity that Israel construed as compliant with the Arab League economic boycott. An expert with deep experience enforcing the international boycott of Iran, Fischer is likely aware of the many active American grass roots campaigns aimed at ending the Israeli occupation of Palestinians through targeted boycotts. These boycotts range from efforts to get retailers to stop carrying manufactured goods produced in the occupied West Bank (Ahava and SodaStream), to overturning contracts with firms providing services in occupied territories (Veolia), to academic boycotts and even efforts to get labor union pensions to divest from Israel bonds. Working more closely with Israel and AIPAC, the Fed could become a vital node for reinterpreting and enforcing old or new laws aimed at outlawing and punishing groups organizing such grass-roots activities by targeting U.S. bank accounts and freezing their financial flows.

Fischer may in the near future also want to launch "exercises" to prepare the U.S. financial system for the fallout of Israeli military attacks on Iran. If Israel decides to attack Iran, it would benefit immensely from having Fischer inside the Fed, protecting the financial flows Israel now regards as its own birthright from its primary global underwriter. Less well known is the Fed's authority to authorize foreign bank acquisitions. Any future Israeli campaign to further entwine its banks into the U.S. financial system through acquisitions would likely find a much more welcoming regulator in Fischer.

Fischer's sudden, inexplicably rushed insertion into the Federal Reserve should have triggered a debate about longstanding Fed policies correctly considering U.S. citizenship preferable for sensitive positions. Fed policies state U.S. citizenship is preferred, "because of the special nature of the supervisory function, the need to ensure confidentiality of information, and the delegated nature of the function." Unfortunately, that policy preference covers only Fed bank examiners rather than top leadership—the Federal Reserve Act is silent on the wisdom of installing a revolving door for U.S. citizens returning from Israel or any other foreign government who took on dual citizenship as a condition of serving abroad.

As mentioned, AIPAC, Fischer's co-author of harmful U.S. economic policies on behalf of Israel, likely sees the Fischer appointment as an important test case to assess American tolerance for openly dual Israeli-American citizens running key U.S. federal agencies. In 2009 former AIPAC research director Martin Indyk, who was at the center of AIPAC's research division during the trade agreement push, said that "the U.S.-Israel Free Trade Agreement served as a wedge that opened up the Congress to free trade agreements across the world, including the NAFTA agreement." Likewise, with Fischer "wedged" into the Fed, it begs the question of why Israel's former ambassador to the U.S. born historian and current Knesset member Michael Oren could not someday lead the Near East division of the State Department.

From AIPAC's perspective, having "qualified Israelis" directly run key divisions of the U.S. Treasury such as Terrorism and Financial Intelligence, rather than indirectly through AIPAC-vetted appointees such as Stuart Levey and his hand-picked successor David Cohen, could probably boost the volume of taxpayer giveaways while improving coordination with Israel. Given AIPAC and Israel's overly large influence on U.S. military initiatives in the region, the lobby may now feel the moment will soon be ripe for appointing Israeli generals into the Joint Chiefs at the Department of Defense. This, AIPAC may well reason, would be much more convenient than constantly arranging the visits of Israeli military and intelligence delegations that increasingly serve as briefers (at times overshadowing the Department of Defense and the American intelligence community) of members of the U.S. Congress.

IAOs are, observably, now immune from regulation under the 1938 Foreign Agents Registration Act, statutes covering espionage, and some other statutes, such as election laws prohibiting charitable organization support for individual candidates. Although there is no known "get out of jail free" card distributed to IAOs outlining their special immunity from investigation and prosecution, the record is now well-enough established that *de facto* immunity could be assumed. The U.S. Department of Treasury has been particularly well stocked with ardent supporters of Israel who look the other way when questions about illegal settlement funding arise. Most immunity rulings occur behind closed doors and are then classified as secrets until the issue becomes moot.

The Zionist Organization of America (ZOA), although originally organized in Pittsburgh in 1918 and created by an act of the New York State Legislature, was legally the U.S. subsidiary of the World Zionist Organization and subject to its direction. The U.S. Department of State politely invited the ZOA to begin registering as the foreign agent of the World Zionist Organization immediately after passage of the 1938 Foreign Agents Registration Act (FARA). The ZOA refused, stating it was an American organization, working to establish a Jewish homeland in Palestine, an objective it noted was supported by (IAO-lobbied) Congressional resolutions. The ZOA cited funds it raised that had flowed to its affiliate organizations, but was adamant that it was not the recipient of international funding. ZOA refused to register on the grounds that it did not receive any subsidies from the World Zionist Congress.

In July of 1941, the Near East Division of the State Department again pushed for ZOA registration, arguing that the ZOA was, on paper, a subsidiary corporation, despite internal cash flows. The State Department sent an employee on an undercover visit to ZOA offices and determined it was an overtly political—as opposed to its self-proclaimed status of "religious"—organization, and therefore could not avail itself of the FARA exemptions available to religious entities such as the Vatican. The State Department also found that ZOA was "subject to the direction" of the WZO. It again ordered the ZOA to register. ZOA again refused, stating that, as a New York corporation, it was merely an "affiliate" of the WZO.

A U.S. Department of Justice official, upon the Justice Department's assumption of FARA enforcement from the State Department, internally found that the ZOA was subject to registration, noting in June of 1943 that the:

> *...threat of prosecution or actual prosecution by the Department of Justice for failure to register seems to be the only remaining effective action. But I doubt that such action would be warranted under the circumstances at this time... In October, the OSS [intelligence agency precursor to the CIA] provided additional information about Zionist activities occurring overseas including arms and people transfers, that supported the registration call, but by November some Justice Department employees began detecting political pressure...the pressure was on somewhere in the government... it would be unwise to do anything further...under the circumstances do not desire for the moment to write to the Zionist Organization of America…*

On February 25, 1948, the DOJ issued another FARA order to the ZOA, citing undue delays in responding to a matter that had been "under consideration for some time." However, with U.S. recognition of the state of

Israel imminent, the attorney general ordered that the registration question be delayed for 60 days. By May, frontline DOJ employees were hearing rumors that a high-level DOJ official privately told ZOA representatives that registration would not be necessary, and that they need not "fear prosecution." Despite ongoing FBI reports of overt public relations and political activities by the ZOA, the Justice Department agreed to quash the registration order if the ZOA altered some of its corporate articles defining relationships with the WZO. However, as documented by the head of the FARA section, the DOJ did not immediately confirm whether such changes to the WZO/ZOA constitutions were made.[427]

In exercising so little real regulatory authority over IAOs, and under so much political pressure, the Justice Department functionaries presumably viewed further attempts to force compliance to be useless and even politically risky. Yet, in hindsight, warranted enforcement of the order and increased scrutiny of ZOA activities could have prevented the theft of U.S. weapons-grade uranium by ZOA operatives two decades later.

On September 10, 1968, the Nuclear Materials and Equipment Corporation (NUMEC) in Apollo, Pennsylvania—run by three ZOA executives—graciously received a key coordinator of Israel's clandestine nuclear weapons program (Avraham Hermoni) and three undercover Israeli intelligence operatives. At that time NUMEC told its U.S. regulator, the Atomic Energy Commission, that the Israeli visitors were "energy specialists." One of them, Rafi Eitan, was a long time intelligence agent who later "ran" spy Jonathan Pollard against the U.S. Pollard served thirty years in federal prison for his massive thefts of highly classified documents.

Lengthy investigations discovered that the NUMEC plant "lost" more weapons-grade uranium than any other federal contractor. CIA officials were unequivocal that the material had been diverted into Israel's secret nuclear weapons program. However, at no time did investigators appear to pursue any ZOA role in the affair, and no criminal charges were ever filed.[428] The Central Intelligence Agency's refusal to share information critical to two FBI investigations thwarted accountability over the so-called "Apollo affair," according to declassified CIA files released in 2015. The case is such a clear-cut example of how Israel used IAO operatives to conduct covert activity of immense damage to the United States that it is worth exploring in this context.

427 "Zionist Organization of America (ZOA) ignores seven (7) Foreign Agent Registration Act orders - 1938-1960," The Israel Lobby Archive http://www.israellobby.org/ZOA/DOJ-149-1603-ZOA/

428 See the author's book *DIVERT! NUMEC, Zalman Shapiro and the Diversion of U.S. Weapons-Grade Uranium into the Israeli Nuclear Weapons Program* [Institute for Research: Middle Eastern Policy, Washington DC, 2012]

The NUMEC nuclear fuel processing company was founded by legendary chemist Zalman Mordecai Shapiro and financed by entrepreneur David Luzer Lowenthal. According to the Department of Energy, during Shapiro's reign at NUMEC the company lost 337 kilograms of weapons-grade uranium after accounting for losses. Much of it was of a unique and high enrichment level. Losses only returned to industry norms after Shapiro, who later unsuccessfully tried to get a job working on advanced hydrogen bomb designs, was forced out of NUMEC.

In the 1940s, Lowenthal fought in Israel's "War of Independence,' serving as a smuggler who developed close contacts with high Israeli intelligence officials. In the 1950s, Shapiro developed vital breakthroughs for U.S. Navy nuclear propulsion systems. An ardent supporter of Israel, Shapiro was Pittsburgh Chapter President of the Zionist Organization of America. According to the *Jerusalem Post*, Shapiro later joined the board of governors of the Israeli Intelligence Heritage Center, an organization that honors spies who secretly took action to advance the cause of Israel. Morton Chatkin, president of NUMEC's holding company, called Apollo Industries, also held a ZOA leadership role, while Apollo Executive Vice President, Ivan J. Novick, went on to become ZOA's national president. David Lowenthal, who raised capital for acquiring NUMEC's facilities (an old steel mill in the center of the village), served as Apollo's treasurer. In 1968, CIA Director Richard Helms sent an urgent request for an investigation to Attorney General Ramsey Clark stating:

> *You are well aware of the great concern which exists at the highest levels of this Government with regard to the proliferation of nuclear weapons...It is critical for us to establish whether or not the Israelis now have the capability of fabricating nuclear weapons which might be employed in the Near East...I urge that the Federal Bureau of Investigation be called upon to initiate a discreet intelligence investigation of all source nature of Dr. Shapiro in order to establish the nature and extent of his relationship with the Government of Israel.*

The FBI investigation documented Shapiro's many meetings with top Israeli nuclear weapons development officials, such as Avraham Hermoni, and wiretapped a conversation between Shapiro and Lowenthal revealing the overall lack of concern for worker safety and the environment after a radioactive spill. The FBI discovered that NUMEC had formed a joint venture with the Israel Atomic Energy Commission called Isorad to supply food irradiators to Israel. The now-defunct Atomic Energy Agency questioned Zalman Shapiro in 1969—never specifically asking if he had diverted any nuclear material—about his many meetings with Israelis known to the FBI to be intelligence operatives. After the AEC defended Shapiro and his continued retention of high security clearances, the FBI terminated its intelligence investigation.

In 1976, the Ford administration reopened the NUMEC investigation in order to determine if a diversion had occurred and whether a government cover-up had ensued. A 130-page CIA file released in mid-2015,[429] is replete with formal CIA denials to Congressional committee investigators, the GAO and the Nuclear Regulatory Commission inquiries about whether the CIA had participated in any illegal diversions, or whether it was aware of any presidential finding authorizing such an operation. Arizona Democratic Senator Morris Udall asked bluntly, on August 23, 1977, "Is it possible that President Johnson, who was known to be a friend of Israel, could have encouraged the flow of nuclear materials to the Israelis?" Citing CIA's role in alerting the attorney general to the problem as evidence that it was not involved, the agency also repeatedly emphasized, "We in CIA are not and have not been concerned with the law enforcement aspects of this problem. Indeed, CIA Director Dick Helms turned the matter over to the FBI in order to avoid such involvement." Rather, exploring the NUMEC-Israel link was part of CIA's intelligence function to substantiate why its National Intelligence Estimate concluded that Israel had a nuclear arsenal.

FBI special agents soon lost morale over being sent unprepared into a second investigation. The CIA, for its part, continued withholding critical information that could have provided both motivation and a tool for confronting hostile interviewees, including the three ZOA executives overseeing the plant. This was, according to the newly released CIA files:

> *...information...of obvious importance in reaching an intelligence decision on the probability of diversion, it is not of any legal pertinence to the FBI's criminal investigation of NUMEC. In our discussions with the FBI we have alluded to this information but we have not made the details available to special agents from the Washington Field Office of the FBI who are working on the case. While Mr. Bush's [then-CIA Director George H.W. Bush] conversations are not known to us, we have had no substantive discussions with officials at FBI Headquarters on this matter.*[430]

[429] "The Nuclear Materials and Equipment Corporation (NUMEC) and the diversion of U.S. government weapons-grade uranium to Israel," Israel Lobby Archive http://israellobby.org/numec/08312015_cia_numec.pdf

[430] "The Nuclear Materials and Equipment Corporation (NUMEC) and the diversion of U.S. government weapons-grade uranium to Israel," Israel Lobby Archive http://israellobby.org/numec/08312015_cia_numec.pdf

It was this sensitive CIA information, made available only to the president, cabinet, and a limited number of top agency officials that led one National Security Council staffer to conclude, "I do not think that the President has plausible deniability."

On June 6, 1977, the CIA's Associate Deputy Director for Operations, Theodore Shackley, briefed the FBI agents in charge of the NUMEC investigation. They grumbled that, since they had not established that the diversion took place, they could not begin to address the second question about a cover-up. They then pleaded for "new information" from the CIA, blithely ignorant that their reasoning was completely backward—it was old information they required, and it was the CIA's withholding of that information that was the true cover-up. The FBI also thought it needed a NUMEC insider willing to blow the whistle in order to finally break the case open.

Unknown to the FBI, every prior serving CIA director was complicit in withholding a key clandestine operational finding from FBI investigators. According to a May 11, 1977 report by Shackley, the "CIA has not furnished to the FBI sensitive agent reporting...since the decision was made by Directors Helms, Colby and Bush that this information would not further the investigation of NUMEC but would compromise sources and methods."

Though carefully redacted from the CIA release, the omitted fact was presumably that highly enriched uranium of a signature unique to NUMEC had been detected in Israel, a country that did not have facilities to enrich uranium. This sensitive information was delivered to former Atomic Energy Commission Chief Glen Seaborg by two Department of Energy investigators, sifting for more facts about NUMEC, in June of 1978. It was powerful enough evidence that the retired Seaborg subsequently refused to be interviewed by the under-informed FBI investigators.

The CIA noted that the FBI investigators "indicated that even if they came up with a case, it was extremely unlikely that Justice and State would allow it to come to trial...they feel that they have been given a job to do with none of the tools necessary to do it." The FBI likely presumed Israeli immunity would prevail. Although, in 1981, special agents finally identified a former NUMEC employee who had personally witnessed the means of the diversion—Shapiro and other NUMEC officials stuffing highly-enriched uranium canisters into irradiators, sealed and rushed to Israel—lacking the missing CIA puzzle piece, the FBI investigation went dormant as the statute of limitations for Atomic Energy Act violations—punishable by death—at long last expired.

At the dawn of 2016, the U.S. Department of Justice is working hard to block further release of secret CIA and its own files on the diversion in order to pass hundreds of millions in cleanup costs to U.S. taxpayers and a company that acquired NUMEC after most of the polluting and illegal activities occurred. In 2012, the Department of Justice denied a Freedom of Information Act request for its criminal and counterespionage investigation report on NUMEC. In 2015, the U.S. Department of Justice secretly began negotiating what share of cleanup costs BWX Technologies of Lynchburg Virginia, which acquired NUMEC in 1971, would pay. In defense of the CIA's position that it did not have to release operations files about the NUMEC affair, in 2016 the Department of Justice asked a D.C. federal court to throw out a case seeking release of the information—presumably since such inconvenient secrets would damage its attempt to pass the cleanup costs of the ZOA-Israel linked NUMEC on to unsuspecting taxpayers.[431]

The Apollo/NUMEC affair is not the only instance in which the Zionist Organization of America served as—if not as the incubator—a matchmaker for Israeli intelligence operations directed against the U.S. According to a 2011 biography about the life of the Hollywood movie producer Arnon Milchan, it was the Tel Aviv office of the Zionist Organization of America where Israeli master spy Benjamin Blumberg first met Milchan.[432] Milchan is an Israeli movie producer who became successful in Hollywood for such movies as Brazil, JFK, and Pretty Woman. FBI files detailing Israel's stealth acquisition of U.S. nuclear triggers, declassified and released on Dec. 28, 2011,[433] reveal how Israel's elite spy networks acquired U.S. nuclear technologies while evading criminal and diplomatic consequences through special pleading.

A krytron is a gas-filled tube used as a high-speed switch. U.S. State Department munitions licenses are needed to export krytrons because they can be used as triggers for nuclear weapons. Between 1979 and 1983, California-based MILCO International Inc. shipped fifteen orders totaling 800 krytrons through an intermediary to the Israeli Ministry of Defense. MILCO obtained them from EG&G Inc. after the U.S. government had rejected several requests for krytron export licenses to Israel.

The book *Confidential: The Life of Secret Agent Turned Hollywood Tycoon – Arnon Milchan* reports that Israeli President Shimon Peres stated, "I am the one who recruited him [Milchan]" in the 1960s. Milchan was an agent for the

---

[431] Grant F. Smith "Department of Justice wears many hats in NUMEC affair: Fighting FOIA, secretly negotiating cleanup payouts and covering for CIA," Antiwar.com, February 2, 2016 http://original.antiwar.com/smith-grant/2016/02/15/department-of-justice-wears-many-hats-in-numec-affair/

[432] Meir Doron and Joseph Gelman, *Confidential: The Life of Secret Agent Turned Hollywood Tycoon Arnon Milchan* [Israel, Gefen Books, 2011]

[433] "FBI investigates MILCO nuclear trigger smuggling to Israel," The Israel Lobby Archive http://israellobby.org/krytons/

Israeli LAKAM[434] under both Blumberg and spy Rafi Eitan until Israel promised to disband the unit after the Jonathan Pollard affair. According to reviews of the book:

> *Blumberg was Milchan's friend, and used him (as well as other Israeli businessmen) to set up straw companies around the world, and to open secret bank accounts for financing the nuclear plant in Dimona and other Israeli security industries...*

Milchan's Heli Trading Company was the originator of brokered transactions for the Israeli Ministry of Defense through the California front company MILCO. The FBI file reveals that after the illicit shipment of krytrons were discovered, a U.S. attorney tried to flip MILCO President Richard Kelly Smyth to implicate Milchan during intense plea bargaining. The gambit failed, and in May 1984, Smyth was indicted on thirty counts of smuggling and making false statements. Smyth and his wife promptly fled to Israel and remained at large until captured in Malaga, Spain, in July 2001, after Smyth applied for Social Security benefits. INTERPOL arrested and extradited him to the United States, where he pleaded guilty to violating the U.S. Arms Export Control Act. In November 2001, Smyth was sentenced to 40 years in prison and fined $20,000, though he was freed within four years because of his advancing age.[435]

The FBI records reveal ongoing interest in Milchan into the mid-1990s. In 1992, a confidential informant relayed details of Milchan's ties to Smyth. The declassified but heavily redacted "secret" communications reveal the Bureau's fascination with Milchan, from his 1996 entry in *Who's Who* to A-list associates such as Robert De Niro and an unsavory Iran-Contra operative.

Like the NUMEC case, the krytron caper benefited from flawed mainstream news coverage that today seems superficial if not suspicious. Among the final pages of the FBI's file is a clipping of Thomas Friedman's May 1985 *New York Times* interview with Milchan, who had suddenly decamped for Jerusalem immediately after the Smyth indictments. Milchan said he had only recently learned "that a krytron was a small little gizmo which anyone can go buy freely in the United States. You can use them for all kinds of things, including, incidentally, making cholent." Friedman clarified for readers that "Cholent is a stew of beans, carrots, potatoes and beef that is a traditional Jewish dish prepared on Friday night for eating on the Sabbath.

---

[434] Bureau of Scientific Relations. LAKAM's mission was to steal, or obtain through deception, military and dual-use technology throughout the world on behalf of Israel's defense industries.

[435] "FBI investigates MILCO nuclear trigger smuggling to Israel," The Israel Lobby Archive http://israellobby.org/krytons/

Mr. Milchan said that with a krytron timer a stove could be set to turn on automatically to heat up cholent on the Sabbath without anyone working to light the fire." He did not explain why, if cooking was to be the end use, the krytrons were destined for the Israeli Ministry of Defense.

Although the files released by the FBI in 2011 also directly implicate current Israeli Prime Minister Benjamin Netanyahu as working inside the smuggling front and meeting with Richard Kelley Smyth in Israel during the operation, no establishment American media has seen fit to investigate and report on this angle.[436] When he was first implicated in the krytron caper, Milchan called his long-time colleague Shimon Peres, then prime minister, soliciting his help to preempt any prosecution by the Reagan administration Justice Department.[437]

One might assume that such a documented history of espionage activities might disqualify the Zionist Organization of America from holding tax-exempt status. This was recently put to the test when the IRS actually revoked its tax-exempt status after the organization failed to file required IRS Form 990s for three consecutive years. The automatic revocation over failure to file that ensnared ZOA did not target any particular organization, but was rather the result of a 2006 law requiring mandatory IRS action that affected hundreds of thousands of nonprofits. However, revocation of ZOA's status meant the organization had to justify anew just what activities it performed were worthy of such tax-exempt status by applying for it again, with all of the substantiation required of an entirely new application. The key question it would presumably have to answer was, "What is the social welfare function of Zionism?"

The ZOA that on October 31, 2012, began the formal reinstatement process was only a shadow of its former self. In 1948, the organization claimed a quarter of a million members; in 2011, it reported only 30,000. Even that figure seems suspect, given a decade of annual revenues averaging only $3 million per year. Like many small nonprofits, ZOA now seemed to exist only to pay a fat salary to Morton Klein, the longtime national president, who had taken over to revitalize the IAO in 1993 after working as a ZOA Philadelphia chapter president. In response to IRS concerns, ZOA's compensation committee outsourced a salary benchmarking analysis that revealed Klein's base pay of $423,500 far exceeded his estimated market value of $186,638to $218,208. The compensation committee told the IRS that Klein was worth the money because, though it had fallen on hard times, ZOA

---

436 Smith, Grant F., "Netanyahu worked inside nuclear smuggling ring," Antiwar.com, July 4, 2012, http://original.antiwar.com/smith-grant/2012/07/03/netanyahu-worked-inside-nuclear-smuggling-ring/

437 Meir Doron and Joseph Gelman, *Confidential: The Life of Secret Agent Turned Hollywood Tycoon – Arnon Milchan* [Israel, Gefen Books, 2011]

was a player—according to another outside consultancy, Quatt Associates, which benchmarked ten much larger organizations in terms of revenue and personnel. In fact, the ZOA told the IRS, Klein was due for a raise:

> *As [consultancy] Quatt Associates pointed out in their study, the median budget of these organizations is greater than that of ZOA. However, the ZOA's reputation, influence, and effectiveness make it comparable to other leading advocacy organizations… We have used the median compensation among the comparator organizations as the appropriate market rate…an increase in the base compensation rate of 10% for Mr. Klein would result in his total compensation placing approximately 11% below the median…His performance continues to be at the highest level, and as a result, the organization continues to enjoy a very effective and visible position as a leader among the advocates on behalf of Israel and the Jewish people. This, in turn, greatly assists the organization's fundraising abilities since many large, like-minded donors are easily motivated to provide financial assistance to the organization's efforts, personified by Mr. Klein.*

A review of ZOA's correspondence with the IRS during its 2011-2013 drive to get reinstatement[438] reveals an organization with a cumbersome and bloated corporate structure designed for the better days of the past that dwarfed current resources. One reason was that ZOA still tried to be in the lobbying game.

Unlike nearly all the other earlier wave IAOs, ZOA did not agree to allow AIPAC to be its umbrella lobby, and both paid and registered its own in-house lobbying team. This led to frequent clashes with AIPAC that had to be managed by the Conference of Presidents of Major American Jewish Organizations. The ZOA spent scarce dollars lobbying to cut federal funding to American universities and colleges allowing pro-Palestinian protests. But unlike AIPAC, ZOA was a 501(c)(3), not a (c)(4), organization which allowed more leeway to lobby. ZOA insisted on lobbying with fully tax-deductible funds. Most of its mandatory lobbying disclosures filed with the Clerk of Congress were even more vague than the Sphinx-like AIPAC's, such as one disclosing only "support for U.S.-Israel political, military and economic cooperation." ZOA was in no hurry to cede the lobbying arena to AIPAC. It could claim to supporters that its more hyperbolic positions made AIPAC follow along. But ZOA was in a hurry to get its tax-exempt status back, lest

---

[438] Zionist Organization of America application for reinstatement of tax-exempt status. The Israel Lobby Archive http://IsraelLobby.org/ZOA/ZOA_taxexempt.pdf

it miss any massive individual donations.

At first, the ZOA attempted to claim that the IRS was in error and had not considered the proper meaning of statutes governing filing deadlines, and that the ZOA may have fallen victim to improper advice from its outside auditors. ZOA submitted a raft of internal emails substantiating poor management and an inability to obtain consolidated accounting data from its chapters. That effort failed, and the ZOA finally had to file a completely new application for tax-exempt status with all of the required exhibits. On December 28, 2012, ZOA's outside tax lawyer, Thomas Korn, urged the IRS to expedite processing, lest the ZOA be unable to receive a tax-exempt contribution from its most ardent supporters. Korn worried:

> *A major, past donor to the ZOA, the Adelson Family Foundation, has pledged to the ZOA a grant of One Million Dollars ($1,000,000). That grant, however will only be made by the Foundation upon the reinstatement of the ZOA's exemption.*

Korn further explained to the IRS why ZOA thought Sheldon Adelson's offer was only good until April, 2013, and that donations from Dr. Robert Shillman of California ($100,000) and Dr. Stanley Benzel of New Jersey ($40,000) were also in jeopardy. Nevertheless, the IRS had further issues. It was unimpressed with ZOA's articles of incorporation passed by the New York State Legislature and signed into law on April 14, 1920. As should have been expected, the IRS sidestepped the entire issue about whether Zionism (as expansively documented in the programs and ZOA's "Narrative Description of Activities'[439] in its application) had any intrinsic social welfare functions. The IRS avoided this by simply requiring a more explicit assertion that ZOA did have such a purpose, as it noted on February 19, 2013:

---

[439] A) To educate the American people about State of Israel's importance as the home of the Jewish people and the spiritual and cultural center of Jewish life. B) To strengthen the concept of Jewish renaissance through the rebirth of Israel as a nation in its ancient homeland; to strive for the survival of Judaism wherever Jews may be, and particularly in the United States of America. C) To foster among its members, and particularly among Jewish youth, the objectives and ideals of Judaism, through a program of Jewish education, and the study of Hebrew culture and language and to strengthen the spiritual unity of the Jewish people. D) To build a bridge of understanding between the Jewish people and others of the United States and the Jewish people in other countries, and especially in Israel. E) To gather and spread information among its members and the public at large, with respect to happenings and events that may affect the Jewish people. F) To foster and encourage among its members an abiding appreciation for the democratic way of life in the United States of America and the ideals upon which it is grounded.

> *Your Articles of Incorporation do not limit your purposes to those specifically described in IRC [Internal Revenue Code] 501(c)(3) or permanently dedicate your assets to purposes specifically described in section 501(c)(3). Therefore, please amend your Articles of Incorporation by filing an Articles of Amendment…*
>
> *Said organization is organized exclusively for charitable, religious, education and scientific purposes, including, for such purposes, the making of distributions to organizations that qualify as exempt organizations under section 501(c)(3) of the International Revenue Code.*

The IRS also noticed that the ZOA filed its application for reinstatement listing only a single board member, scolding that:

> *..to best ensure that your organization will serve the public interest, please modify or expand your Board of Directors to place control in the hands of unrelated individuals selected from the community you will serve.*

Korn made the amendments, certifying by February 28, 2013, that ZOA was "organized exclusively for charitable, religious, educational and scientific purposes…" and other IRS-suggested language. Unlike CUFI, ZOA did agree to have its future lobbying expenses benchmarked, and signed the dreaded IRS Form 5768. Presumably, ZOA was now out of the spymaster/agent matchmaking business or staffing up weapons-grade uranium diversion fronts or was it? ZOA apologized for only submitting one board member, Morton Klein, claiming that it thought the IRS wanted to know only about compensated board members. Among fifty-four of the rest of the ZOA board members faxed to the IRS on February 19, 2013, was Zalman Mordecai Shapiro, former CEO of the Nuclear Materials and Equipment Corporation.

In the end, ZOA did not get two minor demands met by the IRS. It was not until May 15, 2013, that it was granted tax-exempt status. Although ZOA wanted its status to be made retroactive to 2011, the IRS only made the effective date October 30, 2012. For the first time in modern history, for almost a year and a half, the ZOA had officially operated as what it truly was—not a charity.

It is impossible to know what role, if any, IRS commissioner Douglas Shulman might have played in getting ZOA's tax-exempt status restored. Shulman has been evasive in public when questioned about illegal settlements. Any IRS employee looking up through the chain of command probably did not know Shulman's views, but possibly assumed that since Shulman allowed a massive rule change rolling back the transparency of subsidy IAOs, that denying tax-exempt status could have caused forces allied with ZOA to obtain another hearing at the very top of the IRS over the matter.

The Israel lobby has an obvious interest in making sure that the appointed IRS commissioner and other key Treasury Department officials are friendly to Israel, in order to keep charitable funds flowing to (and at times from) Israel. As reviewed in chapter six and mentioned at the beginning of this chapter, the Senate Foreign Relations Committee chartered an investigation in 1961 primarily to unearth—in an effort to properly regulate—the activities of Israel lobbying organizations that were improperly funneling a percentage of the hundreds of millions in U.S. and foreign charitable donations raised for "overseas relief" into political and public relations activities inside the United States. During the course of the investigation and hearings, the committee discovered that the Jewish Agency for Israel, a registered foreign agent, was improperly funding conduits with millions for lobbying and public relations campaigns for Israel. Jewish Agency "conduits" included the American Zionist Committee, its unincorporated lobbying division, the American Israel Public Affairs Committee, the Jewish Telegraphic Agency, and AIPAC founder Isaiah Kenen's *Near East Report* Israel lobbying newsletter, among others.

Getting the IRS to cooperate with the Senate investigation was no easy task. Committee Chair Senator J. W. Fulbright had to obtain two separate executive orders from President John F. Kennedy in order to finally obtain the cooperation of the IRS.[440] Even this cooperation for access to records was extremely limited. By order of IRS Commissioner Mortimer Caplin, the IRS allowed only three Senate staff investigators to review tax records, with the proviso that the Senate Foreign Relations Committee not publicly disclose sensitive information in the open hearings taking place in May and August of 1963.[441]

Following the August hearing, Senator J.W. Fulbright made a broad and comprehensive request for information on Israel lobbying organizations:

---

[440] Senator J.W. Fulbright requests an Executive Order to access tax records (file 10201962), Executive Order (file 11221962), Senator J.W. Fulbright requests ongoing access to tax records from JFK (file 01031963), Executive order 11080 grants Senate Committee on Foreign Relations access to any tax return related to the foreign agent investigation until June 30, 1963 (file 01291963). "Senate Foreign Relations Committee investigates why the IRS granted Israel lobby organizations tax-exempt status, 1962-1964," The Israel Lobby Archive. http://IsraelLobby.org/TEstatus

[441] IRS Director of the Enforcement Division cautions against public disclosure of tax return data (File 04251963). "Senate Foreign Relations Committee investigates why the IRS granted Israel lobby organizations tax-exempt status, 1962-1964" The Israel Lobby Archive

> *I would appreciate information as to whether or not they have tax-exempt status, and if contributions to them are tax-deductible to the donors. In each case where an exemption has been granted I would like to have indicated the facts applicable to the specific organization that brought it under the statutory provisions for tax exemption. I would also like to know if the facts developed during the Foreign Relations Committee hearings with regard to each organization named are consistent with those presented by such organization in its application for tax-exempt status.*[442]

On September 10, 1963, IRS Commissioner Caplin issued a short interim response that IRS tax-exempt status had been granted to the Jewish Agency for Israel, the Jewish Agency-American Section, the American Zionist Council, the Jewish Telegraphic Agency and United Israel appeal, among others, but not the American Israel Public Affairs Committee.

In January of 1964 Commissioner Caplin admitted in a twenty-thee page memo that key Israel lobbying organizations—as a result of facts surfaced during the Senate hearings—had engaged in many activities they did not disclose to the IRS in their applications for tax-exempt status or during periodic IRS reviews.[443]

Caplin confirmed that the Jewish Agency's 1952 application for tax-exempt status failed to disclose that it was registered under the Foreign Agents Registration Act (and had been since 1938). According to Caplin, none of the Jewish Agency's financial statements disclosed "expenditures on behalf of a foreign principal." The IRS was again bamboozled during a 1960 review ruling affirming the Jewish Agency's exempt status when the organization had again failed to disclose it was a foreign agent.

In 1961 the Jewish Agency's New York branch received $1.4 million ($11 million in 2015 dollars) from the Jewish Agency, according to the IRS, in "charitable contributions from all over the world." But of thirty-four publications, only one properly disclosed it was the product of a foreign agent, according to Caplin.

Despite these deceptions, and fully cognizant of major issues raised in the May and August 1963 Senate hearings, Caplin affirmed that "the Service held

---

[442] Senator J.W. Fulbright asks Secretary of Treasury Douglas Dillon about tax-exempt status (file 08131963). "Senate Foreign Relations Committee investigates why the IRS granted Israel lobby organizations tax-exempt status, 1962-1964, The Israel Lobby Archive

[443] IRS Commissioner Mortimer Caplin's final response to the Senate Foreign Relations Committee (file 01161964). "Senate Foreign Relations Committee investigates why the IRS granted Israel lobby organizations tax-exempt status, 1962-1964," The Israel Lobby Archive

in a ruling dated July 26, 1963 that the American Section qualified for exemption pursuant to the provisions of section 501(c)(3) of the Code." The IRS admitted it was unware of any political activities conducted through the American Zionist Council and that AZC was receiving Jewish Agency funds, some of which were then transferred to build the affinity of Christian organizations and a fledgling pro-Israel think tank. In fact, the IRS admitted it had no information whatsoever about the Jewish Agency's massive financial operations that was more recent than 1952. Caplin said the IRS granted the Jewish Telegraphic Agency tax-exempt status in 1939, but was also unaware that its ownership was transferred to a holding company of the Jewish Agency. Caplin did not reflect on many aspects of the Jewish Agency's subsidization of the media through many conduits, which were now public record after having been exhaustively reviewed in open Senate hearings.

But in the end, the IRS Commissioner defiantly stated that, based on the Jewish Agency's formal 1960 announcement that it would reorganize and expand the accountability of its board of directors to include apportionments of U.S. citizens, and implement other reforms, the IRS formally had affirmed—it had done so even before the second Senate hearing took place—the continuance of the Jewish Agency's tax-exempt status. Caplin then left the IRS on July 10, 1964, without the "expanded exempt organizations audit program" ever taking any apparent action on issues raised by the Senate Foreign Relations Committee.

The Jewish Telegraphic Agency, one of the targets of the Senate investigation, breathed a sigh of relief when Sheldon Cohen assumed the mantle as LBJ's newly appointed IRS Commissioner on January 25, 1965, reporting:

> *Sheldon S. Cohen, 37-year-old District of Columbia native, who was nominated this week by President Johnson to be the new Commissioner of the U.S. Internal Revenue Service, said today his two "pet charities" are the local Jewish Social Service agency and the Jewish Community Center.*[444]

The American Zionist Council, as noted, was destroyed by the 1962 Foreign Agents Registration Act order issued by Attorney General Robert F. Kennedy and, just six weeks after the order, the American Israel Public Affairs Committee split off and incorporated as a separate organization. AIPAC did not disclose on its 1967 application for tax-exempt status to the IRS that it had been part of an organization ordered to register as a foreign agent. In 1968, Cohen's IRS granted AIPAC tax- exempt status, retroactive to 1954, the year AIPAC first began lobbying as a division of the American

---

444 "Sheldon Cohen Named Commissioner of the U.S. Internal Revenue Service," *The Jewish Telegraphic Agency*, December 30, 1964

Zionist Council.

It is impossible to know what steps IRS Commissioner Mortimer Caplin would have taken in response to the Justice Department and Senate Foreign Relations Committee's actions against major Israel lobbying organizations had President Kennedy lived. But today two things are clear. Kennedy's assassination on November 22, 1963 took a great deal of pressure off the IRS commissioner to revoke any major IAO's tax-exempt status under the watchful eye of the Senate Foreign Relations Committee, President and Justice Department. It is also now clear—though it was not at the time—that Caplin was an activist who never failed to answer IAO calls to act. From Washington, DC, B'nai B'rith Membership Cabinet Program Director Herbert S. Levy affirmed this in a letter to the editor shortly after Caplin left office, correcting public allegations that Caplin had renounced his religion:

> *Your issue of Friday, June 18, includes an article headlined "Prominent Former Jews Are Named." It refers, among others, to Dr. Mortimer Caplin, former Director of the Internal Revenue Service, as a former Jew. This statement is untrue and does a disservice to a traditional Jew, a founder of the John F. Kennedy Lodge of B'nai B'rith in Washington and who is a prominent and active leader not only in B'nai B'rith but also in the United Jewish Appeal in Washington. Dr. Caplin's father too has been a leader for years in Educators Lodge of B'nai B'rith. I do not recall an occasion when Dr. Caplin's help was required for Jewish causes in which he did not respond. I can categorically state that this outstanding leader of our organization has never even remotely considered the question. He and Mrs. Caplin were appalled when this article was called to their attention. A published retraction in an early issue would be very much appreciated.*[445]

Caplin later won the American Jewish Committee's "Judge Learned Hand Human Relations Award." Caplin's successor, IRS Commissioner Sheldon Cohen, presiding while the IRS recognized and backdated AIPAC's tax-exempt status to 1954, functionally undid the only major IAO regulatory achievement of the Kennedy Administration Department of Justice. Cohen was also an insider Israel activist, who wrote the "strongest" letter to LBJ urging his support for Israel's preemptive attacks during the Six-Day War in 1967.

---

[445] https://newspapers.library.in.gov/cgi-bin/indiana?a=d&d=JPOST19650716-01.1.13 Jewish Post, Indianapolis, Marion County, 16 July 1965.

> *The most dramatic letter President Johnson received came from Sheldon Cohen, the IRS commissioner, writing the day after Hussein and Nasser signed their defense pact…When Cohen thought about Israelis, he saw himself among them…As an American, he believed the United States must stand by the only democratic state in the Middle East. 'We must find a way to help Israel defend itself—hopefully without bloodshed or harm to any of its neighbors, but aggression must be stopped.'*[446]

The next appointed IRS commissioner who was both Jewish and proactive on IAO initiatives was Jerome Kurtz. He helped the movement to socialize and build up pro-Israel identity by working to keep Jewish-only day schools from losing tax-exempt status by being declared racially discriminatory under new IRS regulations.

Douglas Shulman, as explored a bit later, refused to ever take action or respond to petitions and requests from activist groups to meet with him to discuss illegal settlement funding. Shulman's lack of interest extended to calls to review illicit charitable funding for Israel's clandestine nuclear weapons program.[447] Under Shulman's reign, the IRS took a monumental step backwards when it decided that—beginning in 2009—U.S. charities which were required to file IRS form 990 every year no longer had to report overseas recipient organizations, or even their country of residence. This rule change applied to all the organizations included in this study. Subsidy IAOs—particularly those funding illegal settlements—were among the first to take advantage of the IRS rule change, as noted by *The Forward*:

> *That means that an American charity such as One Israel Fund, which in 2003 reported sending tens of thousands of dollars to settlements in the West Bank, now needs only to acknowledge that it sent grants to the "Middle East" for "Security," among other purposes, as One Israel Fund did in its 2010*

---

[446] Tom Segev, *1967: Israel, the War, and the Year that Transformed the Middle East* [New York, Macmillan] 304

[447] Grant F. Smith, "American Committee for the Weizmann Institute: Secret Nuclear Weapons Fundraising," letter to Douglas Shulman, June 31, 2012. Center for Policy and Law Enforcement. http://irmep.org/cfp/06132012_IRS.pdf A response from Manager of Exempt Organizations Guidance David L. Fish urged the author to contact Gregory Schantz. http://irmep.org/cfp/08242012_irs_schantz.pdf Ultimately a form letter from Nanette M. Downing claimed, as Mortimer Caplin did in 1964, that the IRS has robust examination programs, while cautioning that IRS code 6103 "protects the privacy of tax returns and tax return information" even though form 990s are in the public domain. http://irmep.org/cfp/08312012_weizmann.pdf There has been no apparent action taken by the IRS.

> *disclosure...In 2007, American Friends of Hebrew University reported sending $45 million to The Hebrew University of Jerusalem. In 2010, that same group reported that it had sent $34 million to the "Middle East/North Africa" for "general purposes, scholarships, research, capital projects."*[448]

Even Sheldon Cohen, who lobbied the LBJ administration so intensively to support Israel during its preemptive 1967 attacks and in the aftermath of the Six-Day War, professed shock at the audacity of the IRS move: "That's just the opposite of what we were moving towards, which was more accounting responsibility…"[449]

Many professional tax preparers who work for charities are still unaware of the rule change, or why it was made. The IRS has been tight-lipped about its justifications for the move, claiming to the handful of curious journalists that the changes were a result of public input from organizations required to file the form. They were concerned—of course—about their personal "security." The IRS refers all inquiries to a report with the only major IRS statement issued about the change, which reads:

> *Schedule F, Statement of Activities Outside the United States, proposed that an organization list each foreign country in which it conducted activities and requested the name of foreign grantees. This raised concerns about the personal safety of workers, volunteers, and others involved in an organization's work in certain unsafe foreign areas. Many suggested that the Schedule F not require reporting for each country, not be publicly disclosed, have certain identifying information redacted from public disclosure, or be delayed. The IRS may not redact or withhold from public disclosure information reported on the Form 990 unless it is expressly authorized by statute. Because this authority currently does not exist for the information requested by Schedule F, the 2008 Form 990 Schedule F will require reporting on a regional basis (rather than on a country-by-country basis), and will not require reporting of certain identifying information of the grantee. If redaction or withholding from public disclosure becomes feasible in the future, Schedule F will be modified to require*

448 Josh Nathan-Kazis, "IRS rules permit charities to say little about money sent overseas," *The Forward*, April 9, 2013

449 Josh Nathan-Kazis, "IRS rules permit charities to say little about money sent overseas" *The Forward*, April 9, 2013

> *reporting on a country-by-country basis, as well as more specific grantee information.*[450]

Were these "security" concerns cited by the IRS primarily provided by subsidy IAOs? Although the author asked the IRS to substantiate which organizations provided input, and their specific concerns, through a Freedom of Information Act request, the IRS has not responded. A response could reveal whether internal objectives to get out from under public charges that the IRS and U.S. Treasury Department have long aided and abetted illegal settlements by turning a blind eye to U.S. financial flows had any role in the changes.

It is the author's estimate that Israel receives more non-foundation charitable tax-exempt donations from the U.S. than any other country. Verifying this would require a study of the giving patterns of 1.5 million nonprofit organizations, an arduous but possible task given that the poor format of the data distributed by IRS is increasingly being properly digitized and structured by watchdog organizations. But it is undeniable that the IRS has made it possible for the most questionable and evasive IAOs to escape scrutiny. As public attention grows and increasing numbers of lawsuits are filed against the Department of Treasury in general and IRS in particular, both agencies will soon be able to claim—though not legitimately—that they simply do not know what countries or organizations are receiving funding and are therefore not responsible for illegal settlements. From the Israel lobby's standpoint, an IRS commissioner who supports IAO initiatives—but is not too outspoken about it in public before appointment—is an ideal candidate for Commissioner. Once appointed they can than either advocate for Israel (like Cohen and Kurtz), or prevent the IRS from taking any warranted enforcement actions against IAOs (like Caplin and Shulman).

By the author's tally of non-interim IRS commissioners beginning with Mortimer Caplin, commissioners who were IAO members or promoted one or more IAO initiatives have had five terms of office. Commissioners with no visible IAO affiliations or initiatives served for ten terms, including current IRS commissioner John Koskinen. Though only half the number of their non-Israel Affinity, the Israel Affinity commissioners were longer serving, averaging 3.6 years of service versus 3.2 years for the other commissioners.[451]

---

[450] "Internal Revenue Service Form 990 Redesign for Tax Year 2008, Background paper," IRS, December 20, 2007 https://www.irs.gov/pub/irs-tege/background_paper_form__990__redesign.pdf

[451] These figures assume John Koskinen leaves office at the end of the Obama administration in January of 2017

Name	Took office	Left office	Israel Affinity Category	Years in office
Mortimer Caplin	2/7/1961	7/10/1964	Yes	3.4
Sheldon Cohen	1/25/1965	2/20/1969	Yes	4.1
Randolph W. Thrower	4/1/1969	6/22/1971	No	2.2
Johnnie Mac Walters	8/6/1971	4/30/1973	No	1.7
Donald C. Alexander	5/25/1973	2/26/1977	No	3.8
Jerome Kurtz	5/5/1977	10/31/1980	Yes	3.5
Roscoe L. Egger, Jr.	3/14/1981	4/30/1986	No	5.1
Lawrence B. Gibbs	8/4/1986	3/4/1989	No	2.6
Fred T. Goldberg, Jr.	7/5/1989	2/2/1992	Yes	2.6
Shirley D. Peterson	2/3/1992	1/20/1993	No	1.0
Margaret Milner Richardson	5/27/1993	5/31/1997	No	4.0
Charles O. Rossotti	11/13/1997	11/6/2002	No	5.0
Mark W. Everson	5/1/2003	5/4/2007	No	4.0
Douglas H. Shulman	3/24/2008	11/9/2012	Yes	4.6
John Koskinen	12/23/2013	1/20/2017	No	3.1

Figure 41 IRS commissioners and Israel affinity 1961-2017

Researching such behind-the-scenes activities in key agencies is an exercise in patience. Because Congressional records are not subject to the Freedom of Information Act, researchers must often wait fifty years (or more) in order to obtain access to such records. Caplin's interactions with the Senate Foreign Relations Committee records were released in the year 2010. Some records from the Senate investigation, including huge quantities of microfiche, are classified secret or remain unavailable to the public for lack of resources to review them. The IRS is generally unresponsive, if not hostile, to FOIA requests and extremely difficult to research. Just as difficult to research are the agencies that are supposed to enforce counter-espionage statutes and other laws.

Intelligence and law enforcement avoidance of IAO confrontations through an unwarranted presumption of innocence is also well documented. In late 1972, the Pittsburgh, Pennsylvania, FBI field office opened a counter-espionage investigation of an individual conducting suspicious communications with the Soviet embassy in Washington. Rather than intensify the investigation when the individual's connection with Hadassah was uncovered, the FBI instead immediately suspended the case, reporting:

> *The Pittsburgh City and telephone directories disclosed that the Pittsburgh Chapter of Hadassah is located at 6315 Forbes Avenue, Pittsburgh, PA. In this connection it is pointed out that Hadassah is a beneficent organization of the Jewish religion*

> *which functions in a manner similar to the Red Cross. Isasmuch as Hadassah does not appear to present a security risk, no further investigation in this matter appears to be warranted and the case is considered closed.*[452]

Former case officer Victor Ostrovsky, who has written books exposing Mossad practices, would likely advise that IAOs such as Hadassah, with many employees traveling back and forth to Israel, should receive more—rather than less—counterintelligence scrutiny. As an example of how a five-person intelligence team would build a network in London, the former spy said:

> *You open a station in London with five guys...These five guys are the actual case officers. Then what you do is you get people to come from Israel, and they scout the country. And they come up with a lot of names of the Jewish Community in London. And these guys then go out, and they'll approach a doctor, a Jewish doctor in London, and we'll say, 'Listen, we need your help in order to save Jews elsewhere. And we might be turning to you, will you be helpful to us?' Seventy percent turn them down, but nobody will ever turn them in. And that's a very important factor. So you can go to another guy, and another guy, another guy. Before you know it, you got 300, 400 people in London who are supporting the station.*[453]

In 1975, the Ford administration attempted to sell improved Hawk anti-aircraft missiles to Jordan and duly sent notification, containing classified Department of Defense data, to the Senate Foreign Relations Committee and House Foreign Affairs Committee. AIPAC Director Morris Amitay reviewed the classified document after being informed of its existence "secretly by aides of Senator Clifford P. Case, Republican of New Jersey, and Representative Jonathan B. Bingham, Democrat of New York," according to *The New York Times*. Amitay and AIPAC quickly mounted a massive campaign in opposition to the missile sale, telling constituent public pressure groups that the weapons were capable of "providing cover for offensive operations against Israel." After delays, Jordan considered acquiring a similar system from the Soviet Union.

Author and activist Norman F. Dacey was outraged. He dashed off a letter on March 30, 1976, to Deputy Assistant Secretary of State for Near

---

452 FBI counter-espionage case file 105-8221, memo to the Acting Director, FBI, 1/3/1973 released under the Freedom of Information Act on August 15, 2014 The Israel Lobby Archive, http://www.israellobby.org/ADL-FBI/

453 Former Mossad Agency Victor Ostrovsky, undated presentation. https://www.youtube.com/watch?v=-WByQS9SG4I

Eastern and South Asian Affairs Adolph Dubs, inquiring, "Did you initiate action to discover the identity of the individual(s) responsible for the violation and to institute appropriate action to punish the violator?" On April 29, the State Department forwarded Dacey's letter to the Criminal Division of the U.S. Department of Justice, but attempted to downplay the affair by claiming, "A notice of sale is normally not considered by the Department of Defense to require classification and protection.... I would appreciate any comments you could offer on the issues presented by the letter...." On May 19, the State Department seemed to try to extricate itself from the scandal, telling Dacey "we consulted with the Justice Department informally after receipt of your first letter and, at their request, transmitted it to them for further consideration. The matter is still under review in the Justice Department, which expects to provide you with a direct response in the near future."[454]

On June 16, Dacey again pressed the State Department. "We have had no response...There has been a flagrant violation of the U.S. Criminal Code." On June 22, 1976, the litigious Dacey upped the ante. "While we are certain that you have not intended to give the appearance of exhibiting disdain for public inquiries courteously submitted, the lack of any satisfactory response leaves us with no alternative to that conclusion. We do not wish to proceed publicly under sections 2383 and 2384 but you appear to leave us with no other course." On June 25, 1976, the State Department testily warded off Dacey: "We are not aware that any Department of State official has failed to meet his obligations under applicable law and regulation regarding this document."

The Criminal Division of the U.S. Department of Justice initially appeared to think otherwise, and asked the State Department for more details on July 21, 1976. On Nov. 4, the Department of State finally admitted to DOJ that the disclosure to AIPAC was "unauthorized" and had included both the dollar amounts and quantitative configurations of the missile system. The State Department revealed, "Specific details of Jordan's military equipment needs are information provided us in confidence by that government. The classification of the documents in question was, in our view, substantively proper." Worse still, according to State, "Had Jordan actually entered into such a major arms-supply relationship with the Soviets, this would have had a significant adverse impact on U.S. national defense interests and on U.S.-Jordanian relations."

The U.S. State Department then responded to the DOJ's other questions probing the feasibility of criminally prosecuting Amitay. "With the public

---

[454] "U.S. State Department investigates AIPAC Director Morris Amitay's acquisition of classified Hawk missile data," The Israel Lobby Archive http://www.israellobby.org/amitay/

disclosure of the information having already occurred, the authorization of its release for the purpose of prosecution would not be expected to cause damage with our relations with Jordan." However, Amitay was never charged and continued to serve as AIPAC's director until he resigned in 1980 to establish a pro-Israel political action committee (PAC) in Washington. The Department of Defense letter obtained by AIPAC has never been declassified.

Amitay's violations on behalf of AIPAC (and, by extension, Israel) and the reluctance of appropriate law enforcement authorities to do anything about it reveal that even informed citizen action and legal expertise is not enough. Even when they do stumble onto rock-solid cases of Israeli espionage, in coordination with IAOs, law enforcement authorities go to great lengths to isolate Israel from any consequences. This again happened during Israel's quest for duty-free access for exports to the U.S. market.

An AIPAC-Israeli government tag-team and law-breaking-affair is documented in the form of forty-nine declassified FBI files. In 1984, seventy-one major U.S. corporations and worker organizations said "no" to a vast AIPAC economic power grab—a demand to unilaterally lower all U.S. import barriers to Israeli products, while allowing Israel the flexibility to continue blocking U.S. exports. Israeli Minister of Economics Dan Halpern obtained through unknown means a U.S. government document containing proprietary information and business secrets supplied by U.S. industries most opposed to the Israel lobby's economic power grab. Halpern passed it to AIPAC, which made great use of it to undermine the entire advise and consent process. Douglas Bloomfield, AIPAC's top lobbyist, even made an illicit copy of the classified document after AIPAC was explicitly ordered to return it to the U.S. government.[455]

The consequences of this earlier economic crime against U.S. industry slowly became clear. By locking many U.S. products of export quantity out of Israel, the trade agreement delivered, through 2015, a $115 billion cumulative deficit (not adjusted for inflation) since enacted. The U.S. imposes no trade barriers to Israel under the plan. Israel's many rotating barriers—allowed under the agreement—still occasionally make the news. When Israel reinstated a 120 percent duty on imported gefilte fish, it took the involvement of an Illinois congressional representative, the secretary of state, Israel's ambassador and the Israeli Prime Minister to get a "one time" exception and allow the U.S. export.[456] Israel's exports arrive in American ports on greased skids. U.S. exports to Israel, not so much. IAO espionage

---

[455] FBI Investigates AIPAC for espionage and theft of government property in 1984, The Israel Lobby Archive, http://www.israellobby.org/economy/

[456] Aliyah Frumin, "Clinton's gefilte fish mystery, solved," MSNBC, September 1, 2015 http://www.msnbc.com/msnbc/hillary-clintons-gefilte-fish-mystery-solved

has also been deployed to boost Israel's advantage in U.S. funded weapons development projects.

An FBI sting operation against an IAO founder and former NASA scientist, Stewart Nozette, deployed an undercover FBI special agent posing as a Mossad agent. Meeting in the posh Mayflower Hotel in Washington, the undercover agent set up clandestine payments in exchange for highly classified information from Nozette. Nozette began delivering the requested classified national defense information believing it to be destined for Israel, while confidentially assuring the undercover FBI agent that he thought he was already spying for Israel. This activity occurred, according to court documents, under Nozette's prior "consulting" contract with Israel Aerospace Industries, a major Israeli military contractor. The U.S. Department of Justice has traditionally ignored, forgiven, or entirely quashed investigations into Israeli espionage. In this case, in the face of Nozette's blatant misuse of his security clearances to plunder classified information in the greater Washington region, the spy catchers had to carefully isolate IAI so that Congress could continue delivering financial support to Israel's Iron Dome missile defense system—an issue of great importance to the Israel lobby that appeared to supersede the administration's concerns about spying. It had already done service in this arena by failing to properly roll up one of the very first smuggling network that led to IAI's own creation.

Israel Aerospace Industries was once called Israel Aircraft Industries (IAI), a company launched by the flight engineer and entrepreneur Adolph "Al" Schwimmer. Schwimmer was a key man in the vast underground Haganah smuggling effort across the U.S., trafficking in surplus WWII arms, supplies and veteran manpower for war in Palestine. He purchased heavily discounted surplus U.S. military aircraft from the War Assets Administration, violating laws prohibiting their export and use in armed conflict. He did this by creating a fake Panamanian shell corporation and flying an entire transport wing to Palestine to battle for the creation of Israel in 1948. None of the key American financial backers of the effort—who were quickly identified—went to jail, although a handful of small operators, such as Nathan Liff, did eventually appear in criminal court. One of them, Nahum Bernstein, was the Jewish Agency's paymaster in New York who cut checks for the smuggling operations. In July of 1950 Assistant U.S. Attorney Hershel E. Champlin claimed that if the U.S, government "had known of Bernstein's participation in the conspiracy involving Schwimmer et al prior to his admission of it in court, he [Bernstein] would have been indicted along with the others."[457] Instead the low-level operatives all received lenient sentences, pleading they were only giving guns to "young Jewish boys who went to the door of Hitler's

[457] Nahum A. Bernstein FBI File, The Israel Lobby Archive http://www.israellobby.org/Bernstein/

ovens to bring Holocaust survivors to a Jewish homeland."[458] Schwimmer was convicted of a felony but served no prison time. He left the U.S. to become managing director of IAI, with the backing of David Ben-Gurion and Shimon Peres.

IAI contracting with the Israeli Air Force boomed beginning in the 1950s, as did widespread Israeli espionage against U.S. military and industrial targets for vital aerospace expertise and proprietary weapons designs. A formal decision to expunge Schwimmer's smuggling past did not occur until 2000, when his Israel-backer friends in the U.S. successfully lobbied Bill Clinton for a presidential pardon. Schwimmer was unrepentant, explaining to *The Forward* that pardons would require that he:

> *...fill out all sorts of papers asking for forgiveness, telling the Justice Department you're sorry, you did wrong, and you regret it, and you won't do it again. I didn't feel that way, and I still don't. I didn't feel I had done anything wrong, so I never applied.*

In 1990, Stewart Nozette established his intelligence-gathering IAO called the "Alliance for Competitive Technology." It had the publicly stated objective of serving "the national and public interest by conducting scientific research and educational activities aimed at expanding the utilization of National and Government Laboratory resources." By that, Nozette meant utilization by Israel. Nozette still held high-level security clearances after leaving NASA to spy for IAI, which needed secret information—as in the case of the Halpern-AIPAC theft—in order to secure for Israel the best possible negotiating position for the U.S. taxpayer-funded Iron Dome and David's Sling missile defense programs. IAI paid Nozette, according to a criminal indictment, $225,000 for the information.[459]

One former AIPAC leader (and, troublingly, a former Justice Department employee), Neil Sher, claimed he was "shocked by how little the [FBI] agents knew or understood about lobbying and the search for information." Sher urged that before Nozette was prosecuted, "leaders of the Jewish community raise some hell, and not show the timidity which, unfortunately, characterized many responses to the [2005] AIPAC case involving Steve Rosen and Keith Weissman."[460] However, such a public mobilization of Israel supporters

---

[458] Harold Brackman and Giveon Cornfield, "Hawaii residents aided underdog Israel's struggle," *The Honolulu Star Bulletin*, October 15, 2006 http://archives.starbulletin.com/2006/10/15/editorial/special4.html

[459] "Stewart David Nozette convicted for espionage against the United States," The Israel Lobby Archive http://www.israellobby.org/nozette/

[460] Neal M. Sher, "Once again, dual loyalty canard front and center," *The Jewish Press*, March 19, 2013 http://www.jewishpress.com/indepth/opinions/once-again-dual-loyalty-canard-front-and-center/2009/11/04/0/?print

failed to materialize. In hindsight, the taxpaying public should have mobilized.

The FBI instead could have set up a sting of IAI's and the operatives handling Nozette, but instead chose to orchestrate an undercover operation that isolated Israel from culpability. The FBI also carefully edited the surveillance videos used in court and released to the public—fortunately with errors—in which Nozette states he thought he was already spying for IAI. The FBI has fought against full, unedited release of the videos, filed for under the Freedom of Information Act. Although Nozette was sentenced to thirteen years in federal prison, the real victims—U.S. taxpayers—were not made whole and continue to fund Israel's missile programs. Although the Alliance for Competitive Technology is now defunct, we include it as an IAO on a growth trajectory in the Big Israel database because its activities are almost certainly still being replicated in one or more IAOs.

In 2005, when two AIPAC officials were caught passing classified national defense information obtained from Colonel Lawrence Franklin to a friendly *Washington Post* reporter with the aim of precipitating U.S. military attacks on Iran, AIPAC did actually have a plan in place to accuse the FBI of "anti-Semitism" in order to have the charges dropped. AIPAC's secret plan only became public, however, during a related defamation lawsuit that followed the Obama administration's mysterious abandonment of espionage prosecutions against Steven J. Rosen and Keith Weismann. Only the government source of classified information passed along to AIPAC and the Israeli government, Pentagon Colonel Lawrence Franklin, went to prison.

During pretrial maneuvers, the defense team for the two accused AIPAC staffers, Rosen and Weissman, won an unprecedented standard of proof from presiding arbiter Judge T.S. Ellis. In a ruling made shortly before they dropped the case, prosecutors were ordered to prove not whether the two accused were trafficking classified information to the Israelis and friends in the establishment press, but whether they were in a "state of mind" in which they believed they were actually committing a crime. As written, the 1917 Espionage Act, the statute under which the AIPAC duo were accused, is silent on such matters. If things had gone badly, AIPAC's plan was to publicly accuse the FBI of "anti-Semitism" as part of its defense of Rosen and Weisman. The internal AIPAC strategy, released during discovery, stated:

> *Finally, the fact that press reports have indicated that David Szady, a senior FBI counterintelligence official who some Jewish organizations believe has targeted Jews for investigation, is involved in the investigation, has only heightened our concerns. According to these reports, Szady has targeted Jews and blocked or slowed their clearances. He was directly involved in a high profile case involving a Jewish former CIA staff attorney who*

> *sued the FBI, CIA and its top officials for religious discrimination.*[461]

AIPAC later got cold feet and noted on the speech draft, "DO NOT USE UNTIL WE HAVE VERIFIED." AIPAC instead fired Rosen and Weissman rather than defend actions which subsequent court proceedings revealed were standard operating procedure at AIPAC. AIPAC did, however, continue to fund their criminal defense.

In the annals of IAO espionage, no example so clearly documents how secret Israeli intervention, at the highest levels of the U.S. government, can still successfully quash warranted criminal prosecutions and accountability as does the "ADL files case." Though we mentioned the outcome of this case briefly in earlier sections, we explore its implications more fully here.

2013 marked the 20th anniversary of the infamous "Anti-Defamation League (ADL) files controversy," in which the ADL was discovered infiltrating, spying on and otherwise violating the privacy rights of a large number of pro-Palestinian, anti-Apartheid, civil-rights and peace groups through the unlawful acquisition of private data from corrupt local law enforcement officials. The single best retrospective is from long-time Middle East analyst and broadcaster Jeffrey Blankfort, who was among those targeted by the ADL (see the online essay, "The Strange History of the Anti-Defamation League: ADL Spies").

Many Americans were outraged in 1993 after reading mainstream press accounts of a vast national ADL spy network with organelles passing information not only to Israel's Mossad but also to Apartheid South Africa's intelligence service—possibly resulting in the mysterious death of Chris Hani, who was in line to follow Nelson Mandela as South Africa's president, and in the detention and attempted deportation of a number of Palestinians.

FBI files declassified in 2013[462] reveal not only the flood of constituent letters pouring into Congress, and the FBI's unfulfilled assurances that justice would be served, but also the ADL's successful use of proven tactics that the Israel lobby has deployed since the 1940s to skirt accountability for major criminal violations. These FBI files, originally scheduled for declassification in 2038, were suddenly released to the author under the Freedom of Information Act.

A March 16, 1993, memo launched the ADL espionage investigation from the FBI's Los Angeles office. The FBI discovered "unidentified individuals at the Anti-Defamation League (ADL) in possession of [Federal] Bureau [of

---

[461] Grant Smith, "Economic Espionage Haunts AIPAC," Antiwar.com, December 18, 2010 http://original.antiwar.com/smith-grant/2010/12/17/economic-espionage-haunts-aipac/

[462] "FBI investigates the ADL for Espionage," The Israel Lobby Archive http://www.israellobby.org/ADL-FBI/

Investigation] classified information," along with "confidential police reports and files belonging to the San Francisco Police Department," after the ADL's Los Angeles and San Francisco offices were raided and searched under warrant. Until that time, despite public statements to the contrary, Israel was highly interested in preserving close economic and military ties (including sales pitches to sell Israeli nuclear weapons) to Apartheid South Africa.[463] The ADL, in constant contact with the Israeli consulate, which frequently tasked it for help, was eager to pitch in. The FBI discovered that one of its own files in possession of ADL's Los Angeles division was "a summary of activities relating to the African National Congress (ANC)." The FBI immediately noticed that the ADL—which, as previously discussed, had already invested decades securing a forced relationship with the FBI, probably by the usual means of coordinated lobbying of top elected officials—was suddenly "uncooperative" and stalling for time. By month's end, Israel's "heavy guns" were drawn to snuff out the fledgling investigation.

The FBI already had a long history of outside interference in its investigations of Israel espionage and smuggling, and the ADL files affair was no exception. In the 1940s, the FBI had seen the sudden collapse of a pipeline of indictments against hundreds of Americans illegally smuggling conventional weapons to Jewish fighters in Palestine, funded by Jewish Agency paymasters operating out of New York. At that time, it was the intervention of Abraham Feinberg, a major campaign contribution bundler, and Israeli government officials that proved too much for the Justice Department, even as evidence of the lawbreaking continued to pile up. It failed to prosecute, and successfully dodged later demands for justice.[464] A March 31, 1993, FBI memo on the ADL investigation revealed that:

> *...two persons, described as 'Israeli Generals' are in or are about to travel to Washington, D.C...the purpose of their travel is to try to visit the Attorney General to press for an end to the FBI's investigations...The FBI's investigations of these matters are causing a great deal of interference in the U.S. activities of the Anti-Defamation League...and so Israel is seeking to intercede on the ADL's behalf.*

Mailbags of constituent letters to Congress urging the swift criminal prosecution of the ADL were forwarded to the FBI and attorney general. Robert Kerrey, John McCain, Richard Lugar, Hank Brown, Jill Long

---

[463] Chris McGreal, "Revealed: How Israel offered to sell South Africa nuclear weapons," *The Guardian*, May 24, 2010

[464] See "Norman F. Dacey demands Justice and State Department action on credible allegations of Israeli arms smuggling and espionage," The Israel Lobby Archive. http://www.israellobby.org/Dacey/

Thompson, Dennis DeConcini and Ernest Hollings, while often distancing themselves from the substance of the complaints, dutifully forwarded the letters of outrage. The FBI's Legislative Counsel, Charles E. Mandigo, reviewed demands to prosecute both the ADL and "a former San Francisco police officer and former CIA agent [Thomas Gerard]" who "sold police information on Arab Americans to agents of the Mossad." Mandigo assured them "the FBI will actively seek prosecution of any individuals or any enterprise discovered to be involved in illegal activity in violation of federal statutes...." However, those who believed him were all in for a huge disappointment.

After interviewing a disgruntled former ADL "fact finder" librarian who had worked with and curated information gathered by long-time ADL undercover contractor Roy Bullock, the FBI quickly focused in on ADL Regional Director David Lehrer as the prime suspect in acquiring and passing classified FBI files throughout the ADL. The FBI LA office requested several times that the FBI director authorize a formal interview with Lehrer. Nevertheless, FBI Director William Sessions, a holdover from the Reagan administration, left the FBI in July of 1993. Acting director Floyd Clarke took no action before leaving on September 1. Not until September 23, 1993, did the Clinton administration's new FBI Director, Louis Freeh, authorize special agent in command Edward J. Curran to conduct the only interview that could possibly lead to a prosecution: "personally interview David Lehrer, Regional Director—ADL—Los Angeles....The interview is to be conducted according to FCIM 65-5.1 guidelines, and recorded on an FD-302 in the event this matter warrants possible prosecution."

However, by then it was much too late. Israel already had half a year to lobby for closure. On December 1, 1993, Israeli Justice Minister David Libai met for an hour with Attorney General Janet Reno. He spent thirty minutes on a futile attempt to secure Reno's recommendation to President Clinton that the sentence for Israel's spy Jonathan Pollard be commuted. What Libai did for the remaining thirty minutes of the "private" meeting was not disclosed, but, as the FBI feared, he likely demanded an end to the investigation of the ADL. This becomes even more apparent because, on March 22, 1994, the FBI's Los Angeles office formally indicated it was closing the ADL espionage investigation—apparently without ever having interviewed Lehrer. By April, Janet Reno was gushing over the ADL's latest report on militias and the uncomfortable FBI-ADL "special relationship"—ordered by J. Edgar Hoover and renewed by FBI Director William Webster—was back on track.

Until the relevant file declassification and release, it was never clear to outsiders whether the FBI had properly investigated ADL's illegal circulation of classified FBI files. Only now can the ADL "files controversy" formally enter the pantheon of "Israel lobby criminal investigations that were improperly closed." Like AIPAC's ditching of two staffers caught up in espionage, ADL National Director Abraham Foxman fired a "shocked and dismayed" Lehrer in 2002, but without much explanation. Although at the time many speculated that the termination was over the ADL national office's effort to prevent its increasingly autonomous—Hollywood-funded—West Coast offices from splitting off from the national organization, it also could have been the delayed fulfillment of a quiet non-prosecution agreement to finally close the "ADL files controversy." Only the now comfortably retired Abraham Foxman and the Justice Department know for sure.

Whether the ADL also would have accused the FBI of anti-Semitism as a defense is unclear, though it continues to be a primary tool in the ADL toolkit. Certainly ringing the alarm bells about growing anti-Semitism in order to raise funds continues to be an ADL mainstay so much so that other IAOs complained: not that the tactic is used unjustly to destroy innocent people, but that ADL began winning on the fundraising battlefield an oversize share of charitable contributions in the 1990s because of its willingness to sound that ancient alarm. JJ Goldberg reported that:

> *Some critics darkly suggest a link between ADL's 'alarmism' and its dramatic fundraising success. The ADL's budget was about the same as the American Jewish Committee's just 20 years ago. Today, at nearly $30 million per year, it is larger than those of the American Jewish Committee, the American Jewish Congress, the Simon Wiesenthal Center and NJCRAC combined.*
>
> *'People don't give if you tell them everything's O.K.,' gripes an official at a rival agency. But the ADL, in this year's Audit, argues that the rise in anti-Semitic incidents could signal 'a new willingness to engage in direct, provocative confrontation with Jews, a kind of in-your-face' intimidation, reflecting an erosion of the taboo against such open bigotry.*[465]

The most recent major publicly known case of IAO use of classified information to target enemies—with Justice Department deference—is that of United Against Nuclear Iran or UANI. On July 19, 2013, Greek shipping magnate Victor Restis sued UANI, which was incorporated in 2008 and managed and advised by former U.S. and foreign government officials. UANI's advisory board included former Mossad Chief Meir Dagan, long time Israel lobbyist and U.S. "peace process" negotiator and Israel lobbyist Dennis Ross, as well as former Senator Joseph Lieberman and Frances

[465] J.J. Goldberg "How Much Anti-Semitism?" *The Jerusalem Report*, February 20, 1992

Townsend, the former homeland security adviser to President George W. Bush

UANI raised only between $1.3 and $1.7 million a year in tax-exempt donations, but operated out of luxury downtown Manhattan office space. The group lobbied Congress and drafted legislation aimed at thwarting a program that, again, no intelligence agency, including the CIA, claimed existed—an Iranian clandestine program to build nuclear weapons. UANI obtained information about companies it suspected were doing business with Iran in contravention of economic sanctions, then issued accusatory news releases, letters, Facebook postings and blurbs through its Twitter feed as "private sanctions campaigns" designed to pressure a targeted company to cease and desist. UANI, according to Restis court filings, acted as a judge, jury and executioner, demanding:

> *...the targeted company or individual sign a sworn statement under the penalty of perjury refuting whatever charges UANI has made; submit to an examination of the business UANI has targeted by an auditor on its referral list; and subject itself to an audit and review by an 'independent' counsel.'*

UANI's charges that Restis was a "front-man" for Iran were allegedly based on UANI's possession of a proposal letter for Restis to meet Iranian officials in Greece and a second "consultancy engagement agreement letter." UANI refused to publicly release either of the two letters that Restis claimed must have been crude forgeries. On July 3, 2013, lawyers for Restis issued their own "cease and desist" letter to UANI managers which triggered more UANI accusations and adverse publicity, scuttling a planned initial public offering of shipping company shares and other large business deals by Restis.

Restis also received many death threats as a result of UANI's unrelenting campaign, being called "an evil, greasy, greedy bastard," a "Greek fuck," "animal," "crook" and "Christian pig." Restis, who is Jewish and claimed he supported Israel and was opposed to Iran ever developing nuclear weapons, complained about visitor comments on UANI's Facebook page urging others to "hang him," and "just shoot him" and "lock and load torpedoes."

Restis was quietly approached by Rami Ungar, an Israeli shipping executive with no visible public connection to UANI, according to court filings. Restis claimed Ungar was a fixer who mysteriously knew all the details about the UANI situation. Ungar claimed that, on behalf of the group's supporters, he was "authorized to try to resolve the issues." Restis would have none of it. In an April letter to the presiding judge, the Restis legal team claimed they had uncovered information that UANI "is being funded by foreign interests" that, like Ungar, were presumably also from Israel. Restis filed court documents to compel not only Ungar's sworn testimony, but also that of UANI advisor Meir Dagan, the Israeli former Mossad intelligence chief. Restis even claimed it was Mossad that served as the conduit between the source and UANI.

Presumably, at the quiet invitation of UANI, the U.S. Justice Department suddenly became "ex parte" to the case on March 10, 2014, after UANI lost a series of crucial court battles compelling it to release sensitive donor and internal operational information. The Justice Department claimed it was reviewing whether "certain information at issue in discovery is properly protected from disclosure pursuant to the law enforcement privilege," and prohibited Restis from obtaining UANI files through a series of stays granted by the judge.

On July 31, 2014, DOJ asked presiding judge Edgardo Ramos to extend yet another stay on any discovery of UANI's secret files, pending "review of a possible privilege assertion by the Government," until September, 2014. According to reporter Matt Apuzzo at *The New York Times*, Judge Ramos found the government involvement "very curious." Apuzzo subtly posed the obvious question of why the Obama administration's Justice Department was not indicting UANI under its zero-tolerance policy for classified information leaks, which it freely wielded against whistle-blowers and journalists, if UANI, in fact, possessed classified government information.

Restis claimed his shipping businesses lost billions of dollars under UANI's withering public relations assault. UANI's wealthy backers and intelligence sources likely feared exposure. But, in an unprecedented expansion of the so-called "state secrets" privilege, on March 23, 2015, the judge honored the Justice Department's request to quash the lawsuit. No public disclosure of what classified information the IAO possessed, how it obtained it, and from whom was ever forthcoming.

The U.S. Department of Justice action on behalf of UANI exposes the long arc of a circle finally completed. It began with attempts to make IAOs comply with U.S. law. America's top law enforcement agency tried to regulate and curtail illegal IAO activities—in the 1940s, weapons and war material smuggling. Limp efforts were made to investigate NUMEC, AIPAC, ZOA and the ADL. Today the Justice Department is merely an accessory after the fact—protecting an IAO's improper use of taxpayer assets in the form of classified information the Department of Justice is charged to protect, and over which it does rigorously and regularly prosecute when the violators are not as politically enfranchised.

Although the U.S. Congress does not "regulate" the Israel lobby, it passes the laws that do (or, in the case of the Foreign Agents Registration Act, could) regulate lobbying. It controls the purse strings, and is therefore the single most important focus of Israel Affinity Organizations' main lobbying body, AIPAC. While AIPAC is not all-powerful and does not win every single battle, an exhaustive recent study based on interviews of 106 congressional staffers by professor Kirk Beattie reveals it is always a factor:

> *...There is only one richly funded, heavily staffed, highly efficient, and supremely effective lobby; its name is AIPAC. AIPAC is the NRA [National Rifle Association] of any issue affecting Israel. For decades, it has been in a league of its own...no other group successively pressures congresspersons and influences congressional outcomes in this issue area with the same success as does AIPAC. As a current House member noted, poignantly, "When we have some floor votes, some members of Congress will even bring to one another's attention, 'It's an AIPAC vote.'"*[466]

AIPAC, established with foreign funding to advance Israel inside the U.S., has been able to avoid due oversight measures for so long, and secured so much undue influence that many in congress no longer even consider voting against its resolutions and bills.

[466] Kirk J. Beattie, *Congress and the Shaping of the Middle East* [New York, Oakland: Seven Stories Press, 2015], 399

11 MOVING WHERE?

In 2001, Israeli Prime Minister Benjamin Netanyahu, who once characterized the 9/11 attacks on America as "good" for Israel, told West Bank Jewish settlers, in what he thought was a private meeting, "I know what America is. America is a thing you can move very easily, move it in the right direction." Netanyahu's belief that America can so easily be moved is likely grounded in confidence that the Israel lobby will continue to deliver. Another Israeli observer underscored just how critical it is for Israel to maintain privileged access to U.S. government elites in order to make demands in secret and be able to proclaim that there is "no daylight" between the United States and Israel's policies. Historian Michael Oren's 2015 book, *Ally: My Journey Across the American-Israeli Divide,* is an effective documentation of how Israel expects to be treated given the power of the Israel lobby.

Born Michael Scott Bornstein to American parents in 1955, Oren claimed to have suffered anti-Semitic incidents growing up in West Orange, New Jersey. A formative moment was the April 19, 1971 bombing of his synagogue, as recounted in the book:

> *Then, when I was a high school freshman, the phone rang with horrendous news: a bomb had blown up our synagogue. I ran to the scene and saw firemen leaping into the flames to rescue the Torah scrolls.*

As is typical of the errors of omission that permeate the book, Oren neglected to mention that the bombing was linked to Rabbi Meir Kahane's speech at the venue that had been canceled and rescheduled amid controversy. Kahane was the founder of the Jewish Defense League, considered by the FBI to be a terrorist group. He was a suspect in numerous bombings and he was convicted of manufacturing illegal explosives just three months after the attack on Oren's synagogue.[467] Though Oren preferred to let readers believe it was an anti-Semitic attack by unpunished others, synagogue leaders assumed otherwise, as reported by *Mondoweiss*:

> *It really had nothing to do with our synagogue. It was because Kahane was supposed to speak there the following night. There was no reason to bomb our synagogue. We were just a suburban synagogue.*[468]

After scraping together enough money, Oren went to work on a kibbutz in Israel at age 15. He became an elite paratrooper after joining the IDF and participated in Israel's 1982 invasion of Lebanon. After leaving the IDF, he went on undercover missions in the Soviet Union to establish contact and work with dissident Zionist groups. Relying on his U.S. passport for protection and assuming cover as a photojournalist, Oren hinted in his book that he had joined Israel's intelligence service. "Israelis who served in combat units and who held two passports were especially sought after for these missions…" Oren does not clarify who was doing the "seeking." But whenever Oren ran into trouble with the KGB, it was the U.S. ambassador—not the Israeli diplomatic representative—that he demanded to see. After subsequent high-profile teaching and writing stints in America, Oren reluctantly relinquished his U.S. citizenship in 2009—three decades after he emigrated to Israel—in order to become Israel's ambassador to the land of his birth.

In the first pages of his memoir, Oren claims "ally" is a "deceptively straightforward" word, but then only attempts to translate its meaning in Hebrew, as a religious covenant. The attributes most political scientists would use are "a sovereign or state associated with another by treaty or league." Upper echelon U.S. military officials divide the world into "treaty" and "non-treaty" allies. Perhaps Oren avoids such definitions because no such mutual defense treaty between the U.S. and Israel exists, although congressional mandates declare Israel to be a "major non-NATO ally" (1990) and "major strategic partner" (2014). While Oren's book effectively categorizes America's benefactor role toward Israel, he struggles to clarify precisely what—if anything—the U.S. receives in return for its largesse.

---

[467] Morris Kaplan, "Kahane Gets 5-year Suspended Sentence in Bomb Plot," *The New York Times,* July 24, 1971

[468] Philip Weiss, "Michael Oren misrepresents 1971 synagogue bombing that changed his life" *Mondoweiss*, July 10, 2015 http://mondoweiss.net/2015/07/misrepresents-synagogue-changed

Oren confirms that an Israeli ambassador—like an Israeli prime minister—enjoys unlimited access to elite U.S. media, especially at the most crucial times, and can even dictate program format and with whom he will appear. One choice example is Oren's refusal to appear on a split screen with the bombastic former UN ambassador, John Bolton. This earned him a rebuke outside Fox News studios by the walrus-mustachioed Bolton. NBC's Andrea Mitchell was on the cell phone, available for any important opportunity, while *The Atlantic* reporter Jeffrey Goldberg eagerly awaited his next scoop. Oren's own unstoppable stream of output to *The New York Times* and *The Wall Street Journal*, and interviews with a legion of friendly top television and print pundits, likely edged out far more deserving voices, particularly during Israel's attacks on Gaza, drowned out by the Oren-saturated bandwidth.

Oren mostly downplays the Israel lobby as the principal enabler of the U.S.-Israel "special relationship." After even *New York Times* columnist Tom Friedman finally let slip that Israeli Prime Minister Netanyahu's nearly thirty standing ovations in Congress were "bought and paid for by the Israel lobby," Oren rebuked him, ejecting, "You've confirmed the worst anti-Semitic stereotype, that Jews purchase seats in Congress." Oren similarly dismissed Professors John Mearsheimer and Stephen Walt and their findings about the foundations of the relationship as "a conspiracy thesis of undue Jewish influence on Congress and the media." Despite his objections, however, Oren's own recitation of endless meetings with influential members of Congress during daily trips to Capitol Hill (rather than the U.S. State Department) provides far more support for Mearsheimer and Walt's thesis than his own claims of Israel's intrinsic value to America. Oren's most repetitive justifications are purely symbolic and debatable, such as Israel being "the only true democracy in the Middle East."

In his final chapter, Oren reveals what is currently demanded by America's "ally" and why. President Obama's 2009 Cairo speech to Arab youth condemning Israeli settlements, his references to pre-1967 lines as a basis for peace negotiations and a "daylight" policy on diplomacy with Israel generated major trauma for the Israeli government and its diplomat. Obama even told a gathering of Israel affinity group leaders that, "When there is no daylight, Israel just sits on the sidelines..."[469] This public distancing, and the Obama administration's open rebukes of Israel's leadership, must never again happen, according to Oren. Rather, the United States must in the near future officially recognize Jerusalem as Israel's capital, unconditionally support it in the UN Security Council, and refrain from asking for "swift and transparent investigations" of Palestinian civilian casualties routinely perpetrated by

[469] Michael B. Oren, *Ally: My Journey Across the American-Israel Divide*, [New York, Random House 2015] Kindle location 7208

Israel. It must also release convicted spy for Israel Jonathan Pollard.

Oren claims Israel also has some obligations as a U.S. ally, but they are of noticeably lower value, less costly to Israel, and mostly intangible. Israel should refrain from building "isolated" settlements (though East Jerusalem and the larger "blocs" are just dandy), respect "American Jewish pluralism" (which, in clearer language, means that Orthodox Jews who dominate the Israeli religious hierarchy and state treat American Reform and even Conservative branches as legitimate), and give more respect to the "prerogatives of the world's mightiest power."

Most importantly, according to Oren, American leaders must return to a policy of "no surprises, no daylight, and no public altercations." This would be an international redeployment of the "united front" family strategy parents often use to manage their unruly children. It would marginalize and tuck newly energized American intellectuals and activists who oppose the ongoing carnage and costs generated by the "special relationship" back into bed, in the dark, without supper, awaiting parental decisions in which they have no say—yet which will inevitably be claimed are for their own good.

Oren finally admits—in what may be the understatement of the century—that the so-called alliance "is not, of course, symmetrical." In his first pages, he claims "vocal segments" of the American Jewish community are "a vital component of the alliance." Uniting the two provides the book's key unintentional insight. The "special relationship" is not in fact an alliance, because it is all cost and almost no benefit to the U.S. It is rather a linkage that exists only because of the effective programs of a small—and, as a percentage, declining—subset of Americans who work as hard as Oren to bind America to Israel. Unlike Oren, most never have to finally turn over their U.S. passports, put on a uniform, or move to Israel. Some, even the Christian Zionists, would not be welcome if they tried. The actual number of Jewish Americans driving this effort, as mentioned, is probably only around 774,000, or just 0.32 percent of the U.S. adult population.[470] This may be one reason why, over the years, IAOs have grown increasingly reluctant to release their membership numbers—even as strictly defined by the organization—to the public. Even when fairly large membership numbers, such as those released by the federations in Congressional hearings, are divulged, given the propensity of dedicated activists to belong or give to three, four or more IAOs (such as a federation, plus AIPAC, a "Friends of," or hard-core organization, like the Middle East Forum), the numbers do not impress.[471]

---

[470] Author's calculation, assuming 18 percent of the American Jewish adult population is organizationally affiliated, divided by total 2013 American adult population of 243 million.

[471] This is observable when searching for organization news in online databases by keyword and instead finding obituaries for deceased multi-IAO members.

U.S. foreign aid to Israel is a domestic political issue. The American Israel Public Affairs Committee leads the congressional lobbying effort on behalf of the IAO ecosystem. U.S. foreign aid is highly correlated with total IAO revenue. On a chart, such foreign aid emerges as little more than a "matching grant" in which elected officials every year provide an amount more or less equal to the financial might of the Israel lobby as measured by combined IAO annual revenue. Given the revenue trajectory of the Israel lobby, Americans should expect annual foreign aid to reach $6.0 billion by 2020. This amount is comparable to Reagan-administration-level largesse, which when adjusted for inflation was $6.3 billion per year. At that time, aid to Israel was constantly justified by the Israel lobby's assertions that it was a Cold-War ally of the U.S. in the Middle East and a check on Soviet client states. Today the lobby is struggling to define what justifies Israel's position as the leading recipient of U.S. aid. Stripped of assertions of "common values" and other slogans, IAOs resemble mining companies in an extractive industry called the Israel lobby. Taxpayer dollars are merely the ore.

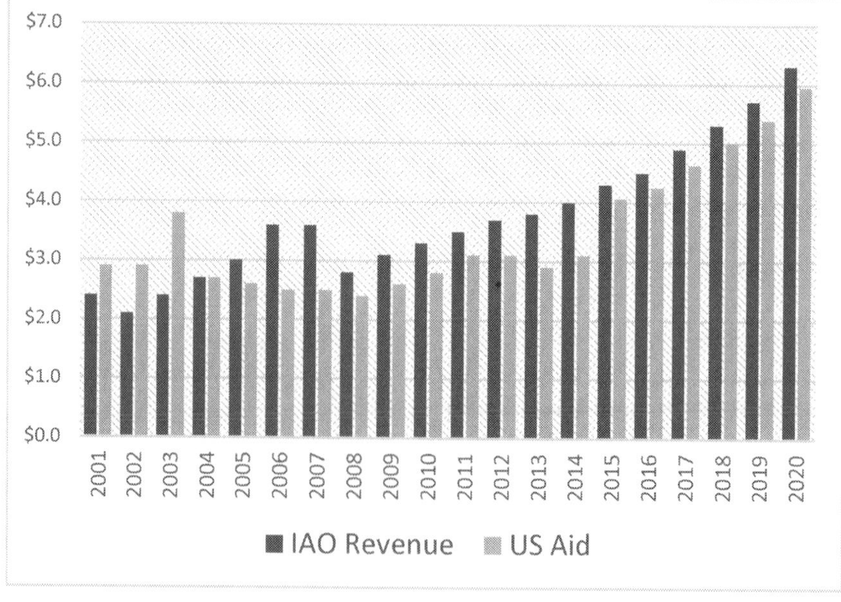

Figure 42 Actual & forecast IAO revenue vs U.S. foreign aid to Israel[472]

[472] Actual IAO revenue through 2012 and forecast through 2020. Actual U.S. foreign aid through 2014, not including secret intelligence or supplemental support.

In the beginning, the Jewish Agency spawned a network of smuggling fronts to illegally purchase, steal and smuggle weapons to Jewish fighters in Palestine. Today, it is the U.S. Department of Defense that must oversee taxpayer-funded weapons shipments to Israel. The Justice Department is tasked with looking the other way as Israeli agents try to increase their share of joint weapons development projects of little value to the U.S.

IAOs continue to pass huge costs on to American taxpayers. American Jewish Committee and Joint Distribution Committee refugee programs are taken on or supplemented by State Department or CIA operations. The Anti-Defamation League has managed to outsource to the FBI its own former task of collecting statistics within categories it wishes interpreted and broadly distributed. The Greater Washington DC JCRC, in what may soon become model legislation pursued across the country, is making Maryland taxpayers fund a Hillel for a small group of economically advantaged students on campus, and as a monitoring station, formerly paid for by IAOs. The list goes on. In aggregate, the impact IAOs have on U.S. taxpayers—ignoring for the moment the costs of Israel-generated appropriations from Congress and state legislatures—is significant. Excluding the capital gains, dividends and interest sheltered from taxes on assets either held by IAOs or residing within their Donor Advised Funds, and calculating only how much tax would have been paid on the annual exempt donations to the 336 organizations in the *Big Israel* database, reveals an enormous "tax externalization:"

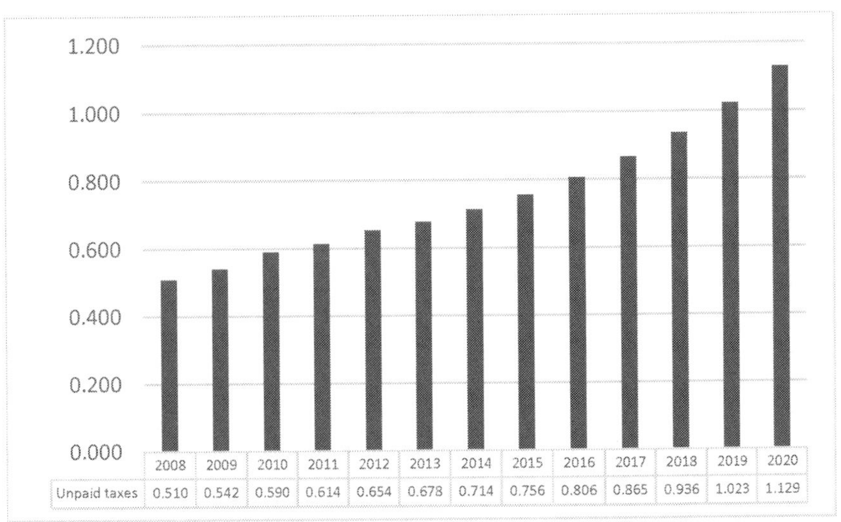

Figure 43 Israel lobby tax burden passed to others ($ U.S. billion)

Some revenue raised within the Israel lobby ecosystem, including federation donations to elderly and healthcare services, clearly has a social welfare benefit. But a great deal of the rest such as unreported lobbying by Jewish Community Relations Councils for state purchases of Israel bonds, influence-peddling payments, transfers of tax-exempt donations to Israeli entities engaged in non-exempt activities like nuclear weapons research and development, and support for illegal settlements—clearly do not.

The estimated $714 million in taxes the Israel lobby shifted to other taxpayers in 2014 is not insignificant, being roughly comparable to the $731 million the leading fifteen major Fortune 500 tax-evading companies—through loopholes, offshoring operations and deft financial maneuvers, taking advantage of U.S. tax code provisions they often helped write—shifted to other U.S. taxpayers despite the companies being highly profitable.[473] However, what term accurately describes IRS-designated charities that engage in few legitimate social welfare activities—and shift the tax burden onto everyone else? Is it relevant in the big scheme of things? For an answer, the author asked 2001 Pulitzer Prize-winning investigative reporter David Caye Johnston, a specialist in tax and economics issues, who replied:

> *A phrase I use in my work and lectures is this: 'When someone gets a tax break it shifts the burden of government onto others (or onto you).'*
>
> *Scale matters here. The federal government expects this fiscal year, which began Oct 1, to take in $1,763 billion in individual income taxes and $473.3 billion [for corporate].*
>
> *That is more than $2.2 trillion so the tax savings from the lobbies you are looking at would [be] minuscule by THAT measure.*[474]

The Israel lobby's $714 million "shift in government burden," which is on track to reach $1.1 billion in 2020, does seem small when only compared to total annual U.S. taxes collected. However, considering that the Israel lobby played a pivotal role promoting the disastrous U.S. invasion of Iraq, it

[473] Eric Pianin, "15 Fortune 500 Companies Paid No Federal Income Taxes in 2014" *The Fiscal Times*, April 9, 2015. Companies cited included CBS, General Electric, Interpublic Group, JetBlue Airways, Mattel, Owens Corning, PG&E Corp., PEPCO Holdings, Priceline.com, Prudential Financial, Qualcomm, Ryder System, Time Warner, Weyerhaeuser, Xerox. http://www.thefiscaltimes.com/2015/04/09/15-Fortune-500-Companies-Paid-No-Federal-Income-Taxes-2014

[474] David Cay Johnston, email message to the author, with permission granted to quote. December 10, 2015.

is also useful to include those costs. The Iraq conflict will cost American taxpayers $1.7 trillion, and an additional $490 billion in "benefits owed to war veterans"[475]—to say nothing of U.S. casualties and the immense death toll and ongoing human suffering in the region. Many IAOs were (and still are) determined to maneuver the U.S. into militarily striking Iran. The costs of war with Iran would almost certainly be far larger than the Iraq fiasco. From this perspective, the tax subsidy given to IAOs adds enormous injury to insult. As mentioned, economic sanctions and insertion of pro-Israel stipulations into trade legislation also prevent U.S. businesses from additional legitimate sales, which are both profitable and taxable.

Intensely studying IAOs and the Israel lobby leads to the realization that laws and regulations applying to most people, and most organizations, do not apply to the Israel lobby. This a reflection of the international scene where laws and norms also do not apply to Israel. Israel's treatment of the Palestinians and settlement policies long ago would have incurred international sanctions were they carried out by any other country. The lobby and the people who run it can pretty much get away with anything. Activities that have put less connected people in jail, or at least led to heavy penalties on normal corporations, do not apply if the entity in question is an IAO. The ongoing corruption that enables all this leads to uncomfortable cracks in the foundation of society. "If that guy didn't go to jail, why should anyone?" "If they don't pay taxes, and mine go for *that*, why am I paying anything?" Societal cohesion and governance soon dissipate when too many people begin to understand the importance of those unanswerable questions.

There are many questions IAOs do not answer, because they are never asked. The simplest is, "who exactly do you represent?" For many decades, top media organizations, including *The New York Times* and others, provided the answer, smugly implying that various IAOs were official representatives of American (and other) Jewish communities. The headlines read:

> *Mr. Bronfman succeeds Philip M. Klutznik as president of the World Jewish Congress, which represents Jewish communities in 66 countries.*[476] *The New York Times*

> *Address by Representative of U.S. Jews, and the Pope's Reply*[477] *The New York Times*

---

[475] Daniel Trotta, "Iraq war costs U.S. more than $2 trillion: study," Reuters, March 14, 2013. http://www.reuters.com/article/us-iraq-war-anniversary-idUSBRE92D0PG20130314#5aumEZ59G4gMrUjq.97

[476] "Bronfman Heads Jewish Congress," *The New York Times*, February 1, 1981

[477] "Address by Representative of U.S. Jews, and the Pope's Reply," *New York Times*, September 12, 1987

But since the present troubles forced their way on to the front pages most major organizations representing America's 6 million Jewish citizens have…[478] *The Guardian*

IRS Sued on Jews' Tax Exempt Status[479] *The Washington Post*

Today, subject to more scrutiny, many no longer make such sweeping claims. Nor can IAOs that have neither the membership rolls, governance structure, observable leadership turnover nor even bona fide elections credibly claim such representation. In addition, strong opposition to caps on the deductibility of donations from large contributors reveals what IAOs will not say—that most rely on a relatively small number of extremely wealthy donors. Those donors drive the organization; they are the Israel lobby's corporate governance. The major IAOs have become the very plutocrats they once accused the local "community chests" of being during the 1940s.

The other demand, which should follow every claim that America and Israel share similar values, is, "Show me a single legitimate survey proving that." There are none, and for good reason. When the next results from an ADL or AJC global survey on anti-Semitism are spread around, a key question must be asked. "Did you also field that survey in Israel?" They will not, because those results also would not likely be favorable. Until such polls, often fielded by IAOs that accuse certain outspoken Jewish and non-Jewish critics of Israel of anti-Semitism or self-hatred, provide a satisfactory explanation for why they refuse to field their global surveys in Israel, their blind redistribution in the news media of domestic and results from other countries should be viewed with skepticism.

At the strategic, global chessboard level, instead of portraying Israel as the regional cop keeping tabs on the Soviet Union in the Middle East, or the valiant ally in the so-called "War on Terror," IAOs are repositioning Israel as a central ally in what will be a long Western confrontation with the so-called "Islamic State." In this new realignment, Israel is working to become both the new ally and a weapons vendor to Gulf states—some of which brutally put down Arab Spring popular movements—while continuing to provide self-serving intelligence and advice to the United States. Because of Israel's poor and declining public image, as J.W. Fulbright long ago feared in his secret memo, Americans and the West should also be on the lookout for resurgent waves of false-flag operations and propaganda masquerading as straight reporting that only seems to prove what Israel wants to be true.

Except for scattered public protests and "new media" reporting, the Israel

---

[478] "Jewish lobby searches conscience," *The Guardian*, December 24, 1987

[479] Al Kamen, "IRS Sued on Jews' Tax Exempt Status," *The Washington Post*, October 8, 1983

lobby has not faced much public backlash over its activities in the United States. However, when people have access to actionable information, the magic cloak of invulnerability begins to slip. This occurs when exposés become public knowledge, such as just how much IAOs collect, take and spend to move America Israel's way. The argument that America acts on Israel's behalf through enlightened self-interest no longer explains Israel's number-one position as a foreign aid recipient. For years, Israel would consolidate and report total charitable contributions received from the United States. This no longer happens, as the country rightfully grows more concerned about how its actions and public image might raise questions about that support, or whether any of it, like in the old days, stealthily finds its way back into the U.S. influence-peddling industry. Many IAOs would like to squirrel away such sensitive information from prying eyes. As mentioned, in 2009 AIPAC tried to report just two donors on its mandatory IRS schedule of contributors giving $5,000 or more: transfers from the captive American Israel Education Foundation for "education" projects, and $48,842,187 for all of the other individual contributions. Though it has not repeated the stunt, it deprived researchers of the ability to see just how lopsided the organization's donor base was in a crucial year. In 2006, just 1,700 AIPAC donors provided 56 percent of revenue. Many fewer probably contributed in 2009, a fact AIPAC likely wanted to hide.

The Sheldon Adelson-dependent Zionist Organization of America may have signed an agreement with a "donor advised fund," the Foundation of Philanthropic Funds, so that it can consolidate large individual donations for disbursement—minus a small fee—into a single transfer to ZOA. ZOA may soon—just as AIPAC attempted—file a single entity on its schedule of contributors, the Foundation of Philanthropic Funds. More importantly, the huge build-up of assets on the sidelines within IAO donor advised funds (particularly at the federation level) is an enormous war chest—poised to launch upcoming propaganda wars for American hearts and minds.

IAOs that send billions in funding overseas are already going dark. As noted earlier, the detrimental 2008 IRS rule change eliminated the requirement that U.S. tax-exempt non-profits individually identify the foreign organizations receiving their grants. A simple reference not to a country, but just a region, now suffices, although subsidy IAOs still must identify the names of American tax-exempt recipients. It is hard to imagine any possible explanation for the rule change on international 501(c)(3) transfers other than the obvious—hiding precisely how much is going to Israel, including to illegal settlements, about which the Treasury has done nothing.

By the time the day arrives that the IRS provides structured digital IRS 990 returns to the public—a day that has been very slow in coming—any independent research compilation of total flows to Israel, as opposed to just the Middle East/North Africa, will be impossible. The rule change has made those embarrassing flows to illegal settlements easier to hide, which is the most likely reason they were implemented, according to Jeffrey Blankfort:

> *...One Israel Fund has no qualms about openly raising funds for projects that are in direct conflict with long standing U.S. policy and yet the government not only has not penalized it but also made it easier to cover its trail. In 2010, on the last available 990, One Israel Fund reported that it had sent $2,340,000 to meet its goals, a $600,000 increase from the previous year. It is not hard to speculate that its donations have grown considerably since then.*
>
> *In its 990 form for 2011, Rabbi Eckstein's International Fellowship of Christians and Jews made no mention of his donations to the Friends of Israel Defense Forces, nor did he do so in its annual report, which was filled with pictures of children, women and the aged in Israel which the Fellowship claims to support out of the slightly more than $100 million it raises annually.*[480]

If the more secretive IAOs also someday wish to retreat into the darkness by becoming "Associations of Synagogues," along the proven CUFI model, the IRS should be expected to continue to show little inclination to stop it. Already, enough significant Jewish Federations have adopted the "hide the foreign country destination" ruling to predict that a future research project building upon this book will be more difficult, if not impossible, to put together.

IAOs strive mightily to avoid becoming the subject of controversy or fighting amongst themselves publicly in order to project the appearance of a unified front. The Israel lobby has long promoted the notion that its core programs are "mainstream," charging that opponents of many stripes are "outside the consensus." This can only work as long as IAOs are able to control or heavily influence the narrative, which, in turn, can manufacture the necessary trust and consent. The European crisis preceding the creation of Israel in 1948 was compelling to Americans. The framing of the 1967 Six-Day War and 1973 crisis were as well, although they have unraveled somewhat as more accurate histories have finally been produced. While the decade-long Iran nuclear crisis led to harsh sanctions on Tehran and a likely boost in U.S. foreign aid to Israel, it has failed—so far—to get the U.S.

---

[480] Jeffrey Blankfort, "Friends of the Israel Defense Forces Raises $27 Million Under NY Media's Radar," *Counterpunch*, April 23, 2013 http://www.counterpunch.org/2013/04/23/friends-of-israel-defense-forces-raises-27-million-under-ny-medias-radar/

involved in yet another Middle East war. Most Americans simply did not believe claims that Israel or the United States were in danger. Some of this surely stemmed from the recent memory of being misled into invading Iraq by corrupt politicians with the full backing of the Israel lobby. However, some skepticism about the Iran nuclear scare was likely due to growing awareness of the Israel lobby's principal role in creating it.

Collectively, IAOs have lodged many claims upon Americans. For the most part, these claims have been met because of lack of awareness about the costs and consequences, along with weak opposition. Most of the information that available to the public was released by IAOs or their supporters. As such it was self-serving, and of little analytical value. Most "investigative reports" aim to see how particular IAO programs affect the American Jewish community (such as the Brandeis study mentioned in chapter 2), rather than the entire American population. But this dearth of information is changing fast due to alternative and social media, which is decentralized, diffuse and difficult to centrally manage. Even a cursory review reveals deep contradictions that cannot be explained away, such as the Israel lobby's long love affair with boycotts, divestment and sanctions—as long as they target Israel's enemies; lavishing IAO and taxpayer largesse on displaced refugees—so long as they are Jewish; keeping the Middle East from going nuclear—unless it is Israel; and publicly pining for peace, while privately supporting policies that unleash chaos and destruction in the Middle East calculated to improve Israel's strategic position.

Some funding extracted from taxpayers and given to IAOs is both wasteful and reinforces unfounded, hurtful accusations. One Israel lobby mantra is that Israel must exist because Jews can never count on being safe in the West. Massive Department of Homeland security grants, earmarked to predominantly Jewish IAOs, serve to reinforce this claim, even casting a shadow of suspicion over those coerced into paying for them—despite little evidence that such locations face any higher threat than many other, similar facilities. The grants subtract from a pool of resources that would be better spent protecting everybody, even while subtly perpetuating a hurtful "not safe in the West" mantra spread by the Israel lobby.

Even the most harmful distortions, claims and disinformation emitted by IAOs flow freely through major media organizations and the Internet. Yet IAOs are extremely concerned that individuals and organizations with opposing views, particularly on campus, may sometimes obtain the same effective distribution. Charges that questioning Israeli policies and human rights record is "incivility" or "makes Jewish students feel unsafe" have sparked a movement to keep unwanted speakers off campus, place pro-Israel monitors and censors at student publications, and substitute foreign policy with other subjects for students to debate—such as T-shirts and fast food chicken dipping sauce, noted one student BDS activist, Ahmad Saadaldin:

> *What message does a university send to its students when they reject a petition from 10,000 of them calling for something? What message does a university send to its students when the student body president sends an e-mail to 46,000 people saying, the referendum you petitioned for, the referendum you voted for is invalidated, but please don't forget to vote for your school T-shirt and have your voices heard? What message does a university send to its students when the student newspaper will not cover the largest petition in support of human rights, but will instead cover a petition to bring Chick-fil-A sauce to our student cafeteria?*
>
> *I'll tell you what message they're sending. They want us to shut up, go to class, pay a lot of money for tuition and for textbooks, don't talk about human rights, don't talk about anything else. The only thing you can talk about is T-shirts and Chick-fil-A sauce…*
>
> *So when AIPAC buys students, when they have one-on-one meetings to undermine the voices of thousands of students, that's not hijacking—but when minorities get involved, not only are we hijacking, we're trying to conquer…*[481]

Another IAO means for dumbing down or diverting the debate is spreading money around and creating dependencies. The Regents of the University of California (not the university system) receive almost a million dollars from the Jewish Community Foundation of San Diego. Is that buying anti-Palestinian activism measures? Does the $2 million it simultaneously gave to the American Civil Liberties Union (ACLU), which advocates for individual rights and liberties guaranteed by the Constitution, keep it away from that particular fight? There is no obvious reason why federations such as the Jewish Community Center of San Francisco cut checks to the Electronic Frontier Foundation (EFF) and the ACLU from the same checkbook that sends funding to the Clarion Foundation and Frank Gaffney's Center for Security Policy. Or, put another way, what business do the Electronic Frontier Foundation, which defends civil liberty in the digital world, and the ACLU have accepting funds from such an IAO?

No 2016 presidential candidate indicated any willingness to stand up to the Israel lobby on any major issue. This signals a future administration that will again be laden with Israel lobbyists within every relevant agency of the U.S. government. However, the exact levels of capture—just like what

---

[481] Ahmad Saadaldin, "Overcoming Obstacles: Students for Justice in Palestine Successes," Speech at the National Press Club, April 10, 2015 http://israellobbyus.org/transcripts/3.3AhmadSaadaldinT.htm

subsidy IAOs actually do with their millions overseas—will be difficult to assess. Under new "national security" guidelines, Office of Personnel Management listings of political appointees holding the top jobs and filling departments and agencies working for Israel and the names of their staffers are no longer released under the Freedom of Information Act. A once-informative list of visitors to the White House, periodically released by the Secret Service under FOIA, has similarly stopped.

Although President Obama has boasted of massive secret support to Israel in the form of intelligence aid, and despite the fact that the U.S. intelligence budget itself is no longer a secret, the current and next administration are likely to continue boosting this secret aid allotment while fighting Freedom of Information Act requests and lawsuits to release the total amount.[482] Israel's drives to involve America in military conflicts on its behalf are poised to continue. Moreover, in wartime, basic information, like the truth, is one of the first casualties. Elected officials, political appointees and government functionaries have been, and must continue to be, publicly challenged over their acquiescence to IAO law breaking and their own bending of rules to accommodate IAOs. Because complaining or insisting on warranted enforcement has not worked in the past, Americans should also begin "withholding consent" from government through nonviolent protest measures until the regulatory capture and corruption exposed in this book is ended. These efforts should be tightly targeted if possible, or general if not.

For far too long America has been easily moved: Toward ever more extreme Israel-centric Middle East policies causing violence and chaos in the region. Toward ever more secrecy in U.S.-Israel policymaking. Away from openness and accountability in the political process. Away from advise and consent by the governed. Far beyond regulatory capture. America has been too easily moved by Israel—toward, ultimately, the loss of its own remaining legitimacy.

---

[482] See the author's federal lawsuit for the CIA's budget to support Israel (and other actions) at IRmep's Center for Policy and Law http://irmep.org/CFL.htm

APPENDICES

In aggregate, Israel Affinity Organizations were the number two "charity" in America in 2012, just behind the United Way, but ahead of the Salvation Army.[483] Given their above-average growth rate, it is reasonable to assume they will soon be number one, if they are not already. That is because the Iran nuclear threat campaign—a manufactured crisis—appears to have mobilized levels of financial support not achieved since the late 1930s through the end of the 1940s.

Most of the financial data in this report and in the following tables has been gathered by examining the IRS form 990 tax returns filed by each IAO. To achieve a common basis of comparison, data reported by an IAO on a year 2012 form 990 is counted entirely as 2012 data, even if an organization's fiscal year does not end on December 31. The figure in the "launch" column is the year the organization was established, incorporated or received IRS tax-exempt status. EIN (employee identification number) is the organization's unique taxpayer ID number. EE is claimed employees for the year 2012, while Vol. is the claimed number of volunteers. Blank spaces indicate the IAO did not provide a response to the IRS.

The revenue figure used in the column "2012" is from IRS form 990 line 12, "total revenue." This line, the net of public and government contributions (most government contributions are negligible), plus any program-related activities, plus or minus investment returns, provides the best snapshot of actual year resources available to implement an IAO's programs. No attempt is made to net out conduit transfers. Therefore, if an IAO solicits and receives $10,000 in public contributions, only to transfer that amount to another IAO, aggregate IAO revenue counted for the year will be $20,000. Figures for IAO employees and volunteers are those reported by the organization's most recent available IRS form 990. Figures for year 2020 revenue are the author's forecast using regression analysis of revenue growth from 2001-2012 (or from the IAO's launch year, if that occurred after 2001).

A blank space in the 2020 column indicates an IAO appears to be on revenue track to become defunct by that year or earlier. Some organizations are listed that have no 2012 revenue or that may have been defunct by that year. Many of these appear in the full online database at IsraelLobby.org if they were involved in interesting activities, such as illegal settlements, or espionage, as mentioned in the case of the Alliance for Competitive Technology.

483 William Barrett and Janet Novack, "The 50 Largest U.S. Charities" *Forbes*, December 9, 2015 http://www.forbes.com/top-charities/ An entry for "the Israel lobby" does not appear between the United Way and Salvation Army, because they are 336 separate corporations, as listed in the following pages.

A. SUBSIDY IAOS

Launch	EIN	EE	Vol.	Organization	2012 $Million	2020 $Million
1962	136192275	31	0	Bar Ilan University of Israel aka American Friends of	343.5	591.7
1914	131656634	154	47	American Jewish Joint Distribution Committee	316.2	527.0
1936	131760102	4	32	United Israel Appeal	193.1	126.0
1983	363256096	97	9	International Fellowship of Christians and Jews	113.5	370.9
1958	136227366	0	0	Feinberg Graduate School of the Weizmann Institute of Science	110.7	163.6
1926	131659627	225	120	Jewish National Fund (Keren Kayemeth Israel)	103.5	138.0
1922	131656651	203	285458	Hadassah, Women's Zionist Organization of America	100.9	51.2
1940	130434195	93	150	American Society for Technion - Israel Institute of Technology	91.7	73.4
1944	131623886	85	40	American Committee for the Weizmann Institute of Science	71.4	47.5
1981	133156445	130	69	Friends of the Israeli Defense Forces	68.3	326.7
1992	136104086	5	29	PEF Israel Endowment Funds	67.8	70.4
1931	131568923	74	210	American Friends of the Hebrew University	47.7	34.3
1972	237182582			American Friends of the Israel Museum	34.1	87.3
1979	942607722	51	270	New Israel Fund	29.7	31.4
1881	135633307	76	90	Hebrew Immigrant Aid Society	25.4	48.3
1955	131996126	29	39	American Friends of Tel Aviv University	24.9	25.7
1940	131790719	49	150	American Friends of Magen David Adom	23.2	30.3
2001	223804152	5	8	Nefesh B'Nefesh Jewish Souls United	20.4	36.4
1969	135562424	104	30	ORT America	16.5	22.9
1979	132995985	0	8	Central Fund of Israel	16.1	74.2
1966	132563745	4	23	Jerusalem Foundation	15.1	17.0
1982	980160122	0	0	Eschel - the Association for the plan and dev svcs Aged in Israel	13.8	17.0
1994	232742482	14	125	Jewish Funders Network	10.7	131.9
1925	135631502	34	43	AMIT	8.5	8.7
1986	133348313	1	0	American Friends of the Israel Democracy Institute	8.2	15.5
1990	223090463	8	26	Friends of Yemin Orde	8.0	23.1
1970	132670365	25	500	Emuh of America	6.1	5.8
1998	113466176	1	0	Friends Of Ir David	5.9	16.3
1988	363441392	315	100	Keshet	5.6	8.7

Launch	EIN	EE	Vol.	Organization	2012 $Million	2020 $Million
2007	562676533	3		American Friends of Shalva Israel	5.5	23.7
1982	133145161	4	1	American Committee for Tel Aviv Foundation	4.9	13.7
1997	133988433			American Friends of Yeshiva Kodshim of Kodshim	4.9	26.4
2000	113533002	3		Batya-Friends Of United Hatzalah	4.9	6.9
2006	208202424	2	0	American Friends Of Leket Israel	4.3	113.8
1951	132572288	22	125	Bnai Zion Foundation	4.2	3.4
1963	135640819	4	0	General Israel Orphan Home For Girls Jerusalem	4.2	2.3
1969	237049727	5	0	American Friends Of Rambam Medical Center	4.1	205.6
1992	133621884	1	0	The Friends Of The Israel Antiquities Authority	4.1	83.0
1974	237443023	2		The American Friends Of The Tel Aviv Museum of Art	3.3	4.3
2004	201933798			Friends Of Tzeirei Chabad In Israel	3.3	32.4
2002	061669917	8	0	World ORT	3.2	45.7
1995	133843506	34		Friends of Israel Scouts	3.1	11.7
2004	201582478	10		American Friends Of Meir Panim	3.1	3.9
1951	131664048	4		American Israel Cultural Foundation	3.1	2.0
1961	316100833			American Friends Of Alyn Hospital	2.7	3.0
1982	133106175	8	10	Friends Of Yad Sarah	2.6	8.3
2003	320081620	0	0	American Friends Of Libi	2.3	27.7
1994	113195338	8	7	One Israel Fund, Ltd.	2.2	1.4
1973	132724055			American Friends Of Kiryat Sanz Laniado Hospital	2.1	0.9
1989	222867329	0	2	American Friends Of Viznitz In Israel	2.1	5.5
1921	135590516	5	17	Na'amat USA	1.9	1.2
1987	133392711			Friends Of Israel Disabled Veterans Aka Beit Halochem	1.8	2.9
2011	275126671			American Friends Of The Israel Sport Center For The Disabled	1.7	8.5
2006	203585888	0	5	American Friends Of The Reut Institute	1.6	3.9
1986	133329462	3		American Friends Of The Israel National Museum Of Science	1.5	24.0
1996	133887075	2	5	US Friends Of Yad Ezrah	1.4	3.4
1997	133962392			American Friends Of The Yitzhak Rabin Ctr For The Study Of Israel	1.4	8.4
2000	522193738	9		American Friends Of Lubavitch	1.3	2.0
1966	526080692	3		American Friends Of Bnei Akiva Yeshivas In Israel	1.3	0.9

Launch	EIN	EE	Vol.	Organization	2012 $Million	2020 $Million
2001	113585917	5	8	One Family Fund	1.2	0.6
1981	133171815	3	0	Elem Israel (ELEM YOUTH IN DISTRESS)	1.1	0.5
2009	260492682			Friends Of Israel Sci-Tech Schools	1.0	2.2
1984	112706563	2	0	American Friends of Ateret Cohanim	1.0	1.1
1982	112623719	5	1	Hebron Fund	1.0	0.5
1984	133244347			American Friends Of The Cntrl Comm For Taharas Hamishpacha In Israel	0.9	1.2
1981	133091674			American Friends Of The Open University Of Israel	0.8	0.3
2002	061652733			American Friends Of The College Of Judea And Samaria	0.8	1.4
2011	590173782			Alexander Muss Institute For Israel Education	0.8	1.2
1992	133691494	0	4	American Friends Of The Israel Free Loan Association	0.7	2.5
1986	133441742	4	21	American Friends Of Neve Shalom-Wahat Al-Salam	0.7	0.6
2010	208021512			Friends Of Yashar L Chayal	0.6	2.9
1951	131940424	2		American Friends Of Reuth Medical & Life Care Centers	0.6	0.2
1994	943201147	0	0	American Friends Of Koret Israel Economic Development Funds	0.5	0.3
1959	135600414	4		American Friends Of Ponevez Yeshiva In Israel	0.5	0.6
1997	311558409	0	0	Gush Etzion Foundation	0.4	0.4
1979	112499314			Friends Of Akim U.S.A	0.4	0.2
1998	134015013	0	.	American Friends Of Yeshiva High School Of Kiryat Arba	0.3	0.8
2005	204015961	0	10	Christian Friends Of Israel America	0.3	0.9
2012	454296987			American Friends Of The U.S.-Israel Binational Science Foundation	0.3	0.0
2003	542091671	0	3	American Friends Of The United Jewish Israel Appeal	0.3	1.0
2007	260620192			Land Of Promise Foundation	0.2	0.1
2013	900794238			American Friends Of The National Institute For Psychobiology Israel	0.2	0.0
2004	581959151	0		American Friends Of The Israel Union For Environmental Defense	0.2	0.3
2004	412109553			Am. Friends Of Elon Moreh	0.2	0.2
1998	113452714		3	Friends Of Yeshiva Chofetz Chaim Kolel-Israel	0.2	0.4
1982	133129249	0		Friends Of The Israel Center For Social And Economic Progress	0.2	0.5
1984	133202264	1		American Friends Of Dvi	0.2	0.5
2012	260572473			American Friends Of WGH Western Galilee Hospital Hariya Israel	0.1	0.0

Launch	EIN	EE	Vol.	Organization	2012 $Million	2020 $Million
2008	264515751	0	0	American Friends Of Israel Emergency Aid Fund	0.1	0.8
1999	522171745	0	9	ELI-American Friends of the Israel Association For Child Protection	0.1	0.3
1988	222757351			North American Friends Of Israel Oceanographic Research Inc.	0.1	0.1
1987	232564116			American Friends Of Israel Elwyn	0.1	0.1
1987	133458345		3	Friends Of-Or-Israel Charitable Trust	0.1	0.1
2001	311740763	1		American Friends Of New Communities In Israel	0.1	0.1
1999	113463752			American Friends Of Chabad Migdal Haemek Israel	0.1	0.7
2008	261463102			Memphis Friends Of Israel	0.1	0.3
2009	141970976			Friends Of The Israel Movement For Progressive Judaism	0.1	0.3
2003	770602999	0		American Friends Of Bat Ayin Yeshiva	0.1	0.0
2005	201935704			Friends Of The Israel Heart Society	0.1	0.0
2007	203394641			Meor Israel Friends Of	0.1	0.0
1978	362937918			American Friends Of Israel War Disabled Foundation	0.0	0.0
2002	300002176			Friends Of Israel Update	0.0	0.0
1986	341486476			American Friends Of Israel College Of Technology For Women	0.0	0.0
2003	510435358	0	0	International Academic Friends Of Israel	0.0	0.0
2006	203540850			Friends Of Israel Galilean Campus For Education And Culture	0.0	0.1
2011	262169840			American Friends Of The Israel National Council For The Child	0.0	0.0
1994	113207262			North American Friends Of Amcha-Israel	0.0	0.0
2005	200298896			Friends Of Israel Fire And Rescue Services	0.0	0.0
2009	261378368			American Friends Of The Israel Chamber Music Society	0.0	0.0
1972	237163245			Ariel American Friends Of Midrasha And United Israel Institutions Ltd	0.0	1.7
2013	264147225			American Friends Of Connections Israel	0.0	0.0
2001	113628160			Am. Friends Of Ahavas Israel	0.0	1.4
1995	113275679			Friends Of Torah Institutions In Israel	0.0	0.1
2002	270013798			American Friends Yeshiva L Tzeirim Ner Israel D Chassidei Goor	0.0	0.6
2000	330401076			Alliance For Competitive Technology	0.0	1.0
2005	202178658			Efrat Development Foundation U.S.A	0.0	
		1,984	287,810	Total	2,005.3	3,831.6

B. FUNDRAISING & LOCAL POLITICAL ACTION IAOS

Launch	EIN	EE	Vol.	Organization	2012 $Million	2020 $Million
1950	362167034	471	12177	Jewish United Fund Of Metropolitan Chicago	93.7	98.8
1964	956111928	29	100	Jewish Community Foundation of the Jewish Federation of Greater Los Angeles	69.6	67.3
1938	590624404	100	2200	Greater Miami Jewish Federation	65.7	42.6
1937	951643388	186	3166	Jewish Federation Council Of Greater Los Angeles	58.8	52.4
1950	520607957	150	7500	The Associated Jewish Community Federation of Baltimore	43.2	46.9
1901	231500085	117	2000	Jewish Federation of Greater Philadelphia	36.7	43.3
1946	520214465	83	7517	The Jewish Federation of Greater Washington	36.5	31.3
1955	221487222	181	719	Jewish Federation of Greater MetroWest NJ	35.3	29.3
1957	251017602	75	736	Jewish Federation of Greater Pittsburgh	33.7	24.8
1968	581021791	67	900	Jewish Federation Of Greater Atlanta	30.8	31.7
1947	390806312	79	700	Milwaukee Jewish Federation	29.2	22.1
1935	470384659	553	602	Jewish Federation Of Omaha	25.8	26.7
1922	210634489	1389	1193	Jewish Federation Of Southern New Jersey	23.2	24.1
1979	591945109	100	90	Jewish Federation Of South Palm Beach County	21.6	19.6
2004	201195592	83	81	UJA Federation Of Northern New Jersey	15.2	11.4
1941	741109654	41	300	Jewish Federation Of Greater Houston	15.0	20.6
1997	311501858	0	0	Foundation For The Charlotte Jewish Community	11.2	12.7
1958	741469465	373	150	Jewish Community Association Of Austin	11.0	9.6
1954	237182057	307	400	Tampa Jcc-Federation Inc.	10.5	11.8
1935	340714442	302	100	Youngstown Area Jewish Federation	10.5	11.7
1947	590967823	27	500	United Jewish Community Of Broward County	10.2	7.5
1942	750800654	49	200	Jewish Federation Of Greater Dallas	9.9	9.4
1945	840402662	34	250	Allied Jewish Federation Of Colorado	9.7	12.3
1941	951319015			United Jewish Federation Of San Diego	8.1	7.9
1934	610444765	387	250	Jewish Community of Louisville	7.7	8.5
1976	880098500	26	500	Jewish Federation of Las Vegas	7.7	12.4
1942	910575950	45	160	Jewish Federation of Greater Seattle	7.5	9.0
1972	237107693	28	1000	Greensboro Jewish Federation	6.6	10.2
1955	31083745	20	345	Jewish Federation Of Columbus	6.6	7.2
1961	160868942	26	200	Jewish Community Federation of Greater Rochester	6.3	6.8

Launch	EIN	EE	Vol.	Organization	2012 $Million	2020 $Million
1910	310537488	78	175	Jewish Federation Of Greater Dayton	5.9	7.7
1952	941167405	13	75	Jewish Federation Of Silicon Valley	5.7	6.8
1966	952407026	52	780	Jewish Federation Orange County	5.7	6.2
1986	222805163	17	500	United Jewish Federation Of Northeastern New York	5.0	5.9
1971	540480621	61	0	United Jewish Community Of The Virginia Peninsula	4.9	2.7
1949	60655482	34	420	Jewish Federation Of Greater Hartford	4.7	4.9
1976	132869041	32	80	Jewish Community Relations Council Of New York	4.5	5.2
1947	860096795	53	500	Jewish Federation Of Southern Arizona	4.3	5.5
1941	231352338	140	20	Jewish Federation Of Greater Harrisburg	4.2	4.6
1945	510064315			Jewish Federation Of Delaware Inc.	4.2	3.7
1993	541653165	8	31	Tidewater Jewish Federation	4.1	0.0
1970	591227747	26	263	The Jewish Federation of Sarasota-Manatee Sarasota, FL	4.1	4.2
1972	941156335	28	300	Jewish Community Relations Council Of San Francisco Marin & Peninsula	4.0	3.7
1942	626077703	16	300	Jewish Federation Of Nashville And Middle Tennessee	3.8	2.6
1948	730579243	110	50	Jewish Federation of Tulsa	3.8	3.8
1945	050259003	0	100	Jewish Federation Foundation (Rhode Island)	3.6	4.3
2000	341884695	14	70	Jewish Community Board Of Akron	3.5	2.3
1942	540524512	11	150	Community Relations Council Of The Jewish Community Federation Of Richmond	3.4	3.1
1939	620475747	13	200	Memphis Jewish Federation	3.4	2.6
1961	344428259	31	30	Jewish Federation Of Greater Toledo	3.3	3.1
1942	720408938	26	100	Jewish Federation Of Greater New Orleans	3.3	3.7
1948	951647830	12	65	Jewish Federation Of Greater Long Beach And West Orange County	3.3	2.7
1920	930386825	17	150	Community Relations Council of the Jewish Federation of Portland	3.2	3.2
1948	236396949	17	200	Jewish Federation Of The Lehigh Valley	3.1	3.2
1959	42105783	12	850	Jewish Federation Of The North Shore Inc.	2.9	2.1
1986	221500549	15	350	Jewish Federation Of Greater Middlesex County	2.8	2.7
1941	60655499	200	0	Jewish Center For Community Services Inc.	2.8	3.2
1977	590637864	13	300	Jewish Federation Of Jacksonville Inc.	2.7	2.5
2002	581384316	108	600	Durham-Chapel Hill Jewish Federation	2.7	3.1
1951	860096784	33	355	Jewish Federation Of Greater Phoenix	2.6	2.5

Launch	EIN	EE	Vol.	Organization	2012 $Million	2020 $Million
1960	237211881	10	49	Jewish Federation Of Palm Springs And Desert Area	2.4	2.4
1949	160743210	13	0	Jewish Federation of Greater Buffalo	2.4	2.7
1973	231728784	20	55	Jewish Federation Of Reading Pennsylvania	2.4	1.1
1979	390867186	176	200	Jewish Federation of Madison	2.4	2.6
1970	631045456	13	55	Birmingham Jewish Federation	2.3	3.0
1944	042104347	30	1000	Jewish Community Relations Council Of Greater Boston	2.3	2.8
1942	741109662	27	100	Jewish Federation Of San Antonio	2.3	2.5
1956	066068624	12	0	UJA Federation of Greenwich	2.2	2.2
1972	237397882	0	32	Jewish Community Foundation of Greater Long Beach & West Orange County	2.1	3.1
1947	590946923	8	100	Jewish Federation Of Greater Orlando	2.0	2.0
2000	10530420	91	26	Jewish Community Alliance Of Southern Maine	1.7	1.8
1956	580566231	4	275	Savannah Jewish Federation	1.7	1.6
1944	42104363	33	200	Jewish Federation of Central Massachusetts	1.5	1.4
1974	237354759	14	110	Jewish Federation Of Greater Santa Barbara	1.5	1.4
1952	576000188	13	15	Charleston Jewish Federation	1.5	1.2
1982	592151725	4	48	Jewish Federation Of Collier County	1.5	1.3
1942	620475677	28	147	Jewish Community Federation of Greater Chattanooga	1.4	1.6
1991	382711480	10	110	The Jewish Federation Of Greater Ann Arbor	1.3	1.4
1942	741168038	57	0	Jewish Federation of El Paso	1.3	1.4
1956	750808797	11	10	Jewish Federation of Fort Worth and Tarrant County	1.3	0.8
1955	350888766	45	150	Jewish Federation Of Northwest Indiana Inc.	1.2	1.2
1964	237174039	2	30	The Jewish Community Foundation Of Princeton Mercer Bucks	1.2	2.1
1914	420835321	43	75	Jewish Federation Of Greater Des Moines	1.2	1.2
1992	620452960	98	100	Knoxville Jewish Federation	1.2	1.3
1987	561553301	49	300	Raleigh-Cary Jewish Federation Inc.	1.2	1.1
1953	520214465	19	58	Jewish Community Relations Council Of Greater Washington	1.1	1.4
1995	521912836	13	150	Baltimore Jewish Council Inc.	1.1	1.2
1983	221668993	5	400	Jewish Federation Of Somerset, Hunterdon, And Warren Counties	1.1	1.2
1964	590697685			Jewish Federation Of Pinellas & Pasco Counties FL	1.1	0.8
1994	042131409	11	300	Jewish Federation of the Berkshires	1.1	1.3

Launch	EIN	EE	Vol.	Organization	2012 $Million	2020 $Million
1942	730579276			Jewish Federation Of Greater Oklahoma City	1.1	1.3
1941	210632971	0	50	Jewish Federation Of Atlantic And Cape May Counties	1.0	1.2
1918	150543614	7	250	Jewish Federation Of Central New York	1.0	0.7
1985	133268920	5	100	Jewish Federation of Rockland County	0.9	1.2
1959	410826434	10	231	Jewish Community Relations Council Minnesota & The Dakotas	0.9	1.1
1990	237300057	15	67	Jewish Federation of Broome County	0.9	0.8
1965	850158242	5	23	The Jewish Federation Of New Mexico	0.9	0.7
1953	350941124	12	100	Jewish Federation Of St Joseph Valley	0.8	0.9
1980	570704341	5	20	Columbia Jewish Federation	0.8	0.0
1978	591774958	2	55	Jewish Federation Of Volusia & Flagler Counties	0.8	0.9
1975	510138674	18	0	Jewish Federation Of Greater Manchester	0.8	0.8
1976	132856699			Westchester Jewish Council	0.7	0.7
1950	381359257	4	100	Flint Jewish Federation	0.7	0.4
1952	240809371	7	101	Jewish Federation Of Northeastern Pennsylvania	0.7	0.7
1969	386099686	48	80	Jewish Federation Of Grand Rapids	0.7	0.8
1994	954443373	21	0	Jewish Federation Of The Greater San Gabriel & Pomona Valleys	0.6	0.5
1978	941156558	11	144	Jewish Federation Of The Sacramento Region	0.6	0.9
1950	150533576	30	100	Jewish Community Federation Of The Mohawk Valley	0.6	0.6
2004	205631988			Jewish Community Relations Council of Saint Louis	0.6	0.6
1971	237084946			Canton Jewish Community Federation	0.6	0.7
1978	141584342	5	75	Jewish Federation of Greater Orange County	0.5	0.7
1937	383011194			Jewish Community Relations Council Of Metropolitan Detroit	0.5	0.5
1977	222140175	6	0	Jewish Federation Of Ocean County	0.5	0.4
1957	870282380	4	24	United Jewish Federation Of Utah	0.4	0.2
1951	720408964	1	0	North Louisiana Jewish Federation	0.4	0.3
1988	042992252	0	0	Merrimack Valley United Jewish Communities	0.4	0.4
1977	310906786	25	100	Jewish Federation of the Bluegrass	0.4	0.4
1975	370662593	4	24	Jewish Federation Of Springfield Illinois	0.4	0.4
1952	486119344	17	100	Mid-Kansas Jewish Federation	0.4	0.4
1912	710245512			Jewish Federation Of Arkansas	0.4	0.4

Launch	EIN	EE	Vol.	Organization	2012 $Million	2020 $Million
1978	237344693	2	0	Champaign-Urbana Jewish Federation	0.4	0.4
1985	222343478	3	0	Jewish Federation Of Cumberland County	0.3	0.4
1955	046006566	3	75	Jewish Federation of Greater New Bedford	0.3	0.2
1992	141751875	3	300	Jewish Federation of Dutchess County	0.3	0.4
1943	586044144			Augusta Jewish Federation	0.3	0.4
1974	237099139			Jewish Community Relations Council Of Indianapolis	0.3	0.4
1972	237208853	1	21	Jewish Federation of Greater Baton Rouge	0.3	0.3
1937	630288849			Jewish Federation Of Central Alabama Inc.	0.3	0.4
1949	420698205			Jewish Federation of Sioux City	0.3	0.2
1948	370661214	4		Jewish Federation Of Southern Illinois, Southeast Missouri, And Western Kentucky	0.3	0.3
1942	350869051	11	15	Fort Wayne Jewish Federation	0.3	0.3
1983	363048783	2		Jewish Federation Of The Quad Cities	0.2	0.2
1950	370697159	4		Jewish Federation Of Peoria	0.2	0.3
2000	161562220	11	30	Jewish Federation of the Twin Tiers	0.2	0.3
1977	133099520			Jewish Community Council Of Pelham Parkway	0.2	0.2
1962	066063384	1	0	Jewish Federation Of Danbury	0.2	0.2
1946	362167845			Jewish Federation Of Greater Rockford	0.1	0.1
1942	250984608	0	35	Jewish Community Council Of Erie	0.1	0.0
1953	221533506	17	476	Jewish Federation Of Central New Jersey	0.0	0.0
		7,701	**57,841**	**Total**	**946.6**	**917.5**

C. ADVOCACY IAOS

Launch	EIN	EE	Vol.	Organization	2012 $Million	2020 $Million
1963	530217164	401	0	American Israel Public Affairs Committee	71.8	157.3
1946	131818723	409	3500	Anti-Defamation League	53.6	67.0
1935	131624240	144	185	Jewish Federations of North America	49.0	37.8
1906	135563393	294	1896	American Jewish Committee	47.9	33.4
1989	521623781	0	0	American Israel Education Foundation	43.7	133.8
2002	230053483	0	5	Jewish Agency for Israel - North American Council	12.2	20.2
1985	521386172	17	50	Republican Jewish Coalition	10.1	11.4
1984	521376034	63	15	Washington Institute for Near East Policy	9.7	16.4
2001	010566033	72	97	Israel Emergency Alliance aka Standwithus	8.7	14.2
2001	134174402	37	32	Foundation for the Defense of Democracies	7.3	38.5
1936	530179971	264	295	B'nai B'rith International	7.0	7.8
2003	371472882	39	10	The Israel Project	5.9	16.1
2007	223951652	19	0	Israeli American Council	5.5	10.2
1997	522068483	19	5	Middle East Media Research Institute	4.9	14.3
1986	237749796	12		Middle East Forum	4.7	10.4
2005	202777557	0	25	J Street Education Fund	4.3	11.5
1976	521233683	15	0	Jewish Institute for National Security Affairs	3.8	7.7
1983	521332702	33	10	Committee for Accuracy in Middle East Reporting	3.6	6.2
1988	521601976	15	21	Center for Security Policy	3.3	11.2
1944	131624104	35	300	Jewish Council for Public Affairs	3.1	2.9
2002	161616489	26		The David Project	2.8	5.7
2006	134331855	0	0	Investigative Project on Terrorism Foundation	2.5	4.3
1920	135628475	28	73	Zionist Organization of America	2.5	3.7
2007	133610041	16		Commentary	2.5	1.9
2008	800263559	0	0	Israel Strategic Alternative Energy Foundation	2.1	5.9
2012	460540994	2		The Israel Institute	2.0	0.0
1978	133509867	10	0	Americans for Peace Now	1.8	1.7
2008	262387657	4		United Against a Nuclear Iran	1.8	5.6
1982	133116652	5		Conference of Presidents of Major American Jewish Organizations Fund	1.6	2.6
2010	273480535	0	0	Friends of Israel Initiative	0.8	3.9

Launch	EIN	EE	Vol.	Organization	2012 $Million	2020 $Million
2010	272572894			Emergency Committee for Israel	1.5	4.9
2006	205845679	6	3	Clarion Fund	1.4	0.2
2009	264392915	15	16	Foreign Policy Initiative	1.3	3.2
2007	262971061	0	0	American Friends of NGO Monitor aka Report	1.2	6.7
2001	061611859	2	0	Middle East Media Watch DBA Honest Reporting	1.2	12.5
2011	300664947	13	6	Israel on Campus Coalition	1.2	0.1
1990	521706068			National Jewish Democratic Council	1.1	0.7
2004	201651102	11		Hasbara Fellowships	1.1	1.1
2012	454724565	10	1	Gatestone Institute	1.1	0.0
2007	260501656	3	4	International Israeli Allies Caucus Foundation	1.1	33.2
1972	132700517	6	0	National Conferences on Soviet Jewry	1.0	1.3
2003	141891915	2	12	Israel Venture Network	0.8	2.4
1964	132500881	9		Conference of Presidents of Major American Jewish Organizations	0.6	0.6
1985	521433850	3	0	National Jewish Policy Center	0.6	0.7
2001	770571579	0	0	Israel21C	0.6	0.6
2008	263402247	0	5	Israel-America Academic Exchange	0.6	4.1
2004	201381912	5	0	Institute for the Study of Global Anti-Semitism and Policy	0.5	0.0
1994	943092706	0	0	Facts and Logic about the Middle East	0.5	0.9
2006	201437733			Secure Community Network	0.4	0.5
1934	131675650	0	0	Jewish Labor Committee	0.4	0.4
2008	261416892			Association for the Study of the Middle East and Africa	0.4	2.4
1993	132679404	6	30	American Zionist Movement	0.4	0.8
2011	451683502			United Nations Watch	0.4	0.0
2010	272402908	5	0	Lawfare Project	0.4	1.8
1932	131679610	0	0	American Jewish Congress	0.4	0.1
1916	135611746	1	11	Religious Zionists of America Mizrachi Hapoel Hamizrachi	0.4	0.1
2010	453204617		4	Louis D. Brandeis Center	0.4	9.7
2011	450949784	4		Jewish News Service	0.3	1.4
2003	421565640	2		Scholars for Peace in the Middle East	0.3	2.8
2006	204329740			Endowment for Middle East Truth	0.3	4.5
1972	510181418	0	0	Americans for a Safe Israel	0.3	0.2
2002	352162870			Minnesotans Against Terrorism	0.2	0.2

Launch	EIN	EE	Vol.	Organization	2012 $Million	2020 $Million
2012	460774311	0	2	AMCHA Initiative	0.2	0.0
1984	680028695	0	20	Jewish Public Affairs Committee Of California	0.2	0.1
2010	263766713			Judaism Alive	0.1	0.3
1996	113259920			Phyllis Chesler Organization	0.1	0.1
2005	270095260			Center for Democracy and Human Rights in Saudi Arabia	0.1	0.1
2003	050538790			Myths and Facts	0.0	0.0
		2,082	**6,633**	**Total**	**403.5**	**762.2**

D. EDUCATION IAOS

Launch	EIN	EE	Vol.	Organization	2012 $Million	2020 $Million
1980	521309391	453	400	United States Holocaust Memorial Museum	124.1	171.9
1999	134092050	53	0	Birthright Israel Foundation	102.0	473.2
1984	521844823	1541	69	Hillel Foundation	27.9	18.0
1985	953964928	121	274	Simon Wiesenthal Center	23.8	19.5
1917	135599486	64	0	Jewish Community Centers Association of North America - JCC Association	21.1	35.7
1980	133041381	13	100	Women's International Zionist Organization	3.4	4.6
2004	113666684	5	0	Aish International - Hasbara Fellowships	2.9	0.9
1914	430769468	16	100	Alpha Epsilon Pi Fraternity	2.8	4.1
1994	521865861	6	0	American-Israeli Cooperative Enterprise	2.6	27.9
1917	130887610	21		Jewish Telegraphic Agency	2.6	3.0
1931	131681984	10	100	Women's League for Conservative Judaism	2.1	2.1
1945	136141078	0	0	Alpha Epsilon Pi Foundation, Inc.	0.9	1.4
1979	521171542	2	0	MERCAZ U.S.A Zionist Organization of the Conservative Movement	0.3	0.2
2006	204903202	4	10	Holocaust Education Center in the Desert	0.2	0.0
		2,309	**1,053**	**Total**	**316.7**	**762.4**

E. IAO CATEGORY TOTALS

EE	Vol.	Israel Affinity Organization Segment	2012 $Million	2020 $Million
1,984	287,810	Subsidy	2,005.3	3,831.6
7,701	57,841	Fundraising and Political Action	946.6	917.5
2,082	6,633	Advocacy	403.5	762.2
2,309	1,053	Education	316.7	762.4
14,076	**353,337**	**Total**	**3,672.1**	**6,273.7**

ABOUT THE AUTHOR

Grant F. Smith lives in Washington, DC where he researches and writes about U.S. Middle East policy formulation. Smith is director of the nonprofit Institute for Research: Middle Eastern Policy (IRmep).

In his thirty-year professional career as a researcher, Smith has investigated financial services and global telecommunications industries, worked in twenty-two countries assessing the impact of regulatory and trade regime changes and managed multi-country research teams. Smith has a BA in International Relations from the University of Minnesota and MIM (Master of International Management) from the University of St. Thomas in St. Paul. Smith's first research experience examining lobbying took place in the late 1980s as a member of a Minnesota Citizen's League committee investigating public entities that used a significant percentage of their taxpayer-funded allocations to lobby elected officials for ever-larger appropriations.[484]

In 2014, Smith sued the Department of Defense in federal court and won release of a detailed report, contracted in 1987, about the advanced state of Israel's nuclear weapons program. *The Nation* wrote about it in the article "It's Official: The Pentagon Finally Admitted That Israel Has Nuclear Weapons, Too." In 2015, Smith sued the Central Intelligence Agency and won release of 131 pages of formerly classified information revealing its overseas agents obtained compelling evidence that Israel stole U.S. government-owned weapons-grade uranium in the 1960s to build its first atom bombs. The CIA's refusal to share this information thwarted two FBI investigations into the diversion. It is the subject of continuing Freedom of Information Act litigation as estimated toxic site cleanup costs approach half a billion dollars.

Smith's essays about the lobby are frequently published at the Antiwar.com news website and the *Washington Report on Middle East Affairs* magazine. *Big Israel* is Smith's eighth book about the Israel lobby.

---

[484] "Because That's Where the Money Is: Why the Public Sector Lobbies" Citizens League Report, June 28, 1990

Made in the USA
Middletown, DE
06 July 2024

56951479R00183